D0205962

In the Matter of

NAT TURNER

Meherrin Road, south of Cross Keys Road, north of Boykins, Virginia

SIC SEMPER TYRANNIS

State Historical Marker U 122

Nat Turner's Insurrection

On the night of 21–22 August 1831, Nat Turner, a slave preacher, began an insurrection some seven miles west with a band that grew to about 70. They moved northeast toward the Southampton County seat, Jerusalem (now Courtland), killing about 60 whites. After two days militiamen and armed civilians quelled the revolt. Turner was captured on 30 October, tried and convicted, and hanged on 11 November: some 30 blacks were hanged or expelled from Virginia. In response to the revolt, the General Assembly passed harsher slave laws and censored abolitionists.

Department of Historic Resources. 1991

In the Matter of NAT TURNER

A Speculative History

CHRISTOPHER TOMLINS

PRINCETON UNIVERSITY PRESS
Princeton & Oxford

Published by Princeton University Press
41 William Street, Princeton, New Jersey 08540
6 Oxford Street, Woodstock, Oxfordshire OX20 1TR

press.princeton.edu

Library of Congress Control Number: 2019953980
ISBN 978-0-691-19866-8
ISBN (e-book) 978-0-691-19987-0

British Library Cataloging-in-Publication Data is available

Editorial: Eric Crahan, Pamela Weidman, and Thalia Leaf
Production Editorial: Nathan Carr
Text Design: Pamela L. Schnitter
Jacket/Cover Design: Pamela L. Schnitter
Jacket images: (Top) Map of Elizabeth City County, VA, from actual surveys by E.A. Semple, Wm. Ivy, and C. Hubbard, 1892. Library of Congress (Right) Marble head of Memnon, student of Herodes Atticus, ca. 170 AD. Photo: bpk Bildagentur / Altes Museum, Belin / Juergen Liepe / Art Resource, NY (Bottom) Green Hill Plantation, slave quarters, State Route 728, Long Island, Campbell County, VA.
Production: Danielle Amatucci
Publicity: Jodi Price and Kate Farquhar-Thomson

This book has been composed in Baskerville 120 Pro and Bodoni Std

Printed on acid-free paper. ∞

Printed in the United States of America

10 9 8 7 6 5 4 3 2 1

FOR ANN, WITH LOVE

One might . . . speak of an unforgettable life or moment even if all men had forgotten it. If the nature of such a life or moment required that it be unforgotten, that predicate would not imply a falsehood but merely a claim not fulfilled by men, and probably also a reference to a realm in which it *is* fulfilled: God's remembrance.

—WALTER BENJAMIN (1923)

And we are witnesses of all things which he did . . . whom they slew and hanged on a tree.

—ACTS 10:39

CONTENTS

PREFACE

O lost, and by the wind grieved, ghost, come back again.
—THOMAS WOLFE (1929)

This book attempts to recover both a historical personage and his way of thinking (his mentalité) from tiny shards of evidence on which—in the absence of anything else—I have pressed as hard as I can, and as often as necessary, guided (both positively and negatively, but always with appreciation) by the labors of others who have been this way before me. Notwithstanding the almost complete lack of the kinds of material from which intellectual history is customarily written, I have come to think of this book as an attempt to create an intellectual history of Nat Turner. As important, the book is also an attempt to demonstrate what the creation of history means to me as an intellectual practice.

My abiding impression of Nat Turner is overwhelmingly one of a person unavailed by history, a person whose very archival evanescence renders him, quite involuntarily, an enigma, a signifier pushed and pulled toward an extraordinary and contradictory array of signifieds.[1] To underline just how tenuous the conditions of Turner's historical existence are, how vulnerable he is to those who would seek him, I have chosen to begin with a prologue that examines the most notorious attempt to construct a knowable Nat Turner—William Styron's best-selling 1967 novel, *The Confessions of Nat Turner*—and its reception.[2] Addressing Styron's interpretive trajectory and the controversies to which it led, the prologue asks the question "*What* is the past?"

The prologue asks this question because it is precisely the question that Styron's book provoked. At the time of its publication, and for years following, Styron's *Confessions* was simultaneously condemned for traducing the historical Nat Turner, and defended as a book faithful in all essentials to the past on which it ostensibly drew. The quarrel pitted African American intellectuals against Styron himself, and against contemporary white historians and others sympathetic to his endeavors. I am critical of Styron's defenders, but my purpose is less to dwell on them than to employ his book and the debates by which it was accompanied as an occasion for entry on concerns of my own—the desires and responsibilities of authorship, and in particular, the meaning of history. On both counts one can learn a great deal from Styron's *Confessions*—from the book's errors of judgment, and from the failure of its central ambition. The errors are less important than the failure. Styron's errors were not few, but they were shallow; they were the errors of a novelist who demanded an imaginative right to take possession of his subject and do as his artistic fancy dictated, no matter the consequences. What resulted was irresponsible, even selfish; but William Styron was hardly the first white man to claim that Nat Turner was his property. Styron's ambition, however, was deep, and orthogonal to his demand that he be accorded a fiction writer's license. It was to escape altogether the fictive terrain of the novel for the profundity of what he called "a meditation on history." Here was no facile creation of some artificially scripted persona; here was a serious attempt to re-create a past, to stand by that re-creation as a philosophically valid exercise, and to propose that the exercise of re-creation was of moral significance to Styron's own present. Here was an intimation that Styron indeed wished to assume responsibility for what he had done because he believed in what he had done. But Styron was never able to explain what his "meditation on history" actually meant. Had he managed to state his ambition coherently, his errors would have been less jarring, more easily forgiven, his book less divisive.

In the Matter of Nat Turner also attempts a meditation on history. But unlike William Styron I am a historian. This means I believe that an actual existing Nat Turner is accessible in remnants or traces that one must attempt to comprehend, a Turner with whom it is possible to communicate if one listens for him and to him with all the powers one can muster. This Nat Turner is something other than the plaything of an authorial imagination. It is a revenant once-was, a living-on, an uncontained remainder that possesses recognizability, fragments of whose truth are recoverable. Having chosen this Turner as my subject it is my responsibility to pursue my attempt at recognition of him respectfully, but also in my own way, believing that using the tools of my particular trade as imaginatively as I can is the only possible route to some degree of success.

That work of recovery and recognition comprises the bulk of this book. It appears in the relatively conventional form (for a historian) of a series of narratives that present empirical evidence and offer arguments about the meaning of that evidence. The reader will find a synoptic guide in the remainder of this preface. But the book as a whole is conceived less conventionally, as a constellation; which is to say, although its narratives are encountered seriatim, as chapters, they fold together both imagistically and dialectically as a succession of layers that together form one montage. Necessarily, this montage is constructed from the standpoint that I occupy. That is what makes the book a constellation. I invite you, reader, to join me and to assume your own critical standpoint in relation to the layers of narrative you will encounter. I invite you to acknowledge how your own work of recognition also constitutes the what-has-been that I am attempting to retrieve, and to admit that what-has-been to your here-and-now so as to form your own constellation—no matter how vertiginous the experience may prove to be. I invite you . . . but it is, of course, for you to determine whether the invitation is worthy of your acceptance, and for you to make of it whatever you wish. As for me, at the book's end, when I am done, I take it on myself to review what I have brought together and to offer an explanation of what it means, at least to me. The book's epilogue is its climax, an attempt to render its constellation visible in a return to the prologue's animating question, "What is *this* past?"[3]

In part I, I begin my work of recovery with the best source, which is also almost the only source, the original *Confessions of Nat Turner*, a twenty-four-page pamphlet published by a thirty-year-old Southampton County lawyer, Thomas Ruffin Gray, shortly after Turner's execution, and the first attempt to convert Nat Turner into the textual property of another. How did Gray fashion this document so that it might perform its possessory role? How has it been understood since its publication by those who have read it? Above all, to what extent can we accept words scribbled in a county jail by an opportunistic white attorney as the true voice of this remarkable captive slave awaiting his trial and inevitable execution? To answer such questions, and to attempt to gain the fullest access to the intellect contained in the text, I read the pamphlet as minutely as possible and with as much "critical theoretical" assistance as possible.

Scott French, who has written with considerable insight of Nat Turner's place in American memory, thinks historians may be ill-served by attending too closely to what Turner had to say for himself in Gray's pamphlet. The original *Confessions* is a document too compromised in the manner of its composition to yield fragments of truth.[4] I disagree. For too many years, historians of slavery disdained as untrustworthy the glimpses of slave consciousness available in autobiographical testimonials, gallows confessions, abolitionist-sponsored slave narratives, folklore, and ethnographic interviews (notably the 1930s WPA narratives of former slaves). They preferred actuarial records, plantation ledgers, planters' diaries, and the observations of northern travelers. John Blassingame's *The Slave Community* broke through the dyke of indifference in 1972. Planters' records "tell us little about slave behavior and even less about the slave's inner life." To counter the biases of planters' records Blassingame sought "the life of the black slave" in "the personal records left by the slave," not because he thought them unvarnished truth but because he thought their interrogation would result in a closer approximation of slavery's multidimensional realities than their dismissal.[5] Were historians to scorn any text that grants access to a historical subject purely because we have reason to distrust the mode of the text's construction, no history would be written, for no text is trustworthy. In Nat Turner's case it seems better to approach Gray's *Confessions* warily, with questions about the manner of its construction and the detail of its narratives uppermost.[6]

French also believes historians who rely on Gray's *Confessions* as the key to Turner and his rebellion are suffering the same illogic as the drunk under the lamppost. Too much attention to that text has crowded out other possible sources of inspiration. "Perhaps," he writes, "we know all we will ever need to know about Turner and his motives."[7] One can only agree that when it comes to Turner and the Turner Rebellion imaginative courage is essential, for the archive is sparse. Still, I do not know how new knowledge might be had independent of continued close attention to the original *Confessions*. Perhaps by purely social history? David Allmendinger, author of the most admirably resolute social history of the Turner Rebellion so far to appear, does not agree; he gives serious attention to the untrustworthy text.[8] In any case, my own impression is that rather than "all we will ever need to know," we actually know very little about Turner and his motives, that throughout its long history the original *Confessions* has not so much been thoroughly drained of all possible knowledge as read without sufficient care or curiosity. In chapter 1 my work of inquiry attempts to show how new meaning may be dislodged from this invaluable document when we add an examination of its structure to consideration of its substance.

Chapter 2 continues the work of inquiry with an extended interrogation of the first half of the text of Gray's *Confessions*, the goal of which is to understand in as much detail as possible the mentalité and motivation of its confessing subject. The consciousness that the exercise of textual analysis reveals is overwhelmingly one of faith—religious faith, a subject that always tends to make scholars uneasy. Far too often, writes Robert Orsi, to the scholar, religion is a phenomenon that exists to be secularized: "Religious practice and imagination [are] about something other than what they are to practitioners. This something else may be human powerlessness, false consciousness, ignorance, hysteria, or neurosis. It may be a social group's shared identity of itself. Whatever it is, religion is not about itself." Historians are not shy of writing about religion, but when they do they usually approach religion as social or cultural history, or in other words as behavioral phenomena embedded in or produced from institutions or practices constructed by human beings. "The confident translation of the stories men and women tell of their encounters with the supernatural into language that makes these stories about something else is based on the pervasive assumption in modern scholarship of the 'always already mediated nature of cultural relations.'" The intellectual orthodoxy of modernity, says Orsi, turns religion into a social construction that "underwrites the hierarchies of power, reinforces group solidarity, and also, if more rarely, functions as a medium of rebellion and resistance."[9] Too often, in my view, this has been the particular fate of the religious life of African American slaves.

I share Orsi's interest in rescuing faith from modernist reductions.[10] I certainly do not claim that faith is free of all forms of cultural embeddedness. There is no doubt, for example, that as Randolph Scully has argued, "Turner, his style of leadership, and his language of righteousness and divine justice really did emerge to a significant degree out of the evangelical culture that had evolved in southeastern Virginia."[11] But in this book, Nat Turner is not a puppet dangling on strings of culture and sociality. He is first of all a Christian. He is "inspired by God," by "Christian faith and the Bible."[12] We should not read his confession with eyes whose only desire is to explain what we take to be the secular occurrence with which it is associated, his "slave rebellion." First and foremost Turner's confession is an exercise in ideation, a confession of faith.

But, even if the primary key to Turner is faith, still one must attempt to explain the apparent transfiguration of that faith, the bloody violence with which the name "Nat Turner" is indelibly linked. How does faith become "kill all the white people?" One might answer "resistance" and have done with it. But that answer is far too easy. Resistance is another reduction.[13] It makes faith into something other than itself. In this case, I argue in chapter 3, faith deals death precisely *because* it is faith.[14] What we know as "the Turner rebellion" begins in an act not of self-liberation but of divine violence.

We cannot determine this objectively—the same action that may be divine for those engaged in it will likely appear, to an external observer, merely irrational mob fury.[15] Nor, in any case, can we be at all certain that the action had the same macrocosmic meaning for all those who became involved in it. Some participants embraced other outcomes, some were merely opportunistic, some joined only reluctantly, some were actively coerced, some departed as soon as chance allowed.[16] All who took part had to be persuaded to join, and persuasion could not be grounded on a shared cosmology, for none is in evidence. Persuasion, chapter 3 holds, required something different of Turner than public rehearsals of his own faith. To translate faith into action in which others could share required that he invent a politics that could enunciate faith's intentions but in a distinct language, that could supply a way to understand the objectives of the action for which he called that might be comprehended by all those who decided to follow.[17]

Turner's translation of his faith into a politics of action meant that the foundational singular causality of faith necessarily yielded to the multiplicity of reception in the minds of those persuaded. In other words, what we know as the Turner Rebellion is an instance of overdetermination, in relation to which Turner is the essential precipitating supplement.[18] I mean here "overdetermination" in a form akin to Freud's usage. As Ben Brewster explains, Freud used the term to describe "the representation of . . . dream-thoughts in images privileged by their condensation of a number of thoughts in a single image . . . or by the transference of psychic energy from a particularly potent thought to apparently trivial images."[19] As such, Turner's rebellion is best grasped less as in itself the result of a specific cause, or a wellspring of specific meaning, than as an *event*—an effect in excess of any particular trigger or circumstance, the logic of which is to work a transformation. In chapters 3 and 4 I try to explain this event with reference to the faith that began it, to the persuasion that realized it, to the transformative violence by which it is best known, and to the answering repression that was the established response of the profane order that faith and persuasion and violence had all targeted. Where in part I of this book my most important guides are primarily biblical text and commentary, in part II they are primarily philosophical, sociological, and anthropological. The goal is to understand both the evental site brought momentarily into being by the mentalité that part I suggests was truly in play, and in the actuality of the action that transpired, the event itself that flickered into existence on that site.[20]

Part III attends to the ripples of the event. In part III I ask the reader first to ponder the meaning of what Nat Turner undertook on his terms, and then to ponder the impact of the event on the Virginia of his time. In chapter 5, I propose that we think of Turner's rebellion as an instance of countersovereignty, violence deployed in the hope of changing a regime. "By putting the right to take life in their own hands, the perpetrators of religious violence [make] a daring claim of power on behalf of the powerless, a basis of legitimacy for public order other than that on which the secular state relies. In doing so, they [demonstrate] to everyone how fragile the public order actually is."[21] In an act that was an act both of faith *and* of politics, to the sovereignty of the profane Turner had counterposed the sovereignty of God.

In chapter 6 we reconnoiter the wider terrain on which Turner's rebellion took place, the political and economic terrain of white Virginia. This Virginia, of course, did not understand itself as in any sense answerable to Nat Turner. This Virginia was a secular polity, uneasy and apprehensive, a Virginia of brittle eastern slaveholders and resentful western yeomen, occupied in incessant squabbling over the terms of its own modernization. To contemplate the impact Turner's rebellion had on this Virginia, to understand the consequences of rebellious disorder for such a frail polity, we must consider how white Virginia understood itself—its "aristocratic" tidewater slaveholding past, its "democratic" yeoman transmontane future, the suspicions and antagonisms that divided them, and the political institutions that, notwithstanding suspicion and antagonism, were supposed to oversee Virginia's transition from the old version of itself to the new. All three—remembered past, imagined future, present politics—together composed the conditions of white Virginia's fragile sovereignty, the order of things on which the event of August 1831 burst. Virginia in 1831 was a polity and an economy seeking an escape from its own apparent declension without quite knowing how. Turner's rebellion bit deep into the debates that assessed its capacities to do so.

As chapter 6 continues, we will see that in the aftermath of Turner's rebellion white Virginia reacted by failing to agree on how to react. White Virginia had debated the extent of its obligations to the east's slaveholders, covertly, in a state constitutional convention in 1829–30. It did so again, overtly, early in 1832, when in the aftermath of Turner's rebellion the House of Delegates took up the question of slavery's future in the state. Those who resented slaveholders' political ascendancy declared slavery pernicious; they sought gradual emancipation of the enslaved and their expulsion from the state. Slaveholders resisted, threatening to divide the state in two. The inability of Virginia's political institutions to weather the debate brought talk of gradual emancipation to a chaotic halt, and in the aftermath white Virginia dressed itself in new clothes, the conjectural and providential clothes of political economy. These were clothes that bypassed legislative politics altogether, that explained white Virginia's immobility to itself not as crippling political irresolution but as historically ordained and economically appropriate. Political economy became white Virginia's new faith, a faith to answer faith that sanctified renewed dedication to Virginia's old slaveholding self, that replied to the event of Turner's rebellion in providential language shorn both of Providence and of proprietorial duty; market society's brutal language of the bottom line.[22]

Ultimately, then, Turner's rebellion became a confrontation between cosmologies, a disjunctive dialectic that countered the Christian enthusiasm to which Turner himself credited the event "for which I am about to atone at the gallows"[23] with the profane enthusiasm of political economy, Virginia's eventual answer to the rebellion. This is the gloss I offer in this book's epilogue. Political economy commodified slavery on a grand scale, mollifying alike both anxious slaveholders and those in whose debt anxious slaveholders lived. And so it seemed to provide the solution that Virginia's fragile sovereigns sought. But it was a cosmology haunted at its dissembling disenchanted core by the very presence that it was its purpose to efface, the selfsame slaves whose hands gripped the fibers of white Virginia's life, the inescapably real slaves from whom Virginia's brutalities had already wrung one violent response, and might yet provoke more of the same.

I should probably add a word about my title. I have chosen "In the Matter of Nat Turner" rather than plain "Nat Turner" because this book is not a biography in any conventional sense, and because its object of attention is not just Nat Turner the person materialized in text but Nat Turner the historical phenomenon—"a fact or occurrence," as the *OED* defines it, "the explanation of which is in question." Likewise, I have chosen to describe what I have written as a *speculative* history because it is a work of conjecture. My compatriot, the late Teresa Brennan, once wrote that speculation "connotes the art of wondering about the connections between events, causes, origins, possible outcomes."[24] That is a fine summary of what the reader will come across in the pages that follow. I treasure the scraps of empirical evidence on which this book relies. They are the only means to recover the revenant Turner who is the book's reason for being. Yet most of the answers the book seeks are not to be found by mobilizing empirical evidence, whether because of the nature of the questions I have chosen to ask, or because there is so little of the kind of evidence that historians normally employ from which to fashion the answers. As a result, my answers will probably not silence the questions. Nor should they.[25]

In the Matter of

NAT TURNER

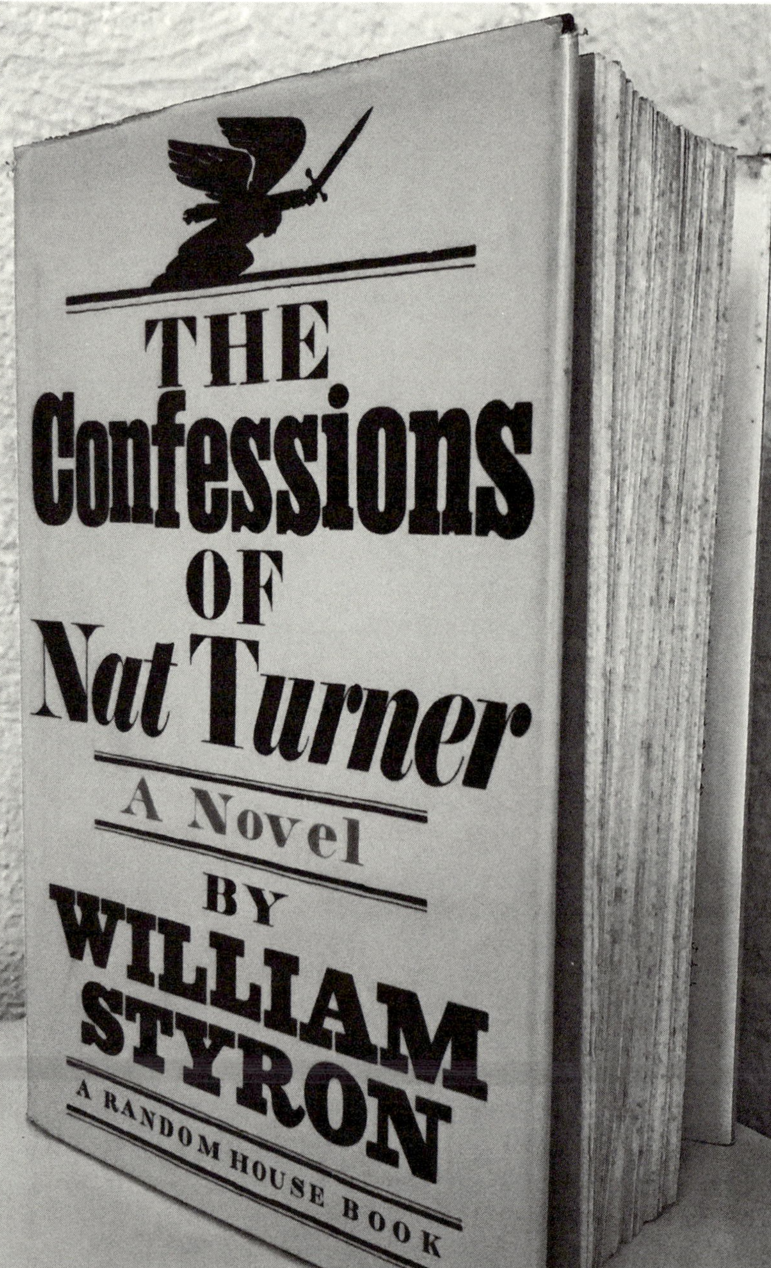
THE
Confessions
OF
Nat Turner
A Novel
BY
WILLIAM
STYRON
A RANDOM HOUSE BOOK

PROLOGUE

What's Past?

> The story of Nat Turner had long been gestating in my mind, ever since I was a boy—in fact since before I actually knew I wanted to be a writer.
>
> —WILLIAM STYRON (1993)

In 1967, the American novelist, William Styron, published his third major work of fiction, a book entitled *The Confessions of Nat Turner*.[1] Styron's *Confessions* represented itself as the autobiographical narrative of an African American slave, known as Nat Turner, who in August 1831 had led a slave revolt (known as the Turner Rebellion) in Southampton County, Virginia, not far from Virginia's southeastern tidewater region where Styron himself had grown up. Both Turner and the event that bore his name were real enough—Styron took his title from a pamphlet account of Turner and of his rebellion that had been published in November 1831, a few days after Turner's capture and execution;[2] his book's point of departure was the series of conversations between Turner and the pamphlet's publisher, a Southampton County lawyer named Thomas Ruffin Gray, that had occurred while Turner was in jail awaiting trial, and on which Gray drew heavily in constructing his pamphlet. But for Styron the man revealed in those conversations was a person with whom he wished to have nothing to do, "a person of conspicuous ghastliness,"[3] utterly beyond moral reclamation. The Turner of record, Styron emphasized—confidently, consistently, repeatedly—was "a ruthless and perhaps psychotic fanatic, a religious fanatic," a "madman," a "dangerous religious lunatic," a "religious maniac, a psychopath of almost fearful dimensions," a "demented ogre beset by bloody visions," who had led "a drunken band of followers on a massacre of unarmed farm folk."[4]

FIGURE P.1. Cover of William Styron's *The Confessions of Nat Turner*, 1st ed. (1967). Reproduced by permission of Penguin/Random House. Photograph by Christopher Tomlins.

And so, claiming "a writer's prerogative to transform Nat Turner into any kind of creature I wanted to transform him into,"[5] Styron invented his own Nat, a sexually inhibited, homoeroticized celibate, whose actions were driven not by eschatological fervor but by an "exquisitely sharpened hatred for the white man" learned over many years from the quotidian mortifications of his dehumanizing and emasculating condition of enslavement.[6]

Styron's objective, he explained, was to demonstrate that Turner (his Turner) was inspired by "subtler motives" than those manifested by Gray's Turner, and so enable the man to be "better understood."[7] Casting aside the "apocalyptic and deranged visions . . . heavenly signs and signals . . . divinely ordained retributive mission" allegedly on display in Gray's pamphlet,[8] Styron instead gave Turner's impulses "social and behavioral roots."[9] Styron's Nat is religious, but his religiosity is "stern piety" not "demonic fanaticism."[10] His violent rebellion is not mindless slaughter but a rational, though tragically misguided, response to the behavioral degradations, disappointments, and humiliations of his enslavement.[11] In Styron's eyes it assumes the comprehensible form of "Old Testament savagery and revenge,"[12] to which the novel counterposes at its climax a redemptive and forgiving "New Testament charity and brotherhood" that melts Turner's anger and allows his humanity fully to appear.[13] The agent of Turner's redemption is the young and virginal Margaret Whitehead, the one person the historical Nat Turner is recorded as killing during the rebellion that bears his name, who becomes in Styron's hands both object of Turner's sexual desire and his sacrificial savior, through whom (in a masturbatory fantasy minutes before his execution) Turner recovers his unity with the God he believes has abandoned him because of his bloody rampage.[14] "Perhaps," wrote Styron, "she had tempted him sexually, goaded him in some unknown way, and out of this situation had flowed his rage. . . . It was my task—and my right—to allow my imagination to range over these questions and determine the nature of the mysterious bond between the black man and the young white woman," for in their bond (and their mutually determined fate) lay the symbol he sought, the "dramatic image for slavery's annihilating power, which crushed black and white alike."[15]

Why, one might wonder, did the William Styron who had been obsessed by the story of Nat Turner since he was a boy, and who had felt an urge to explain him to modern America ever since he became a writer, nevertheless make no attempt to comprehend the Turner whom he actually encountered in the sources he consulted ("I didn't want to write about a psychopathic monster")?[16] Why "re-create" Turner in a persona that might be "better understood"?[17] The answer lies in what Styron represented as an act of self-expiation that was also and simultaneously an act of regional and even national expiation, an act that led him to claim that his *Confessions* was not a "'historical novel'" but a "meditation on history."[18] By re-creating Nat Turner and his motives, Styron sought respite from American history's violent racial storm in cathartic reconciliation with (through knowledge of) "the Negro":

> No wonder the white man so often grows cranky, fanciful, freakish, loony, violent: how else respond to a paradox which requires with the full majesty of law behind it, that he deny the very reality of a people whose multitude approaches and often exceeds his own; that he disclaim the existence of those whose human presence has marked every acre of the land, every hamlet and crossroad and city and town, and whose humanity, however inflexibly denied, is daily evidenced to him like a heartbeat in loyalty and wickedness, madness and hilarity and mayhem and pride and love? The Negro may feel it is too late to be known, and that the desire to know him reeks of outrageous condescension. But to break down the old law, to come to *know* the Negro, has become the moral imperative of every white Southerner.[19]

Styron's "social and behavioral" explanation pulls Turner into Styron's present in order to capture and complete him. By explaining this particular Negro, Styron will come at last to know and to explain *the* Negro. He will fulfill the felt moral imperative; overcome the old law of suppression, suspicion, and separation; lay the ghost; and earn redemption for himself, every other white Southerner, and arguably the nation as well. Completion of the past relieves and completes the present.

The attempt was, of course, hopeless. *The Negro* was a wholly white ideological-cultural construct (albeit one with a very long history), nonexistent as such, hence unknowable in any form that could satisfy Styron's desire "to know the Negro."[20] Styron's Nat was the figment of a white authorial imagination that, notwithstanding Styron's insistence that he had respected "the *known* facts," sedulously refused to listen to any of Turner's own explanations of himself.[21] Yet this fatally flawed exercise was neither uninfluential nor unimportant. As a published book Styron's *Confessions* was a major commercial success. It became one of the principal channels through which white America, in the midst of its confrontation with civil rights agitators, Black Power, and the urban riots of 1967 and 1968, renewed its acquaintance with slavery and slave rebellion. It generated intense controversy within late 1960s academic and "public intellectual" circles, largely in the form of a series of confrontations between African American intellectuals who attacked Styron's depiction of Turner and of slavery, and Styron's self-appointed defenders, notably the bumptious polemicist of American slavery and defender of the American South, Eugene Genovese. And it stimulated critical assessment of the novel's fictive realities and their relationship to the representation of historical events. In all these respects, Styron's claim that his work was no "historical novel" but a "meditation on history" was, perhaps intentionally, deeply provocative, for it ensured that his fictive depiction of reality would continuously challenge, rather than simply be haunted by, the shadowy presence of that with which the depiction did not accord.

Styron's attempt to "humanize" Turner, to make him understandable—and worthy of understanding—in Styron's present, locates him in time (as a slave in antebellum Virginia) but treats him as if exempt from time (as an essence or being intelligible at any time). Such a "metaphysics of presence," a problematic endemic to historical explanation, has long been considered philosophically suspect, an ontological denial of time in that it treats all modes of being as modes of presence, hence all modes of temporality as facets of a single primordial present.[22] "The past and the future are always determined as past presents or future presents," Jacques Derrida writes. Being is "already determined as being-present."[23] Derrida's deconstructive response is *différance*—a nonmetaphysical past, irreducibly in time and irreducibly past, a past that has never been and could never be present.[24] Among historians, the poststructural equivalent has been the turn to critical historicism, the basic proposition that "a social practice or a document is a product of the preoccupations of its own time and place, and that if it survives to be reenacted or reread at a later time, it will acquire a new set of meanings from its new context."[25] Historicism in this vein is an antifoundational philosophy of history. By pinning phenomena to time and place we render their meaning entirely a consequence of their circumstances, and so rob them of numinous possibility.[26]

Must one, though, treat the past as never capable of anything but being-past?[27] Might not the past inject itself into our here-and-now, precisely at moments in which it becomes recognizable, and is recognized by us?[28] Might it not at those moments become both enlivened by our recognition, and enlivening of our recognition, of the interest we discover in the past precisely because it has managed to force recognition upon us?[29] Styron desired to put the past to a present use by completing it on his own terms, but he also groped for something else, a way to express that desire as recognition and relation, which is to say as something other than simply fictive manipulation. Hence his rejection of the label "historical novel"; hence his "meditation upon history."

As prologue to this speculative inquiry into the matter of Nat Turner, I ask what called William Styron's fictive realities into being, and how they were crafted. I also ask what made his work a "meditation on history"—and why it failed. Finally, I ask whether it might be possible to redeem Nat Turner from endless deferral—the effect of our attempts to "understand" him as a figment of text without listening to (or for) him as a person.[30] From William Cooper Nell and Martin Robison Delany to Sharon Ewell Foster, from Kyle Baker to Nate Parker and Nathan Alan Davis, African American popular culture has tried, with some success, to retrieve Nat Turner, to recognize and assimilate him to itself, without deferral.[31] Might he ever achieve a *historical* presence of his own that is other than past?[32] How?

I

William Styron was born in 1925 in Newport News, Virginia. He lived in Newport News until he was fifteen years old, when he was sent to an Episcopalian boarding school near Urbanna, Virginia, some fifty miles to the north. College followed, first at Davidson in North Carolina—a conservative Presbyterian school, chosen by his father, where Styron remained only one year—then at Duke under the auspices of a Marine Corps training program. Styron was called up in October 1944, never saw combat, returned to Duke, and graduated without distinction in 1947. Through connections made at Duke he secured a junior editorial position at McGraw-Hill in New York where he remained for a few months, then quit to embark on a career as a writer.[33] His first novel, *Lie Down in Darkness*, was published four years later, his second, *Set This House on Fire*, in 1960. Both were Faulknerian, gothic, and preoccupied with doom, despair, entrapment, and particularly the latter, existential angst.[34] Both, also, were florid and portentous in style and in substance, particularly *Set This House on Fire*, in which Styron began his twenty-five-year, three-book struggle with the depiction of evil.[35] Styron's protestations notwithstanding, both were perceived as representative of a "southern" literary tradition, characterized as one that "looks to the past, is deeply concerned with race relations and class differences, the force of superstition and religious belief over the rational mind," and by obsession with "disorder, psychological disturbance, defeat, and unnaturalness."[36] The first was greeted with considerable acclaim, the second, in some quarters at least, with derision.[37]

All this time—ever since he had concluded to be a writer—Styron had been toying with transforming boyhood curiosity about Nat Turner into a book.[38] In the immediate aftermath of *Lie Down in Darkness* he decided Turner would be his next subject, noting, "It'll probably take a bit of research," but also that "when I'm through with Nat Turner . . . he will not be either a Great Leader of the Masses—as the stupid, vicious Jackass of a Communist writer might make him out—or a perfectly satanic demagogue, as the surface historical facts present him, but a living human being of great power and great potential who somewhere, in his struggle for freedom and for immortality, lost his way."[39] Styron was dissuaded from proceeding further at this time by his editor, Hiram Haydn, who advised against involvement "in subject matter as purple as your own imagination."[40] So instead he wrote *Set This House on Fire*. But in 1960 Styron turned back to Nat Turner. Turner was to be his voyage of discovery, the means to satisfy "his powerful curiosity about black people,"[41]—people who had "barely existed" in his boyhood South "except as shadows which came daily to labor in the kitchen, to haul away garbage, to rake up leaves," people who were "simply a part of the landscape," who would "blend with the land and somehow melt and fade into it," people whose collective presence haunted Southern whites "like a monstrous recurring dream populated by identical faces wearing expressions of inquietude and vague reproach," yet who were as individuals irremediably absent, people who had surrounded him but with whom he had had no intimate connection, people of whom he was utterly ignorant. "Whatever knowledge I gained in my youth about Negroes, I gained from a distance, as if I had been watching actors in an all-black puppet show."[42] Here was the collective "Negro" whom Styron now thought it his moral duty to know.

Early in his Turner inquiries, Styron by happenstance became personally acquainted with James Baldwin, who became in effect his "first" Negro.[43] Knowing Baldwin helped Styron create the autobiographical Turner that was so striking—and controversial—an aspect of his *Confessions*: much of the characterization of Styron's Nat can be read as an adaptation of the "small, tightly wound, very dark, articulate and intense . . . unattached homosexual" Baldwin.[44] The larger part of Styron's preparatory work, however, consisted of research on the historical Nat Turner, on slavery, on the event of the rebellion, and on the psychology of rebelliousness.

Research on the Turner of record and his rebellion was the easy part. Styron quickly concluded that what he took to be the sum of available materials—Gray's *Confessions*, a few contemporary newspaper stories, William Sidney Drewry's 1900 monograph *The Southampton Insurrection*—were easily mastered and mostly slim pickings.[45] He would remark on one occasion that "any C+ history student" could learn all there was to know in "official sources" about Nat Turner in a few days; on another that it would take only a day; on yet another, that twenty minutes would suffice.[46] Nor, from his first encounter with those materials in 1952 until his final commentaries on his book fifty years later, did Styron ever change his mind about the Turner they revealed: "A ruthless and perhaps psychotic fanatic, a religious fanatic who, lacking any plan or purpose . . . takes five or six rather bedraggled followers and goes off on a ruthless, directionless, aimless, forty-eight hour rampage of total destruction, in which the victims are, by a large majority, women and little children."[47] This was the Negro Styron could not understand and apparently did not wish to try to know, the Negro whom he wished to replace with a different *knowable* Negro.

To re-create Turner as a Negro he could know, indeed of whom he could take complete possession ("I supplied him with the motivation. I gave him a rationale. I gave him all the confusions and desperations, troubles, worries")[48] Styron turned to three mid-twentieth-century sources: the existentialism that had already influenced *Set This House on Fire*, notably in this case Albert Camus's *L'Etranger* (1942);[49] the history of slavery—in particular Stanley M. Elkins's psychology-influenced *Slavery* (1959);[50] and the newly fashionable genre of psychohistory, specifically Erik Erikson's *Young Man Luther* (1958).[51]

From *L'Etranger* came the book's broad plan, its beginning and end—Part I, "Judgment Day," and Part IV, "It Is Done . . ."—and the idea of an autobiographical narrative. All were sparked by the situational parallel that Styron saw between Nat Turner and *L'Etranger*'s central character, Meursault:

> About 1962 . . . I was up on Martha's Vineyard and I had just read for the first time Camus' "The Stranger." It is a brilliant book, the best of Camus, and it impressed me enormously: there was something about the poignancy of the condemned man sitting in his

> jail cell on the day of his execution—the existential predicament of the man—that hit me. And so did the use of the first person, the book being told through the eyes of the condemned. The effect of all this was so strong that I suddenly realized my Nat Turner could be done the same way: that like Camus, I would center the novel around a man facing his own death in a jail cell, which of course was true of Turner and how his life ended. And so there, suddenly provided, was the architecture of the book, its framework, along with the idea of telling the story in the first person.[52]

From Elkins, meanwhile, came a conception of slavery so insidiously dreadful that it could dwarf, hence explain, even justify, the savagery of the rebellion, and at the same time render comprehensible the haunting absence—that elusive otherness—of the Negro Styron desired so urgently to know: a North American slavery distinct from that of any other time or place; a despotic slavery produced by an utterly unrestrained agricultural capitalism; a slavery so total in its domination that it produced in its victims the perpetual submissive childishness of "Sambo," not as racist stereotype but as psychological actuality; a slavery that rendered the plantation analogous to the Nazi concentration camp:

> Both were closed systems from which all standards based on prior connections had been effectively detached. A working adjustment to either system required a childlike conformity, a limited choice of "significant others." Cruelty per se cannot be considered the primary key to this; of far greater importance was the simple "closedness" of the system, in which all lines of authority descended from the master and in which alternative social bases that might have supported alternative standards were systematically suppressed. The individual, consequently, for his very psychic security, had to picture his master in some way as the "good father," even when, as in the concentration camp, it made no sense at all. But why should it not have made sense for many a simple plantation Negro whose master did exhibit in all the ways that could be expected, the features of the good father who was really "good"? . . . For the Negro child, in particular, the plantation offered no really satisfactory father-image other than the master.[53]

If *L'Etranger* provided the book's framework, *Slavery* provided much of its substance—the "black shit-eating people" that Styron's adult

Nat so despises, "faces popeyed with black nigger credulity," and of whom he despairs, "lacking even the will to destroy by their own hand their unending anguish"; the "cheap grins and comic shufflings" to which even his closest confidant is prone; and Nat's own early unawakened life as "a pet, the darling, the little black jewel of Turner's Mill," the "spoiled child" of saintly Marse Samuel's plantation household.[54]

How does the spoiled child of *Confessions* Part II, "Old Times Past," become the avenging Old Testament rebel of Part III, "Study War"? Here Styron turned to Erikson's *Young Man Luther*, a psychobiographical case study of late adolescent/early adult "identity crisis." Identity crisis, for Erikson, referenced "that period of the life cycle when each youth must forge for himself some central perspective and direction, some working unity, out of the effective remnants of his childhood and the hopes of his anticipated adulthood."[55] Styron's Nat experiences his identity crisis as a moment of collapse and betrayal—the failure and disintegration of his home, Turner's Mill, and with it the end of Marse Samuel's plans for Nat's advancement—a new life in Richmond, apprenticeship, and eventual emancipation (the hopes of his anticipated adulthood). Here lie the beginnings of what would become Nat's "exquisitely sharpened hatred,"[56] in Erikson's terms the birth of his "new world perspective" in a moment of "total and cruel repudiation" of his former understanding of the world (literally "old times *past*"). Here too lie the beginnings of the transformation of naïve adolescent religiosity into "Old Testament vengeance."[57] Erikson observes:

> We will call what young people in their teens and early twenties look for in religion and other dogmatic systems an *ideology*. At the most it is a militant system with uniformed members and uniform goals; at the least it is a "way of life" or what the Germans call a *Weltanschauung*, a world-view which is consonant with existing theory, available knowledge, and common sense, and yet is significantly more: an utopian outlook, a cosmic mood, or a doctrinal logic, all shared as self-evident, beyond any need for demonstration. What is to be relinquished as "old" may be the individual's previous life; this usually means the perspectives intrinsic to the life-style of the parents, who are thus discarded contrary to all traditional safeguards of filial devotion. The "old" may be a part of himself, which must henceforth be subdued by some rigorous self-denial in a private life-style or through membership in a militant

> or military organization; or it may be the world-view of other castes and classes, races and peoples: in this case these people become not only expendable, but the appointed victims of the most righteous annihilation.[58]

This, the righteous annihilator, is the new Nat of "Study War."

How, though, to separate this righteous Old Testament annihilator from the religious fanatic Styron did not wish to know, and from the reader's reproach and condemnation? How to make him, despite his acts, worthy of knowing? Here Styron drew further on Erikson, and on two psychological impulses of his own, sexual desire and conflicted love, united in the character of Margaret Whitehead.[59] The moment Styron's Nat, goaded by the insane, rape-obsessed, rebel "Will,"[60] consummates his hate/love longing for Margaret Whitehead (with which we have become familiarized through Nat's own serial rape fantasies)[61] by killing her, his rebellion loses direction and meaning, and Nat himself begins a headlong slide from righteous annihilation to grief and guilt-ridden despair, utterly estranged from God.[62] And the moment he acknowledges and consummates his unconflicted love of Margaret (the preexecution masturbation fantasy) he surmounts his last Eriksonian crisis, the integrity crisis, which "leads man to the portals of nothingness . . . to the station of *having been*,"[63] and in Nat's case points him toward death finally united with a New Testament God of brotherhood and forgiveness, forever severed from the Old Testament's primitive desert God of rage and terror. Styron's Nat exits the world a rather conventional Christian sinner saved.[64]

By integrity, Erikson means a state of mind in which the ego has achieved "assurance of its proclivity for order and meaning." He continues:

> It is a post-narcissistic love of the human ego—not of the self—as an experience which conveys some world order and some spiritual sense, no matter how dearly paid for. It is the acceptance of one's one and only life cycle as something that had to be and that, by necessity, permitted of no substitutions. . . . Before this final solution, death loses its sting.[65]

In the final moments of his life, Styron's Nat becomes the Negro the author desires so urgently to know, the bearer of a promise of acceptance and reconciliation, the embodied hope of the author for himself and for an America healed of racial violence, ignorance, and hatred.[66]

II

To re-create Nat Turner, to make him his own (so as to make him the embodiment of an integrated self and nation), Styron had to displace two other Nat Turners, the Nat Turner of Thomas Ruffin Gray's original *Confessions*, and the Nat Turner of oral legend, particularly of African American legend. In each case Styron's displacement strategy was the same—denial and rejection. The two denials, however, were quite distinct.

Styron's denial and rejection of the Turner of Gray's *Confessions* was not based on any carefully reasoned conclusion that he was a fabrication.[67] Rather, Styron insisted that this Turner was an insane monster, a religious fanatic who did not deserve attention or comprehension.[68] Styron's impression thus reproduces precisely what Gray desires his reader to see, "a gloomy fanatic . . . bewildered and overwrought . . . endeavoring to grapple with things beyond [his] reach," so described by a man who advertises his own repulsion at "the expression of his fiend-like face when excited by enthusiasm . . . daring to raise his manacled hands to heaven." As "I looked on him" says Gray, "my blood curdled in my veins."[69] Unlike Gray, however, it is not Turner's religiosity as such from which Styron recoils.[70] "Old Testament vengeance" is a central and essential component of Styron's Nat.[71] But enthusiasm—evangelical Christian faith—is not. Like Gray, Styron treats Turner's enthusiasm as insanity.[72] To domesticate him, Styron simply relieves Turner of his enthusiastic ideation, substituting in its stead those "subtler motives" suggested by social and behavioral explanation.[73] Styron's Nat is a noticeably calculating, a highly rational, strikingly modern intelligence.[74]

In small part, Styron separated his Nat from religious enthusiasm the better to use the book as an opportunity to inveigh against institutionalized Christian hypocrisy. "I've always been partially intent on contrasting the spiritual impulse as it is defined by Christianity with the hypocritical ritual and hypocritical shallowness and thought that surround much of [its] manifestations in life."[75] In *Confessions*, Styron's attack on Christian hypocrisy takes the form of an attack on denominational churches (notably the Methodist Church) on the grounds that "in Turner's time" the church was one of the two institutions (the other was the legal system) "which sold the Negro down the river" by promising salvation but failing to deliver.[76] "Basic psychology dictates that when you are offered the sweetest of promises and you experience only total frustration of it, you're driven round the bend. . . . It was perhaps the cruelest sell-out of all time."[77] Much more important, however, the separation of Turner from religious enthusiasm was a device that enabled Styron to insert a quite different Christian sensibility in its place, by having his Old Testament warrior first abandoned by the God of the prophets, then saved at the last by the intercession of Margaret Whitehead's Christian love.[78] "He was an avenging Old Testament angel. . . . I intentionally avoided the mention of Christ as much as I could throughout the book. He is almost never mentioned. Because if the book does have a sense of redemptive quality, it is only at the very end that it comes."[79] This is by any measure an extraordinarily perverse treatment of the Turner of Gray's *Confessions* (a treatment, one should note, for which Styron was commended by C. Vann Woodward),[80] whose religiosity is couched almost entirely in New Testament discourse, and who is himself his own redeemer.[81] It is explicable only by Styron's (and Woodward's) refusal (or inability) to recognize that Turner's New Testament did not belong to the "charity and brotherhood" species of Christian "spiritual impulse" espoused by twentieth-century white liberals, but to the martial and ascetic evangelicalism of eighteenth- and early nineteenth-century Anglo-American Protestantism, whose history of salvation began before the Fall and hence rejected any distinction between Old Testament and New.[82] Styron appears not to realize that in this species of Christian faith, the avenging angel is Christ himself.[83]

Styron's other displacement—the displacement of the Turner of legend—was more straightforward. Styron simply denied there was any such Turner.[84] His 1965 *Harper's Magazine* essay, "This Quiet Dust," tells of a day trip to Southampton County in May 1961 in search of a legendary Turner who completely fails to materialize. "What research it was possible to do on the event I had long since done. . . . It was not a question, then, of digging out more facts" but of savoring local mood and landscape, and probing for local lore.[85] But whomever he questions on local knowledge of Turner and his rebellion, white or black, disappoints him. "The native Virginian, despite himself, is cursed with a suffocating sense of history. . . . Yet it was as if Nat Turner had never existed."[86] People seemed "simply unaware."[87] If there were no recollection here, where he had once lived and wreaked bloody havoc, then there could be none anywhere. Turner "had been erased from memory."[88] The story is entirely bizarre: Accompanied by his father and his wife, Styron tours backcountry Southampton in the county sheriff's squad car, "with its huge star emblazoned on the doors . . . its riot gun protectively nuzzling the backs of our necks over the edge of the rear seat," in search of passersby whom they can stop and quiz on what they know about the Turner Rebellion.[89] Styron describes how the sheriff himself enthusiastically joined in the interrogations. "I think it tickled him to perplex their foolish heads, white or black, with the same old leading question: 'You heard about old Nat Turner, ain't you?' But few of them had."[90] Small wonder. Ironically, Styron's essay itself provides epigraphic evidence that gives the lie to his claim of the absence of folk lore—two verses from what was labeled an "Old-time Negro Song," the refrain of which was the impossibility of suppressing Nat Turner.[91]

After his *Confessions* was published, Styron would return repeatedly to the sparseness of fact and the erasure of memory to elevate the product of his own creative imagination above both.[92] This earned him, largely, congratulation and commendation from white commentators,[93] and—again largely—disdain and outrage from black commentators.[94] In a *New Republic* review remarkable for the seamlessness of its many transits back and forth between historical and imaginative depiction, the doyen of white Southern historians, C. Vann Woodward, awarded Styron the mantle of complete and utter scholarly respectability. "The picture of Nat's life and motivation the novelist constructs is, but for a few scraps of evidence, without historical underpinnings, but most historians would agree, I think, not inconsistent with anything historians know. It is informed by a respect for history, a sure feeling for the period, and a deep and precise sense of place and time."[95] A man one might consider Woodward's African American counterpart, John Henrik Clarke, did not agree.[96] "No event in recent years has touched and stirred the black intellectual community more than this book. They are of the opinion, with a few notable exceptions, that the Nat Turner created by William Styron has little resemblance to the Virginia slave insurrectionist who is a hero to his people."[97] Nine other black intellectuals joined Clarke in publishing a book of essays claiming the existence of a potent African American history (and lore) of Nat Turner ignored by Styron, and attempting to reclaim the historical figure of Turner from him. With perhaps two exceptions,[98] their rebuttal—*William Styron's Nat Turner: Ten Black Writers Respond*—though heated, was not unduly rancorous. Nonetheless they were speedily condemned by Styron's defenders, notably Eugene Genovese, for a collective exhibition of "ferocity and hysteria" that revealed the black intelligentsia was on course for a "moral, political, and intellectual debacle."[99] Nothing had ever prevented "black intellectuals, who claim to have the living traditions of black America at their disposal, from creating their own version" of Turner, Genovese wrote, even as he busily set about denying that black America's living traditions actually contained any memory of Turner, and excoriated the ten's attempts to defend an African American "version" as mere pandering to the Black Power movement.[100] "If white historians—for whatever reasons—have been blind to whole areas of black sensibility, culture, and tradition, then show us. We can learn much from your work but nothing from your fury."[101] Subsequently, Styron himself would claim the ten black writers were no more than a front for the U.S. Communist Party and its *apparatchik* theoretician, Herbert Aptheker, the white historian of slavery whose work Styron—like Genovese—publicly derided.[102]

III

The Confessions of Nat Turner was published, to considerable demand, in October 1967. Random House had prepared the ground carefully. Styron "would have a great many readers and make a great deal of money."[103] Book club and paperback rights had been sold long in advance, bringing $250,000. Movie rights went for $800,000. *Harper's* and *Life* bought serial rights to publish substantial excerpts coinciding with the book's publication.[104] By release day (October 9) Random House had 125,000 hardback copies in print; many more would follow.[105] The next three years saw multiple foreign editions, a Pulitzer Prize (1968), and the Howells Medal (1970).[106] Styron's *Confessions* was another "orgy of commerce"—this time a real one.[107] Commenting on the book that preceded *Confessions*—*Set This House on Fire*—Norman Mailer had written in 1959, prior to the book's appearance, "The reception will be a study in the art of literary advancement. For Styron has spent years oiling every literary lever and power which could help him on his way, and there are medals waiting for him in the mass-media."[108] *House on Fire* had not been the major commercial success Mailer had anticipated. *Confessions*, it seemed, would prove him right the second time around.

The first reviews were fulsome indeed. "A stunningly beautiful embodiment of a noble man, in a rotten time and place, who tried his best to save himself and transform the world."[109] No one was more admiring than the literary critic Philip Rahv in the *New York Review of Books*. Styron had successfully matched his subject—chattel slavery and its consequences—to the moment—"the political and intellectual climate of the Sixties." The novel's historicity did not exclude, but rather invited, contemporaneity in a way that "only a white Southern writer" could have managed. A Northern writer would have been too much of an outsider, Rahv argued, "and a Negro writer, because of a very complex anxiety not only personal but social and political, would have probably stacked the cards, producing in a mood of unnerving rage and indignation, a melodrama of saints and sinners." Styron had surpassed Faulkner in "ability to empathize with his Negro figures." His book was "a radical departure from past writing about Negroes"; it fulfilled its author's desire "to know the Negro."[110]

The helpless, hapless, condescension of reviewers like Rahv helps explain the appalled reaction of John Henrik Clarke and his compatriots, whose essential complaint was pithily summarized in Vincent Harding's essay title, "You've Taken My Nat and Gone."[111] Rahv seemed to think of "the Negro" as an object of study, from which truth might better be extracted by expert white observation than by attention to self-description. But, however unintentionally, Rahv had also put his finger on *Confessions*' core ambition—and the difficulty it was to cause the book's author.

The issue at hand was raised by Styron himself, twice over, in the author note accompanying his *Confessions*. First, he addressed the inevitable tension for one writing on a historical subject between historical research and creative imagination:

> During the narrative that follows I have rarely departed from the *known* facts about Nat Turner and the revolt of which he was the leader. However, in those areas where there is little knowledge in regard to Nat, his early life, and the motivations for the revolt (and such knowledge is lacking most of the time), I have allowed myself the utmost freedom in reconstructing events—yet I trust remaining within the bounds of what meager enlightenment history has left us about the institution of slavery.[112]

Second, and immediately following, Styron alluded to his embrace of a philosophy of history that, in effect dialectically, overcame the tension between fact and creative imagination that he had just acknowledged:

> The relativity of time allows us elastic definitions: the year 1831 was, simultaneously, a long time ago and only yesterday. Perhaps the reader will wish to draw a moral from this narrative, but it has been my own intention to try to re-create a man and his era, and to produce a work that is less an "historical novel" in conventional terms than a meditation on history.[113]

Styron's desire to escape the low-earth orbit of the "historical novel" and its subjective, moralistic standpoint on indubitably past events for the Proustian elasticities of "the relativity of time" is clear.[114] Unfortunately for him, he would find it enormously difficult to explain precisely what he meant by "a meditation on history,"[115] or how it had helped him overcome the fact/imagination tension, or how it gave him a standpoint different—more serious, more worthy of respect, more authentic—than that of the historical novel. As a result, when challenged—first by Aptheker,[116] later by the ten black writers and others—Styron became stuck in an increasingly petulant defensive crouch. When his creative imaginings of Turner and of slavery were challenged, Styron would cite his research, his mastery of facts and sources.[117] When his mastery of facts and sources was challenged, Styron would cite his creative imagination.[118] Some months into the controversy, Styron discovered Georg Lukács's book, *The Historical Novel*,[119] which—still unable to explain his own philosophy of history—he began citing with abandon.[120] There was a certain irony in this, given that Styron had wished to distance *Confessions* from the historical novel, but Lukács was no defender of convention, and in any case Styron thought he had found in *The Historical Novel* impeccable authority—"the greatest Marxist literary critic" or "the great Hungarian Marxist critic"[121]—for artistic license, for respectable intellectual radicalism, and above all for freedom from "the dead baggage of facts," from "particular historical facts."[122] And indeed Lukács had written that "the novelist must be at liberty to treat [particular historical facts] as he likes, if he is to reproduce the much more complex and ramifying totality with historical faithfulness."[123] But Lukács was, of course, distinguishing here between "real historical fidelity to the whole . . . fidelity in the reproduction of the material foundations of the life of a given period" and "the pseudo-historicism of the mere authenticity of individual facts."[124] It was precisely the "real historical fidelity" of Styron's representation of Turner and of slavery that was at issue.[125]

Styron's self-defense would eventually turn *The Historical Novel* into a sort of fiction writer's checklist, which also gave the unfortunate impression that he had read *The Historical Novel* before writing *Confessions* rather than come across it afterwards. Lukács "should be read by all who attempt to write in the genre" he observed in 1992:

> A bad historical novel leaves the impression of a hopelessly over-furnished house, cluttered with facts the author wishes to show off as fruits of his diligent research. Georg Lukács . . . views the dis-

> regard of facts as a state of grace: the creator of historical fiction, he argues convincingly, should have a thorough—perhaps even a magisterial—command of the period with which he is dealing, but he should not permit his work to be governed by particular historical facts. . . . At the time of writing *Nat Turner*, I felt that as an amateur historian, I had absorbed a vast amount of reading on slavery in general, not only by way of a great number of antebellum books and essays but through much recent scholarship in the exploding field of the historiography of the slave period; thus, while my command may scarcely have been magisterial, I felt I reasonably fulfilled the first of Lukács's conditions. It was perhaps serendipitous that Lukács's other condition, regarding the relative unimportance of facts, made my task easier since I had chosen a man about whom so little was known.[126]

All that said, Styron credited Lukács in his 1992 essay with helping him in his struggle to articulate what he meant by "a meditation on history." But the statement of meaning he allowed himself on that occasion—that "historical novels which have no resonance in the present are bound to prove of only 'antiquarian' interest"[127]—was banal.

Styron struggled to articulate what his "meditation" meant because, being neither philosopher nor historian, he actually had no idea what it meant, and so took his cue from the views of whatever authoritative and apparently supportive voice he happened to encounter. In the course of a postpublication conversation about *Confessions* with C. Vann Woodward and his Yale colleague, the literary scholar R.W.B. Lewis, for example, Styron started out agreeing with Woodward that his goal had been to make "valid and authentic use of history for the purposes of fiction," and to be faithful to, and respectful of, "the period, the time, the place." Lewis then asked whether "meditation on history" meant "a meditation on the mysterious processes of history." Styron answered that his goal had been to distance himself from the "curse" of the historical novel—a return to Woodward's contention that his goal had been to write a book that was an authentic and respectful invocation of history—then added that he had also aspired "to encompass a meditative quality as I wrote." Lewis took this to mean that Styron was not after all himself meditating on history, but rather that he wished to convey a sense of his subject, Nat, meditating on *his* history—"brooding about the entire adventure while waiting to be hanged." Styron agreed with that too.[128] When, later, Genovese argued (inveighing against Aptheker and the ten black writers) that one should look to history not for ideological reassurance but for truth, and that Styron had told the truth about Turner and about slavery, Styron agreed with that.[129] Then, when Seymour Gross and Ellen Bender argued the opposite—that Styron like all other writers had simply produced his own partial Turner, "reading into him, and out of him, those usable truths which seemed to him to coalesce about the image he was contemplating"—Styron agreed with that too.[130] Although throughout he stubbornly insisted on the integrity of his depiction, by 1992 Styron seemed ready to surrender to the predilection for contingency that over the previous twenty-five years had become uppermost in historical scholarship. Turner "utterly evaded a consistent portrayal." He "was truly a chameleon."[131]

In fact, the meaning of Styron's "meditation" had always been clear and available, in his own words, for all to see, at the end of his 1965 *Harper's* essay, "This Quiet Dust." At the end of his long and disappointing day in Southampton County, Styron discovers what he takes to be the home of Margaret Whitehead, and describes a vision of her death. What he wrote then had nothing to do with tensions between "facts" and "creative freedom." But it does help explain why Styron clung so tenaciously to both history and art, despite his inability to articulate why. Styron's meditation was on the impossibility of living imaginatively within history's decisive separation of "the past" from his "now":

> I leaned against the rotting frame of the door, gazing out past the great trees and into that far meadow where Nat had brought down and slain Miss Margaret Whitehead. For an instant in the silence, I thought I could hear a mad rustle of taffeta, and rushing feet, and a shrill girlish piping of terror; then that day and this day seemed to meet and melt together, becoming almost one, and for a long moment indistinguishable.[132]

Fittingly, the passage is a good stand-in for so much that is maddening about William Styron's *Confessions*, and simultaneously for so much about the book that was misunderstood. First, the house from which he gazed "into that far meadow" was not actually the Whitehead house at all. His "facts" were wrong.[133] Second, the idea central to the passage was conveyed with all of Styron's familiar florid profundity—every noun carefully attended by a posse of guardian adjectives. But, third, the idea itself, Styron's "long moment indistinguishable," was well worth the trouble.

The title of the *Harper's* essay reveals its meaning only in the essay's last paragraphs, as Styron explores the "Whitehead" house, choking on the dust "that lay everywhere in the deserted rooms, years and decades of dust, dust an inch thick in some places." The title is taken from Emily Dickinson's poem *The Single Hound* #74, a muse on being and nothingness:

This quiet Dust was Gentlemen and Ladies,
And Lads and Girls;
Was laughter and ability and sighing,
And frocks and curls.
This passive place a Summer's nimble mansion,
Where Bloom and Bees
Fulfilled their Oriental Circuit,
Then ceased like these.[134]

Styron's words embrace Dickinson's temporal cycle of life and death, but restate it as one not simply of presence and absence, but of memory and recognition. Amid the dusty ruin of what he thought was the Whitehead house, his "lustrous and golden day" in Southampton County "seemed to find its only resonance in the memory, and perhaps a premonition, of death."[135] Here was the "long moment indistinguishable," a rebuke to those who would labor to create as "history" a separated past from which the present had departed. Styron, who bitterly resented the common critical comment that he was his generation's William Faulkner, was nevertheless having a Faulknerian moment. "The past is never dead," Faulkner famously wrote in *Requiem for a Nun*. "It's not even past."[136]

Styron's long moment sets him apart, philosophically, from those to whom he had turned, so gratefully, for professional assistance: from C. Vann Woodward, for whom Styron's novel was *history*—a reconstruction of a particular past;[137] from Eugene Genovese, for whom Styron's novel was less history than *art*—and for that reason able to claim access to transcendent truths as no history ever could;[138] and even from Georg Lukács, for whom "a real historical novel" was one "which contemporaries would experience as their own pre-history."[139] It puts him instead in the company of Walter Benjamin, for whom the goal of history was to represent "our age"—the age that examines historical events—"in the age during which they arose."[140] As Michael Jennings has noted, Benjamin's point is liable to be misunderstood. It does not mean "that we bring a previous age to representation in our own," but the reverse—that "we bring the salient . . . features of our own age to consciousness" by recognizing their representation in that to which we give our attention.[141] In Benjamin's own words the contrast with Lukács is clear. For Lukács the object of historical inquiry was to recover the reality of an object situated temporally and spatially in the past.[142] For Benjamin the object of historical inquiry could only exist in a condition of constellation with the moment—the "now"—of its observation:

> It is said that the dialectical method consists in doing justice each time to the concrete historical situation of its object. But that is not enough. For it is just as much a matter of doing justice to the concrete historical situation of the *interest* taken in the object. And *this* situation is always so constituted that the interest is itself preformed in that object and, above all, feels this object concretized in itself and upraised from its former being into the higher concretion of now-being [*Jetztsein*].[143]

This is a semblance of the intent attributed to Styron by his biographer, who argues that by employing a narrative voice "not . . . limited by time or place" Styron intended to create a collision between Turner's language, and world, and his own, "to bring the past into direct confrontation with the present," to possess it and transform it in "an unruly, uncooperative" fashion.[144]

One might wonder why, if this was indeed Styron's intent, he had not made it clear years before. Though it is unlikely it would have saved him from controversy it might have assisted comprehension of his purposes. In fact, apart from the conclusion to "This Quiet Dust," Styron was unwilling, more likely unable, to explain himself. First, in interviews accompanying publication, perhaps because his publisher was so determinedly insisting that the book was a commentary on the present, Styron preferred to distance himself from any desire to create a collision between the late 1960s and the Turner Rebellion: "I began the book and was concerned with the subject back in the forties, long before the civil-rights struggle was truly joined. The central meaning of the book is not consciously contemporary."[145] Second, throughout his life after *Confessions*, Styron struggled for words from which to fashion a self-reflective account of meditative intent. He managed to convey a sense of temporal doubleness, but the two elements—history and representation—remained obstinately apart. The book dealt with history but was also "a separate entity"; it had "its own autonomy . . . its own metaphysics, its own reason for being as an aesthetic object." It was simultaneously engaged with history and "a metaphorical diagram for a writer's attitude toward human existence."[146] In 1982 he appealed to the same discourse of doubleness, calling the book "an imagined vision within a vision," but then discounted "meditation on history" by divorcing the book from "the detritus of fact" or any pretensions to "truth."[147] Ten years later Styron had become more willing to let the worlds collide: "Certainly I was never anything but intensely aware of the way in which the theme of slave rebellion was finding echoes in the gathering tensions of the Civil Rights movement," and "certainly in the back of my mind I had hoped that whatever light my work might shed on the dungeon of American slavery, and its abyssal night of the body and spirit, might also cast light on our modern condition . . . [on] the agony that has bound the present to the past."[148] He would reemphasize the collision another decade on:

> Americans have a penchant for historical amnesia. Very few Americans are aware of the continuity that exists between slavery and the racial dilemma we still live with in this country. Without an understanding of slavery I don't think there can be any true perception of the complexity of the racial agony in the nation. And any legitimate story, such as the one that involves Nat Turner, or any other aspect of slavery, could be an illumination for our society. Most people don't understand the extent of the utter dehumanization created by American slavery, the almost uniquely monolithic emasculating quality that slavery possessed. If a story like Nat Turner could be made part of the general consciousness of Americans at this time, I think it would be of enormous value.[149]

But this was not constellation—the creation of a dialectical image.[150] It was instead a description of hauling a piece of the past into the present so as to inform a current conjuncture with moral reflection on a prior atrocity. Here was no escape from the low-earth orbit of the "historical novel" into "the relativity of time." It suffered, moreover, from Styron's fatal persistence in simultaneously seeking a black audience that would appreciate his work, while failing to realize how completely he had excluded that audience from his imagination. Could one defensibly maintain that very few *African* Americans were "aware of the continuity that exists between slavery and the racial dilemma we still live with in this country"?[151] Still, as its author's final plea for his book's "passion and . . . honesty . . . [and] integrity,"[152] it was not without grace.

CONCLUSION

What remains is the question how one might deliver Nat Turner from those, like William Styron, who would befriend him by giving him "rational dimensions" so that he might be yanked into the American present to teach it a lesson it could understand on its own terms. How might Turner instead be encountered on *his* terms, such that "what has been comes together in a flash with the now to form a constellation," the moment of a specific recognition that teaches the present not a moral lesson about itself, but instead that it is itself a montage fashioned from dialectical images—from "critical constellations in which precisely this fragment of the past finds itself with precisely this present"?[153] How does one overcome the metaphysics of presence—which dictated both the construction and the reception, on all sides, of Styron's Nat—without surrendering the past to the past?

First we have to recognize that the Turner whom Styron rejected, the Turner he met in Gray's *Confessions*, the psychopath afflicted with "crazed visions," is just as much Styron's invention as the rational Turner, gifted with human complexity, whom he created to take the psychopath's place in the modern mind.[154] The psychopathic visionary is no more Turner on his own terms than the rational calculating Turner of Styron's *Confessions*. It is instead what results from a complete refusal to engage in inquiry into those terms and to substitute instead a lazy modernist cliché—as Eugene Genovese so helpfully put it in his assault on the ten black writers, "one of those religious fanatics whose single-minded madness carried him to the leadership of a popular cause"—that excuses one from undertaking the investigation.[155]

Nor is Styron alone in that refusal. Though historians have found Turner's rebellion historically significant,[156] even praiseworthy,[157] as an event, most have contented themselves with entirely superficial assessments of Turner himself.[158] The best that Kenneth Stampp could manage was that Turner, whom Stampp thought "a rather unimpressive" slave, whatever that meant, "somehow . . . came to believe that he had been divinely chosen to deliver his people from bondage."[159] For the more censorious, ever opinionated, Genovese, "those who read the record could not be faulted for concluding that Nat Turner, unlike Gabriel Prosser and Denmark Vesey, was a hate-driven madman who had no idea of where he was leading his men or what they would do when they got there."[160] Nor was Genovese by any means alone in preferring those who better conformed to his understanding of what the leader of a slave rebellion should look like—Gabriel Prosser and Denmark Vesey—to the "fanatic" Nat Turner. The major African American literary figure Arna Bontemps, author (amongst many works) of *Black Thunder* (1936), a novel about Gabriel's Rebellion, tells us he had first considered writing about Turner, but had been troubled by Turner's "'visions' and 'dreams,'" his "trance-like mumbo-jumbo."[161]

As the words of Genovese (and Bontemps) suggest, "reading the record"—which means reading Gray's *Confessions*—is taken to be a straightforward process that, inevitably, reveals the man that Gray presented, a madman confused and overwhelmed by visions, dreams, and "mumbo-jumbo." Literary scholars, in contrast, have shown us how to read Gray's *Confessions* with a far more subtle appreciation of the connotations of Turner's Christian-inflected discourse.[162] If Nat Turner is to be delivered from cartoonish caricature, the attempt must begin in a careful recovery of the layered meaning of his own speech, the soterial speech of an ascetic evangelical Protestant, not a dismissal of it as "impossibly elevated and formal," or of its speaker as fanatic or insane.[163] Here, one might say, the historian is required to encounter Derrida's past, the past that never can be present.

But, second, this "contextualization" of Turner's intellect—recognizing it the way it really was—is only the initial step in his rescue. For "articulating the past *historically*" means much more than simply "recognizing it 'the way it really was.'"[164] Historical perspective *dispels* "self-contained facticity."[165] Articulating the past historically "means appropriating a memory as it flashes up in a moment of danger," at "the moment of its recognizability," which is the here-and-now.[166] In other words, if we understand history as an enlivened understanding of an object of contemplation, which is to say an object rendered intelligible, we must recognize that the contemplated object is not enlivened by the relationalities within which it allegedly belongs (the relationalities of *its* time) but by the fold of time that creates it in constellation with the present. "The lines of perspective in this construction, receding to the vanishing point, converge in our own historical experience."[167] That which we recognize, and to which we give our attention, is enlivened by our recognition; it also enlivens us.

Dimly, I think, William Styron recognized that an enlivened Nat Turner could not be a Turner of self-contained facticity but had necessarily to be a Turner brought into a relationship with Styron's own present. In attempting to create that relationship, Styron so thoroughly uprooted Turner from Turner's past as to reinvent him completely in the terms of Styron's present. Rather than "recognize" Turner he preferred to exchange one self-contained facticity for another.[168] And so he failed. But his failure was not complete. His error lay in the execution, not in its animating idea.

Contemporary historicism, the historicism whose intellectual contribution has been to pin phenomena in temporal and spatial place, would not have much time—literally—for William Styron's "long moment indistinguishable." Such a moment that melts distinct spatio-temporal locales into one and the same makes no sense to a historicism whose purpose is relentless temporal separation. Fortunately there are other ways of doing history that may help us make sense of indistinguishable moments. They will help us produce an enlivened Nat Turner who is no longer merely enigmatic spectator.

PART I

Perpetually Thirsting

I
am a stranger
lurking alone
In my own vicious wilderness
while the meat in my chest
squeezes and teases a hulking hunger
groping in motion
balance is
but a shimmering notion
and lurching compelled
my soul in its
special hell
of wet mortal limits
perpetually thirsting . . .

—VIC CHESNUTT,
"GLOSSOLALIA" (2007)

THE

CONFESSIONS

OF

NAT TURNER,

THE LEADER OF THE LATE

INSURRECTION IN SOUTHAMPTON, VA.

As fully and voluntarily made to

THOMAS R. GRAY,

In the prison where he was confined, and acknowledged by him to be such when read before the Court of Southampton; with the certificate, under seal of the Court convened at Jerusalem, Nov. 5, 1831, for his trial.

ALSO, AN AUTHENTIC

ACCOUNT OF THE WHOLE INSURRECTION,

WITH LISTS OF THE WHITES WHO WERE MURDERED,

AND OF THE NEGROES BROUGHT BEFORE THE COURT OF SOUTHAMPTON, AND THERE SENTENCED, &c.

Baltimore:
PUBLISHED BY THOMAS R. GRAY.
Lucas & Deaver, print.
1831.

1

Confessions: Of Text and Paratext

Whosoever shall confess me before men, him shall the Son of man also confess before the angels of God.

—LUKE 12:8

This Speaking Man . . . there is need of him yet! The Speaking Function, this of Truth coming to us with a living voice, nay in a living shape, and as a concrete practical exemplar.

—THOMAS CARLYLE (1843)

Some facts are not in dispute. Over the course of twelve hours beginning around 1:00 a.m. on Monday, August 22, Nat Turner led a group of fellow blacks—mostly slaves[1]—in an armed attack on some fifteen white slaveholding households in St. Luke's Parish, Southampton County, Virginia, resulting in the deaths of fifty-five women, children, and men. During the following twenty-four hours, members of Turner's band engaged in a series of confrontations with white militia and armed inhabitants, at the end of which Turner was the only active participant in the massacre who had managed to avoid death or capture. Remaining in his old neighborhood, in hiding, Turner continued to avoid apprehension for more than two months, until he was finally discovered on Sunday, October 30. On Monday, October 31, he was taken to Jerusalem, the county seat, where he was examined before two county magistrates, James W. Parker and James Trezvant. Parker and Trezvant found sufficient evidence to warrant committing Turner to the county jail to await trial by the Southampton County Court, sitting as a court of Oyer and

---

FIGURE 1.1. Title page of Thomas Ruffin Gray's *The Confessions of Nat Turner*, 1st ed. (1831). Photograph by Special Collections, Swem Library, College of William & Mary.

Terminer, on charges of conspiring to rebel and making insurrection. Turner's trial took place five days later, on the morning of Saturday, November 5, before a bench of ten magistrates. He was convicted, and sentenced to death. He was hanged on Friday, November 11.[2]

More detail was forthcoming, and as a result questions, because on the evening of October 31, following Turner's examination and committal, a local attorney named Thomas Ruffin Gray gained access to him in jail by permission of the jailor and ascertained "that he was willing to make a full and free confession of the origin, progress and consummation of the insurrectory movements of the slaves of which he was the contriver and head." Gray "determined for the gratification of public curiosity to commit his statements to writing and publish them." By agreement with Turner (and the jailor) Gray returned the next day, Tuesday November 1, to hear Turner's account of what had happened. Turner's narrative continued the following Wednesday and Thursday. Then, "having the advantage of his statement before me in writing," on Thursday evening Gray "began a cross examination." He found Turner's statement corroborated, to his satisfaction, "by every circumstance coming within my own knowledge or the confessions of others . . . whom he had not seen nor had any knowledge since 22d of August."[3]

Following Turner's trial on November 5, Gray left Jerusalem for Richmond, 70 miles to the north, where on November 7 (a Monday) he attempted to arrange the printing of his manuscript. Unsuccessful in Richmond, he rode on to Washington, DC, a further 110 miles to the north, where on November 10 he obtained copyright for his pamphlet. The pamphlet itself was printed in Baltimore, another 40 miles northeast of Washington, by the firm of Lucas and Deaver. It was published on November 22 and advertised for sale, priced twenty-five cents. A second edition, newly typeset and with minor typographical corrections, was printed by the firm of T. W. White and published in Richmond the following year. All told, rather more than fifty thousand copies may have circulated.[4]

Gray's pamphlet is entitled, in full, *The Confessions of Nat Turner, the Leader of the Late Insurrection in Southampton, Va. As fully and voluntarily made to Thomas R. Gray, In the prison where he was confined, and acknowledged by him to be such when read before the Court of Southampton; with the certificate, under seal of the Court convened at Jerusalem, Nov. 5, 1831, for his trial. Also, An Authentic Account of the Whole Insurrection, With Lists of the Whites who were Murdered, And of the Negroes Brought before the Court of Southampton, and there Sentenced, &c.* It "immediately became the standard account" of the event that became known as the Turner Rebellion.[5] The event has spawned many commentaries, both historical and literary. Without exception all grant considerable prominence to Gray's pamphlet.[6] But like all documents generated in the course of master-class investigations of slave revolts, alleged or actual, *The Confessions of Nat Turner* raises obvious evidentiary quandaries: credibility, reliability, authenticity. Precisely what kind of historical source is this document? How should it be interrogated? What can it tell us?

These questions are not posed idly. In 2001, the historian Michael Johnson aimed devastating criticism at three new histories of the Denmark Vesey slave conspiracy, thought to have occurred in 1822 in Charleston, South Carolina, because in Johnson's view their authors—and by extension every other historian of the Vesey Conspiracy—had relied far too credulously on the *Official Report* of the inquiry into the alleged plot undertaken by the Charleston Court of Magistrates and Freeholders.[7] Invited to review the authors' books, but moved by their facile (to Johnson) celebrations of Vesey as "a bold insurrectionist determined to free his people or die trying," as well as by his own mounting doubts about the evidentiary basis on which he had himself once taken much the same position, Johnson had undertaken a thorough examination of the manuscript sources from which the *Official Report* had been constructed. He discovered that, "far from being an impartial account of court proceedings, the *Official Report* is a document of advocacy, a public, retrospective statement of the prosecution's case against Denmark Vesey and the many other defendants. It must be read and interpreted with the suspicion warranted by special pleading." Unfortunately, in their reliance on this dubious document, historians of the Vesey Conspiracy had "failed to exercise due caution in reading the testimony of witnesses recorded by the conspiracy court." They had depended uncritically on the very sources used to convict those accused for information about who they were, what they did, and what they hoped to do, and so had become "unwitting co-conspirators with the court" in perpetuating the court's claim that there was indeed something called "the Vesey Conspiracy." They had trusted law to produce empirical—though not political—truth, but in fact the court had "colluded with a handful of intimidated witnesses" to create an insurrection plot out of nothing more than suspicion and rumor. The Vesey Conspiracy was a juridical witch hunt, prosecuted by the court in defense of its reputation after its initial peremptory accusations and hasty executions were criticized within Charleston's white community. "Vesey and the other condemned black men were victims of an insurrection conspiracy conjured into being in

1822 by the court, its cooperative black witnesses, and its numerous white supporters." The empty conspiracy claim had been "kept alive ever since by historians eager to accept the court's judgments while rejecting its morality." Historians seeking heroes in rumors of revolt were better advised "to pay attention to the 'not guilty' pleas of almost all the men who went to the gallows, to their near silence in the court records, to their refusal to name names in order to save themselves. These men were heroes not because they were about to launch an insurrection but because they risked and accepted death rather than collaborate with the conspiratorial court." Johnson's conclusion challenged all historians of American slavery to cease their moral and ideological posturing and to use their sources—particularly their legal sources—more critically. "Surely it is time to read the court's *Official Report* and the witnesses' testimony with the skepticism they richly deserve and to respect the integrity of a past that sometimes confounds the reassuring expectations generated by our present-day convictions about the evil of slavery and the legitimacy of blacks' claims to freedom and justice. Surely it is time to bring the court's conspiracy against Denmark Vesey and other black Charlestonians to an end."[8]

There are, of course, important differences between *The Confessions of Nat Turner* and *The Official Report*. First and most obvious, the event that would become known as the Turner Rebellion actually took place. We are dealing with something that happened, rather than a plot to cause something to happen, alleged or actual. Second, *The Confessions of Nat Turner* does not purport to be an official report of an investigation undertaken by a public body and prepared at its request by its presiding officers. Still, the pamphlet does represent itself (like the *Official Report*) as a faithful record of Turner's verbal account of his actions and motivations, an account given voluntarily, without the prompting of his white interlocutor, while under detention awaiting trial on capital charges, and though not commissioned, certified as accurate after the fact by the Southampton County Court. Hence, Johnson's admonitions are as relevant to those who would rely on *The Confessions* as the ur-text of the Turner Rebellion as they are to those who would write of the Vesey Conspiracy using the materials generated by the Charleston Court of Magistrates and Freeholders. Narrowly, what trust can one have in the substance of Gray's pamphlet as truthful description and explanation of the event, and as guide to its leader's mentalité and motivation, given that it was compiled hastily and in camera by an opportunistic and impoverished local white attorney, hoping to cash in on the notoriety of the

Southampton County insurrection, while its subject was under legal duress?[9] More broadly, accepting Johnson's case for skepticism in the historian's encounter with historical evidence, but also accepting that the document itself (like the *Official Report*) remains a valuable historical resource, how can it be used? Gray's pamphlet is undoubtedly evidentiary, but evidence of what?

The narrow question—of trust—can be answered in different ways. First, one can examine the content of the pamphlet. In substance it appears as a firsthand narrative account of the motivation for, and events of, Turner's rebellion. Gray acknowledges his own intellectual presence in, and influence on, Turner's statement. He reports that he forbore from frequent questioning while listening to Turner's narrative, but that once Turner had finished "I . . . had much conversation with and asked him many questions."[10] He does not represent the published statement as verbatim Turner but rather as one "with little or no variation, from his own words."[11] Alternatively, one can ask whether the narrative account that appears in the pamphlet is plausible in light of other evidence. Noting that the text "is riddled with difficult problems of authenticity and intentionality," Eric Sundquist, for example, advises that "corroborating evidence must be pieced together and even then remains highly speculative."[12]

Answers to the broader question—of what, precisely, is the pamphlet evidence?—turn to a considerable extent on what kind of text one determines it to be. As a text *The Confessions* has attracted detailed attention from both historians and literary scholars, whose approaches to it, however, have been quite distinct. Once past the "evidentiary reliability" barrier, historians have tended to take the pamphlet at face value: *The Confessions of Nat Turner* is an impressionistic but largely accurate narrative account of the coming-to-be of a slave rebellion, based, invaluably, on extended conversations with the rebellion's leader and architect, supplemented by commentary written by his opportunistic white interlocutor. Gray frames Turner's narrative with observations of his own calculated to make the narrative acceptable and appealing to a curious white public, and to serve the interests of Southampton County's legal and slaveholding elites by representing the rebellion as an isolated and purely local affair, conjured into being by one "gloomy fanatic," easily contained and justly punished, demonstrating "the policy of our laws in restraint of this class of our population" and their guardians' "watchful eye."[13] Gray's framing notwithstanding, the narrative itself emerges in the pamphlet as "definitive."[14]

Literary scholars, in contrast, have worked to assimilate the *Confessions* to one or other available category, or genre, of text, holding that the meaning of the pamphlet, hence its significance, lies in the modes or techniques of its composition and self-presentation, no less than in the "authenticity" and empirical reliability of its substance. Texts are created in critical compositional contexts that situate them spatially, chronologically, and qualitatively, and influence what they can and cannot do or say. This is to reach beyond the source as an empirical account of an event that is or is not "accurate" and to ask instead after its intended function as a document.

In one of the earliest and most inspired literary commentaries on the pamphlet, Eric Sundquist held it to be a "remarkable combination of autobiography, religious reflection, and political oratory," composed in dialogic collaboration between Turner and Gray, whom Sundquist figured as antagonists locked in a dialectical struggle in which Turner's "revolutionary energy" escapes Gray's attempts at "countersubversive containment."[15] Sundquist thus assimilated the pamphlet to the genres of both slave narrative and revolutionary tract. Twenty years after Sundquist, Jeannine DeLombard situated *The Confessions*' "highly interiorized account of the birth, growth, and maturation of the leader of the bloodiest slave uprising in American history" chronologically between "the early American scaffold tradition" of gallows literature and the "fugitive slave narratives promoted by the antebellum abolitionist movement." Turner, she argues, appears as the epitome of criminal mens rea, like the confessing subjects of gallows literature, but refuses to play the confessional role of communitarian tradition through public acknowledgment of his guilt, thereby restoring communal order, and instead tips over into the aggrieved "I" forced to labor who is the speaking subject of the antebellum slave narrative.[16] It will be apparent that interpretive purchase, not a quest for ontological "authenticity," is DeLombard's primary concern. In her reading, unlike Sundquist's, Turner is a wholly textual creature, hence wholly defined by genre, not a life form existing *de hors-texte*.[17] Just as he once was entirely "Styron's Nat" here he is unequivocally "Gray's Turner."

Other literary readings recoil somewhat from Derridean mistranslations.[18] William L. Andrews, Laura Thiemann Scales, and John Mac Kilgore all grant an extratextual Turner authorial influence over his own narrative, albeit the narrative itself remains limited by the radius of genre's expressive leash. Andrews and Scales concentrate on his religious persona: his self-presentation is "Christological," his confession one not of guilt but of faith;[19] his speech is a mode of prophecy—continuous revelation—common amongst self-divinizing contemporaries.[20] In both cases Turner escapes the gloomy "gothic" cage erected by his amanuensis.[21] Kilgore, meanwhile, assimilates Turner's "enthusiasm" less to messianic faith than to Byronic politics: enthusiasm means not pathological religiosity but the outgrowth of "a prophetic tradition of inspired resistance to tyranny."[22]

A final literary reading returns us, and somewhat dogmatically, to interpretation. It speaks to the constraints rather than the opportunities of genre. Breaking in particular with Sundquist, but also with all other readings of the pamphlet, historical or literary, Caleb Smith asserts that *The Confessions* is neither historical narrative nor autobiography, nor dialogic struggle. The pamphlet was "composed by the Virginia lawyer Thomas Ruffin Gray" and is addressed "to the public culture of justice." The pamphlet, "it should be clear, is a trial report."[23]

It is certainly true that the pamphlet performs "ritualized speech acts of religion and the law."[24] Legality and religion infuse *The Confessions*. But Smith can assimilate the pamphlet to the genre of "trial report" only by ignoring virtually all of its narrative content so as to concentrate the reader's attention on the final two pages. These indeed purport to be a report of Turner's trial. Smith emphasizes the final two pages because it is only here, he argues, that Turner encounters his real dialogic adversary—not Thomas Ruffin Gray at all, whose work of composition becomes no more than the scribbling of a clerk, but Jeremiah Cobb, the Southampton County magistrate who presides over Turner's trial. It is a rather one-sided dialog. Turner's narrative (the bulk of the pamphlet) becomes important only insofar as it furnishes material that Cobb can hurl back in the convicted defendant's (silent) face during the trial's declamatory climax, Cobb's "vehement" death sentence, which "links worldly statutes to the law of God."[25]

Another, different, evaluative technique is available, which also reaches beyond the narrow question of evidentiary accuracy to the broader issue of textual construction: what does an examination of the *form* of the pamphlet, rather than of its substance or its genre, tell us about the pamphlet's purpose and identity as a text? This question—thus far unasked in examinations of Gray's pamphlet—allows us to access aspects of the pamphlet that have not attracted much attention, aspects that fall within what the structuralist literary theorist Gérard Genette has called "the paratext."[26]

Genette argues that every text comes accompanied by a paratext, within which the text is enfolded, which exists, as it were, as the fringe of the text, and which informs and indeed attempts entirely to control how the text will be read. Genette divides paratext into two structural categories that he denotes the *peritext* and the *epitext*. Peritext refers to those paratextual elements that position text and reader in relation to each other: title, authorial identification, dedication, chapter titles, epigraphs, preface, design, typography, and so forth. Each is a manipulation that functions to point the text in a particular direction. Epitext refers to those paratextual elements that surround and inform the production and reception of the text—that is, its circumstances: print run, modes of dissemination, advertisements, reviews, authorial interviews, commentaries on the text, critical disquisitions, and so forth. Genette also employs the term *hypotext* to denote the sources of the text, the text before the text.

Here I will concentrate on the peritext. How is *The Confessions of Nat Turner* constructed as an artifact that creates (or attempts to create) the conditions on which a reader enters into an engagement with it, and hence the conclusions that will be drawn from it?[27]

The original Baltimore edition of *The Confessions of Nat Turner* is twenty-four pages long. Though short, it is a complex document of multiple components. In order, it is composed as follows:

(a) A title page, which doubles as the front outside cover (page 1, the recto of page 2). The title page is not uniform in appearance, employing multiple fonts of multiple sizes. As well as title, the page includes information about the pamphlet's origin: publisher, printer, year and place of production (see figure 1.1).
(b) A statement of copyright (page 2).[28]
(c) A 2½ page preface, headed "TO THE PUBLIC." The preface is signed, in capitals, "T. R. GRAY" (pages 3–5).
(d) A statement of time and place, which appears immediately under Gray's signature, set in italics except the numbers, which are set in roman, "*Jerusalem, Southampton, Va. Nov.* 5, 1831." (page 5).
(e) A signed and sealed certification by six Southampton County Court Justices, appearing below Gray's signature and the statement of time and place, but separated from them by one blank line. The certification attests to the provenance of the confession. It too is stamped with a declaration of time and place, "at Jerusalem, this 5th day of November, 1831" (page 5).[29]
(f) A second certification appearing below the first, but separated by one blank line, also dated November 5, confirming that the

justices in question were indeed Justices of the Peace in and for Southampton County, signed and sealed by the Clerk of Court (pages 5–6).[30] With the exception of the continuation lines of the clerk's certificate, page 6 is blank.

(g) A section of 13½ pages, entitled "CONFESSION" (pages 7–20). A short, centered, intermediate line appears under the title, separating the title from the text (page 7). The first five lines of text comprise a brief introduction written by an "I" who is Thomas Ruffin Gray (page 7). They are separated by one blank line from the remainder, which comprises a narrative spoken by an "I" who is Nat Turner, addressed to Gray as amanuensis (pages 7–18). After 11 pages of narrative (which include three interrogatory interruptions, twelve parenthetical clarifications and one footnote) the "I" who is Turner ceases to speak, and is abruptly replaced at the beginning of the next paragraph by the "I" who is Gray. This "I" then offers 2½ pages of commentary on the preceding narrative (pages 18–20). Typographically, the 2½ pages of commentary on pages 18–20 are indistinguishable from the preceding confession narrative and continuous with it. No blank or intermediate line separates the "I" who is Turner from the resumption of the "I" who is Gray. The CONFESSION section ends on page 20. Here a second short, centered, intermediate line, which matches the first, on page 7, appears below the last line of the section.

(h) A section of 1¼ pages in the form of an unattributed and undated trial report (pages 20–21) entitled *The Commonwealth,* vs. *Nat Turner.* This section begins on page 20 below the short, centered, intermediate line that signifies the end of the "Confession" section, separated from it by a blank line.

(i) A section entitled *A list of persons murdered in the Insurrection, on the 21st and 22d of August, 1831* (page 22).

(j) A section entitled *A List of Negroes brought before the Court of Southampton, with their owners' names, and sentence* (pages 22–23).

(k) A blank outside back cover, which is the verso of page 23 (page 24).

Let us begin at the beginning, with the title, and examine each of its several elements. (*i*) *The Confessions of Nat Turner, the Leader of the Late Insurrection in Southampton, Va.* The first element of the title announces that Turner, identified as the leader of the Southampton insurrection, has confessed. Hence, what the reader will encounter within the pamphlet is not description or argumentation about the insurrection but instead a species of intimate and presumptively truthful knowledge of it.[31] The statement that Nat Turner was "leader" of the insurrection is not contentious. Newspaper reports named Turner as the leader of the insurgency virtually from the moment of the event, and witnesses in early trials had confirmed "Nat" as "the head of the insurgents."[32] *(ii) As fully and voluntarily made to Thomas R. Gray, In the prison where he was confined, and acknowledged by him to be such when read before the Court of Southampton; with the certificate, under seal of the Court convened at Jerusalem, Nov. 5, 1831, for his trial.* This phrasing both adverts to the wording of the justices' certificate, which the reader will encounter within the pamphlet, and employs its language (which includes the plural "confessions"), but with two emendations: first, the justices' certificate is not under seal of the Southampton County Court as such, but of the plural individual seals of six of the ten justices present at Turner's trial.[33] What is under seal of the Southampton County Court is the clerk's certificate, which attests that the six signatory justices were (by name) members of the court that tried Turner, and requires "that full faith and credit are due, and ought to be given to their acts as Justices of the peace aforesaid."[34] Second, the title states explicitly what is left implicit in the justices' certificate, that the confession had been read before the court. *(iii) Also, An Authentic Account of the Whole Insurrection, With Lists of the Whites who were Murdered, And of the Negroes Brought before the Court of Southampton, and there Sentenced, &c.* Here we encounter the title's real puzzle. The pamphlet indeed includes lists of whites murdered and blacks charged. But it supplies no distinct "authentic account" of the whole insurrection, to which the lists are appended, as the sentence beginning "*Also*" leads the reader to anticipate. The only account of the "whole insurrection" is that which appears on pages 12–18 of the section entitled "Confession" narrated by the "I" who is Turner. In other words, in a pamphlet of multiple interlocked component parts, each performing a single function, each carefully identified as such, in this one case we encounter instead a single component part ("Confession") performing multiple functions—that of "Confession" and, separately and simultaneously but only partially (pages 12–18, but not pages 7–11), that of "Authentic Account of the Whole Insurrection." The double duty done by pages 12–18 as, simultaneously, "Confession" and "Also, An Authentic Account," is underscored by Gray's statement on page 19, which explicitly demurs from adding further to what has already been recorded: "I will not shock the feelings of humanity, nor wound afresh the bosoms of the disconsolate sufferers in this unparalleled and inhuman massacre, by detailing the deeds of [these wretches'] fiend-like barbarity." While the plural certificates become a single stamp of truth, the single account of the insurrection is made to serve two purposes.

The title page is notable for the absence of a clear authorial claim. Confessions of one person (identified in large type) are made to another (identified in smaller type). Their provenance is acknowledged in the title by the confitent and certified by the invoked authority of the county court. Authorship of the whole is not claimed by the amanuensis. Instead he signifies authorship only of one component part of the text—the preface—and does so within the body of the pamphlet by adding his name to the end of that part.[35] Gray also adds a self-identifiable (but unsigned) closing commentary to the section narrated by the "I" who is Turner. The commentary is continuous with the confession narrative. It elaborates on the procedure followed in taking the confession, the character of the confitent, and the reactions of the amanuensis; it adds some details of the insurrection that go unmentioned in the confession narrative.[36] Neither confitent nor amanuensis signs the "Confession" section.[37] Gray records a claim of possession, of intellectual property, when he obtains his copyright in the federal district court for the District of Columbia, but he does so as "proprietor" of the work in question, not as author. The proprietary claim is realized on the pamphlet's title page in the phrase "published by Thomas R. Gray." All this suggests ambivalence about authorship, or a concern to disguise authorship, or distinctly, an indirect acknowledgment that the text actually has multiple intermingled authors.[38]

Following the statement of copyright (page 2) comes the one section to which Gray explicitly lays claim as an author in his own right, the 2½ page preface, which addresses a definitive audience, "To The Public" (pages 3–5). The preface instructs the reader in how the remainder of the text is to be read and understood, and what conclusions are to be drawn from that reading. It represents the text as, variously: a response to "public curiosity"; the answer to a "mystery"; a "useful lesson as to the operations of a mind"; a demonstration of "the policy of our laws in restraint of this class of our population," and of the law's watchful guardianship of the security of all; proof that the events detailed in the body of the text (the "account of the whole insurrection") were "entirely local," and that they were motivated not by "revenge or sudden anger" but were the offspring of one man's "gloomy fanaticism"; and finally, a means to the removal of "doubts and conjectures from the public mind which otherwise must have remained."[39] Along with the title page these instructions create the framework of conditions on which the text is to be encountered. The care with which Gray instructs the reader in how to read what is to come evidences concern that the text the reader is about to encounter may otherwise escape, that an uninstructed reader may respond to what is being presented in a fashion other than the author of the preface desires.

The preface is followed immediately (pages 5–6) by not one but two avowals of textual authenticity—the certifications of the six Southampton County justices and of the clerk of court. By confirming that the text is indeed what Gray says it is, these certifications add to the text's empirical authority. By conforming in appearance to standing gubernatorial instructions that evidence in the trial of slaves charged in connection with the revolt "be taken verbatim as given in Court and that it be so certified," they also grant Gray's pamphlet a quasi-official status.[40] They also add weight to the cage that Gray is building around the text, to control it, to shape its meaning, for their position—situated immediately after Gray's signed preface and separated from the next section, headed "Confession," by nearly a full blank page—makes them as much a certification of the authority of Gray's prefatory instructions as of the authenticity of the confession narrative that the reader is still waiting to encounter. In substance the first certification repeats what Gray has just told the reader about the circumstances in which the text has come to be, while the second certification authenticates the first. The positioning of the statement of time and place that follows the attribution of Gray's authorship of the preface, and appears to anchor that attribution, "*Jerusalem, Southampton, Va. Nov.* 5, 1831," is such that it could just as well stand as the header for the first certification as time/place stamp of Gray's signature, particularly as it is not positioned under Gray's name (right justified) but instead matches both in position (left justified) and type (set in italics) the header on the second certification, *State of Virginia, Southampton County, to wit:*. In other words, both certifications are linked typographically at least as much to the preface as to what they are ostensibly authenticating, which is the confession narrative that follows the preface.[41]

The confession narrative finally begins on page 7 and runs for 13½ pages (pages 7–20), in a section of the pamphlet entitled not "Confessions," as in the pamphlet title, but "CONFESSION." The narrative is divisible into four component parts: a five-line introduction written by the "I" who is Gray (page 7); an 11-page narrative spoken by an "I" who is Turner (pages 7–18), which is itself divisible into two sections, the break between them occurring from the bottom of page 11 to the top of page 12; and the 2½ pages of commentary (pages 18–20) by the "I" who is Gray, which follow on seamlessly from the end of the narrative attributed to the "I" who is Turner.

Gray's introduction to the "CONFESSION" narrative serves as yet another component in the cage of control built around the text of the confession. It is very carefully phrased:

> Agreeable to his own appointment, on the evening he was committed to prison, with permission of the jailer, I visited NAT on Tuesday the 1st November, when, without being questioned at all, he commenced his narrative in the following words:–

Gray's introduction puts in place the final set of conditions on which the narrative is to be "released" to the reader—the sixth component condition of the narrative's existence, all of which have collectively monitored its coming-to-be and its encounter with a waiting reader.[42] By describing the circumstances (exact time and place) under which the narrative was obtained the introduction stresses once again the text's authenticity.[43] It also stresses that the narrative was not produced as an answer to a prompt but was offered spontaneously ("without being questioned at all"), that it came directly from its source as an unmediated, volunteered ("agreeable to his own appointment") stream of consciousness ("he commenced his narrative in the following words"), and that the narrative was the authored possession of the identified narrator ("*he* commenced *his* narrative"). The narrator himself is given a large, direct, and animate presence ("NAT") but is also secured, controlled ("with permission of the jailer"). Only after obtruding these final conditions, all not only stated below the heading, "CONFESSION," but also *below* the intervening intermediate line rather than above it, hence an intrusion into the typographical space reserved for the confession narrative itself, does Gray finally permit the actual narration to begin. It concludes on page 18, in a sentence that stresses that the narrator who has been released to narrate has been taken back under control, both physical and moral: "I am here loaded with chains, and willing to suffer the fate that awaits me." Gray then underscores the resumption of that control by immediately beginning his own concluding commentary, without any distinguishing break save only a new paragraph, with a sentence that stresses he is back in charge. "I here proceeded to make some inquiries of him, after assuring him of the certain death that awaited him." Just as Gray's introduction intrudes into the space of the confession narrative, so does his commentary on it. Gray pushes himself directly into the typographical space of the confession narrative itself.[44]

Thus, the "Confession" section is itself bracketed by an introduction and conclusion written by Gray, just as it is also bracketed in the pamphlet by Gray's preface, which matches his conclusion to the "Confession" section (they are almost exactly the same length—the preface is 995 words, the commentary 1,105) and by the final substantive component of the pamphlet, the trial report. All this underscores how the confession narrative itself is surrounded, caged, by multiple controlling devices, all of which urge the reader to read it in a particular way. The composition of the pamphlet suggests that the confession narrative is an unruly, potentially dangerous text, release of which requires the deployment of multiple rings of security and imposed meaning. The urgency of retaining control of the text is emphasized by the typographic immediacy that Gray's concluding commentary assumes in relation to the narrative. No break is allowed. Typographically—structurally—Gray is a participant in the confession narrative.

Just how much Gray is participating in the confession narrative becomes clear from the division in the narrative. This division occurs at the point of transition from the narrator's account of his life, beliefs, thoughts, and motivations during the thirty years of his life prior to the commencement of "the late insurrection" (pages 7–11) to the narrator's account of the sequence of events—inception, killings, encounters, movements from place to place, skirmishes, and final flight—that comprised "the late insurrection" itself (pages 12–18). We should note that the first section of the narrative contains four of Gray's self-identified interventions in the narrative—an explanatory interjection in the text on page 7,[45] a footnote on page 8,[46] and interrogatories on pages 9 and 11.[47] It also contains one parenthetical comment on page 9, written in a manner that attributes the comment to Turner,[48] and three on page 11 identifying people or events mentioned in the narrative. The narrative itself appears without any paragraph breaks, except at the point of transition on pages 11–12. A short paragraph that ends in Gray's third and final interrogatory at the top of page 12 provides the transition.[49] The narrative then, quite abruptly, changes character.

The two parts of the confession narrative, either side of the bridging paragraph, are quite distinct in textual appearance, in punctuation, grammar, and syntax. Pages 7–11 are roughly drafted: discontinuous, staccato, and nonlinear. Sentences interrupt and spill into each other; punctuation, grammar, and syntax are all sloppy. Major parts of the narrative are presented in multiple incomplete sentences joined together with dashes. The following is representative:

> —My grand mother, who was very religious, and to whom I was much attached—my master, who belonged to the church, and other religious persons who visited the house, and whom I often saw at prayers, noticing the singularity of my manners, I suppose, and my uncommon intelligence for a child, remarked I had too much sense to be raised, and if I was, I would never be of any service to any one as a slave—To a mind like mine, restless, inquisitive and observant of every thing that was passing, it is easy to suppose that religion was the subject to which it would be directed, and although this subject principally occupied my thoughts—there was nothing that I saw or heard of to which my attention was not directed—The manner in which I learned to read and write, not only had great influence on my own mind, as I acquired it with the most perfect ease, so much so, that I have no recollection whatever of learning the alphabet—but to the astonishment of the family, one day, when a book was shewn me to keep me from crying, I began spelling the names of different objects—this was a source of wonder to all in the neighborhood, particularly the blacks—and this learning was constantly improved at all opportunities—when I got large enough to go to work, while employed, I was reflecting on many things that would present themselves to my imagination, and whenever an opportunity occurred of looking at a book, when the school children were getting their lessons, I would find many things that the fertility of my own imagination had depicted to me before; all my time, not devoted to my master's service, was spent either in prayer, or in making experiments in casting different things in moulds made of earth, in attempting to make paper, gunpowder, and many other experiments, that although I could not perfect, yet convinced me of its practicability if I had the means.[50]

From page 12 onward, the narrative is a lincar progression, written in complete sentences, carefully composed, and punctuated in standard form, separated by periods, with only one outbreak of dashes.[51] The following is typical:

> We remained some time at the barn, where we paraded; I formed them in a line as soldiers, and after carrying them through all the manœuvres I was master of, marched them off to Mr. Salathul Francis', about six hundred yards distant. Sam and Will went to the door and knocked. Mr. Francis asked who was there, Sam replied it was him, and he had a letter for him, on which he got up and came to the door; they immediately seized him, and dragging him out a little from the door, he was dispatched by repeated blows on the head; there was no other white person in the family. We started from there for Mrs. Reese's, maintaining the most perfect silence on our march, where finding the door unlocked, we entered, and murdered Mrs. Reese in her bed, while sleeping; her son awoke, but it was only to sleep the sleep of death, he had only time to say who is that, and he was no more. From Mrs. Reese's we went to Mrs. Turner's, a mile distant, which we reached about sunrise, on Monday morning. Henry, Austin, and Sam, went to the still, where, finding Mr. Peebles, Austin shot him, and the rest of us went to the house; as we approached, the family discovered us, and shut the door. Vain hope! Will, with one stroke of his axe, opened it, and we entered and found Mrs. Turner and Mrs. Newsome in the middle of a room, almost frightened to death. Will immediately killed Mrs. Turner, with one blow of his axe. I took Mrs. Newsome by the hand, and with the sword I had when I was apprehended, I struck her several blows over the head, but not being able to kill her, as the sword was dull. Will turning around and discovering it, dispatched her also.[52]

The two sections are also marked by completely distinct temporal rhythms. The first section is relatively indifferent to sequential time. The narrator states at one point, "Several years rolled round, in which many events occurred to strengthen me in this my belief."[53] The events themselves are not described. But relative indifference to temporal linearity in the first section is accompanied by close attention to particular moments of significance, and to the emphatic compression of time that accompanies them.

> And on the 12th of May, 1828, I heard a loud noise in the heavens, and the Spirit *instantly* appeared to me . . . And *immediately* on the sign appearing in the heavens the seal was removed from my lips.[54]

In contrast, the second section—like the profusion of notarial place/date stamps that accompany the pamphlet's various authorizing components—is obsessed with linear temporality and sequence. From page 12 onward the narrative is a highly methodical, highly detailed, one-thing-after-another account of the progress and ultimate collapse of the insurrection.[55]

The contrast between the two sections of the confession narrative attributed to Turner suggests that Gray's pamphlet actually conjoins two relatively distinct texts (hence, perhaps, *Confessions*).[56] The first part is a confession of faith. It discourses on matters of which Gray could have had little prior knowledge—Turner's childhood and upbringing, his beliefs and motivations. Its central theme is the maturation of an ascetic personality, its achievement of a state of ecstatic religious grace, and the ideational consequences attending that outcome. The untidy syntax and ungrammatical composition suggests haste in writing, notes taken verbatim as the narrator spoke, with explicitly recorded clarifications (the interrogatories, the interjection, the footnote: matters which caught Gray unawares, about which he sought amplification). The second section takes the form of a criminal confession, an empirical record of the progress of a crime or crimes. It discourses on matters of which, by the time he met with Turner, Gray had already accumulated considerable independent knowledge. It too contains clarifying parenthetical comments, but the most significant of these add details of which Gray was aware but Turner was not.[57] The writing in this section is relaxed, confident, and grammatically and syntactically sophisticated.[58]

Gray had been with the first party of militia who rode out from Jerusalem on the morning of Monday August 22 in search of the rebels, and he had spent days on the scene, followed by weeks at the Southampton County Courthouse during September and October.[59] He had served as counsel to four defendants, he had observed the trials of others, and he had heard the testimony of witnesses.[60] He had already written one lengthy and detailed report on the insurrection, published by the Richmond *Constitutional Whig* in the form of an anonymous letter from "a gentleman well conversant with the scenes he describes."[61] He had had access to other published reports and to local people. Whether Gray attended the preliminary examination of Turner undertaken before Southampton magistrates James Trezvant and James W. Parker by Commonwealth Attorney Meriwether Broadax that took place on October 31 immediately following Turner's capture is unclear, but he would certainly have known what had occurred at that meeting.[62] Armed with this profusion of sources, Gray had already had ample opportunity prior to his meetings with Turner to construct an account of the events that would comprise the "Turner Rebellion." The second half of the narrative, literally a blow-by-blow, real time, account of the rebellion, bears all the signs of careful, methodical preparation.[63]

This analysis answers the puzzle of the title. The phrase *Also, An Authentic Account of the Whole Insurrection* suggests Gray sought, indirectly, credit for the composition of the confession narrative's account of the rebellion by distinguishing it from the confession narrative itself. The "also" betrays pride of authorship. Gray's goal in interviewing Turner was to improve on the account he had already authored (anonymously) in the *Constitutional Whig*, to seek confirmation and supplementary detail on the progress of the insurrection itself. The careful composition of the second half of the narrative suggests that this was the part of the document about which Gray cared the most. It was likely relatively complete, at least in draft, prior to Gray's encounter with Turner. The two appended lists "of persons murdered in the Insurrection, on the 21st and 22d of August, 1831" (page 22), and "of Negroes brought before the Court of Southampton, with their owners' names, and sentence" (pages 22–23) are entirely Gray's composition, added as proof positive that this was indeed the fullest "account of the whole insurrection" available.

In turn, all this suggests that the comparatively rough and hasty composition of the first section of the narrative signifies this section was indeed Turner's own account of his upbringing, beliefs, and motivations, heard for the first time during the jail cell encounter. In this section Gray is truly amanuensis taking notes, rather than would-be author seeking confirmation. Given the demands of travel to Richmond, and thence to Washington and Baltimore—approaching 250 miles, all told, the first 200 traveled in four days—Gray would have had little opportunity to make this section of the narrative more artful. Nor had he any real motivation to do so. From Gray's point of view Turner had conveniently condemned himself as a confused religious fanatic.[64]

The bridging paragraph between the two sections describes the meeting at which the insurrection is set in motion—a meeting of which Gray had independent knowledge from the testimony of others already tried who had been there, but about which he had one question: "Why were you so backward [late] in joining them."[65] This interrogatory, situated at the end of the bridging paragraph, is the last explicit interrogatory in the entire confession narrative.[66]

When Gray's "I" resumes full control on page 18, after the narrative's close, he reports that many more questions were asked, and a cross-examination undertaken, all confirming the account given in the narrative. Unlike the interrogatories cited in the text of the narrative, which are open inquiries, the purpose of this reported questioning is to press the reader once more toward the reading of Turner's rebellion already announced in the preface—an isolated local event, not part of "any extensive or concerted plan," the offspring of "a complete fanatic."[67] Gray's concluding commentary ends by assuring the reader that all is over, and all is well. It repeats the stress in the preface on "removing doubts and conjectures," and on the law's watchful guardianship, by invoking "the hand of retributive justice" which, "fortunate for society . . . has overtaken them." The law has indeed exercised watchful guardianship. "Not one that was known to be concerned has escaped."[68] The structural cage that contains the potentially unruly and dangerous confession narrative and directs its reception is complete.

There follows the final component of the pamphlet, the section of 1¼ pages that takes the form of an unattributed report of *The Commonwealth vs. Nat Turner* as heard in the Southampton County Court (pages 20–21). This section confirms the claim entered in the immediately preceding section on behalf of remorseless retributive justice, in that it rings down the curtain on the only one "known to be concerned" who had until that moment escaped, namely Turner himself. The pamphlet's consummation is his trial and conviction.

The trial report has occasioned much comment, directed to the extent to which it departs from the trial record that appears in the Southampton County Court "Minute Book," primarily by presenting the confession "as given to Mr. Gray" that appears in the pamphlet as if it had been entered into evidence.[69] Because there is no indication in the trial record that it was so entered, the trial record is held to cast doubt on the elaborate string of authentications obtained by Gray prior to his departure for Richmond, and so on the credibility of the pamphlet itself. Perhaps Gray made the whole thing up.[70]

The discrepancies between Gray's report and the trial record indicate that Gray indeed wrote up his own trial report, and used it to highlight the confession he had obtained. But if that is the case, Gray was doing no more on this occasion than early nineteenth-century court and newspaper reporters did routinely. He was approximating and elaborating on the bare record of a proceeding kept by the clerk of court, based on personal observation.[71] The certificate of the six Southampton County Court justices attests "that the confessions of Nat, to Thomas R. Gray, was read to him in our presence," and that when called on to state why sentence of death should not be passed on him, Turner had "replied he had nothing further than he had communicated to Mr. Gray." The certificate strongly implies, but does not state explicitly, that all this occurred publicly in court rather than in camera. For its part, Gray's trial report states that sworn evidence given by Levi Waller during the trial was given "(*agreeably to Nat's own Confession*)" and that, testifying as one of the examining and committing magistrates, James Trezvant "narrated Nat's Confession to him, as follows (*his Confession as given to Mr. Gray.*)" The italics and parentheses suggest dissimulation, even deceit, but not fabrication. They suggest a desire to create, shorthand, the impression of similitude and harmony between what occurred in public during the trial and what was recorded in the pamphlet, hence authority for the pamphlet. They suggest—particularly the parentheses, and the word *agreeably*—that the material in the pamphlet was a reliable stand-in for what had been given in evidence in court, not that the material in the pamphlet was what had actually been given in court. Concretely, they suggest that Turner "confessed" (gave an account of himself) before Parker and Trezvant on October 31, and again before Gray during their encounter between November 1 and 3, and that his serial confessions were not much different in substance, although they may well have been different in length and detail given Gray's considerable independent knowledge of the rebellion and the extent of his conversations with Turner.[72]

Thomas Ruffin Gray's pamphlet is a closed, self-authenticating world. Its multiple components serve as a controlled iterative string intended to substantiate all the claims made in the pamphlet's title: that *The Confessions* were those of *Nat Turner*, that Turner had been *the Leader of the Late Insurrection in Southampton, Va.*, that the Confessions had been *fully and voluntarily made to Thomas R. Gray, In the prison where he was confined*, that they had been *acknowledged by him to be such when read before the Court of Southampton*, and arguably most important to Gray, that the pamphlet was, independently of Turner, *Also, An Authentic Account of the Whole Insurrection*. Structural critique allows one to penetrate this self-authenticating world through a process of textual mortification—not, that is, by evaluating or interpreting the text as a thing in itself but by corroding it, rendering it a rubble of fragments such that its fragments of truth may be extracted.[73] By exposing the paratextual conditions of the pamphlet's existence, and their frictions and inconsistencies, one can produce from amid Gray's interlocutions and interpolations the likelihood that, in Eric Sundquist's words, "Nat Turner's voice remains strongly present."[74]

Still, it is another voice, adverse to Turner's, that lends independent support to the proposition that Gray's pamphlet is indeed a fruitful source through which to engage with Nat Turner, with his rebellion, and with the legal response to both man and event. More than half of the trial report that concludes Gray's pamphlet is given over to a speech attributed to the presiding magistrate, Jeremiah Cobb, sentencing Turner to hang. The trial record contents itself with a banal boilerplate statement of the death sentence: "Therefore it is considered by the Court that he be taken hence to the Jail from whence he was taken therein to remain until . . . taken by the Sheriff to the usual place of execution and there be hanged by the neck until he be dead. And the Court values the said slave to the sum of three hundred and seventy five dollars."[75] In contrast, as Caleb Smith has noted, the speech that Gray's report attributes to Cobb is "a vehement oration," an elaborately per formative summoning of "the transcendent voice of the law" that "transforms a rote legal procedure into a dramatic ceremony of justice."[76]

Smith's conclusion, as we have seen, is that what matters here is recognition that as such the pamphlet is performing the genre of trial report, speaking to "the public culture of justice," not whether it is a "true" confession, or a trustworthy account of the insurrection. Smith, however, misstates the reported speech in one key aspect. "Quoting from Gray's version of the confession," he writes, "the judge uses Turner's words against him: 'your own confession tells us that [your hands] were stained with the blood of a master; in your own language, "too indulgent."'" But these words ("too indulgent") do not appear anywhere in Gray's version of the confession. Gray, as trial reporter, appears to be recording faithfully what Cobb the presiding magistrate actually said, referencing words given in evidence before him—words from the preliminary examination placed in evidence by James Trezvant.[77] So doing, Gray has revealed the degree of his own dissimulation: the confession he had taken was not before the court. But in exposing himself he has furnished us with reasonable grounds for believing that his pamphlet indeed conveys to us something of the reality of the charged voice of Jeremiah Cobb, just as we have reasonable grounds for believing it conveys something of the reality of the charged voice of Nat Turner.

Thus we discover yet another author lurking in the iterative multiplicity of *The Confessions of Nat Turner*. Jeremiah Cobb joins Nat Turner and Thomas Ruffin Gray. Small wonder that when Gray obtained his copyright he labeled himself the text's proprietor rather than its author. His was a text crowded with authors—far too many to claim authorial rights for himself alone.

CONCLUSION

What Gérard Genette has to say about the importance of a text's paratextual aspects has an especial force when applied to legal, or in this instance quasi-legal, texts. Legal texts almost invariably possess a hugely elaborated, grandly formulaic peritext of structural and compositional authority. They also move constantly within an epitextual penumbra of production, projection, reception, interpretation, and reinterpretation. In this, *The Confessions of Nat Turner* performs all the functions of a composite legal text.

However, to read the pamphlet's legalities entirely through the trial report, as Caleb Smith recommends, is to allow the tail to wag the dog, to discern legality only in official discourse. It is to affirm that only at the trial were "worldly statutes" linked "to the law of God," and only by a magistrate speaking his own authority into the void of Turner's silence. It is to deny that Turner's speech has its own legal content and its own perception of the relationship between the order of the profane and the Kingdom of God.

Perhaps most important, it is to accept without examination that we know what the "Turner Rebellion" was. Here again genre is critically important: from the moment of its occurrence the event has without question been assimilated wholly to the "genre" of slave rebellion. Which raises the question whether that is, in fact, all of what it was.

Gray knew what the event was—or at least he thought he did. The first line of his introduction to Turner's narrative names its subject as "The late insurrection in Southampton." He also knew the purpose of his text. The pamphlet fastens Turner's narrative to the panoptics of secular law and its administration: "It is calculated . . . to demonstrate the policy of our laws in restraint of this class of our population, and to induce all those entrusted with their execution, as well as our citizens generally, to see that they are strictly and rigidly enforced. Each particular community should look to its own safety, whilst the general guardians of the laws, keep a watchful eye over all." But this was not a perspective Turner shared. The legalities of his narrative, rather than of Gray's account of it, and the genre to which they belong, take their shape in his first sentence: "You have asked me to give a history of the motives which induced me to undertake the late insurrection, *as you call it*."[78] From the outset, that is, Turner denies that he and his interlocutor share a common understanding of what had occurred. From this moment we know that while Gray calls the event an insurrection Turner does not. To discover what Turner calls it, we can read the first half of his narrative—the half that I have argued bears unmistakable signs of composition in the moment of interlocution—for clues.

In the early 1990s, the literary critic Marie Maclean situated paratext in the study of thresholds and liminality.[79] As she wrote then, the signs and fringes that accompany a text constitute a threshold, or frame, that interposes between the text and any context within which it find itself, and that bends (or attempts to bend) its reception by that context, just as an apparently transparent (hence notionally invisible) lens bends light. Maclean cites the philosopher Michel Serres's observations on liminality:

> A door opens or closes a threshold which is held to be such because at this spot a law is overturned: on one side reigns a certain rule, on the other begins a new law, so that the door rests on its hinges on a neutral line where the two rules of law balance and cancel each other. . . . The singular site is a part of neither this world nor the other or else it belongs to both.[80]

What is so important about the paratext is the possibility of alterity in reading that it anticipates, and which it is its task to bend and thus deflect. Now that we have called attention to the paratext of *The Confessions*, and thereby penetrated its deflection, what alterities can we recover from the text itself that will help us understand the life of Nat Turner, and the events of August 1831?

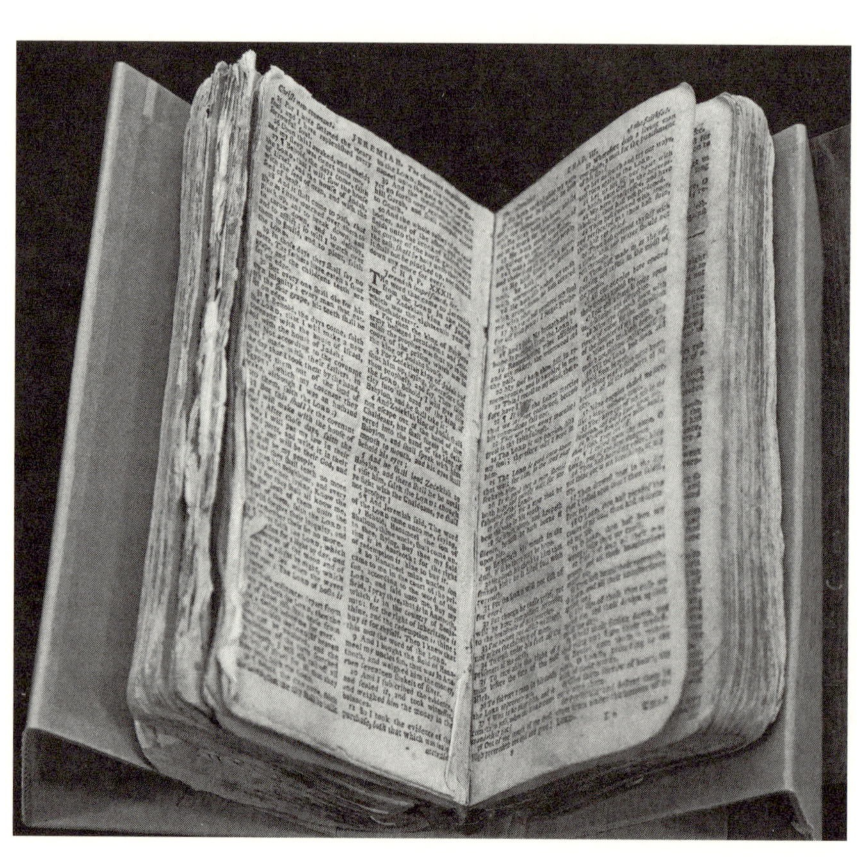
JEREMIAH

2

Reading Luke in Southampton County

> Cry for pardon, cry for washing
> In the blood which cleanses all.
>
> —ANN GRIFFITHS (1806)

> Take him, ye *Africans*, he longs for you,
> *Impartial Saviour* is his title due:
> Wash'd in the fountain of redeeming blood,
> You shall be sons, and kings, and priests to God.
>
> —PHILLIS WHEATLEY (1773)

Nat Turner, it has been said, "demonstrated a mastery of scripture."[1] Necessarily, the observation is based on *The Confessions*: this is the only available guide to Turner's religious mentalité. But there the matter generally rests. The question of *what* scripture Turner had mastered, and for what purposes, has not been canvassed in any detail. Observers content themselves with generalities, or propose idiosyncratic textual interpolations that accord with what they assume *The Confessions* reveal Turner's formative beliefs and intentions to have been. Turner, says Caleb Smith, believed that "the slaveholding legal order rest[ed] on an unjust foundation," and "represent[ed] himself as a prophet and an exhorter, communicating a message of divine justice." In light of what transpired in August 1831, the assumption seems entirely reasonable on its face, but it is nevertheless an assumption: Turner says nothing explicitly about the justice or otherwise of the slaveholding legal order, and Smith leaves unstated the theological detail, or scriptural basis, of the divine justice his message countenanced.[2] Daniel Walker Howe tells us, rather more

FIGURE 2.1. Nat Turner's Bible. Photograph by Michael Barnes/Smithsonian Institution.

definitively, that Turner was inspired by Isaiah "to proclaim liberty to the captives . . . and the day of vengeance of our God." Again the assumption is reasonable on its face, but in actuality Turner makes no reference to this particular text, or indeed to any text from Isaiah, in *The Confessions*. Like William Styron, Howe takes Turner to be partial to the main currents of Old Testament prophecy.[3] He presumes Isaiah to have been uppermost in Turner's religious imagination because Isaiah's prophecy that the Redeemer will proclaim liberty to the captives accords with Howe's own interpretation of the intent and meaning of Turner's actions. Even the most detailed and sophisticated reading of *The Confessions*, by Eric Sundquist, interprets Turner's theology through its supposed foundation on a quest for secular freedom. The authenticity of *The Confessions* is to be found in "its enunciation of a speaking subject whose messianic and ideological messages are one, in which mania and performance coexist in the desire for liberty."[4]

Smith, Howe, and Sundquist may all be entirely justified in the arguments they offer and the conclusions they draw. My own arguments and conclusions will differ from theirs, but the reader may judge at the end of the day that the differences do not much matter. That outcome, however, is less important to me than the purpose to which this chapter is dedicated—an attempt to establish from the few fragments of evidence that exist what Nat Turner thought he was doing in the years leading up to August 1831, and why. To such an inquiry into a mentalité, Turner's "mastery of scripture" is central. As Sundquist comments, "Turner's biblical exegesis was far from simplistic or haphazard."[5]

Turner's biblical exegesis, in its entirety, is to be found amid the 2,200 words that comprise the first half of Thomas Ruffin Gray's narrative of their jail cell conversations—what Sundquist describes as "the rhetorically-charged and passionate account of Nat's divine inspiration," which in Gray's pamphlet is counterposed to "the factual, cold-blooded, recital of the killings."[6] That first half is fundamental to any attempt to explain Turner's motivation that is other than mute synecdoche of his behavior. In it, Turner refers entirely to New Testament texts. He exhibits a fondness for Revelation, which is perhaps predictable, but also, and more pronouncedly, a fondness for the Gospel of St. Luke, which is not.[7]

Why Luke? Initially, one might offer two reasons. First, Nat Turner was an evangelical Christian visionary who had lived his entire life in Southampton County's St. Luke's Parish. In Christological terms, he may have considered the sacred name of the place of his own birth and life of significance in guiding the extended adult effort to comprehend the relationship between himself and the Saviour that the first half of *The Confessions* describes. Second, considered as a narrative of Christ's life and works, Luke is by far the most complete of the synoptic gospels. It is the longest gospel; it contains material that exists nowhere else in the Bible—material that is absolutely essential to Turner's own self-representation and self-comprehension; and when conjoined with Acts (by the same author) it provides the New Testament with its spine.[8] "Only Luke-Acts tells the story of Jesus Christ from his birth through the beginning of the church into the ministry of Paul." Luke tells that story, moreover, as a progressively unfolding narrative "that allows who Jesus is to dawn on the reader."[9] Like Luke's life of Christ, Turner's account of himself begins with events prior to his own birth, describes an emerging awareness of "some great purpose," and culminates in a climactic sacrificial act of atonement. Throughout, Turner employs typological reasoning for the messianic purpose of re-creating himself as the Redeemer returned.[10]

Given Turner's narrative purpose, it is perhaps not surprising that Luke should figure so prominently as both source and inspiration. But we may take the matter further than general descriptive similarities to the question of theological and soteriological hermeneutics. In examining Turner's resort to Luke, and Revelation, as textual inspiration, what conclusions can we draw about his understanding of himself, and his messianic purpose? For example, one reason for Turner's attention to Luke may lie less in the Gospel's narrative substance than in Luke's allusion to themes from Isaiah, specifically Isaiah's servant songs. To some commentators, notably Hans Conzelmann, Luke is distinctive amongst the gospels in representing Christ as a subordinate to God. "The plan of salvation is exclusively God's plan . . . Jesus' function within it is that of an instrument."[11] Given that one crucial quandary with which Turner wrestles explicitly is the reconciliation of his sense of "some great purpose" with the actuality that he is a slave, it is conceivable that he is drawn to Luke because Luke's Gospel addresses and resolves that precise spiritual tension. Other commentators on Luke have disagreed with Conzelmann's emphasis on Christ's subordination, but they too recognize parallels between Christ and the Isaianic servant. Luke's infancy narrative establishes that "Jesus is uniquely from God. . . . But the details are to be worked out in what Luke does in the rest of his narrative."[12] In that work, "the ideas of servant, chosen, and beloved are tied together," particularly in Luke's narration of Christ's baptism. "The Spirit descends in bodily form, and a voice connects Jesus to a role as regal son and as the Servant of God who declares and brings deliverance."[13] Luke's account underlines that Jesus is a far more important figure than John the Baptist, who is not even present in Luke's account of the baptism. Still, returning from the wilderness after his baptism and "in the power of the Spirit," what Jesus takes on in preaching "his mission and its fulfillment" in Nazareth is the mantel of Isaiah's servant: "The Spirit of the Lord is upon me, because he hath anointed me to preach the gospel to the poor; he hath sent me to heal the brokenhearted, to preach deliverance to the captives, and recovering of sight to the blind, to set at liberty them that are bruised." Here, says Bock, "Jesus is the Servant par excellence."[14] In Christian iconography, Luke's symbol is the ox, a figuration of service as well as sacrifice.[15]

In this chapter I will first survey Turner's account of himself and of what inspired him, with particular attention to his account's pattern of scriptural citation, in order to substantiate the claim that Turner indeed blended invocation of Revelation with a fondness for Luke. I will argue that in fact Turner based much of his understanding of himself and of the significance of his actions on Luke's account of the life and ministry of Christ. I will also examine other possible influences on Turner's narrative of what inspired him. I will end by indicating how this examination of Turner's biblical exegesis might influence our perception of his narrative of the events leading up to August 1831.

I

The first half of Nat Turner's confession grants us access to Turner's life history as a narrative of three braided threads. The first thread tells of the ascent of a severely ascetic personality to a state of grace. This is a story of self-isolation, of withdrawal from others, of "austerity of . . . life and manners," of "fasting," continual prayer, spiritual maturation, and at last assurance of sanctification.[16] The second thread, a crucial component of an ascetic Protestant life, asks life's central question: What is my calling? This is a question, for obvious reasons, acutely problematic for a slave to answer. It is doubly problematic for Turner, of whom it had been remarked in his childhood by "my master, who belonged to the church, and other religious persons who visited the house" that "I had too much sense to be raised, and *if* I was, I would never be of any use to any one as a slave."[17] Finding that he had become an adult "and was a slave" nonetheless, "I began to direct my attention to . . . the purpose for which, by this time, I felt assured I was intended."[18] The third thread comes from Turner's eventual formulation of an answer to his question of purpose. A maturing consciousness of messianic mission will eventually find fulfillment in the life story from its inception.

It is important to keep these threads distinct. Most historical readings do not—the confession is usually read as Gray designed it, as a single linear account in which the life's final events appear as an outcome ordained virtually from infancy.[19] This is an error. In Turner's account his painful struggle for spiritual maturity and his search for his calling become utterly central in his life long before the confession turns to any clear intimation of interracial violence.[20] Indeed, the moment the confession does make that turn is precisely the moment when Gray's rationalist and empirical prose takes the place of Turner's language of faith.

Turner's quest for his life's spiritual meaning begins in early adulthood.[21] "Hearing the scriptures commented on at meetings," Turner reports he was struck by the passage, "Seek ye the kingdom of Heaven and all things shall be added unto you."[22] Turner does not cite the passage cleanly, but the closest biblical reference is Luke 12:31, "Seek ye the kingdom of God; and all these things shall be added unto you." Matthew 6:33 is also a close match, "Seek ye first the kingdom of God, and his righteousness; and all these things shall be added unto you." But it contains more variations from Turner's version than Luke.[23] In Matthew the text is from the Sermon on the Mount; in Luke it is part of a sermon delivered "before an innumerable multitude of people" (the Sermon on the Plain) during Christ's journey out of Galilee to Samaria and Judea, and finally to Jerusalem. For Conzelmann, the journey motif is Luke's editorial construction and expresses Christ's "awareness that he must suffer."[24] To the extent Turner sensed he was embarking on a spiritual journey of his own, the precise scriptural circumstances of the phrase that attracted his attention will have had bite. In both Matthew and Luke the meaning of the passage appears the same: God will provide for those who seek him. But Howard Marshall argues that whereas in Matthew the teaching of the Sermon on the Mount is that spiritual virtue will be rewarded, in Luke the meaning of 12:31 and associated passages is "that there will be a reversal of places in the kingdom of God." One who lays up treasure for himself "and is not rich toward God" will find no welcome. "It is . . . the attitude towards God which matters."[25] Luke, we will find, is replete with images both of authority (God's authority, Christ's authority), of obedience (of Christ toward God, of the disciples toward Christ, of man toward God), and of the reversal of places. The Gospel may have resonated with Turner on all these counts.

Intense prayerful contemplation of the admonition to seek God's kingdom brings Turner his first revelation—"the spirit spoke to me"—that affirms the scriptural injunction.[26] Continual prayer over the following two years brings a repetition of the same revelation (circa 1822), "which fully confirmed me in the impression that I was ordained for some great purpose in the hands of the Almighty."[27] But *what* purpose? This remained unknown, while "several years rolled round," even though "many events occurred to strengthen me in this my belief."[28] At this point (circa 1824) Turner first fully confronts the apparent contradiction between his quest for his calling and his enslavement. The "many events" have made him confident of his eventual ordination "for some great purpose." Yet he carries with him that childhood prediction that he "would never be of any use to any one as a slave." The second proposition blocks the first.[29] Turner's sensible solution is to abscond.[30] By running away Turner would cease to be a slave and hence remove the obstacle to the realization of his great purpose. He is so confident in the correctness of his solution that he boasts to his "fellow servants" that "something was about to happen that would terminate in fulfilling the great promise that had been made to me."[31]

Belatedly, however, Turner realizes he has misunderstood God. And so, "after remaining in the woods thirty days, I returned." God had made no promises. He had simply instructed Turner that his purpose lay in seeking His kingdom. Turner had failed to obey. "The reason of my return was, that the Spirit appeared to me and said I had my wishes directed to the things of this world, not to the kingdom of Heaven, and that I should return to the service of my earthly master."[32] For a third time in as many years, in other words, Turner had been admonished to seek God's kingdom, and this time with the unmistakable injunction to do God's will rather than interpret that will to suit himself as if it were a "promise" with earthly consequence.[33]

This moment calls forth a second biblical citation. It is unambiguously Lukan. "And that servant, which knew his lord's will, and prepared not himself, neither did according to his will, shall be beaten with many stripes."[34] Also from Luke 12, it reinforces the Lukan gloss on Turner's first citation, for it expresses Turner's self-reproach at his failure to appreciate that what matters is the attitude toward God. In his spiritual immaturity Turner had taken "all things shall be added unto you" as a promise of earthly reward. "I had my wishes directed to the things of this world, not to the kingdom of Heaven."[35] Luke 12 emphasizes that the servant must always stand ready, "for the Son of man cometh at an hour when ye think not."[36]

This key passage of the confession has been interpreted as a kind of tu quoque: Turner the rebel in chains reminds his white interlocutor of the fate of those who would defy God's will by keeping slaves in bondage. Turner, God's agent, has indeed "beaten [them] with many stripes."[37] But although this reading is available, it is implausible. Turner here is speaking of his own abject failure to understand God's will, his shallow interpretation of his revelations as worldly "promises" rather than injunctions pointing him toward grace. His reappearance at his master's plantation after a month's absence is an act of penitence. No doubt it earned him punishment, as well as the incredulity of his fellow slaves, who, he says, were "astonish[ed]" at his reappearance and "found fault and murmurred [*sic*]" against him,[38] "saying that if they had my sense they would not serve any master in the world."[39] Turner is at this point profoundly isolated, humiliated, and quite conceivably—given God's reproof—unable to comprehend the meaning of his revelations. He has been chastened spiritually while in the wilderness, and perhaps, physically on his return. Yet we should also note that by requiring that he return to his earthly master, God has quite pointedly dissolved the blockage that led Turner to abscond in the first place. He has indicated not that Turner must cease to be a slave before he can be of use, but rather that it is *as a slave*, as a subaltern, that he must pursue his calling.[40]

This moment of acute psychological crisis and self-examination, of fault and contrition, of "promise" dueling with "purpose," produces Turner's most intense vision to this point. "I saw white spirits and black spirits engaged in battle, and the sun was darkened—the thunder rolled in the Heavens, and blood flowed in streams—and I heard a voice saying, 'Such is your luck, such you are called to see, and let it come rough or smooth, you must surely bare it.'"[41] The vision is something of a collage. Most of its visual cues come from Revelation, which from this moment onward becomes a major influence on Turner's eschatology. One of these visual cues, however, is a direct quotation from Luke's description of the climax of Christ's crucifixion—"and the sun was darkened."[42] The vision also has a voice, which again is a mixture of Revelation and Luke. First comes the Book of Revelation's fundamental command: witness and reveal: "Such is your luck, such you are called to see."[43] The resonance of the remainder—"let it come rough or smooth, you must surely bare it"—is Lukan. The voice here is Luke's voice of John the Baptist, preaching repentance and the coming of the Messiah: "The voice of one crying in the wilderness, Prepare ye the way of the Lord, make his paths straight. Every valley shall be filled, and every mountain and hill shall be brought low; and the crooked shall be made straight, and the rough ways shall be made smooth."[44] Once again Turner is being summoned to seek and to serve. The injunction "rough or smooth you must surely bare [bear] it" alludes to Luke at 14:27, particularly in light of the Lukan passages to which Turner has already adverted that underline the absolute necessity of the disciple's total commitment: "Whosoever doth not bear his cross, and come after me, cannot be my disciple." Well prior to the act of crucifixion, Luke turns to the cross as Christ's means to stress apostolic discipline and obedience. "In Luke 14:25–27, Jesus warns the 'many crowds' pressing about him of the journey of discipleship that demands their total allegiance. . . . Whoever does not carry his or her cross in this journey to death cannot be Jesus's disciple. But the converse is also true. Whoever bears Jesus' cross and shame as faithful to the end will be rewarded with the life of heaven."[45]

Onto this moment of intense eschatological anticipation and commitment, Turner imposes a specific coding—"white spirits and black spirits engaged in battle." Almost invariably these words are read phenotypically, as an intimation of racial violence experienced some seven years (in Turner's recollection) before the actual event.[46] To serve that purpose, however, the vision must be detached from its biblical referents and turned on its head. "Spirits engaged in battle" suggests Revelation 12:1–11—"And there was war in heaven" (12:7)—which describes Christ's defeat of Satan at the climax of the crucifixion (invoked by Turner in "the sun was darkened") and the expulsion of Satan from heaven to earth, marking "the coming of God's kingdom and of his Christ's authority."[47] In Christ's war against Satan, in which Turner here is being enlisted, the white spirits of Revelation are those that have been washed "in the blood of the Lamb." They are "a great multitude, which no man could number, of all nations, and kindreds, and people, and tongues, stood before the throne, and before the Lamb, clothed with white robes," who serve God "day and night." It is they who cry out "with a loud voice, saying, How long, O Lord, holy and true, dost thou not judge and avenge our blood on them that dwell on the earth?"

> And white robes were given unto every one of them; and it was said unto them, that they should rest yet for a little season, until

their fellow servants also and their brethren, that should be killed as they were, should be fulfilled.[48]

Christ's own appearance in Revelation is described in the same terms—"His head and his hairs were white like wool, as white as snow; and his eyes were as a flame of fire"—as it is by Luke on the occasion of the transfiguration: "As he prayed, the fashion of his countenance was altered, and his raiment was white and glistering." In his visions, Turner appears to associate darkness with error.[49] White and black spirits engaged in battle is as likely to describe his own internal struggle to understand his purpose and its realization. "It must start from the violence of being struck blind, like Paul on the road to Damascus."[50]

Turner's vision is thus an unlikely anticipation of interracial violence. It follows immediately on explicit divine warning *against* involvement with the creaturely world. He has been told repeatedly that his sole purpose is to learn God's will, and obey it. In the vision, what he has been summoned to witness is Christ's great victory at the crucifixion. In the vision's aftermath, his response is not engagement with the world, but—as far as possible for one in his situation—a more complete withdrawal from it. His purpose becomes "serving the Spirit more fully."[51] As they commune, Turner at last begins to understand the meaning of God's creation—"the elements, the revolution of the planets, the operation of tides, and changes of the seasons."[52] He becomes more confident of his own spiritual maturity, his capacity to obtain the "true holiness" that he seeks, to receive "true knowledge of the faith." He finally experiences grace. "And from the first steps of righteousness until the last, was I made perfect; and the Holy Ghost was with me." It is difficult to read these words as anything other than the description of an experience, and a temporality, at once sacral and ecstatic. Turner is describing himself as at one with the—necessarily eternal—will of God.[53]

What is that will? From this point on, Turner's theology relies on the compound of Revelation and Luke from which his intense vision of the crucifixion was constructed. His experience of sanctification—"made perfect" in the company of the Holy Ghost—is accompanied by a second intense vision for which Revelation's redemptive promise of Christ's second coming supplies the essential imagery. "Behold me as I stand in the Heavens" the Holy Ghost commands him.[54] "Behold" says Revelation of Christ, "he cometh with clouds; and every eye shall see him, and they also which pierced him: and all kindreds of the earth shall wail because of him."[55] In relation to the figure of Christ, Turner in his vision assumes as before the position of Revelation's author, John of Patmos, "in the Spirit," called upon to witness and reveal.[56] Like John, he witnesses the "lights of the Saviour's hands" stretched across the sky "even as they were extended on the cross on Calvary for the redemption of sinners."[57] Revelation says "he had in his right hand seven stars," and explains the seven stars are "the angels of the seven churches" of Asia Minor to which Christ instructs John of Patmos to write.[58] Turner says that the "children of darkness" name the lights wrongly ("gave other names than what they really were").[59] His observation recapitulates Revelation 2 and 3, throughout which Christ, through John, warns the seven churches to repent "from whence thou art fallen." Only those who "have not defiled their garments . . . shall walk with me in white: for they are worthy."[60] Turner tells of the "drops of blood" he has discovered "while laboring in the field . . . as though it were dew from heaven," which he determines was "the blood of Christ" that "had been shed on this earth, and had ascended to heaven for the salvation of sinners, and was now returning to earth again in the form of dew."[61] His words reproduce Luke's description of Christ's Passion on the Mount of Olives—"And being in an agony he prayed more earnestly: and his sweat was as it were great drops of blood falling down to the ground"—and marries it to Revelation's celebration of the souls of the faithful in heaven, who had been "slain for the word of God," and "come out of great tribulation," washed "in the blood of the Lamb."[62]

In his description of the vision, Turner also speaks of seeing "the forms of men in different attitudes" in the heavens and then of finding the same figures, and hieroglyphic characters, and numbers all represented in the blood returned to earth.[63] Revelation's account of humanity's tribulation (not to mention Methodist camp meetings, with which Turner would have been familiar) is, of course, suffused with men in different forms and attitudes—agonized, contorted, condemned, saved, worshipping—accompanied by a profusion of symbols, characters, numbers, and blood images.[64] Another possibility, more prosaic, is that Gray, listening, misheard the word *beatitudes*, which might (consistent with Matthew 6:33 above) have been an invocation of St. Matthew's rendition of the Sermon on the Mount, or alternatively of the four beatitudes and accompanying woes of Luke's Sermon on the Plain (6:20–26), in which Luke again stresses the theme of reversal—the poor, the hungry, the weeping, and the rejected shall take the place of the rich, the replete, the smug, and the self-righteous. Yet another possibility is that here, as elsewhere in his narrative, Turner may have been elaborating his description by drawing on almanac knowledge—astronomical, astrological, and meteorological.[65]

The meaning Turner ascribes to his vision is understandably apocalyptic. Having earlier witnessed the crucifixion, he now anticipates the imminent return of Christ (Parousia). "It was plain to me that the Saviour was about to lay down the yoke he had borne for the sins of men, and the great day of judgment was at hand."[66] As the coincidence of second coming and Last Judgment indicate, Turner's eschatology here takes on a distinctly postmillennialist slant.[67] "About this time" he shares his revelation with a white man, parenthetically identified in the confession as Etheldred T. Brantley, "on whom it had a wonderful effect . . . he ceased from his wickedness, and was attacked immediately with a cutaneous eruption, and blood ozed [*sic*] from the pores of his skin." After nine days of prayer and fasting together, Brantley is healed of his stigmata,[68] "and the Spirit appeared to me again, and said, as the Saviour had been baptised so should we be also."[69] Turner's account of his baptism "by the Spirit" replicates Luke's account of Christ's baptism as "the bringing together of Jesus and the Spirit,"[70] and for the first time in the confession he renders his typology explicitly, for the Spirit has told him "*as the Saviour has been baptised so should we be also.*"[71] Turner's description of the "many who reviled us" as he and Brantley underwent their baptism also hints at Christ's foretelling of his own crucifixion.[72]

The narrative's apocalyptic tension tightens appreciably in the wake of Turner's baptism, when "on the 12th of May, 1828, I heard a loud noise in the heavens, and the Spirit *instantly* appeared to me and said the Serpent was loosened,[73] and Christ had laid down the yoke he had born for the sins of men, and that I should take it on and fight against the Serpent, for the time was fast approaching when the first should be last and the last should be first."[74] The Spirit's message that "the time was fast approaching when the first should be last and the last should be first" is Luke's message—again—of reversal, that at the time of judgment "there shall be weeping and gnashing of teeth, when ye shall see Abraham, and Isaac, and Jacob, and all the prophets, in the kingdom of God, and you yourselves thrust out. . . . And, behold, there are last which shall be first, and there are first which shall be last."[75]

From this point onward Turner is living entirely in sacred space and time, beyond Armageddon, his calling—at last clarified—to fight the final battle against Satan "loosed a little season," and all those Satan had deceived, so that the Last Judgment could take place,[76] completing humanity's redemption, and the New Jerusalem appear. He must wait, in silence, for the sign to commence the battle with Satan, "to arise and prepare myself, and slay my enemies with their own weapons," just as Christ had called *his* enemies to account—"those mine enemies, which would not I should reign over them, bring hither, and slay them before me."[77] And just as Luke has been his companion and source of inspiration throughout the narrative, Luke also supplies the "signs in the heavens" that will inform Turner when he should commence "the great work laid out for me to do," for they are Luke's "great signs . . . from heaven."[78] When the first sign appears—an eclipse of the sun that occurred in February 1831—the "seal" is removed from Turner's lips. Here too Luke is his point of reference: the seal on Turner's lips preventing communication of "the great work" to others, which was removed by the appearance of the first sign, is the seal that was placed on the lips of Zacharias, father of John the Baptist. "Thou shalt be dumb, and not able to speak," Gabriel tells Zacharias, "until the day that these things shall be performed," that is until the birth of John; upon which "his mouth was opened immediately, and his tongue loosed, and he spake, and praised God."[79]

Turner communicates his God-given purpose to four others.[80] The enormity of the task defies imagination—"Many were the plans formed and rejected by us."[81] Turner nearly buckles under the burden; he becomes sick with tension and distress.[82] A plan is finally concocted, hurriedly and haphazardly, only after a second unambiguous sign.[83] The event that we now know as the Turner Rebellion begins immediately.

Asked by Gray whether, chained in his cell, his fate does not prove him mistaken in his convictions, Turner's curt reply—"was not Christ crucified"[84]—confirms the third and final thread of his narrative. The account Turner has composed as he awaits trial is of a life, as was Christ's, of preparation: a precocious infant gifted with uncanny knowledge;[85] an adult tested in the wilderness,[86] come to grace and baptism,[87] confronted in his maturity by an immense task that nearly breaks him,[88] on the outcome of which rides the salvation of all. In Gray's company, Turner awaits the final and most important Christological act, his own sacrificial atonement.[89]

The life that Turner has recounted is Luke's life of Christ. Although individual elements of what Turner had to say refer to other gospels, or other elements of the Bible, the consistency of his reliance on Luke for inspiration is indisputable. This pattern is only reinforced when we look beyond similarities in words to wider matters, of content and meaning.

II

Quite apart from the biblical exegesis that shows Nat Turner was indeed a "master of scripture," two aspects of his narrative are particularly noteworthy. The first is its emphasis on prayer; the second is the emphasis it places on the central role played by "the Spirit" in his journey of self-discovery. To those who are not observant, neither characteristic may seem remarkable in one who is religious. Both, however, are characteristically Lukan.

Turner refers directly to himself engaged in prayer seven times in the course of *The Confessions*. All indicate that prayer was utterly central to his life. "All my time, not devoted to my master's service, was spent either in prayer, or in making experiments."[90] As this first mention underlines, when Turner refers to "my time" he means time not spent working. Still, Turner also finds opportunities to pray while at work: "As I was praying one day at my plough." In fact he prays "continually, whenever my duty would permit." His purpose is devotional—"[I devoted] my time to fasting and prayer"—but also inquisitorial: "I prayed daily for light on th[e] subject . . . [I] prayed to be informed of a certainty of the meaning thereof." And it is instrumental: "After praying and fasting nine days, he was healed."[91]

We imagine that the Bible is full of prayer. But it is not. Of the 23,505 verses that comprise the Old Testament in the Authorized (King James) Version, the Standard English translation available in the early nineteenth century, only 152 verses mention prayer in the sense of supplication or worship addressed to God. The New Testament is substantially more prayerful—148 verses of 7,597. Of these, 62 verses occur in the four gospels and 30 in Acts. Luke contains 27 of the 62 gospel verses devoted to prayer, substantially more than the next gospel, Matthew (18). Together Luke-Acts contain nearly 40 percent of all New Testament verses mentioning prayer in its supplicatory sense.

Commentators have drawn attention to the incidence of prayer in Luke in comparison to other biblical texts. Luke's Gospel begins with Zacharias at prayer, it ends in prayer, and at key moments throughout—baptism, transfiguration, crucifixion—Christ prays. "As is well known," write Craig Bartholomew and Robby Holt, "prayer is a major theme in Luke as it is not in the other gospels." The incidence is not simply numeric. "Luke foregrounds prayer in a way that the other gospels do not."[92] Prayer has a particular role in Luke, for it is "closely associated with the self-disclosure of Jesus." Bartholomew and Holt point to the transfiguration (9:28–36) as an example. "It is *as* Jesus is praying that his true status is disclosed."[93] As such, prayer is associated "with the movement of God's redemptive drama, with gaining or disclosing insight into the reality of that drama and its central character, and with preparation for participation in that same drama."[94] That is, prayer is the sign that one is cognizant of God's purpose. God "is already guiding salvation-history, and prayer is a means of human perception of, and thus participation in, what God is doing."[95] Such, indeed, is the fruit in Turner's own narrative of his years of prayer: "It was plain to me that the Saviour was about to lay down the yoke he had borne for the sins of men, and the great day of judgment was at hand." Prayer has trained him for the part he will play.[96]

If prayer is a central and essential element of Turner's life, so is "the Spirit." Turner refers once to "communion of the Spirit," as if the Spirit were a frequent or even constant companion.[97] But if we simply count explicit references, "the Spirit" appears seven times in the course of *The Confessions*—first in answer to Turner's prayerful meditation on Luke 12:31, subsequently as a source of revelation, reproach, instruction and guidance, as an object of devotion, and as an agent of sanctification. Separately, Turner also refers twice to "the Holy Ghost," distinguishing Holy Ghost from Spirit. Turner associates the Holy Ghost specifically with the actual presence of Christ in his most potent vision, which is inspired by Revelation and which imparts particular knowledge of the work of redemption.[98]

In all these respects, Turner's interactions with the Spirit appear very Lukan. Max Turner reports "consensus" among commentators that "of the synoptic writers, it is Luke who evinces the strongest redactional interest in the Spirit."[99] Consensus extends to identification of the Spirit as "the uniting motif and the driving force" in Luke's soteriology, in which the Spirit represents prophetic legitimation (and empowerment) for mission, rather than simply a force for the ethical and religious renewal of the individual.[100] Luke's pneumatology is rooted in the Old Testament's Judaic spirit of prophecy,[101] but extends further to grant the Spirit "Christocentric functions."[102] In Luke's birth narratives and infancy material the Spirit's Christocentric functions are those of initiation and conversion,[103] visible at first in the person of John the Baptist, who is "filled with the Holy Ghost, even from his mother's womb," then in the person of the infant Jesus, who is immediately recognized by Simeon as "the Lord's Christ" (that is, the Lord's anointed one), the long-awaited agent of salvation, "A light to lighten the Gentiles, and the glory of thy people Israel."[104] In Luke's baptismal narrative, the Christocentric function of the Spirit is greatly intensified. John pointedly contrasts himself and his ministry of water baptism with "one mightier than I . . . the latchet of whose shoes I am not worthy to unloose" who "shall baptize you with the Holy Ghost and with fire."[105] John, says Bock, "is only a precursor. . . . The stronger one to come baptizes with the Spirit."[106] As we have seen, Christ's superiority to John is underlined by John's absence from Christ's own baptism in the Spirit, which initiates Christ's own mission of messianic restoration, to which, "being full of the Holy Ghost," he will apply himself.[107] But the larger point of the promised baptism of spirit and fire is that it "represents two sides to Jesus's offer of God's promise. It divides people into two groups." As Luke has it, "He will throughly [*sic*] purge his floor, and will gather the wheat into his garner; but the chaff he will burn with fire unquenchable." Those people who accept Jesus's offer, "by accepting the one who brings it, are purged and taken in. Those who do not accept it are thrown to the wind."[108] The "pouring out" of the Spirit, by God on Christ, by Jesus on all people, throughout Luke-Acts, fulfills God's plan; it "fulfills the promise pointing to the last days and to the Messiah's mediation of salvation from God's side."[109]

Initially Turner encounters the spirit of prophecy. He identifies the Spirit as "the Spirit that spoke to the prophets in former days."[110] But in his narrative, as in Luke's, the Spirit becomes increasingly Christocentric as Turner himself, like Christ, grows beyond prophet (the voice of John the Baptist in his first vision), achieves his own sanctification, and is eventually called by the Spirit to his own baptism "as the Saviour had been baptised." This crucial description is at once a claim to typological identity and an announcement that Turner's own mission has been initiated, for which he must stand ready: "Christ had laid down the yoke he had borne for the sins of men, and . . . I should take it on."[111]

In taking it on, Turner too will offer baptism of spirit and fire. He will pour out the Spirit. He will divide people into two groups. But his mission is not a replication of that undertaken by Jesus following his baptism, the *initiation* of humanity's redemption. His mission is to "fight against the Serpent," the serpent of Revelation, "loosed a little season."[112] Turner's task is to *complete* the redemption of humanity begun by Jesus.

Once more, then, we encounter the conjunction of Luke with Revelation that permeates Turner's biblical exegesis. Luke's Gospel itself points precisely to that conjunction. "The Kingdom of God need not be searched for with signs," Christ tells the disciples in Luke's famous first eschatological discourse, "for it already is in their midst." But "before the consummation of the kingdom comes, the Son of Man must suffer." Then, when the Son of Man returns "judgment will appear suddenly and obviously like lightning. . . . It will be a day of separating people, and it will be a place of death, where vultures gather."[113]

III

When asked by Thomas Ruffin Gray whether, as a body in a cell wearing chains, his fate had not proven him mistaken, Turner's reply—"was not Christ crucified"—likens his situation to that of the Saviour. As the climax to his narrative, in fact, the reply signifies more than likeness. It signifies his own transfiguration as Christ; or—in a sense the same thing—as Christ's typological antitype. In soteriological terms, Turner is revealed as who he *really* is. To understand the implications of this requires that we delve a little into Protestant hermeneutics.

The roots of evangelical Protestantism in antebellum southeastern Virginia lay in the revivals of the 1750s and particularly of the 1760s, when Virginia's dominant Anglican church was challenged first by the influence of Baptist dissenters spreading northward across the border from North Carolina, and then by an internal rupture as Methodism (originally a largely, though by no means entirely, Arminian reform movement within the Anglican church) split off to create a separate denomination.[114] Nat Turner's original master, Benjamin Turner, was an Anglican-turned-Methodist, whose home was frequently used for Methodist class meetings—in *The Confessions* Turner refers to "religious persons" who visited his master's house when he was a child, "and whom I often saw at prayers." Turner himself has been linked to Barnes Methodist Church, located on the border of Southampton County with Northampton County, North Carolina.[115] In the wake of the events of August 1831, local opinion labeled Turner a Baptist preacher.[116] But Turner's own account of his experience of sanctification, notably his statement that he had been "made perfect," is classically Methodist.[117] Methodists were generally not, unlike the Baptists, Calvinist; that is, disposed to believe in predestination.[118] The two denominations also differed in principles of church organization, the Baptists congregationalist, Methodists cleaving to Wesley's looser system of class meetings and circuits. Ideationally, however, they were not dissimilar.[119] Both were intensely ascetic and pietistic. Both "modeled their churches on the primitive Christian communities of the New Testament, fellowships knit together by emotional intimacy and spiritual equality, godly discipline and self-abasement." Both placed "unsparing emphasis on mankind's sinfulness, hell's torments, and Satan's wiles." Both emphasized "close study of the Bible" and "constant inward scrutiny." Both harvested souls in mass gatherings of "collective enthusiasm" that included very substantial numbers of African Americans.[120] Both—but particularly the Baptists—were millenarian in eschatology. Baptists were largely premillennialist; Methodists inclined to millenarianism were postmillennialist or amillennialist in sensibility.[121] Both—but particularly Methodists—lived in a religious world of portentous dreams and visions, and of physical extremity.[122]

Virginia Methodism was one element in the great transatlantic evangelical movement that had begun in the 1730s and would dominate the next hundred years. This was the age, as Mark Noll has labeled it, of Jonathan Edwards, George Whitefield, and the Wesleys, John and Charles.[123] At its inception, the evangelical revival was eclectic. One strand, best represented by Jonathan Edwards, remained Calvinist in orientation and emphasized the importance of correct doctrine. Another strand, typified by the Calvinist Whitfield and the Arminian Wesleys, subordinated doctrinal precision to the urgency of preaching the "good news" of Christ, and the importance of holy living. This strand was not theologically innovative. It gave primary attention to "the existential issues of conversion and sanctification."[124] But at least at its inception, evangelicalism was a broad and constantly intercommunicative Euro-American front, holding basic concerns and commitments in common: conversion—"the belief that lives need to be changed"; scripture—the belief that "all spiritual truth" was to be found in the Bible; activism and mission—"the dedication of all believers . . . to lives of service for God"; and "crucicentrism"—the certainty that Christ's atoning death was the key event in the history of human redemption, and that God's work of redemption was the principal expression of His relationship to the world.[125] Here we can see all the essential elements of Turner's messianic comprehension of his own purpose.

In all of these respects, nothing was more important to the development of transatlantic evangelicalism than the interaction, beginning in the 1730s, of continental European pietists with English and American evangelicals. These contacts, Noll argues, "would have the most far-reaching consequences imaginable." By far the most consequential was the impact of the Moravian Renewed Unity of Brethren on the progenitors of Methodism.[126] In this synthesis we may discover further hints of Turner's self-comprehension.

The Renewed Unity of Brethren, better known simply as the Moravians, was the surviving remnant of the pre-Reformation Hussite Church of Bohemia, and one component in the stream of Protestant refugees driven from the Catholic Habsburg domains of central Europe between 1690 and 1730. Arriving in Saxony in 1722, the Moravians were sheltered and given assistance by Nikolaus Ludwig, Count von Zinzendorf, at his estate "Herrnhut" (the Lord's Protection) where their "revivalistic faith" combined with Zinzendorf's own "pietistic Lutheranism" to form a potent religious movement.[127] Initially, the Herrnhut community embraced continental pietism's principle of *Bußkampf*, or penitential struggle, as the key to saving grace. Bußkampf had much in common with both Calvinistic revivalism and Wesleyan Methodism. "Before we can be saved," writes Frederick Dreyer, "we must be convinced of our own sinfulness, of our utter dependence on the grace of God." Believers must confront their own damnation and experience hopelessness. "Faith begins with despair." But this is not the saving faith that will bring rebirth. Not until despair at one's own guilt is complete will the believer be brought to *Durchbruch* (breakthrough)—the "saving faith" that is the realization of one's salvation through Christ's sacrifice.[128]

A despairing confrontation with one's own sinfulness as the preliminary means to authentic faith and salvation would become a central theme in Wesleyan Methodism. But during the 1730s Zinzendorf and the Herrnhut Moravians moved beyond it. "*Bußkampf* came to be thought of as a legalistic, unevangelical institution" in the sense that it identified conversion as a process of acknowledging one's own guilt: one proceeded haltingly in supervised stages (classes) through degrees of wretchedness, self-awareness, and awakening, to faith. For the Moravians, "real truth" was instead to be found only through *Versöhnungslehre*, the Moravian doctrine of atonement, which proclaimed "the radical significance of Jesus' atonement on the cross [as] the first fact of Christianity, to which everything else was subordinated." Conversion should be directed not to self-condemnation, to "the law of God and our guilt under it," but to "knowledge of our redemption:"

> To effect conversion, we must begin with the knowledge of Christ's sacrifice, not with the knowledge of our own guilt. We must start with the Gospel, not the law. In the *Bußkampf*, conversion begins with the hatred of sin. It begins with terror and fear. In the conversion implied in the *Versöhnungslehre* we start with knowledge of our redemption, only afterward feeling sorrow for our sins. From the

> suffering of Jesus on the cross, it is seen how gravely we have offended God. We know that we once were damned only when we have learned of our forgiveness. We experience contrition only after we learn that our sins no longer matter. Sorrow is the result of our salvation—not, in any sense, its precondition. The *Bußkampf* conversion commences in fear and proceeds with hesitation and doubt; the Moravian conversion starts joyful and remains confident.[129]

For Zinzendorf, Bußkampf could not be performed by humans. It had already been performed "once and for all," by the innocent suffering of Jesus atoning on humanity's behalf on the cross. By far the most important signifier of Christ's penitential struggle was the blood and the wounds with which he had purchased human redemption. As Zinzendorf would write: "When the dear Savior died and his blood poured out, When his side was opened up, then the Holy Spirit, like a dammed stream, broke out again. She burst through and made the entire earth a streambed. As a part of its surface is covered with water, so is the entire world, at least by and by, covered with the Holy Spirit."[130] Conversion was acceptance of the redemption purchased by Christ's blood and wounds. This was the meaning of Versöhnungslehre. In 1744 Zinzendorf oversaw the composition of a *Wundenlitanei* (Litany of the Wounds) that would become a central and essential element of Moravian theology for the remainder of the eighteenth century. The litany uses graphic language to recount Christ's suffering during the Passion, and venerates his blood and wounds as the very real embodiment of Christian salvation.[131]

John Wesley had been exposed to Bußkampf pietism when in the company of Moravians during his journey to Georgia in 1735 and his sojourn there for two years while at work as a missionary for the Society for Promoting Christian Knowledge.[132] Then and later he struggled with his own conversion, until in 1738 both he and his brother Charles became directly acquainted for the first time with Zinzendorf's Versöhnungslehre through a Moravian mission led by Peter Böhler that stopped for several months in England en route to Georgia. Böhler counseled both Wesleys to "seek God's grace through faith alone." God had "but one primary injunction: *believe*. There is also only one primary sin: unbelief. Through the blood of Jesus, this sin is conquered." Böhler's teaching brought both Wesleys "special reassurance of divine grace."[133] Charles expressed his joy in hymn, the words of which clearly show the influence of Zinzendorf's theology of blood and wounds:

Come, O my guilty brethren, come,
Groaning beneath your load of sin;
His bleeding heart shall make you room;
His open side shall take you in:
He calls you now, invites you home;
Come, O my guilty brethren, come!

For you the purple current flow'd
In pardons from his wounded side;
Languish'd for you the' eternal God;
For you the Prince of Glory died:
Believe, and all your sin's forgiven;
Only believe, and yours is heaven![134]

John Wesley also found it possible for the first time to express belief in the wake of Böhler's visit, although (characteristically) he would quickly retreat to doubt his own assurance of grace. But he was clearly affected by Zinzendorf's theology. Traveling to Herrnhut in August 1738, he was seized there by a sermon preached by the veteran Moravian Christian David, "which made such an impression upon me that when I went home I could not but write down the substance of it." In Frederick Dreyer's description, what Wesley learned was that "What reconciles us to God, 'wholly and solely'" is "'the blood of Christ.'" One could not obtain justification by grieving over one's sins. "The impediment of our own contrition must be removed, before the right foundation for faith can be laid. 'The right foundation is, not *your* contrition . . . not *your* righteousness, nothing of *your own*, nothing that is wrought *in you* by the Holy Ghost.' It is 'something *without you* viz. the righteousness and the blood of Christ.'" Returning to London, Wesley represented himself in correspondence with Herrnhut virtually as a Moravian missionary: "We are endeavoring here . . . to be followers of you, as you are of Christ. . . . We now have eight bands of men, consisting of fifty-six persons; all of whom seek for salvation in the blood of Christ."[135]

Wesley learned much from the Moravians. He would subsequently model the Methodist connection on the Moravian diaspora, Methodist itinerancy on Moravian itinerancy, and Methodism's embrace of mission on Moravian missionary commitments. The division of Methodist societies into self-appraising classes replicated the Bußkampf pietism Wesley had learned in Georgia, while the nonsectarian relationship of Methodism to the Anglican Church reproduced that of the Moravians to Lutheranism. "Like Moravianism, Methodism was intended to complement the work of other denominations. Wesley entertained no wish to challenge the Church of England" just as Zinzendorf "pretends to be a good Lutheran."[136]

How much Wesley retained from his excursion into Zinzendorf's theology is less clear. Justification by faith alone remained central to Methodist teaching, but so did Bußkampf pietism. Christian perfectionism hardly reproduces "only believe," yet for some its "aspiration for entire sanctification" performed the same role as Zinzendorf's "continual meditation on the bleeding form of Christ and the spiritual experience of being washed in that blood," namely "preserv[ation] of the believer from despair and from sin."[137] Prevenient grace did not focus on the blood of Christ, but it did convey something of the same message that Wesley discovered at Herrnhut in 1738, that "the right foundation" for grace was not human contrition or righteousness, "nothing of your own," but "something [from] without you."[138] As Wesley's brother Charles would himself write on the first anniversary of his own conversion, "His blood can make the foulest clean / His blood avail'd for me."[139] Perhaps that is why Wesley remained attached to Zinzendorf's hymns, which depicted the believer rapturously adorned in garments soaked in the Saviour's blood:

Jesus, thy Blood and Righteousness
My beauty are, my glorious dress:
'Midst flaming worlds, in these array'd,
With joy shall I lift up my head.[140]

Both Methodism and Moravianism were Christocentric. But Wesley criticized the Moravians for their quietist self-insulation from the world—"humans had the responsibility to *actively* observe the means of grace . . . in the process of seeking justification."[141] Methodism's devotion to Christ's saving blood became paired with violent physical struggle against sin and Satan. Christian life was "a form of warfare" that "demanded a willingness to sacrifice, suffer, and die." Methodism "spoke of bloody battles against the minions of evil and slayings at the hands of a warrior God." It enjoined Christians to "take 'the kingdom of heaven by violence.'"[142]

Wesley's religion of violent struggle and Zinzendorf's theology of blood and wounds both made their way to North America, where both underwent a degree of transformation. If anything, American Methodism's was an intensified violence, as its camp meetings—assemblages of shrieking, jerking, contorted bodies—made clear.[143] Doctrinally pragmatic and socially fluid, a religion of "practical piety available to all . . . unmediated by an educated elite,"[144] American Methodism was nevertheless apocalyptic in its visions of impending divine judgment—the wrath to come, of which sinners were to be warned—and in its identification of the human body's flesh and blood as the site of physical and not just spiritual battles with Satan. Methodism's language, whether in exhortation or hymnody, was that of physical aggression; its ideological commitment to "the God of battles" transformable into a willing resort to violence to achieve divine ends:[145]

Urge on your rapid course,
Ye blood-besprinkled bands;
The heavenly kingdom suffers force;
'Tis seized by violent hands:
See there the starry crown
That glitters through the skies!
Satan, the world, and sin, tread down,
And take the glorious prize![146]

As for the *Wundenlitanei*, it was brought to the Moravian settlement at Bethlehem, Pennsylvania, in 1744, by August Gottlieb Spangenberg, "vicar general for the *Brüdergemeine*'s work in America," where it became "the centerpiece" of Moravian theology, "central to Moravian missions," particularly those to native peoples.[147] Too often dismissed as a bizarre and short-lived phenomenon in Moravian worship, the blood and wounds of Christ was in fact "the great Moravian discovery for the evangelization of the world."[148] It was certainly part of Moravian worship in the North Carolina Piedmont settlements of the Wachovia tract, established in 1753, taken there by migrants from Bethlehem, and underscored in communications from Spangenberg: "Be commended to the lamb of God: his death, the nail prints—so red—the wounded side, the sweat in his agony."[149] This was indeed a theology not of Christ's glory but of the cross—the redemptive suffering of the crucifixion: "The Savior has endured the death grief on his head," wrote Zinzendorf, "by which his sweat broke out, and with such a quantity that finally instead of the usual watery moisture, blood came out of his veins and pores, and fell like water drops on the earth."[150] The image is a striking recapitulation of Luke. As striking, it is replicated in the blood imagery that is so important a component of Nat Turner's theology.

Wachovia was two hundred miles from Southampton County, and as it had developed during the second half of the eighteenth century the settlement had become enmeshed in transregional networks that were both commercial and religious. "Blacks in Salem [Wachovia] were part of a larger web of Afro-Christians in Piedmont North Carolina and beyond, who worshiped, learned from each other, and exchanged ideas in many settings." Jon Sensbach thinks "blood and wounds" a temporary and outlandish aspect of Moravian worship, and indeed, by the end of the eighteenth century, Moravian commitment to the Litany of the Wounds appears to have been in decline. Even so, if indeed "the Moravian 'pedagogy of conversion' served as a model for future Methodist success" amongst Caribbean and mainland slaves, it is by no means impossible that some strand of the Moravian web of exchange and influence may have transported elements of this extraordinary theology into the southern Virginia borderlands, where it brushed against Methodists in Southampton County, Nat Turner among them.[151]

IV

Nikolaus von Zinzendorf's theology of blood and wounds was perhaps the most extreme invocation of Christ's saving blood in the evangelical soteriology of redemption, but it was certainly not isolated. Indeed, one finds Zinzendorf's litany referenced—even celebrated—in one of the most famous of all evangelical hymns, "Rock of Ages," composed in 1763 by the "stiff" English Calvinist, Augustus Toplady:

> Rock of Ages, cleft for me,
> Let me hide myself in Thee;
> Let the water and the blood,
> From thy wounded side which flow'd,
> Be of sin the double cure,
> Save from wrath and make me pure.[152]

Other Calvinist evangelicals were less easily convinced. In his 1746 *Treatise Concerning Religious Affections*, examining Christian conversion, Jonathan Edward, the Northampton, Massachusetts Congregationalist cleric,[153] dismissed those "made to believe, through some delusion of Satan" in "a counterfeit faith, from impressions on their imagination," those who "say they know that there is a God, for they have seen him; they know that Christ is the Son of God, for they have seen him in his glory; they know that Christ died for sinners, for they have seen him hanging on the cross, and his blood running from his wounds."[154] Yet Edwards's own writings on the Apocalypse were not backward in mobilizing Christian blood imagery for his own purposes. Edwards emphasized that Revelation's souls of the faithful—"that innumerable multitude of all nations that have been martyred, since the beginning of the Reformation"—had been "washed . . . in the blood of the lamb" and (like Charles Wesley) "purged from all filthiness of sin," and "their garments, that were stained with their own blood, are now made white in the blood of the Lamb; and they are perfectly freed from all manner of trouble and affliction." It was "the blood of the Lamb" that had enabled Revelation's martyrs to overcome Satan, for "in shedding their [own] blood they shed the blood of Christ."[155]

Edwards's discourse on the Apocalypse was central to his millenarian hermeneutics, which in turn were of the first importance to the theology of redemption promoted in the evangelical revivals of the eighteenth and early nineteenth centuries wherever they occurred across Europe and America.[156] The central figure in Northampton's own revival of 1734–35 (he was then thirty years old), Edwards was the single most important religious intellect anywhere in the eighteenth-century Atlantic world. He enjoyed lasting influence on American evangelicalism far beyond Massachusetts, through writings published during his life and after his death.[157]

Of all Edwards's works, the most comprehensive eschatological statement is his *History of the Work of Redemption*, which originated as a series of thirty sermons on the work of redemption preached in Northampton in 1739 but was not published until 1774, in Edinburgh, in an edition prepared from the sermons by Edwards's son Jonathan and the Scottish clergyman John Erskine.[158] The *History* was republished frequently in the later eighteenth and early nineteenth centuries, both in its original edition and in augmented editions.[159] It has been credited with "enormous influence" on American popular culture between the Revolution and the Civil War, both as "a manual of Calvinistic theology suited for lay readers and popular preachers" and as an explanation of evangelical thought that helped to diffuse a millenarian sensibility throughout American Protestantism, nurturing "the numerous religious groups, movements, and subcultures making claims to instant or living redemption that so flourished in the antebellum years."[160] The *History* "set up exceptionally long-lived and significant resonances within the popular culture." It "securely anchored American experience in a cosmic setting, locating it by means of reference to sacred Scripture, and investing it with preeminent significance for concluding the drama of Christian redemption."[161] Without mentioning the *History* specifically, Christine Heyrman notes that Edwards was "a perennial favorite among Southern evangelicals" who absorbed his emphasis on "the divine origin of revivals."[162]

The hermeneutics of Edwards's *History* are essentially as follows: First, throughout the entire span of scriptural time, from the Fall to the Last Judgment and the end of the world, God's principal relationship to the world is expressed in His work of redemption—that is salvation—of humanity,[163] of which the most visible expression is "remarkable pourings out of the Spirit at special seasons of mercy."[164] All other of God's works, from the creation through all His works of providence, were reducible to the work of redemption: "'tis the end of it" Edwards wrote, "as the use of an house is the end of the building of an house."[165] Redemption is the greatest of God's works because its culmination is a renewal of creation that extends for all eternity.[166]

Second, all God's work of redemption belongs to an eternal covenant entered into between Father and Son, God and Christ, before the beginning of the world, which elected Christ as mediator between God and humanity.[167] Throughout scriptural time, Christ as mediator protects the survival of his church whether invisible or visible.[168] Third, the entire span of scriptural and human history is manifested in three phases: the first phase from the Fall until Christ's incarnation in human form is to be understood as one of preparation for the purchase of redemption. The second phase, which is that of Christ's first coming, lasting from his incarnation until his death and resurrection, is the phase in which the purchase of redemption is actually accomplished through the perfection of Christ's obedience to God, his humiliation and crucifixion, and his resurrection. At this point, for the first time, Christ's kingdom of heaven becomes a reality on earth. The third phase, which lasts from Christ's resurrection until the end of the world, is to be understood as a time of constant struggle to complete the work of redemption by extending Christ's kingdom on earth until it encompasses all humanity, a struggle necessarily undertaken in constant confrontation with Satan, just as the work of preparation had been undertaken in confrontation with Satan.[169] This is, of course, an entirely teleological history of salvation (*Heilsgeschichte*) that knits all time into one determinate era—albeit an era divided into three distinct periods of preparation, purchase, and completion, as well as into additional shorter "dispensations," or distinct and successive periods conforming to scriptural and human history (the Jewish dispensation, the evangelical dispensation, the dispensation of the covenant of grace, and so forth).

To create a detailed historical account of the work of redemption, Edwards relied on scriptural evidence, notably the currents of prophecy (revelation of what would come to pass) that recur throughout Old and New Testaments, and on what he terms "profane" history, that is, nonscriptural chronicles of events.[170] To establish the meanings and connections that rendered scriptural time holistic, he employed several distinct hermeneutical strategies: first, the interpretation of certain Old Testament events as betokening the presence of Christ in scriptural narrative prior to his New Testament incarnation;[171] second, prophecy;[172] and third, a quasi-allegorical theory of "shadows" or "images" in which one scriptural or historical reality discloses or represents another more fundamental or higher reality. The strongest and most detailed form that this quasi-allegorical hermeneutics takes is typology, which expresses a broad Protestant literalist and historical rejection of Catholic scriptural exegesis. Essentially, typology is a figuralist hermeneutics that unifies the Bible by identifying Old Testament events and individuals as prefigurations of Christianity.[173] According to Eric Auerbach, figuralism "establishes a connection between two events or persons in such a way that the first signifies not only itself but also the second, while the second involves or fulfills the first."[174] Protestant typology literalized figuralism—a common example is that the Old Testament figure of David is read as the type fulfilled by Christ as antitype.[175] Edwards greatly expanded the range of typological interpretation by treating the New Testament—notably the Book of Revelation—and the recorded history of the Christian church in secular time as sources for types that would be fulfilled by future antitypes, and hence as means to predict the course of the work of redemption during that part of his third period, from the resurrection until the end of the world, yet to occur.[176]

How does this help us understand Nat Turner? Consider two interrelated propositions. First, as I have already argued, Turner believed himself to be the fulfillment of Christ at the moment of his second coming. Turner's account of himself in the first part of *The Confessions* is not simply an account of a figure that is Christ*like*. Considered typologically, Turner creates himself as the antitype of the Christ of the New Testament, as the materialization in human form of the Christ whose return in a postmillennial eschatology coincides with the Last Judgment.[177] The significance of this proposition can best be appreciated if one is prepared to accept a second proposition, which is that Turner was acquainted to some unknowable extent with Edwards's redemptive soteriology. This second proposition cannot be directly substantiated, but given the *History*'s wide circulation and immense resonance among "lay readers and popular preachers"—or in other words people like Nat Turner who populated the networks from which he may have gained scriptural knowledge—it is not as eccentric as might at first appear. Turner has been widely identified as a lay preacher.[178] He was highly intelligent (this is generally accepted), and he was highly literate.[179] We have already seen that *The Confessions* evidences his claims to possess the kind of knowledge that familiarity with widely circulating texts such as almanacs would impart.[180]

In fact, a circumstantial case for Turner's acquaintance with Edwards's *History* can be made. Consider, initially, Edwards's representations of Christ in his human form and compare Turner's self-description. First Edwards: Christ was born into "uncommon humiliation and sufferings. . . . He suffered in his birth as though he had [been] meaner and viler than a man, and not possessed of the dignity of the human nature, but had been of the rank of the brute creatures." He was "persecuted in his infancy. They began to seek his life as soon as he was born." He was subjected to "great humiliation" by his "servile, obscure life in a mean, laborious occupation." He spent "the first thirty years of his life . . . among mean, ordinary men, as it were, in silence." He lived a life of "spotless purity and eminent holiness . . . in great measure hid in obscurity . . . he was little taken notice till after his baptism."[181] Now Turner: he was born into slavery, "the property of Benj. Turner, of this county." He carried with him into adulthood a memory of conversation among white onlookers who casually remark of him as a child (whether jest or threat, how was the child to know) that "I had too much sense to be raised, and *if* I was, I would never be of any service to any one." As a slave, his labors were devoted entirely "to my master's service." His "life and manners" bespoke both "austerity" and obscurity—avoidance of "mixing in society," devotion to "fasting and prayer." Turner's claim to a precise knowledge of his date of birth—October 2, 1800—is noteworthy, not only because such knowledge was extremely rare among slaves, but also because the date he claimed meant that like Christ he too was thirty years old when the time came to "arise and prepare myself."[182]

Consider, second, certain turns of phrase or images that Turner uses in his narrative. One, obviously, is his frequent invocation of "the Spirit," which parallels Edwards's repeated reference to "the remarkable pouring out of the Spirit"—of God, of Christ, or just "of the Spirit"—throughout the *History*.[183] A second example is to be found in Turner's references to blood.[184] Like Turner, Edwards drew widely on Revelation for his *History*, but as we have seen he also treated Old Testament events as typological figurations ("types") for Christ, notably (in this case) the waters of the Flood for the crucified Christ's saving blood. His description of a sinful world drowned in a tempest of blood resonates with Turner's first intense vision, which Turner likens to a storm—darkened sun, thunder in the heavens, and blood flowing in streams:

> That water that washed away the filth of the world, that cleared the world of wicked men, was a type of the blood of Christ that takes away the sin of the world. That water that delivered Noah and his sons from their enemies is a type of that blood that delivers God's church from their sins, their worst enemies. That water that was so plentiful and abundant that it filled the world and reached above the tops of the highest mountains was a type of that blood the sufficiency of which is so abundant baptismal for the whole world's baptism, to bury the biggest mountains of sin. The ark that was the refuge and hiding place of the church in this time of storm and floods was a type of Christ, the true hiding place of the church from the storms and floods of God's wrath.[185]

Likewise, we find elsewhere in the *History* blood images that closely match those used by Turner to describe Christ's blood "shed on this earth . . . ascended to heaven for the salvation of sinners . . . now returning to earth again in the form of dew." As Moses redeemed his people "from hard service and cruel bondage" when others were destroyed by "the sprinkling of the blood of the paschal lamb," says Edwards, so Christ saves his people and his church "from the cruel slavery of sin and Satan" by "the sprinkling of the blood of Christ when the rest of the world is destroyed."[186] Compare, finally, Turner's description of Etheldred Brantley's stigmata—"blood ozed [*sic*] from the pores of his skin"—with Edwards's description of Christ's agony in Gethsemane: "So violent was the agony of his soul as to force the blood through the pores of his skin."[187]

A more particular example arises from the turn of phrase that Turner uses to specify "the great work laid out for me to do" (itself of course redolent of Edwards's multiple references to God's "great work" of redemption). It is to "slay my enemies with their own weapons."[188] This seems innocuous for the expression is now familiar. But its familiarity is deceptive. Despite its biblical ring it is not a biblical phrase. Etymological evidence suggests the phrase had no extended currency before the mid-nineteenth century. The conceit conveyed by the phrase does have an etymological history that predates Turner and his rebellion, first appearing in the early seventeenth century,[189] but the sources in which it appears are few and far between, and in most cases the form of expression and the meaning of the phrase are quite distinct.[190] Jonathan Edwards, however, employs virtually the same phrase as Turner, and uses it to convey precisely the same auspicious redemptive meaning: "God preserved him [David] from him [Goliath], and gave him the victory over him, so that he cut off his head with his own sword and made him therein the deliverer of his people, *as Christ slew the spiritual Goliath with his own weapon, the cross, and so delivered his people*."[191] In Edwards's *History* this sentence appears in the paragraph immediately following a disquisition on David as type to Christ's antitype that describes David as "low of stature and . . . of despicable appearance," whereby God showed how Christ, who was "despised and rejected [of men]," would "take the kingdom from the great ones of the earth. . . . Thus was that frequent saying of Christ fulfilled, 'The last shall be first and [the first last].'"[192] In *The Confessions*, the same three ideas are intimately associated—that Turner was reviled of men, that "the time was fast approaching when the first should be last and the last should be first," and that "I should arise and prepare myself, and slay my enemies with their own weapons."[193] They occur in the same order as in the *History*, on the same page of Gray's pamphlet, and within a very few lines of each other. If the first part of Gray's *Confessions* is indeed a reasonably accurate record of what Turner said, in the order he said it, the conjunction of the three ideas, reproducing the same conjunction in Edwards's *History*, is noteworthy indeed.[194]

Consider finally the tenor of Turner's postmillennialism. Where does it come from? That he should have embraced a millenarian worldview is not itself remarkable (although more unusual for a Methodist than a Baptist)—millenarianism was a central element of early nineteenth-century American popular culture, and of a religious culture dominated by the morphology of revival-driven conversion.[195] Nor was postmillennialism a rare eschatology in the early republic. "A minority position in earlier generations" writes Daniel Walker Howe, "postmillennialism became the most widely held viewpoint on eschatology . . . among Protestants in antebellum America."[196] But Howe is writing here of the period's "middle-class mainstream," the urbane white citizenry that embraced progress and uplift, whose celebration of "reformers, inventors, and Christian missionaries" folded evangelical religion seamlessly together with lyceums and mechanics' institutes, with utopian communities and collegiate education, with commerce and capitalism, to compose an antebellum civic identity of respectable bourgeois expectation.[197]

Was this a mentalité one should expect to find amid the fetid squalor of small-scale rural slavery in decaying southside Virginia?[198]

Remarkably, Turner does offer us hints of that folding together of religion and inventive curiosity that Howe holds typical of antebellum postmillennialism. Of his unawakened youth, for example, he tells Gray "all my time, not devoted to my master's service, was spent either in prayer, or in making experiments in casting different things in moulds made of earth, in attempting to make paper, gunpowder, and many other experiments, that although I could not perfect, yet convinced me of its practicability if I had the means."[199] Gray adds, "When questioned as to the manner of manufacturing those different articles, he was found well informed on the subject."[200] Still, Turner's was not the complaisant postmillennialism of Howe's emergent bourgeoisie, but the altogether more urgent, revolutionary eschatology of Edwards's *History*, in which Christ's Kingdom does not await his second coming but is a reality on earth from the moment of his resurrection, and in which human history from that moment onward becomes a history of the struggles of Christ's suffering visible church to advance his kingdom against the earthly powers of Satan, struggles attended by extraordinary danger and by miraculous successes against impossible odds brought about by the glorious "pouring out of the spirit of God,"[201] struggles accompanied throughout by Revelation's chorus of martyred souls slain for their faith, "How long, O Lord, holy and true, dost thou not judge and avenge our blood on them that dwell on the earth?"[202] struggles that are constant and continuous until the moment when "It is done," when "the whole work of Redemption is finished," when "that new heaven and new earth . . . that renewed state of things that had been building up ever since Christ's resurrection [shall] be completely finished after the very material frame of the old heavens and old earth are destroyed."[203] This is the revolutionary postmillennial sensibility that Turner brings to the extraordinary moment of supreme danger to the whole work of redemption that precedes finality, the moment when Satan is "loosed a little season,"[204] when "the church of Christ . . . shall be reduced to narrow limits again" and "shall seem to be imminently threatened with a sudden and entire overthrow" by a measure of human wickedness and apostasy incomparably greater than ever before seen.[205] This is the moment, Edwards insists, of Christ's second coming, once again "in his human nature," when "the wickedness of the world will remarkably call for Christ's immediate appearing in flaming fire to take vengeance."[206] This is the moment Turner describes, but winds to an even more exquisite level of eschatological tension: "I heard a loud noise in the heavens, and the Spirit *instantly* appeared to me and said the Serpent was loosened, and Christ had laid down the yoke he had borne for the sins of men, *and that I should take it on* and fight against the Serpent." Suddenly, the entire burden of Christ's original purchase, the fate of the entire work of redemption, the salvation of humanity, has been laid on the thin shoulders of a thirty-year-old southside slave.[207]

In light of all this, what then was "the great work laid out for me to do" that Turner finally shared with his confidants in February of 1831? It was, he tells us—although before they actually begin he says it only once—"the work of death."[208] We must ask, who were to be the slain? As it turned out, a dozen wretched southside farmers and their families. But in Turner's intent, at least, were these not the "blasphemous, murtherous enemies" pressing in on Christ's church, "wicked persons . . . not fit to live," people who had mocked his baptism, people whose threat to the final realization of the work of redemption Turner had been charged to end, against utterly impossible odds, in what one might therefore represent as the most wonderful "pouring out of the spirit of God" of all?[209] Just as Christ crucified had been brought "under the power of death" to complete the purchase of human redemption, as Edwards repeatedly noted, so Christ's enemies had themselves finally to be brought under the power of death to complete the work of redemption itself.[210] "Those mine enemies, which would not I should reign over them, bring hither, and slay them before me."[211]

CONCLUSION

It is tempting to read *The Confessions of Nat Turner* knowing that at the end of the spiritual odyssey they detail lies a massacre of white slaveholding families undertaken by a group of (mostly) slaves, to identify that massacre as a "slave rebellion," and to assume that *The Confessions* is a narrative of how that slave rebellion came to be. Indeed, it is not simply tempting but perhaps also inevitable to read the pamphlet in that manner, given that it was constructed after the event, that both of the participants in its composition were fully aware of—intimately involved in—the massacre that had taken place, and that at least one of them (Gray) had spent the previous two months thinking both personally and professionally of the massacre as a "slave rebellion," as indeed had virtually the entire population of St. Luke's Parish, of Southampton County, of Virginia, and probably anyone in the United States or beyond who had read or heard of the affair. It is nevertheless remarkable that virtually nothing that Turner says during the first part of his confession (and nothing at all directly) either embraces, or even hints, that the outcome he planned, or intended, or imagined was a "slave rebellion"—an insurrection "*as you call it*." So far as Turner was concerned, it was not insurrection that had "terminated so fatally to many, both white and black" but "enthusiasm."[212] To discover a slave rebellion in the making in *The Confessions* we have to accept Gray's own gloss, read Turner's narrative backward, and then ignore his actual words. We have to treat his apocalyptic eschatology as if it were a secret code referencing something other than itself, not as a confession of faith.

Like Thomas Ruffin Gray, Nat Turner had more than two months to think back on what had happened on August 22 and 23, 1831. When the time came for him to explain what had happened, and why, he had resort not to a language of revenge, or revolution, or self-expiation, or guilt, but to an eschatological cosmology of revelation and judgment. His discourse of revelation and judgment was not some ethical assessment that tried and found wanting the profane slaveholder legalities in which the Southampton County Court trafficked; it was judgment in furtherance of redemption, a sacred and tempestuous instant of justice.[213] We have seen Caleb Smith argue that in sentencing Turner, Jeremiah Cobb created a linkage between "worldly statutes" and "the law of God."[214] In fact there is not one shred of any such linkage to be found in anything Cobb has to say. The worldly Cobb speaks of "valuable citizens" done to death under circumstances "shocking to humanity." He speaks a secular and sentimental nineteenth-century language of "sympathy" that pities Turner for his delusory "fanaticism"—which is to say his Christological religiosity.[215] Smith invokes "Old Testament cadences" that he professes to detect in Cobb's declamation,[216] but there are none; only a facile intimacy that seeks to smother what Turner actually *is*.

Biblical cadences do suffuse *The Confessions*, but they are not to be found in the speech of Jeremiah Cobb, and in any case they are not Old Testament cadences, but New. They situate the profane and tawdry worldliness of St. Luke's Parish slaveholders next to the Last Judgment, to the profound and terrible detriment of the former. The cadences are those of Nat Turner.

PART II

A Sword in the Sunlight

But I
bask in a
beautiful byproduct
from twisting torque
of dichotomy
what my eyes do see
in this spilling, dead wicked desert
it dances
born of babble
is now raison d'etre
for the rabble
I sing my soul with tongue
A sword in the sunlight
thrashing and flashing . . .

VIC CHESNUTT,
"GLOSSOLALIA" (2007)

3

The Shudder of the Thought

> If any man come to me, and hate not his father, and mother, and wife, and children, and brethren, and sisters, yea, and his own life also, he cannot be my disciple.
>
> —LUKE 14:26

> Clarify the value of the exception, of the event, of rupture.
>
> —ALAIN BADIOU (2003)

How do you respond when God makes it known that He requires you to kill? We know what Nat Turner *did*—he killed, and he persuaded others to kill. But we know little of how he understood what God asked of him, or how he reached the decision to obey. Of this *The Confessions* tells us next to nothing.

We can surmise that at some point between May 1828 and August 1831, in my view later rather than sooner,[1] Turner realized that the instruction "to fight against the Serpent," the injunction to slay his enemies "with their own weapons," was meant to be taken literally; that "the great work laid out for me to do" was work "of death."[2] *The Confessions* hint that the prospect was shocking, that it caused Turner distress: "Many were the plans formed and rejected by us, and it affected my mind to such a degree, that I fell sick." Irresolution—"time passed without our coming to any determination how to commence"—was overcome only by an unambiguous reminder from God of what was expected of him.[3] But this is all we are told. Turner's narrative in *The Confessions* turns as if on a hinge at the paragraph break on page 11/12 of the pamphlet. On one side of the break we encounter hesitation, perhaps doubt, perhaps dread. On the other, action. Evidently a decision has been taken, but it is a decision that the text does not discuss. Instead we exit a metaphysical cosmos to find ourselves immediately enveloped in the utter reality of massacre.[4] How has this onto-epistemological break occurred? What exists in this temporal and textual cleft between worlds, this "caesura of the work," in which "everything pauses," that can explain so abrupt a transition?[5]

Thomas Ruffin Gray offers us a clue, in his own recoil from "the calm, deliberate composure with which he spoke of his late deeds and intentions," from "the expression of his fiend-like face when excited by enthusiasm, still bearing the stains of the blood of helpless innocence about him." Turner, helpless, "clothed with rags and covered with chains," still "raise[s] his manacled hands to heaven, with a spirit soaring above the attributes of man." Realizing, perhaps, the fatal attraction to an audience of a tragic hero, Gray assures his readers that in fact he beholds a monster. As "I looked on him . . . my blood curdled in my veins."[6]

Gray need not have worried. The Turner whose invisible decision exists in the text's cleft is not a tragic hero. Everything that Turner has revealed of himself in the first part of *The Confessions* underlines not tragic heroism, but faith. Clothed in rags in his squalid jail cell, faith is what raises his manacled hands to heaven, faith is what soars above the attributes of man. Gray recoils because faith is not part either of his irreligious world or of the shallow gothic melodrama that his prologue and epilogue seek to make of Turner's narrative by folding it within layers of rival text that attempt to turn the narrator into an utterly corrupted, hence utterly illegitimated, challenger to the established order of things. "It will thus appear," Gray informs his readers, as he ushers them carefully toward Turner's words, "that whilst everything upon the surface of society wore a calm and peaceful aspect . . . a gloomy fanatic was revolving in the recesses of his own dark, bewildered, and overwrought mind, schemes of indiscriminate massacre to the whites."[7] But here was no gloomy fanatic. Here was what Søren Kierkegaard calls "the knight of faith."[8]

Kierkegaard's knight of faith appears in his book *Fear and Trembling* (written when Kierkegaard was thirty years old).[9] *Fear and Trembling* is profoundly relevant to my attempt to comprehend Turner's response to God's instruction to kill, because it is a meditation on the identical decision that Abraham must make in the wake of God's instruction that he kill his son Isaac. That Abraham does not ultimately kill Isaac makes no difference: Abraham's *willingness* to sacrifice Isaac is what makes him a paradigm of faith.[10] "He knew it was God the Almighty who tested him, he knew it was the hardest sacrifice that could be demanded of him, but he also knew that no sacrifice was too hard when God demanded it—and he drew the knife."[11] For one does not bargain with God. "Without faith it is impossible to please him: for he that cometh to God must believe that he is, and that he is a rewarder of them that diligently seek him."[12] We have already seen that this precise injunction was the focus of Turner's prayers from the moment of his earliest encounter with religious instruction; the injunction, once accepted, that created the route to his own sanctification. "Seek ye the kingdom of Heaven and all things shall be added unto you."[13] Faith, says Kierkegaard, transcends worldly understanding. It transcends hope, or resignation, or barter. All of these states of mind are left behind. Faith is acceptance—of the impossible, of the absurd—"by virtue of the fact that for God everything is possible."[14]

The hardest problem of faith lies in its relation to ethics. Or, what is the same, the absence of any relation. "The ethical expression of what Abraham did is that he intended to murder Isaac."[15] How does faith absolve Abraham of intent to murder? Kierkegaard draws an absolute distinction between ethics as the highest stage of a worldly morality—the expression of a Hegelian universal—and faith. The distinction births the paradox "that the single individual is higher than the universal."[16]

Abraham is no tragic hero: the tragic hero remains within the parameters of ethics. That is why the hero is tragic.

> The case is different with Abraham. By his act he transcended the whole of the ethical and had a higher telos outside, in relation to which he suspended it. . . . Why does Abraham do it then? For God's sake, and what is altogether identical with this, for his own sake. He does it for God's sake because God demands this proof of his faith; he does it for his own sake so that he can prove it.[17]

C. Stephen Evans comments that Kierkegaard was "well aware of the dangers of a faith that is not subject to society's rules."[18] Abraham, says Kierkegaard, "arouses my admiration" but "he appalls me as well," for if in giving up the universal to grasp something higher he made a mistake, "what salvation is there for him?" Yet he believed, and in believing he stood for the absurd, in defiance of a social order, a reality, that would elevate itself above "an authentic message from God."[19]

Inside the cleft in the text, then, what we discover is the separation of faith from ethics in an encounter with the Real—with the Lacanian Real, that is, which is the naked actuality of the death-work to be done, and the terrifying majesty of the God who orders it done—and with it "the ontological disintegration of reality itself."[20] Inside the cleft, "The ethical relation is reduced to the relative in contradistinction to the *absolute* relation to God." Doing the deed "is the expression for the most absolute devotion (doing it for God's sake)." Faith thereby becomes a paradox, inexplicable in ethical, which is to say universal human, terms. "Faith itself cannot be mediated into the universal, for it is thereby annulled. . . . The single individual is utterly unable to make himself intelligible to anyone." Faith is an explanation that "can be given by the single individual always only to himself."[21] The knight of faith "walks alone with his frightful responsibility."[22]

Turner, though, is unlike Abraham in one crucial respect. He does not act alone. And his comrades are not knights of faith; or at least they offer no clear sign of it.[23] In their company, the knight of faith does not vocalize his frightful responsibility; that he continues to bear alone. But he must still persuade them to come with him on the journey he began in faith. To persuade them he must enter the creaturely world that they inhabit, and he must address them on its terms: he must take men, rather than God, as his criterion.[24] He must discover a politics that will allow them, collectively, to *act*—beyond ethics, beyond legality, act to confront what they already know, their impossible reality, the social order in which they are forced to live that elevates itself above God. "This is where the political impact takes place. . . . Knowledge falls to the rank of symptom, seen from another perspective. And this is where truth comes in."[25]

To act is to redefine one's situation, untie from fictions and ideology, leap into the unknown, experience "absolute disarray." This is why Turner must invent a politics that is for the moment and of the moment, a politics that will enable each of them to see through what surrounds them, shrug off hesitation, take the plunge, and act, *in the real*.[26] He must invent a new universal.[27] He becomes, to that extent, demonic: which means (another paradox) that he is in the world but not of its ethics. He will face worldly judgment, but without in any sense accepting it. Natures like his "cannot be saved by mediating them into an idea of society. Ethics really only makes a fool of them. . . . The fact of originally being placed outside the universal by nature or historical circumstance is the beginning of the demonic, *for which the individual, however, is not personally to blame*."[28]

Early newspaper reports of the Southampton event stated, "Nat, the ringleader . . . declares to his comrades that he is commissioned by Jesus Christ, and proceeds under his inspired directions."[29] Later reports, based on trial testimony, stated more prosaically that the original group had agreed they would "rise and kill all the white people."[30] In the fissure between these two statements lies the demonic, the invention of the new universal, the politics of the moment that will enable them to begin.

Turner, the lonely knight of faith, had to enter the moral world of captivity created by slaveholders to persuade the oppressed of that world—Will, and Jack, and more, all those who were the last who should be first, all those who were the outcasts of "the structured social field"[31]—to accompany him. We cannot know the precise content of the politics he invented for that moment, but we do know that Turner's politics enabled their collective, violent defiance of the enslavement that had wrapped them all in its coils. This was the serpent, the wicked social order that had elevated itself above God, the immediate embodiment of all the wickedness not fit to live that it was Turner's charge to end, against all odds, by pouring out God's spirit so that human redemption might be realized. His charge, human redemption, depended on his comrades' capacity for self-redemption.

Eventually—after the death-work has been done—he will resume the silence of the knight of faith.[32] But although the world of captivity is a world whose historical circumstances place him, as slave and outcast, outside its universal, it will make a fool of him just the same, for it will hold him accountable to itself and to its wickedness. Though he is not of that world's ethics, its ethics will convict him. Though he is silent "ethics condemns him, for it says: 'You must acknowledge the universal, and you acknowledge it precisely by speaking.'"[33]

"The genuine tragic hero sacrifices himself and all that is his for the universal; his deed and every emotion within him belong to the universal, he is open and in this revelation the beloved son of ethics."[34] He speaks. He explains himself. But this was not Abraham. Nor was it Turner. Abraham does not speak, "for he indeed knows that God demands Isaac for a sacrifice, and he knows that he himself precisely at this moment is ready to sacrifice him."[35] And Turner does not speak, because he knows that God had insisted that he kill, and that God had not relented, and that his faith had answered God's demand.

Kierkegaard, says Evans, "was convinced that the reduction of the life of faith to the ethical life was disastrous" because reduction meant the loss of any opportunity to transcend guilt—"the fundamental problem posed by the ethical life." Faith answered guilt because faith enabled the individual to "become an authentic self by responding in faith to God's call."[36] The call's demand was both frightful and great. It was to be found in Luke 14:26: "If any man come to me, and hate not his father, and mother, and wife, and children, and brethren, and sisters, yea, and his own life also, he cannot be my disciple." When subjected to trial, Turner answered the accusation of guilt with his confession of faith. He had been placed outside the universal by nature, by historical circumstance. He did not "feel" guilty.[37] And of the matter before the court he had nothing more to say.[38] So, confronted by his silence, slaveholder ethics judged him, and condemned him, as murderer and insurgent, to an emphatic death, "hung by the neck."[39]

> What did he achieve? He remained true to his love. But whoever loves God needs no tears, no admiration; he forgets the suffering in the love. Indeed, so completely has he forgotten it that there would not be the slightest trace of his pain afterwards if God himself did not remember it; for he sees in secret and knows the distress and counts the tears and forgets nothing.[40]

HORRID MASSACRE IN VIRGINIA.

The Scenes which the above Plate is designed to represent, are—Fig 1. a Mother intreating for the lives of her children.—2. Mr. Travis, cruelly murdered by his own Slaves.—3. Mr. Barrow, who bravely defended himself until his wife escaped.—4. A comp. of mounted Dragoons in pursuit of the Blacks.

4

The Work of Death: Massacre, Retribution

> Think not that I am come to send peace on earth: I came not to send peace, but a sword.
>
> —MATTHEW 10:34

> And now also the axe is laid unto the root of the trees: every tree therefore which bringeth not forth good fruit is hewn down, and cast into the fire.
>
> —LUKE 3:9

To pass through the cleft in the text is to leave the metaphysics of faith and enter immediately the profane, creaturely world, where persuasion must occur if the death-work is to be done, and where, once it is done, ethics will judge. It is where the knight of faith becomes demonic, where the transcendent breaks into time. But on what terms does Turner become demonic, enter the creaturely world? How does he persuade? What human self does he become? And by which universal shall this self be judged? By the universal of freedom—the servant's freedom? Or by the universal of ethics—the master's ethics?

The self's recognition of itself as a self for-itself, says Hegel, comes about only through struggle with another, a struggle in which each risks all in attempting "the destruction and death of the other." Struggle initiates awareness "that *life* is as essential to [the self] as pure self-consciousness," and, simultaneously, awareness of the other as distinct, "unlike and opposed." In struggle, self and other "stand as two opposed forms or modes

---

FIGURE 4.1. *Horrid Massacre in Virginia* (1831). From Samuel Warner, *Authentic and Impartial Narrative of the Tragical Scene Which Was Witnessed in Southampton County*. (New York: Printed for Warner and West, 1831). Library of Congress.

of consciousness," the one independent, "its essential nature . . . to be for itself"; the other dependent, "its essence . . . life or existence for another." The one is lord [*Herr*], the other bondsman [*Knecht*]. "A form of recognition has arisen that is one sided and unequal."[1]

The consciousness of lordship, "existing on its own account," as independence, obtains its recognition by negation of the other, which "cancels itself as self-existent." In obtaining recognition through the other, however, lordship achieves only dependence. Its "truth" is "the consciousness of the bondsman." And just as lordship's essential nature stands revealed as the reverse of its desire, so bondage, upon completion, will "pass into the opposite of what it immediately is."[2] Hitherto apprehending bondage only as a relation to lordship, we come to consider it in and for itself. "Being a consciousness repressed within itself, [bondage] will enter into itself, and change round into real and true independence." The other, in which self-consciousness is initially formed, is cancelled; negation is negated.[3]

How does this dialectical sublation come about? It begins in fear: fear as such, fear of the Real, "of death, the sovereign master"; and fear of the lord. Fear as such is pure self-existence; fear of the lord is "the beginning of wisdom."[4] But it is not this "beginning of wisdom" that overcomes the bondsman's cancellation of self-existent awareness. Rather "th[e] consciousness of the bondsman comes to itself" through work and labor. "Labour . . . is desire restrained and checked, evanescence delayed and postponed . . . labour shapes and fashions." By labor, the bondsman's consciousness attains "direct apprehension" of its self as independent:

> In the master, the bondsman feels self-existence to be something external, an objective fact; in fear self-existence is present within himself; in fashioning the thing, self-existence comes to be felt explicitly as his own proper being, and he attains the consciousness that he himself exists in its own right and on its own account [*an und für sich*]. By the fact that the form is objectified, it does not become something other than the consciousness moulding the thing through work; for just that form is his pure self existence, which therein becomes truly realized. Thus precisely in labour where there seemed to be merely some outsider's mind and ideas involved, the bondsman becomes aware, through this re-discovery of himself by himself, of having and being a "mind of his own."[5]

Hegel's dialectic is justly famous, "finding a place in Marxism, psychoanalysis, and postcolonial studies," indeed "in any critical discourse that wrestles with some idea of the 'other' as that against which you define yourself."[6] The question arises, however, to what extent the dialectic of lordship and bondage should be considered an ahistorical abstraction—"some kind of phenomenological retreat from materiality"—or grounded in a material history. In a notable critique of the tradition of phenomenological readings of the *Phenomenology* dating to Alexandre Kojève and Jean Hyppolite, Andrew Cole demonstrates that Hegel situated the dialectic in a specific historical frame, the history of German feudalism, and concludes that "if we are to understand the lord/bondsman dialectic as the signal instance of modern self-consciousness, then we need also to appreciate its central generator—that struggle [between 'ownership' and 'effective possession' of land] toward which antiquity leans, and out of which the 'modernity' of capitalism grows."[7]

From Cole it seems to follow that the correct reading of Hegel is a historicist reading. "Critics who dehistoricize Hegel's meaningful vocabulary obscure the sort of social phenomenology he is striving for."[8] But historicism's quest for meaning in the particular really only shifts the problem from "reading" to "context,"[9] where, in place of Cole's emphasis on Hegel's materialist critique of feudalism as the key to what the dialectic of lord and bondsman "really means," Susan Buck-Morss can substitute the master/slave conflict of the Haitian Revolution, of which Hegel was well aware, or David Brion Davis (following Kojève) can invoke the guns of Jena and Napoleon's revolutionary ascendancy over Europe.[10] More important, there is no necessity that Hegel be "dehistoricized" in order to obtain a universalizing conceptual vocabulary from the dialectic. One can acknowledge that his ideas had originating specificities—and Cole's account of those specificities is by far the most thorough and convincing of the various alternatives—but this does not entail surrendering to those specificities. Arguably, it was precisely Hegel's objective to break beyond the interpretive constraints of any given social formation.[11] The point, as Slavoj Žižek writes, is to recognize and realize the universal that is immanent therein:

> The commonplace according to which we are all thoroughly grounded in a particular contingent lifeworld, so that all universality is irreducibly coloured by and embedded in that lifeworld, needs to be turned round. The authentic moment of discovery, the

> breakthrough, occurs when a properly universal dimension *explodes from within a particular context and becomes "for-itself," and is directly experienced as universal.*[12]

My interest in dislodging the lord/bondsman dialectic from historicist specificities is quite straightforward. The dialectic assists me in both exploration and explanation of the event known as the Turner Rebellion—the "taking the lives of divers free white persons of the Commonwealth" over the span of approximately twelve hours on Monday, August 22, 1831, in St. Luke's Parish, Southampton County, Virginia; the taking of the lives of some twenty-five slaves and free people of color that followed over the next twenty-four hours; and the subsequent *juridical* putting-to-death of a further eighteen slaves, variously accused of "feloniously counselling, advising and conspiring with each other and divers other slaves to rebel and make insurrection and making insurrection."[13] It does not assist because the dialectic is specific to the relation of master and slave, for as we have seen it is not. It assists because certain components of the dialectic are helpful in explaining the massacre that took place, notably the centrality of work (in this case death-work) to the bondsman's formation of self-consciousness and self-possession; its "direct apprehension" of its self as independent.[14] For John Locke, for example, labor is the means to propertied independence: killing those who would maintain one in relations of dependence is a means to obtain a property in oneself. For Hegel, on the other hand, property is not that on which one has expended labor so much as that in which one has invested one's will.[15] One invests one's will in one's self through the work of willfully killing those whose standing claim to have invested *their* will in one's self blocks one's own claim. As we will see, the dialectic also helps to explain the specific juridical form of retributive killing that was the central white response to the work of death done by Turner and his comrades.

Nat Turner used that pungent phrase, "the work of death," to describe the action that he initiated.[16] The phrase was, if not commonplace, not uncommon.[17] It meant killing, and its associated experiences.[18] But what kind of killing? The killings that are indelibly associated with Turner's name were not a "spree." Nor were they the shambolic nightmare imagined by Eugene Genovese, mindless slaughter conjured by "a hate-driven madman who had no idea of where he was leading his men or what they would do when they got there."[19] The killings were not indiscriminate, but purposeful.[20] They followed a logic. But what was their logic? Was it instrumental—revenge? Was killing incidental to some overriding purpose, such as flight, or revolution?[21] Or was it in itself a central and essential redemptive act? And what did it mean, particularly to a slave, to describe dealing death as "work?"[22]

I. THREE DAYS IN AUGUST

Us neber shot a hog . . . us always used an axe.
—JOSEPH HOLMES, 1937

The killing began in the early hours of Monday, August 22, at the house of Joseph Travis, approximately five miles west of the hamlet of Cross Keys. "We determined to enter the house secretly, and murder them whilst sleeping."[23] Nat Turner scaled a ladder, opened a second floor window, descended the stairs and unbarred the door. Prevailed on by his companions to strike first, Turner attempted to kill Travis with a hatchet as he lay asleep, but managed only a glancing blow. "He sprang from the bed and called his wife." Turner's comrade, Will [Francis], "laid him dead with a blow of his axe." Travis's wife, Sarah, was killed the same way as she lay in bed. So too were Sarah's son, Putnam Moore, and Travis's apprentice, Joel Westbrook, their heads hacked off. Recalling after their departure an infant child left alive in the house, "Henry [Porter] and Will returned and killed it."[24]

The killing had been decided at a meeting near Cabin Pond, less than a mile from Travis's house. The meeting had begun the previous afternoon, only a few hours before the invasion of the Travis house. "It was agreed between Henry, Hark [Moore] and myself," Turner reported, "to prepare a dinner the next day for the men we expected, and then to concert a plan, as we had not yet determined on any." Hark slaughtered a pig, Henry brought brandy, and "they prepared in the woods a dinner, where, about three o'clock, I joined them."[25] Four others came to the meeting, two of whom—Nelson [Edwards] and Sam [Francis]—had been confidants of Turner's for some time, two of whom, Jack [Reese] and Will, were new to the group. "I saluted them on coming up, and asked Will how came he there, he answered, his life was worth no more than others, and his liberty as dear to him." The other newcomer, Jack, was the younger brother of Hark's wife. "I knew [he] was only a tool in the hands of Hark."[26] Tool or not, on learning that the meeting had been called to agree on a plan "to rise and kill all the white people," Jack became alarmed, objecting that those present were "too few." Notwithstanding Hark's retort that "as they went on and killed the whites the blacks would join them," Jack continued to display extreme reluctance at the thought of participating in serial acts of murder. He "complained of being sick and wanted to go home but . . . Hark would not let him go." After the group adjourned to the Travis house, Jack continued to display obvious distress and incapacitation; "his head between his hands resting on his knees," he remained "in the yard sick."[27]

Jack Reese's anguish at the prospect of involvement in an episode of mass killing was the most overt sign of stress among the initial group of perpetrators, but it was not the only sign.[28] The original five had already tried once to nerve themselves to begin, six weeks before: "It was intended by us to have begun the work of death on the 4th July last." But indecision had prevailed amid disagreements and distress. This time, during the afternoon meeting, prior to any collective discussion of what was to be done, Turner was observed to take each man aside, one by one, "and hold long conversations," a pattern of deliberate and careful persuasion designed to quell anxieties and gain trust. Once open discussion began among the group and Jack had "denied the possibility of effecting" the plan, Turner answered and "assured them of its practicability—saying that their numbers would increase as they went along."[29] To others present who might also have been shocked by the prospect of mass killing, Turner reportedly "stated, that his reasons for not telling of it before, was, that the negroes had frequently attempted similar things, confided their purpose to several, and that it always leaked out . . . his resolve was, that their march of destruction and murder, should be the first news of the insurrection."[30] The group then agreed to commence at the Travis house, and to do so immediately ("on that night"); the men further agreed that "until we had armed and equipped ourselves, and gathered sufficient force, neither age nor sex was to be spared."[31]

Still, on arrival at Travis's the group appears to have delayed for several hours, while all except Turner "went to the cider press and drank."[32] Finally steeled to begin, the group looked to Turner to lead, but Turner was no more anxious to kill than anyone else. After entering the house and unbarring the door Turner reportedly told the others "that the work was now open *to them*."[33] This was unacceptable. "It was then observed that I must spill the first blood." Turner tried, but failed. "I entered my master's chamber, it being dark, I could not give a death blow, the hatchet glanced from his head." Travis awoke, screaming. In the excitement and alarm, Will split Travis open with his axe, and then did the same to his wife. Thus was the die cast.[34]

Turner had faltered at the first hurdle, but his leadership survived. No matter how hesitant or clumsy they had been, the group of slaves had managed to kill five whites in their own house—an extraordinary occurrence in itself. With guns and muskets recovered from Travis's, and with two new recruits,[35] the group could take on the appearance of a fighting force; it could acquire some esprit de corps. "I formed them in a line as soldiers, and . . . [carried] them through all the manœuvres I was master of."[36]

After Joseph Travis, master of Turner and of Hark, the next target was Salathiel Francis, master of Sam and Will, whose cabin was approximately half a mile from the Travis house. "Mr. Francis asked who was there, Sam replied, it was him, and he had a letter for him, on which he got up and came to the door, they immediately seized him." Sam and Will dragged Francis from his cabin and beat him to death in the yard—"repeated blows on the head."[37]

As it proceeded, the group became more resolute, "maintaining the most perfect silence on our march."[38] Now that the killing had begun it became easier to contemplate and so easier to perform. The men were becoming more practiced at what they did, and, crucially, they were encountering little opposition. On arriving at the Reese house, about a mile from Francis's cabin and the home of Jack, of Hark's wife, and possibly of Turner's own wife, they found the door unbarred, entered silently, "and murdered Mrs. Reese in her bed, while sleeping." They also killed her son, William, quickly, competently: "He had only time to say who is that, and he was no more."[39] Another mile across country took the group to the plantation occupied by Mrs. Elizabeth Turner, widow of Nat's sometime master Samuel G. Turner, where they arrived at sunrise. "Henry, Austin, and Sam, went to the still" where they surprised Hartwell Peebles, the plantation overseer. Austin shot him—the ninth white to die and the first to be shot. The rest of the group headed for the house where they found themselves discovered, probably by the noise of the gunshot, and the door barred. "Vain hope!" Turner said to Gray, a sardonic comment, perhaps a memory of unaccustomed power. Will smashed through the door with his axe and cut down Mrs. Turner where she stood, huddled "almost frightened to death" with a visitor, Mrs. Sarah Newsom. Turner, following, flailed at Mrs. Newsom with the sword he had been carrying since the group left the Travis house: "I struck her several blows over the head." But she did not die—"the sword was dull."[40]

Instead Will killed Mrs. Newsom with his axe. She was the eleventh victim: four men, four women, three children; all but one (Peebles) stabbed repeatedly, beaten to death, or hacked apart.

Four households had been wiped out in four hours. The group had doubled in size—there were now fifteen men[41]—and it had developed a pattern of activity: a stealthy approach, a surprise attack, reliance on knives and axes rather than guns, and following the killing, "a general destruction of property and search for money and ammunition."[42] These were not random, indiscriminate attacks. The group had purpose and method. Its course was deliberately conceived.[43]

After four successful raids the men had gained enough self-confidence for more complicated manœuvres. Six men on foot made their way to Henry Bryant's house, about a quarter mile east, where they killed the entire family: Henry; his wife Elizabeth; Elizabeth's mother Mildred Balmer; and the Bryants' child. Nine men mounted on horses gathered from the Reese and Turner farms headed for the Whitehead property, a mile beyond Bryant's. Near the house they encountered Richard Whitehead, a Methodist minister, son of Katherine Whitehead. "We called him over into the lane" where Will, now nicknamed "the executioner," decapitated him "with his fatal axe."[44] Turner reported that he left the group to pursue someone he saw running off, "thinking it was some of the white family." But it was a servant girl. "I returned to commence the work of death" but all had been dealt with in his absence, save only Katherine Whitehead and her eldest daughter, Margaret. Turner watched as Will dragged Mrs. Whitehead from the house, "and at the step he nearly severed her head from her body." Turner himself flushed Margaret from her hiding place and after battering her with his sword "I killed her by a blow on the head, with a fence rail."[45] In all seven Whiteheads—one man, five women and a child—had been killed.[46] Two more households had been destroyed. Two more rebels recruited.[47]

Once more the group divided and attempted a more elaborate maneuver, this time encompassing four households, the larger part "going to Mr. Richard Porter's, and from thence to Nathaniel Francis's," the remainder "to Mr. Howell Harris', and Mr. T. Doyles."[48] Turner, as leader, became responsible for coordinating their movements. This was about to become a particularly important role, for on reaching Porter's it became clear that news of their activities had preceded them: the white family (twelve in all) had fled. "I understood there, that the alarm had already spread."[49] Turner instructed the party heading for the Nathaniel Francis property to wait for him "in that neighborhood," and left to make contact with those "sent to Mr. Doyles, and Mr. Howell Harris.'" Turner met them returning from their mission. They reported they had encountered Doyle (Augustus "Trajan" Doyel) "on the road" and had killed him there. But they had proceeded no further, "learning from some who joined them, that Mr. Harris was from home."[50] Howell Harris, the local constable, was most likely on his way to Jerusalem to raise the alarm.

Turner and the Doyel/Harris group did not bother to visit the Nathaniel Francis farm, assuming that the others "would complete the work of death and pillage" there. They were correct. Francis's overseer was shot dead and his two orphaned nephews decapitated; Louisa Williams, a visitor, and her infant child were also killed.[51] Instead, Turner and his companions tracked their comrades through several other devastated farmsteads: the Edwards farm, which they found deserted, the family gone; the Barrow farm, where John Barrow had exchanged shots with the rebels before his throat was slashed open, and where his brother-in-law, George Vaughan was also killed; and finally the farm of Newit Harris, where they caught up with the main body whom they had last seen heading for the Francis property.[52]

The scene at the Harris farm was one of extreme excitement. The family had fled, its property had been destroyed: the house, as elsewhere, had been ransacked for "money and other valuables." When Turner appeared "the men now amounting to about forty, shouted and hurraed . . . some were in the yard, loading their guns, others drinking."[53] It was now approximately 10:00 a.m. on Monday morning. Eleven households (if one includes Porter's) had been destroyed; thirty whites had been killed, their corpses left "mangled."[54] Turner ordered the company "to mount and march instantly." There was no longer any point in stealth—the opening phase of accumulating participants and weapons was over. Turner now chose to follow a very different, very public, path of brute intimidation by spreading "terror and devastation" throughout the countryside, "wherever we went."[55]

Since the attack on the Whitehead property, the southernmost of the households destroyed in the first phase, Turner had directed his company steadily northward, toward the Barrow Road. After Porter's, however, he had lost contact with the main body, which, in targeting Newit Harris's plantation, had strayed westward. "I never got to the houses, after leaving Mrs. Whitehead's, until the murders were committed, except in one case."[56] After catching up with the main body at Newit Harris's, Turner's awareness that they were discovered and time was passing, his terse command "to mount and march instantly," all suggest some concern at the detour.

The entire body headed for Waller's farm, four miles directly eastward from Harris's along the Barrow road in the direction of Jerusalem, which lay some eight miles beyond Waller's. As befitted the role of commander, Turner took his station "in the rear" and directed about half his force ("fifteen or twenty of the best armed and most to be relied on") to advance on the farm at full gallop, their task to prevent escape and to "strike terror to the inhabitants." The remainder followed behind.[57] At Waller's seventeen whites awaited them—two adult males, two adolescent males, the remainder mostly women and small children. The men possessed loaded guns but chose flight over resistance. Ten were killed at Waller's, the women and children, mostly hacked or beaten to death, brains "knocked out," bodies "piled in one bleeding heap."[58] One more, an infant child, would die two days after. Six fled or hid, and survived, Levi Waller among them.

At Waller's the company paused to drink at the still, then continued eastward. At Williams's farm they cut down William Williams Jr. and two hired boys, then captured Williams's fleeing wife, "brought her back, and after showing her the mangled body of her lifeless husband . . . told [her] to get down and lay by his side, where she was shot dead."[59] Allmendinger comments that Turner's account of Mrs. Williams's death "suggests a growing boldness on the part of her assailants."[60] A quarter mile further east lay the property of Jacob Williams where the company repeated its full-tilt approach, surprising a visiting overseer, Edmund Drewry, there on business—"pursued, overtaken and shot"—along with Jacob Williams's wife, Nancy, and their three small children, all killed in the kitchen, and the wife and child of Williams's overseer, Caswell Worrell.[61] Rebecca Vaughan's house was the next target: Vaughan was shot to death, along with her son and niece. Vaughan's was the final assault of the day on a farm household—the fifteenth if Porter's and Edwards's are included.[62] Twelve hours had passed since the murder of the Travis household. Fifty-five whites were dead or mortally injured; twenty-five had been killed in the previous two hours alone. "Our number" meanwhile "amounted now to fifty or sixty, all mounted and armed with guns, axes, swords and clubs."[63] It was early afternoon and Turner decided they were ready for the next phase. "I determined on starting for

Jerusalem." He would contemplate no more delays or detours. "I had a great desire to get there to procure arms and amunition [*sic*]."[64]

The company proceeded three miles east along the Barrow Road to the junction with the road from Cross Keys to Jerusalem, then a half mile northeast on the Cross Keys Road as far as James W. Parker's plantation. "It was proposed to me to call there, but I objected." Turner was convinced the whites would be long gone, "and my object was to reach [Jerusalem] as soon as possible." But others wanted to recruit from among Parker's slaves, and Turner reluctantly agreed to a delay while the majority of the group approached the plantation. "After waiting some time for them, I became impatient."[65] Turner left sentries at the road and headed for the house where he rounded up his men, but on their return toward the road they were surprised by a party of armed whites. This group—eighteen strong—had answered the alarm carried by Howell Harris to Jerusalem and had been following the trail of wrecked households from the Whitehead plantation.[66] "I ordered my men to halt and form." The whites approached but at about one hundred yards one of them fired accidentally, whereupon several others began backing off, outnumbered and fearful. "I then ordered my men to fire and rush on them." Turner planned a repetition of the terrifying spectacle they had presented to such great effect at Waller's, and his expectations seemed justified, for "the few remaining stood their ground until we approached within fifty yards, when they fired and retreated." Turner's men rushed on "and overtook some of them who we thought we left dead."[67] None was, in fact, killed,[68] but the rout continued until the fleeing men met a second party of whites who had been in the vicinity after riding out from Jerusalem about two hours earlier, "who knew the negroes were in the field," and had heard the gunfire.[69]

Reinforced, the fleeing whites halted, and both parties began firing on Turner's advance. "I saw them re-loading their guns, and more coming up than I saw at first, and several of my bravest men being wounded, the others became panick struck and squandered over the field; the white men pursued and fired on us several times." None of the rebels was killed, but half a dozen were wounded and others had scattered. Still, the whites did not press their advantage and Turner took the setback in his stride. No longer able to use the Cross Keys Road, "I instantly determined to go through a private way, and cross the Nottoway river at the Cypress Bridge, three miles below Jerusalem, and attack that place in the rear."[70] But the bridge was guarded, and too many of his men had run off. And so, "after trying in vain to collect a sufficient force to proceed to Jerusalem," Turner and the remainder of his company (twenty or twenty-five men) retreated to the southwest, following in the footsteps of those who had fled. "I was sure they would make back to their old neighborhood." The plan became to regroup overnight in the vicinity of Cross Keys, "make new recruits, and come down again." They had suffered a reverse, but the country had been thoroughly cowed by twelve hours of slaughter. The farms through which they passed were deserted. "The white families having fled, we found no more victims to gratify our thirst for blood."[71]

At some point late in the afternoon of Monday 22, Turner changed his mind. Since turning for home the group had recovered some of its lost strength.[72] Turner abandoned the retreat back toward Cross Keys and instead the group headed north to Major Ridley's Buckhorn Quarter, thus remaining no more than an hour's ride from Jerusalem. Turner, evidently, was determined to try to reach the town the next day. He estimated his numbers had grown to forty again, but alarms during the night caused some to run off, so instead of riding on Jerusalem immediately the next morning (Tuesday, the twenty-third) the objective changed to more recruitment.[73]

Early on Tuesday morning the company approached the nearest house (Dr. Blunt's). They fired a gun "to ascertain if any of the [white] family were at home." They were answered by concentrated gunfire "and retreated, leaving several of my men."[74] This second engagement was decisive. The group's fragile commitment to raid Jerusalem collapsed and the men fled southwest, their original course the previous afternoon, back toward Cross Keys. At the Harris farm, where twenty-four hours earlier they had celebrated the incredible success of the first phase, they encountered a swarm of white cavalry, and what remained of the group's cohesion disintegrated. "All deserted me but two." The three hid for the rest of the day, then Turner attempted one final rally, sending his last companions to find his original confidants—Henry, Sam, Nelson, and Hark—with instructions to regroup at the place of their Sunday meeting. But when Turner made his own way back to Cabin Pond nothing was to be seen but patrolling whites. Seventy-two hours had passed since the decision to attack Travis's had been taken, "and none of my men joining me . . . I gave up all hope for the present."[75] Turner would spend the next ten weeks in hiding, alone.

II. MASSACRE

Harrowing was the squealing of the victims; quick was the stroke that slew them.

—JOHN SERGEANT WISE, 1899

To call what took place on August 22 in Southampton County a "massacre" is to invoke a particular way of understanding this episode of concerted—and, under the circumstances, unprecedented—killing.[76] Begin with the word itself. Etymologically, the meaning of the English word *massacre* is derived from the Middle French *massacre*, meaning butchery, and Old French *maçacre/maçacle*, meaning a slaughterhouse or butcher's shop. *Maçacre/maçacle* glosses postclassical Latin *macella*, meaning a shambles or butcher's shop, which is a variation on classical Latin *macellum*, meaning a provision-market. The common first syllable mass/maç/mac tracks postclassical Latin *macia*, meaning a bludgeon or club, *mace* in Anglo-Norman, which is a variation on vulgar Latin *matteuca*, or cudgel, itself derived from classical Latin *mateola* meaning an agricultural implement, from which the English words *mattock* and *maul* are derived. "Massacre" thus unites several otherwise distinct concepts: killing in the manner of animal slaughter, or butchery, in which those killed lack means of self-defense; killing in the manner of a vocation that requires the expenditure of bodily effort, as in the work of slaughtering animals and butchering meat, or agricultural work such as felling trees, hammering posts, or chopping firewood; close proximity between killer and killed, as within the confines of a slaughterhouse or a butcher's shop; and the use of physical force to overwhelm those killed, as in stabbing, slitting, chopping, or bludgeoning.[77] In origin associated with the slaughter of animals for food, massacre came in the late sixteenth century to be associated with the killing of people in the manner of animals—a repetitious process of slaughter—with ritual, purgative connotations.[78] In current usage massacre means a form of killing that occurs "in a precise place and during a limited time," in which "the relations of physical force" between those who kill and those who are killed are asymmetrical, and in which the killed have the character of defenseless, even innocent, victims.[79] Massacre is taken to imply multiple or repeated killings but the etymological emphasis on the *manner* of killing means that it can also describe single killings, such as exemplary and ritual executions, or extravagantly theatrical murders.[80]

Applied to the killing of people, massacre is thus associated with physical excess: "So inhuman has been the butchery, so indiscriminate the carnage, that the tomahawk and scalping knife have now no terrors."[81] Or as the principal modern student of massacre, the French sociologist Jacques Semelin, puts it, "blood spewing everywhere, unthinkable atrocities, bodies torn asunder." Still, to Semelin massacre is hardly indiscriminate, for it is at least as much a mental or ideological as a physical process. It is a dialectic of recognition, "a way of seeing some 'Other' being, of stigmatizing him, debasing him, and obliterating him before actually killing him." Before massacre can take place, a "prophet[ic]" intellectual construction of the other as enemy must occur.[82] Semelin describes this as a discursive process composed from three elements—identity, purity, and security. Identity means the creation of a collective self as "one" against the "other" from a "common past of suffering"; purity defends the integrity of the newly created collective self against the corruption of the other; security is the undertaking to rid the collective self of the threat posed by the extreme difference of the other, to destroy the other in order to forestall the inevitability of its violence.[83] To Semelin, the inflammatory process of identity formation creates a mythic *imaginaire* of omnipotence and destruction focused on the other, "a sacrificial violence that aims to 'regenerate' the group at the expense of an 'other.'"[84] He calls this a crystallization of identity through purification, a "logic of the sacred through murder."[85]

Semelin stresses that massacre is less a *murderous* process than a physically *destructive* process, "an organised process of destruction" directed not just at persons but also at their property.[86] As such, massacre is extremely demanding on the perpetrator, both psychologically and physically. Psychologically, massacre demands that some ordinary people learn how to kill others—others whom they know, amongst whom they live, with whom they may enjoy some degree of amity until the process of destruction is initiated.[87] "It is not easy for a man to resolve to kill a fellow human, even if he gives himself good reason for doing so."[88] Perpetrators must become inured, they must learn how to routinize their capacity to destroy so that it can be repeated as often as required. Some learn quickly, expressing "pleasure . . . unconcealed glee."[89] Such a perpetrator, according to Wolfgang Sofsky, "wants to wallow in blood, to feel with his own hands, with his fingertips, what he is doing. The knife affords him a direct, tactile sensation. . . . By crushing, cutting, dismembering, he is in contact with his own violence."[90] Others experience profound unease, traumatic stress.[91] Some mitigate their stress with alcohol.[92] Others obfuscate their participation, or quietly abscond.[93]

Most simply persist, assimilating the process of killing and destroying to "work."[94] There are at least three reasons why massacre becomes "work" in this way. First, killing (particularly repeated killing) is extremely laborious: "To slaughter human beings requires a high degree of physical and above all mental exertion."[95] Second, killing on the scale of massacre borrows its methods from work: it borrows both the means (tools),[96] the tendency to develop habitual practices (repetition and routine),[97] and the mode of organization—a division of labor amongst leaders who direct but rarely kill, executioners who kill frequently, and ancillary personnel who kill on occasion but mainly assist those who kill frequently.[98] Third, the most populous segment of perpetrators of massacre corresponds sociologically to a "workforce"—overwhelmingly male, single, and young, even adolescent, in the age range of thirteen to twenty-five years old.[99]

Massacre is analogous to work for a fourth reason: it is a transformative process. On one side, victims become something other than merely corpses. It is quite common (and not at all inappropriate) to argue that massacre involves a transformation of the living body into something *less* than it was. Thus, Semelin observes that "the very conditions of neighborhood massacre, which *de facto* implies the physical proximity of executioners to their victims, [are] necessarily conducive to the committing of atrocities. . . . Perpetrators of massacre feel a need to 'disfigure' this fellow human as quickly as possible" to forestall the possibility that recognition of a common humanity will stand in the way of killing the victim. "Cruelty is truly a mental operation on the body of the other, intended to destroy his humanity."[100] But chopping, crushing, decapitating, disemboweling, dismembering, hacking, mangling, mutilating, slitting, scalping, turning bodies into waste, into rubbish to be devoured by wild beasts,[101] all also represent much *more* than killing. These are somatic transformations that "expose, penetrate, and occupy the material form—the body—of the . . . other." They are a "vivisectionist" exhibition that puts new personal realities on display.[102] "Extreme bodily violence may be seen as a degenerate technology" by which new intimacies are fashioned between former social intimates, a "counterperformance" of their former relationship that destroys a prior order of life and re-creates the victim as something drastically different than before—helpless, weak, and vulnerable; *opened* for inspection.[103] Here we should recall the repeated usage in Southampton witness reports of the adjective "mangled" to describe the bodies of victims.[104] The victim and the victim's body have become the site on which prior relational uncertainties or antagonisms are resolved "through brutal forms of violation, investigation, destruction, and disposal."[105]

Just as it transforms victims' bodies, massacre transforms its agents. One can argue with justification that massacre renders its agents *less* than human—and indeed, unsurprisingly, in this case that was the consensus of white opinion. Though many descriptions were applied to them—monsters, savages, brigands—most commonly the rebels were referred to as "wretches" and "bandits," or "the banditti"; that is, as outcasts from human society.[106] But, however briefly, massacre can also mean the formation amongst perpetrators of a new identity, whether individual or collective, a new consciousness, endowed with a new integrity and new capacities. This is what the "logic of the sacred through murder" means.[107] Here, then, is "death" as "work" in its Hegelian mode, in which "self-existence comes to be felt explicitly" as the agent's "own proper being" through the action of fashioning; in which labor, where formerly "there seemed to be merely some outsider's mind and ideas involved," creates awareness, a "re-discovery of himself by himself, of having and being a 'mind of his own,'" a "will."[108]

Notable in the earliest accounts of the Southampton massacre, before the conventions of the symbolic order began concealing actuality beneath layers of descriptive discretion, is the sheer raw shock of white commentators both at its deadliness and its ferocity: families destroyed in an infection of madness;[109] horrible massacres;[110] horrible ferocity;[111] bloodthirsty wolves preying on helpless women and children;[112] knives and axes, knocking out brains, cutting throats;[113] corpses horribly mangled;[114] blind purposeless fury;[115] inhuman butcheries;[116] whole families butchered, left in heaps;[117] bodies chopped to pieces, "buzzards preying on the carcasses."[118] White commentary attempted to deny the massacre any meaning other than madness and degeneracy—an exhibition "more marked by its ferocity than its force."[119] But if meaning is to be sought we will find it, precisely, in ferocity. Turner's "work of death" was death-work that he and his comrades performed in the service of their self-transformation, through a cancellation and destruction of the other, from bondsmen subordinated by fear, "consciousness repressed within itself," into willful actors possessed, however fleetingly, of "real and true independence."[120]

III. INSURRECTION

> He knocked some honky down and beat him to death, and then laid his wife down and killed her, right next to him. He wasn't afraid of white men; he killed white men, white babies, white women, white cats, white dogs, everything that was in the neighborhood.
>
> —SECOND QUESTIONER, 1969

If the logic of the Southampton massacre lay in Turner's attempt to transform its perpetrators from subservience to self-awareness through self-redemptive "destruction and death of the other," it remains to ask whether the event itself had any distinct instrumental purpose. Examining individual instances of massacre, Semelin discerns three fundamental political dynamics, or rationalities, on display: subjugation, eradication, and insurrection.[121]

Killing in the service of subjugation means "to annihilate a group partly in order to force the rest into total submission."[122] A population is subjected to the terror of destructive example—massacre, pillage, and rape—to produce an effect, such as surrender, or subservience, or the abandonment of resistance to established authorities. Wars of colonial conquest, modern "total" warfare, wars of enslavement and the institution of chattel slavery itself, all have the character of exemplary mass violence intended to induce capitulation.[123]

Killing in the service of eradication means killing not to subjugate or suppress a population but to destroy it in order to remove it physically from a position in command of resources desired by another, or from a position in which it is perceived as a threat.[124] Killing in the service of eradication may be exemplary, in that it is designed to induce an existing population to move elsewhere so that its territory can be claimed for use by others,[125] or it may be totalized, its objective completely to destroy, to eliminate, the entirety of a population.[126] In either case, whether by departure or death, the territory in question is "cleansed" of the other's presence.[127]

Killing in the service of insurrection is distinct from killing in the service of subjugation and/or eradication in two respects. First, subjugation and eradication are usually the work of state actors, or state sympathizers; killing in the service of insurrection is not. Second, subjugation and eradication both exhibit a capacity to escalate into elimination; state actors usually possess the resources to make escalation a viable possibility if less intense forms of coercion prove ineffective. Insurgents rarely possess the capacity to escalate. At most they can multiply—do what they are already doing but with greater frequency.

The objective of killing in the service of insurrection is "to strike the target group in a single blow to provoke an intense traumatic shock likely to influence its leaders' policies."[128] To terrify the target population is an objective in all three of Semelin's rationalities of massacre. In the third case, however, the perpetrators' weakness—lack of alternative resources—renders terror not simply an objective to be accomplished but a primary rule of engagement.[129] Insurgents are fully aware that they have no presence in the relevant public sphere, either because they are an excluded minority or because the armature of the target group is too formidable to penetrate: spectacular violence enables them to gain sufficient purchase on the target group's attention to shock the system it dominates.[130]

In appearance, the Southampton massacre was, using Semelin's terms, killing in the service of insurrection.[131] As Turner explained himself, the first objective was to gather resources—weapons and participants—sufficient to secure freedom of movement while killing to preserve secrecy. Once secrecy had been lost, killing became more explicitly part of the design, and movement was subordinated to killing: "My object to carry terror and devastation wherever we went." Corpses became expressive—shocking—and their own silent propaganda: "mangled bodies" to intimidate those who would pursue "our blood-stained track."[132] Finally, resources gathered, opponents cowed, the moment arrived to intensify the traumatic shock. "I determined on starting for Jerusalem."[133] Why? The massacre had become a rolling snowball: begin; repeat; hope. Turner sought new resources—supplies of arms and ammunition—to multiply both frequency and freedom of action. Jerusalem was the logical source.

What followed was failure; the insurgents did not reach Jerusalem. But failure had little to do with any fault in Turner's plans, which he pursued boldly with everything he had at his disposal.[134] Eugene Genovese to the contrary, he knew what he was doing, and why.[135] Failure lay, rather, in the relationship between the insurgents' "struggle for life" and the circumstances—the grid of constraints—that bound them. Circumstance was by no means all to their disadvantage: the spatial geography of slavery in Southampton County enabled them to overcome the obstacles inherent in what Donald Black has called "the social geometry of terrorism."[136] But they could not overcome the crucial distinction that Michel de Certeau draws between "tactics" and "strategy" in their struggle for life.[137]

To invoke Certeau is to leave the sociology of massacre for social anthropology, in particular "the models of action characteristic of . . . the dominated element in society," those fated to use only what is left over by the dominant rather than to produce for themselves.[138] This is less of a leap than it might seem, for a moment's reflection will show that we remain within the terms of Hegel's dialcctic. Certeau's "users" are analogous to Hegel's unawakened bondsmen, confronted by lordship "existing on its own account," their own will to exist for themselves deferred or canceled. Just as the bondsman begins to attain self-consciousness through work, Certeau's users "make [*bricolent*] innumerable and infinitesimal transformations of and within their cultural economy in order to adapt it to their own interests and their own rules."[139] The verb here, *bricoler*, is not insignificant.[140] Semelin's killers are also *bricoleurs*, attaining self-consciousness through *their* work, makers of meaning from what lies at hand, whose violent practices assert identity.[141] "A bricoleur is a kind of 'jack-of-all-trades' in the sense that he or she uses whatever materials are at hand to perform given tasks. Like bricoleurs, perpetrators . . . draw upon a toolkit of personal and cultural knowledge to overcome their hesitations and to make sense of the murderous deeds they are carrying out."[142] Turner and his comrades move through space, engaged in an "efficacious meandering" of their own construction built from their own ways of using what comes to hand, from local, practical knowledge (*mētis*)—"clever tricks, knowing how to get away with things, 'hunter's cunning,' maneuvers":[143]

> Sam and Will went to the door and knocked. *Mr. Francis asked who was there, Sam replied, it was him, and he had a letter for him*, on which he got up and came to the door, they immediately seized him, and dragging him out a little from the door, he was dispatched by repeated blows on the head.[144]

Still, they are unable to overcome the positionality of the weak. Theirs is not the realm of "strategy" but of "tactics."

For Certeau, strategy is "the calculus of force-relationships which becomes possible when a subject of will and power can be isolated from an 'environment'"; that is, when the subject becomes for-itself (*propre*) and thereby attains an autonomous spatiality, a "basis for generating relations with an exterior distinct from it."[145] Tactics, by contrast, is "a calculus which cannot count on [an autonomous spatiality], nor thus on a borderline distinguishing the other as a visible totality. *The place of a tactic belongs to the other.* A tactic insinuates itself into the other's place, fragmentarily, without taking it over in its entirety, without being able to keep it at a distance. It has at its disposal no base where it can capitalize on its advantages, prepare its expansion, and secure independence with respect to circumstances." In the calculus of tactics the actor is a creature of circumstance. It "must play on and with a terrain imposed on it and organized by the law of a foreign power. It does not have the means to *keep to itself*, at a distance, in a position of withdrawal, foresight, and self-collection."[146]

Turner's rebellion is, from the very beginning, a calculus of tactics, undertaken "'within the enemy's field of vision' . . . within enemy territory."[147] Turner and his confidants do not have the option of strategy. They acknowledge this quite explicitly, from the outset. "Many were the plans formed and rejected by us . . . the time passed without our coming to any determination how to commence . . . forming new schemes and rejecting them." When they decide to begin it is not a strategic (autonomous) decision, but one taken in answer to a temporal demand imposed from elsewhere (God)—"the sign appeared again, which determined me not to wait longer."[148] And even then they must still decide *how* to begin, "to concert a plan as we had not yet determined on any."[149] Once under way, the rebellion "operates in isolated actions, blow by blow." It has no place of its own, no secure base from which to operate, to which to return. It must rely on mobility, seizing "the possibilities that offer themselves at any given moment . . . vigilantly [using] the cracks that particular conjunctions open in the surveillance of the proprietary powers."[150] It must surprise its adversaries, poach on their territory. Begin. Repeat. Hope.

The fate of the rebellion is a manifestation of the limits inherent in the calculus of tactics. Lacking place, tactics rely on "a clever utilization of time." The rebellion follows a definite trajectory; it is "a temporal movement through space," its unity as event fashioned from the "diachronic *succession* of points through which it passes" rather than from the synchronic/achronic figure that the points form on a space. It is "a *temporal* articulation of places" rather than "a *spatial* sequence of points."[151] It unfolds in three successive phases: an initial phase of accumulation, conducted largely on foot; a phase of intimidation, from horseback; and a phase of vindication and multiplication—pressing toward Jerusalem—that turns to dismount and defeat. Turner's account exhibits a growing sense of dispatch as phase succeeds phase. Once they have been discovered, "I ordered [my men] to mount and march *instantly*" to begin the sequence of attacks that will terrify the countryside. After the last of these attacks and Turner's decision to start for Jerusalem he becomes "impatient" at delays that prevent achieving his objective "as soon as possible." Turned away in the skirmish at Parker's field, "I *instantly* determined to go through a private way . . . and attack that place [Jerusalem] in the rear."[152] Throughout, Turner communicates a preoccupation with time rather than with the occupation of space. He repeatedly uses the word *immediately* to describe his own actions and those of others—"they *immediately* seized him . . . Will *immediately* killed Mrs. Turner . . . the alarm had already spread, and I *immediately* returned to bring up those sent to Mr. Doyles . . . learning from some who joined them, that Mr. Harris was from home, I *immediately* pursued the course taken by the party gone on before . . . [I] *immediately* started in quest of other victims . . . *Immediately* on discovering the whites, I ordered my men to halt and form."[153]

The rebels' defeat is a victory of space over time, of strategy over tactics, of *techné* over *mētis*, of power over trickery and local knowledge ("private ways"). The terror of the rebellion empties the terrain of white men and their families. Gradually, inexorably, the whites fill it again, with armed men. By reestablishing their command of place they block the rebellion's trajectory. They fill the channels connecting place to place, neighborhood to neighborhood. Their obstructions "reduce temporal relations to spatial ones."[154] One group follows the rebels' tracks; another group rides into their faces. When the rebels try to regroup and go around "through a private way, and cross the Nottoway River at the Cypress Bridge" they find the bridge guarded, the way blocked. They spend the night in a state of constant fear of white patrols converging on them. When they attempt to recruit the next day they are "immediately fired upon" and retreat headlong. Their retreat falls foul of yet another "party of white men" squarely in their path, and what remains of their cohesion disintegrates. The whites take back the roads; they force the rebels onto footpaths; they patrol everywhere—"riding around the place as though they were looking for some one." One by one Turner's last companions desert and he finds himself alone. "On this I gave up all hope for the present."[155]

IV. "THAT PLACE"

O Jerusalem, Jerusalem, which killest the prophets, and stonest them that are sent unto thee.

—LUKE 13:34

Nat Turner's "work of death" describes a particular kind of human labor—the violent destruction of others—in the service of a redemptive struggle for life: what one might call a process of destructive creation. The logic of the attempt was dialectical, an explosive collective realization of life through release from the circumstances of a particular lifeworld, the lifeworld of enslavement, of the serpent, the wicked social order that God had charged Turner to end, such that life could become "for-itself," and directly experienced as a universal flourishing, perpetrators and abettors and circumspect involuntary beneficiaries of massacre enlivened and empowered.

But the attempt did not succeed. Some of the insurgents were killed, some were captured, some ran off. Rather than produce the desired universal, the dialectic collapsed back into mere circumstance. Or, to put it differently, no crowning sublation occurred. Instead the course of the dialectic proved disjunctive, lurching from *Knecht* back to *Herr*, Bondsman to Lord, Slave to Master.[156] Hegel had argued that the consciousness of lordship, "existing on its own account," obtained its recognition through negation of the other, the bondsman, and that in doing so lordship demonstrated its dependence on the negated. In what Alexandre Kojève called the "existential impasse" of lordship and the oppression to which it gave rise lay the beginnings of the bondsman's wisdom, the seeds of antithesis and eventual sublation.[157] But Orlando Patterson argues differently. The master was not so dependent on the slave. True, "the degradation of the slave nurtured the master's sense of honor," but "as a ready object for the exercise of his sense of power." And beyond the relationship of master and slave lay other fountains of honor and recognition. "The poorest free person took pride in the fact that he was not a slave. By sharing in the collective honor of the master class, all free persons legitimized the principle of honor and thereby recognized the members of the master class as those most adorned with honor and glory."[158] An ambivalent, circumspect, black minority,[159] a timocratic white majority:[160] these were tough nuts for rebellious slaves to crack.

Still, Southampton slaveholders could not rest easy. Turner had only given up hope "for the present." The dialectic was disjunctive rather than nonexistent. It might lurch back again. To secure their lifeworld they had their own work of death to do.

Here again, we see strategy ascendant over tactics. Retribution was not immediate—no continuation of *massacre* in the form of answering mass *atrocity*. Revenge killings certainly took place, but they were not legion.[161] Rather, the slaveholders' work of death was "a triumph of place over time." Slaveholders invested in what was already their established advantage, the *techné* of legal process, on display in a specific place, the town of Jerusalem.[162] For Turner the town ("that place") had been an objective only because he thought arms and ammunition might be found there—resources that could buy him more time. For those he sought to destroy, the town was a different kind of resource, not temporal but spatial, a strategic knot in a net of authority that extended across all the counties of the state, and stretched as well above and beyond to Richmond, the state capital. As Southampton's county seat, Jerusalem was an empowered place, home to the Southampton County Court and its special trial jurisdiction of Oyer and Terminer, reserved for the capital crimes of slaves.[163]

Jurisdiction underwrote strategy but also answered massacre in kind. The tactics of massacre had wrought somatic transformation on its victims; correspondingly, the court opened the bodies of slaves up for inspection. At least temporarily, massacre had stunned and invaded the lifeworld of slavery. The task of the court was to restore the lifeworld to proper (*propre*) place by terminating those found to have conspired to rebel and make insurrection against it, and to have killed others in insurrection's service. The court's process was panoptic, a resumption of mastery through sight, specifically the sight of those who had witnessed. Witnesses transformed what was foreign to the lifeworld of slavery (insurgent slaves) into objects "observed and measured, and thus control[led] and 'include[d]'" within the court's "scope of vision."[164] Such were the ways of strategy. Such was *its* work of death.

Fifty-four slaves and two free men of color were either killed in the course of Turner's rebellion, or sentenced to death in its aftermath, an exacting response to the fifty-five whites who died, but not in outcome an exact one, for twelve of those sentenced to hang had their sentences commuted by Virginia's governor, John Floyd. Of the fifty-four slaves at least fifteen and as many as twenty-three died in circumstances deemed atrocities by contemporary white authority. Six were bystanders, some of whom may have been implicated in the rebellion. Two were insurgents killed before capture—Nelson Edwards and Henry Porter—whose bodies were mutilated (decapitated). Seven others were suspected insurgents killed on capture. A further eight suspected insurgents (including Will Francis) died during the rebellion, in circumstances unknown. One suspected insurgent died in jail. One free man of color (Billy Artis) died in what was either a reprisal killing or a suicide. Another (Berry Newsom) was convicted in April 1832 in the Southampton Circuit Superior Court of conspiracy to make insurrection, and hanged.[165] Including Newsom, fifty-five blacks appeared before the Southampton County Court on charges of participating in an insurrection. Five were free people of color of whom one was discharged and four remanded to superior court trial. Newsom apart, all of these were acquitted. Of the fifty slaves, seven were discharged without further proceeding and forty-three committed for trial. At trial before the county court thirty were convicted and sentenced to hang, of whom eighteen were indeed hanged; the remainder had their sentences commuted to transportation. Thirteen were acquitted and discharged.

Of the forty-three defendants committed for trial before the county court, thirty-five were tried individually and eight in three small groups.[166] All had counsel appointed by the court as required by statute; all pleaded not guilty. The court proceeded expeditiously, not because time was of the essence to its processes, but because delay would invite the mob to substitute atrocity (tactics) for the court (strategy) and so undo the net of juridical authority.[167] Trials began on Wednesday August 31, exactly one week after Turner "gave up all hope for the present." During the following nine days, twenty-three trials (twenty-seven defendants) took place, 60 percent of the total. Only four of the trials were continued to a second court date, in one case because the defendant was not present. Most trials lasted only an hour or two. On Friday, September 2, for example, the court conducted four complete trials; on Saturday, September 3, its busiest day, it conducted six trials (one continued). During this initial phase, ending Thursday, September 8, twenty-one of the twenty-seven defendants were condemned to death, nine with recommendations of commutation.[168]

During the first week of trials (ending Tuesday, September 6) only one defendant was discharged; the remaining eighteen were all condemned to death (seven with recommendations of commutation). On Wednesday, September 7, the court finished two trials adjourned from the day before, both resulting in death sentences with recommendations of commutation. During the remainder of that day and the next the court conducted another three complete trials (five defendants) all of which resulted in discharges. At this point—a turn away from the relentless flow of convictions—the court adjourned as a court of Oyer and Terminer for ten days. It came back into session on Monday, September 19, and sat for four days, during which it held nine trials (ten defendants) resulting in five death sentences (one with a recommendation of commutation) and four discharges.[169] It adjourned again, for a week, held one trial on Wednesday, September 28 (another discharge), then adjourned again until Monday, October 17, when it held three trials over two days (two death sentences, one with a recommendation of commutation, and one discharge). The court did not reconvene again until Saturday, November 5, when a bench of ten magistrates, double the required quorum, met to try Nat Turner and, inevitably, sentence him to hang. Its last trial of an alleged insurgent slave occurred two weeks later, on Monday November 21. The result was one final death sentence, not executed until December 20.[170]

The court had done exactly what courts do when confronted with serious social disorder. It had established cold, clear authority over alleged miscreants; it had administered (by its lights) a just measure of pain, mingled—as it proceeded—with an admixture of mercy and evenhandedness; and on November 5 it had answered the social demand for "closure" with righteous, wrathful condemnation of the elusive ringleader. David Allmendinger holds that throughout, "in trial procedure the magistrates observed the letter of the law."[171] That is to say, defendants had counsel appointed to represent them, a record of proceedings was kept, and the required quorum of five justices was always present. Thomas Ruffin Gray commended the court for its work, "listening with unwearied patience to the examination of a multitude of witnesses and to long and elaborate arguments of counsel." Though by his estimation the numbers of the condemned, added to those already killed during the affair, "exceed the number attributed to the insurgents," he held the legality of the court's labors unimpeachable. The court had "reflect[ed] credit upon our county."[172]

Some disagree. Daniel Fabricant's examination of Turner's trial alleges improprieties in that case—notably trial testimony offered by sitting magistrate James Trezvant in the capacity of a prosecution witness, in which he reported Turner's responses to questions put by himself and by James W. Parker (also sitting on Turner's trial) during their committal examination conducted a few days previously, on Monday, October 31, the day after Turner's capture.[173] To prove his point Fabricant cites William Waller Hening's *The Virginia Justice*: "The confession of the defendant, taken on an examination before justices of the peace, or in discourse with private persons, it is said, may be given in evidence against the party confessing. . . . But it should be observed, that this examination of the offender, being taken in pursuance of the statute of England of I & 2 P. & M. c. 13 which is not in force in this country, the trial of a criminal in this state must be governed by the rules of the common law, and our own acts of Assembly; neither of which will justify his own examination in order to convict him."[174] In fact Trezvant was not the only witness called in Turner's trial. Levi Waller also testified to the effect that Turner had been in command of the company when it destroyed Waller's household. But Trezvant's testimony did establish that Turner had killed Margaret Whitehead, as well as confirm his leadership of the rebellion and responsibility for "the bloody scenes which took place."[175]

Fabricant concludes, "By hearing Trezevant's [*sic*] testimony, the Southampton court disregarded the longstanding obligation justices of the peace were under to safeguard the integrity of their office and ensure that the public's trust and confidence in it was not betrayed."[176] Yet for all that, he cannot argue that Trezvant's testimony was legally inadmissible, for it was not.[177] And here we approach the heart of the matter. The point is not, as Fabricant puts it, that "Nat's trial" or any of the other trials "must stand as a whitewash of justice." It is not that "the requirements of the law were commonly set aside . . . when they came into even remote conflict with the need to control blacks," for they were not.[178] Rather the reverse. The court was proper in its legality. The law was not in conflict with "the need to control blacks"; it was precisely "the need to control blacks" that the law expressed. Law, not the mob, was the agency of control and of retribution. It was the oil in the hinge on which the direction of the dialectic swung from *Knecht* back to *Herr*. This was strategy ascendant over tactics.

Alfred Brophy offers a more sophisticated summation. "The trials reveal the legal system's concern for restoration of order, sorting the most guilty from those with less guilt, and providing vengeance for the slave-owning community."[179] Everyone performed according to his appointed task. The prosecutor prosecuted, the defense lawyers "attempted to limit convictions and executions in the trials," the magistracy "served a critical function of negotiating between competing considerations of the desire for vengeance, the need for punishment to terrify future rebels, and the need for some restraint in the violence," and the governor considered the magistracy's actions and recommendations, and supplied a further check.[180]

But even Brophy falls a little short. "Negotiate" is a modern, poststructural concept that expresses the postfunctionalist orthodoxy of critical legal history: that relations between legal systems and social orders are culturally and historically contingent; that law and society are "mutually constitutive"; that law is an "an arena of social struggle."[181] It does not quite do the justices justice. Turner's rebellion was an instance of countersovereignty, "insurrectory" force deployed by members of a despised population who had discovered their own capacity for willful action and were intent on expressing it through the destruction of a regime that oppressed them.[182] By its very nature, "insurrectory" force called the regime's own sovereign legality into question. The justices' job was to restore that sovereign legality by doling out death to whatever extent necessary to do so.

> Whereupon the Court after hearing the testimony and on due consideration thereof are unanimously of opinion that the prisoner is guilty in manner and form as in the information against him is set forth and it being demanded of him if anything for himself he had or knew to say why the court should not proceed to pronounce judgment against him according to law and nothing being offered or alleged in delay of judgment it is considered by the Court that the prisoner be taken hence to the place from whence he came there to be safely kept until . . . taken by the Sherriff to the usual place of execution, and there be hanged by the neck until he be dead.[183]

Just as in the insurgency itself, here was no indiscriminate work of death. Indeed, the two were at one in the end—punishment—to which their work was dedicated, albeit those punished by the rebels and by the courts were of different sorts and conditions, and were punished for different reasons.[184] The point is that as Southampton County slaveholders' answering agent of retribution, their modality of rule, law was not negotiator but, like the rebels, *perpetrator*. Some would live, some would die. Law would decide which.[185]

And so what we have here is another "authentic moment of discovery," another "breakthrough," another moment when "a properly universal dimension *explodes from within a particular context and becomes "for-itself," and is directly experienced as universal.*"[186] In its moments of "due consideration," of decision, law is no arena of struggle. Those moments instead reveal law for-itself. "Violence crowned by fate, is the origin of law . . . where the highest violence, that over life and death, occurs in the legal system, the origins of law jut manifestly and fearsomely into existence." Law for-itself does not negotiate. Rather, "in the exercise of violence over life and death, more than in any other legal act, *the law reaffirms itself*."[187]

V. THE USUAL PLACE

Meat is the common zone of man and the beast, their zone of indiscernibility.
—GILLES DELEUZE, 2003

The eighteen condemned were hanged on eight different dates in September, November, and December 1831. Most were dead before September was half over. The first executions—of Daniel Porter and Moses Barrow—took place at noon on September 5, a Monday. Though the court was in the midst of its busiest stretch of trials of insurgents, September 5 was a relatively quiet day. The justices finished Jack Reese's trial, held over from the previous Saturday (sentenced to death, recommending commutation), tried and sentenced Dred Francis (death, no commutation), and considered whether Arnold Artes, a free man of color, should be remanded for trial in the Southampton Circuit Superior Court as an alleged insurgent (discharged). Quite likely the court adjourned to watch as Porter and Barrow were turned off. The following Friday, September 9, another five men were hanged. After a pause for the Sabbath, six more were thrown over on Monday the twelfth. The court had adjourned on Thursday 8, leaving Friday free except for the executions. It met briefly on Monday the twelfth to consider whether Thomas Hathcock, another free man of color, should be remanded for trial in the superior court as an alleged insurgent, but "for reasons appearing to the Court" Hathcock's examination was quickly adjourned until the first day of the next session (September 19), permitting the justices, if they chose, to attend that day's batch of hangings. No more executions took place until Monday, September 26, when Joe Turner was hanged, along with Lucy Barrow, the only woman tried as an insurgent. The court was not in session that day. The next to die was Sam Edwards, hanged on Friday, November 4, while Nat Turner sat in jail awaiting his trial. Turner himself followed Edwards a week later on Friday. The last was Ben Blunt, on Tuesday, December 20.

Few accounts of the hangings exist. Turner's execution, the likeliest to attract attention, is marked by two brief reports that squabble over the details. "We learn by a gentleman from Southampton, that the fanatical murderer, Nat Turner, was executed according to sentence, at Jerusalem, on Friday last, about 1O'clock," said the Petersburg *Intelligencer* for the week of November 14, reprinted in the Richmond *Enquirer* for November 22. "He exhibited the utmost composure throughout the whole ceremony, and although assured that he might, if he thought proper, address the immense crowd assembled on the occasion, declined availing himself of the privilege, and told the sheriff in a firm voice, that he was ready. Not a limb nor a muscle was observed to move. His body after death was given over to the surgeons for dissection." Four days earlier the *Enquirer* for November 18 had published a very different account, this one taken from the Norfolk *Herald*. Turner had been "launched into eternity" at twelve o'clock precisely, not "about 1O'clock." The "wretched culprit" had "betrayed no emotion," but he had seemed "utterly reckless in the awful fate that awaited him, and even hurried the executioner in the performance of his duty!" The two reports agreed that Turner's corpse was to be dissected, but according to the *Herald* this was at his own initiative: "Nat sold his body for dissection, and spent the money on ginger cakes." Perhaps most important, according to the *Herald*, "but a few people" had been present, not the *Intelligencer*'s "immense crowd." With ponderous sarcasm the *Herald* requested Northerners to note "that Nat was not torn limbless by horses," like Damiens the regicide, "but simply 'hanged by the neck till he was dead.'"[188]

These two accounts of Turner's death offer radically different assessments of the conduct of the condemned. In the first, execution is a solemn ceremony in which Turner comports himself in accordance with the gravity of the occasion. This account makes absolutely no mention of the technique by which death is procured. It focuses instead entirely on the art of dying. Turner is composed, he is firm of voice, he is in physical control of himself, and his death is dignified, implicitly instant and painless: "Not a limb nor a muscle" moves. His demeanor is that of one who has prepared himself for death, and although he refuses the invitation to deliver a scaffold homily he dies well, exemplifying—as far as a condemned man can—the *ars moriendi*.[189] His role is to draw all that has occurred to a close, to completion. He plays the part well, and his reward is the crowd's presence—an "immense" number of people are there to watch him.

The *Herald*'s account is very different; it is irritated, it implies dissatisfaction with the spectacle, and it vents its dissatisfaction on the condemned.[190] Turner is a "wretched culprit," which is to say he performs the role of culprit wretchedly. He is shallow (betrays no emotion), heedless of the solemnity of the occasion (utterly reckless), and behaves with cowardly impropriety (hurries the executioner to make an end of things). He has no respect for the occasion, no respect for himself, and in his irresponsible profligacy no respect even for his own body, which he sells for cakes. His death will have no dignity because he has no dignity. Instead, he is a mean and insignificant man who dies a mean and insignificant death. Not for him the notoriety of being "torn limbless by horses." He is simply to be "hanged by the neck"—stretched, in "a riot of motion"[191]—for as long as it takes to satisfy his executioners that he is dead. The absence of the crowd underscores both the newspaper's contempt, and the implicit absence of completion in what it has seen.

Though their reports differ in what they see, both newspapers underscore the importance of *seeing* to execution. In nineteenth-century public hangings, witnessing—seeing and hearing—are both crucial elements. They are what make the occasion a spectacle. This would have been as true of the execution of the Southampton insurgents as of any other executions of the period. Still, both reports are utterly incomplete as guides to what was actually seen. Both reports concentrate on the conduct of the condemned in the final moments of life. Both represent that conduct as an index of the life the condemned has lived—in one the condemned is a great criminal who dies well; in the other he is a wretched culprit who does not. Both represent the moment of death (dignified/undignified) as an extension of the last moments of life. All of this is entirely to be expected, for these are morality tales, a routine accompaniment of execution. But what of the actuality of hanging by the neck at the end of a rope until one died? What did *that* "riot of motion" actually look like?

"A man who is hanged suffers a great deal . . . he is not at once stupefied by the shock, suffocation being a thing which must be gradual and cannot be forced on instantaneously . . . a man is suffocated by hanging in a rope just as by having his respiration stopped by having a pillow pressed on the face, in Othello's way, or by stopping the mouth and nostrils . . . for some time after a man is thrown over he is sensible and conscious that he is *hanging* . . . in three minutes or so he is stupefied."[192]

The mechanics are not complicated. Hanging is death by strangulation, a halter around the neck of the condemned, cinched tight by the weight of the suspended body, and then tightened further by its struggles against suffocation. Death resulted from asphyxia or apoplexy, or most often from an indistinguishable combination of the two; only rarely—until long ropes and long drops became common—from a ruptured spinal cord; and even then, unless judged perfectly according to the length of the rope and the weight of the condemned, the length of the drop might prove inadequate to snap the condemned's neck, or if excessive might tear off his head.[193] Like all the others, Turner was hanged from a tree branch not a scaffold; no careful calculation of bodyweight, rope length, and drop here. Their deaths were slow suffocation.[194] But that was not all. Compression of the neck forced blood into the brain, resulting in "lividity and swelling of the face," grotesque distortion of facial features, especially of the lips and ears, swollen eyelids, protrusion of the eyes "sometimes partially forced out of their cavities," a distended, livid tongue, either protruding or "compressed" between the teeth, rupture of blood vessels, a "retracted" lower jaw, the appearance of "a bloody froth or frothy mucous" from mouth and nostrils, laceration and contusion of the neck, muscular contractions and convulsions, involuntary urination and defecation.[195] Men might become erect and ejaculate; women bled from the uterus. Like any other violent, mutilating death, suspended strangulation was physical destruction of the body. Hanging re-created the condemned as something drastically different: a body jerking and vibrating on the end of the "strangling cord";[196] helpless, weak, and vulnerable; "choking, pissing, and screaming."[197]

And of course in Turner's case, like many before him, hanging was not the end of it. His body was to be dissected, insides turned out, opened for inspection. Dissection was a postmortem reenactment of the distinctly premortem emasculation, disemboweling, decapitation and quartering of the body to which stretching by the neck had been merely a preliminary in statutory English punishments for high treason. In England, punitive dissection became the fate of murderers in 1751, a clinical alternative to gibbeting (hanging in chains), meant as "a further terror and peculiar mark of infamy."[198] Just like gibbeting, the intent was to destroy the corpse of the condemned so completely that nothing was left for burial. This is what happened to Turner. William Sidney Drewry writes that Turner's body was flayed, its flesh rendered into grease, its skin used to make mementos, its skeleton claimed for anatomical purposes by one Dr. Massenberg (James D. Massenburg was a Southampton County justice).[199] Whether all this is actually so cannot be proven—Drewry relied on local lore so far as the mementos and the fate of Turner's skeleton were concerned—but it seems entirely likely, for Drewry's account is in conformity with criminal dissection practices. In England, for example, the meat of the dissected murderer John Holloway, hanged in 1831 in Lewes, was separated from the bones, and the skeleton preserved for anatomical use in the Sussex County Hospital. Three years before, Suffolk General Hospital had become home for the skeleton of William Corder, hanged in 1828 in Bury St. Edmunds for the murder of Maria Marten.[200]

Corder is of particular interest, because the well-documented treatment of his body, postmortem, is as good a guide as one might obtain to the undocumented treatment of Turner's body. Cut down from the scaffold, Corder's body was taken to the Bury Shire Hall, where it was first "exposed to public view,"[201] and then opened up by the county surgeon:

> The first step of dissection was to examine the parts of the sternum, and accurately to describe them to the gentlemen present, which from the fine state of the subject, and his great muscularity, were well marked; the external and internal abdominal wings were exposed to view, as well as the fascias, &c. &c. . . . A quantity of serious fluid was effused into both sides of the chest, (about two or three ounces), and the lungs were gorged with blood.

As the dissection proceeded the gentlemen debated "whether it was *suffocation* or *pressure* upon the spinal chord" that had been the cause of death. They wondered, too, what the dead body might reveal about living behavior. They voiced regret that they could not examine Corder's brain "as the determination of making a skeleton prevents any part of the bones being destroyed."[202]

At length, the body's secrets exposed as best they could be, its bones were "cleared of the flesh" in preparation for re-wiring as an anatomical skeleton, and the gentlemen turned their attention to Corder's other parts. "A great portion of the skin has been tanned, and a gentlemen connected to the hospital intends to have the Trial and Memoirs of Corder bound in it."[203] The gentleman made good on his intentions. As Drewry found out, public hangings create a demand for souvenirs.[204] The volume in question remains on public display, in Moyse's Hall Museum, Bury St. Edmunds, to this day.[205]

Like William Corder, Nat Turner brought his hide to court and received—a hiding.[206] Law, says Michel de Certeau, "engraves itself on parchments made from the skin of its subjects. It articulates them in a juridical corpus. It makes its book out of them."[207]

VI. THE RADIANCE OF JUSTICE

It's a peculiar apparatus.
—FRANZ KAFKA, 1919

At law's core lies the body scourged with words.[208] Law's penalties incise the bodies of the condemned.[209] Kafka's punishment machine wrote with a harrow. At about the sixth hour of the harrow's work, too exhausted to scream any more, the condemned would begin slowly to comprehend his sentence. "You've seen that it's not easy to figure out the inscription with your eyes, but our man deciphers it with his wounds."[210] As death approached and realization dawned, the face of the condemned would begin to glow with the radiance of justice.[211] "There is no law that is not inscribed on bodies," says Certeau. "Law 'takes hold of' bodies in order to make them its text."[212]

Massacre also scourges bodies to create script. In Southampton County, "bodily brutality perpetrated by ordinary persons against other persons with whom they may have . . . previously lived in relative amity"[213] created a text that followed Semelin's "logic of the sacred through murder" to its own—distinct—radiance of justice. This justice owed nothing to law; its text was one of "brutal intrusions of justice beyond law."[214] Turner's death-work was what Walter Benjamin would later call divine violence.[215]

Law answered massacre with its own work of death. For Hegel, penality followed the same dialectical logic as the birth of consciousness: "Crime logically implies its punishment . . . the dialectic naturally moves from crime to punishment as punishment follows crime." For Hegel, in fact, crime was self-contradictory; it was "a mere negation of right [*Recht*]" that as such "carrie[d] within itself its own negation—the reaffirmation of right through punishment."[216] Punishment was the negation of a negation.[217]

But law's retribution could not cancel what brutal intrusion had created. The Southampton dialectic, we have seen, was disjunctive. And this was as true of its lurch from slave back to master as in its initial lurch from master to slave. Punishment could not negate the crime of massacre, because massacre, though the work of wretches and bandits, had not been a negation of right. It had been, rather, a rupture of the reality endured by wretches and bandits, the reality of their enslavement; it had torn into that reality and its attendant ethics, its logic of right. It had put in their place, however ephemerally, something entirely distinct: an *event*.[218]

The evental site "is a figure of the instant." It appears only to disappear. But consequences endure.[219] "An event is the creation of a new possibility. An event changes not only the real, but also the possible. An event is at the level not of simple possibility, but at the level of possibility of possibility."[220] At the level of "possibility of possibility" the Southampton dialectic's disjunctions could persist. They did.

PART III

Glossolalia

Speak he cannot;
he speaks no human language.
Even if he understood all the languages of the world,
even if those loved ones also understood them,
he still cannot speak —
he speaks in a divine language, he speaks in tongues

—SØREN KIERKEGAARD,
FEAR AND TREMBLING (1843)

5

On the Guilt of Fragile Sovereigns

> But all these puerile conceits fall far short of surmounting the great difficulty which, like Memnon, is eternally present and cannot be removed. "*Sedet eternumque sedebit.*"
>
> —THOMAS RODERICK DEW (1832)

I have described Turner's rebellion as an instance of countersovereignty, force deployed in the hope of changing a regime. To the sovereignty of the wicked—the profane, the unregenerate, the "children of darkness"—Turner counterposed the sovereignty of God. He persuaded others to join him in work of death that gave expression to the instant of countersovereignty.[1] His was an act of faith, an expression of "(in)human boldness in the face of impossibility."[2]

The only means available to Turner to give his faith political effect were the conspiracy of persuasion and the example of self-sacrifice. Regime change, as we know it, is of course saturated with conspiracy—covert action, misrepresentation, lies, dissembling, intrigue. It is no less saturated with self-sacrifice. The wild risk of change—the bid to chop off the head of the king—always creates martyrs on one side of the attempt or the other, depending on its success or failure.

By adding his own prologue and epilogue to Turner's narrative of the attempt, Thomas Ruffin Gray encased Turner within a melodrama of his own devising, its object to reverse the narrative's polarity by using conspiracy and self-sacrifice *against* their author. "It will thus appear," we have seen Gray inform his readers, "that whilst everything

---

FIGURE 5.1. *Capitol of Virginia, Richmond* (1831), site of the Virginia Constitutional Convention of 1829–30, and of the Virginia Slavery Debate of 1831–32. Engraving by Fenner Sears and Co. after the painting by William Goodacre. Reproduced by permission of the Virginia Museum of History and Culture.

upon the surface of society wore a calm and peaceful aspect . . . a gloomy fanatic was revolving in the recesses of his own dark, bewildered, and overwrought mind, schemes of indiscriminate massacre to the whites."[3] The very disjunction between Turner's thought process and his imputed worldly situation—a calm and peaceful environment, a kindly master, no provocation given, no vengeance sought—proves him insane. Gray's melodramatic emplotment is intended to deprive Turner of the rebel's elemental dignity, to display him instead as nothing more than a composite of shallow and corrupted characters: intrigant, tyrant, and martyr; a tripartite threat to the suddenly fragile sovereigns who ruled Southampton County, Virginia—indeed, who ruled the entire slaveholding South.[4] Turner is condemned as artless intrigant, says Gray, by his own words: "His own account of the conspiracy is submitted to the public, without comment. It reads an awful, and it is hoped, a useful lesson, as to the operations of a mind like his, endeavoring to grapple with things beyond its reach."[5] As ideas yield to actions, the cartoon conspirator "bewildered and confounded, and finally corrupted" becomes cartoon tyrant; perpetrator "of the most atrocious and heart-rending deeds," hideous invader of peace and innocence: "No cry for mercy penetrated their flinty bosoms. No acts of remembered kindness made the least impression upon these remorseless murderers. Men, women and children, from hoary age to helpless infancy were involved in the same cruel fate." In Gray's melodrama, Turner has become an atrocious butcher who forces the helpless dead "from Time to Eternity." He is a monster from beyond civility who "will be long remembered in the annals of our country . . . many a mother as she presses her infant darling to her bosom, will shudder at the recollection of Nat Turner."[6]

Melodrama presses us to distinguish evil from good, fanaticism from wisdom, as black from white. It supplies narrator and audience with the moral compass they need to countervail divine inspiration with the deranged irrationality of its implementation. It produces on cue the sickly romance of slaveholder humanity, rendered in the reported words of the Southampton County Court's presiding magistrate, Jeremiah Cobb. "From my soul I pity you; and while you have my sympathies, I am, nevertheless called upon to pass the sentence of the court."[7] Cobb's sentimental "sympathy" underscores that Gray has pacified the ingenuous Turner—reduced him to a pitiable martyr, not to slavery but to his own lost cause. "Nat has survived all his followers, and the gallows will speedily close his career," writes Gray, sanctimoniously lauding "a mind capable of attaining any thing" had it not been perverted by obsessive religiosity.[8]

Whom does Turner threaten, that he must be so reduced? Southampton's fragile sovereigns. They are a constant presence in Gray's melodrama, both audience and players. In his opening peroration they are "Public curiosity" agape at this "first instance in our history of an open rebellion of the slaves," and "on the stretch to understand [its] origin and progress . . . and the motives which influence[d] its diabolical actors." They are the litter of slaughtered innocents left in Turner's wake, and the few who escaped: "A little girl who went to school at Mr. Waller's"; Harriet Whitehead, the only member of her immediate family (mother, brother, three sisters, a nephew) to survive; Lavania Francis, who concealed herself in the recesses of an attic; Mary Barrow, her escape deliberately hindered by her faithless slave Lucy, but covered by a brave husband who "scorn[ed] to fly." They are the resourceful Dr. Blunt whose firm resistance broke the rebellion's back, and brave Benjamin Phipps, "armed with a shot gun well charged," who captured Nat.[9] Above all they are the magistrates of the Southampton County Court, who presided over Turner's trial (as they had "with unwearied patience" over the trials of all the other captured rebels),[10] who certified (with no sense of irony?) his confession to be "free and voluntary," who sought "full faith and credit" for their acts of just condemnation, and who doubtless listened and nodded as their appalled chairman denounced Turner for "plotting, in cold blood, the indiscriminate destruction of men, of helpless women, and of infant children," for slaughtering "many of our most valuable citizens" while they were asleep and defenseless—the old, the young, his own master, a man "in your own language 'too indulgent.'"[11] The fragility of these fragile sovereigns was precisely their innocence, their acts of kindness, their indulgence, their trust, their sympathy, their gullibility, their very defenselessness. No more. Turner was to be "hung by the neck until you are dead! dead! dead."[12] As for the remainder of "this class of our population," it was past time to ensure that the laws restraining them were "strictly and rigidly enforced."[13]

But these vulnerable, fragile sovereigns were also guilty sovereigns. They—some of them, at least—had been quietly contemplating their guilt for decades. "Whilst America hath been the land of promise to Europeans, and their descendants, it hath been the vale of death to millions of the wretched sons of Africa," wrote St. George Tucker, in 1796. "Whilst we adjured the God of Hosts to witness our resolution to live free, or die, and imprecated curses on their heads who refused to unite with us in establishing the empire of freedom; we were imposing upon our fellow men, who differ in complexion from us, a *slavery*, ten thousand times more cruel than the utmost extremity of those grievances and oppressions, of which we complained."[14] At the Virginia Constitutional Convention of 1829–30 their contemplation became somewhat more open. Fears for the security of their property in slaves underlay eastern resistance to representatives of the nonslaveholding western section of the state, who sought reform of suffrage qualifications and reapportionment of representation hitherto biased in favor of the slaveholding east. But eastern delegates were loath to speak out in defense of their slaveholding as such. Instead they wrung their hands and lamented their misfortune. Take as exemplary this from the convention's chair, former U.S. president James Monroe:

> What has been the leading spirit of this State, ever since our independence was obtained? She has always declared herself in favor of the equal rights of man. The revolution was conducted on that principle. Yet there was at that time, a slavish population in Virginia. We hold it in the condition in which the revolution found it, and what can be done with this population? If they were extinct, or had not been here, white persons would occupy their place, and perform all the offices now performed by them. . . . If you set them free, look at the condition of the society. Emancipate them, and what would be their condition? Four hundred thousand, or a greater number of poor, without one cent of property, what would become of them? Disorganization would follow, and perfect confusion. They are separated from the rest of society by a different colour; there can be no intercourse or equality between them; nor can you remove them. How is it practicable? The thing is impossible, and they must remain as poor, free from the control of their masters, and must soon fall upon the rest of the society, and resort to plunder for subsistence.

Slaves could not be emancipated unless the emancipists were removed from Virginia. But the cost of removing them was too great. What to do? No one knew. Plaintively, Monroe blamed the British. Colonial Virginia had attempted to prohibit slave importation but the Crown had refused to accede. "No imputation, then, can be cast upon [Virginia] in this matter. She did all that was in her power to do, to prevent the extension of slavery, and to mitigate its evils."[15] Slavery was Virginia's burden, not her fault. It was all so unfair.[16]

Turner's brusque intervention in white Virginia's affairs caused a panic that only heightened public anxiety.[17] On October 14, 1831, the Richmond *Constitutional Whig* printed a memorial addressed to the state legislature (one of a large number circulating in the state) noting with alarm the growth of the state's black population over the previous forty years. "Will you wait until the land shall be deluged in blood, and look alone to the fatal catastrophe, of the extinction of the black race by force as the only remedy, or rather will you begin the great and good work [of ridding the state of 'the unhappy and degraded race of Africans'] by kind, gentle, gradual, and sure means?" On December 20, the Richmond *Enquirer* enjoined the legislature not to rise "without ordering the police of the State on wise and secure principles." On January 7, it encouraged the legislature in its efforts to address "the greatest evil" by debating gradual emancipation. "Something must be done."[18]

But nothing was done. A debate took place, but the regime did not change. Instead the regime changed its description of itself. Slavery, it decided, was not an evil to be lamented, a historic injustice done to Virginia by an uncaring imperial metropolis, an alien blot on her ideals with which Virginians had somehow by the necessities of the situation to cope. Slavery was an ingredient essential to Virginian identity: a good to be defended, a responsibility to be fulfilled. Slavery, wrote Benjamin Watkins Leigh, was "a dispensation of Providence."[19]

The argument was rammed home in a pamphlet published in December 1832 by Thomas Roderick Dew, St. George Tucker's successor in George Wythe's chair of law and police at the College of William and Mary. Dew's pamphlet drew an emphatic line under the convulsive uncertainty that had followed Turner's rebellion. Simultaneously, it ejected from discussion both previously dominant genres of expression—Providence, whether in the shape of Turner's divine violence or Leigh's Christian dispensationalism, and legislative politics. It gave matters over, decisively, to a distinct form of knowledge: political economy.[20]

In Virginia, then, epistemological change defeated ontological change. By giving slavery over to political economy, Virginia's sovereigns forestalled regime change by changing their definition of the regime. They shook off political conflicts by locating epistemological authority elsewhere. They placed their regime in a realm beyond politics and guilt altogether. And so, it seemed, the disjunctive dialectic had finally sublated; the regime, disembedded, refurbished, redefined, stood intact.[21] Neither the ripples of Turner's cosmology or the state's own querulous siren song of lamentation that "something must be done" would move the rule of law. In antebellum Virginia, law and political economy stood *for* the tyranny of the state's fragile sovereigns, not for confrontation with it. *Sic Semper Tyrannis.*

Thus we encounter a tyrannical regime that does not change, that resists the politics of change, that ends up decrying the messages of politics altogether and embracing political economy to explain and justify its stasis.

And what of Virginia's slaves? Only a tiny and localized minority had joined Turner's rebellion. Most had stood aloof, many in dismay.[22] The speed with which the regime had concentrated its forces and crushed Turner's little band testified to the slaves' knowing assessment of its brutish capacities. Under such circumstances, what else could they have done but look to themselves, no matter the extremity of their lives?[23] The tradition of antebellum slave collectivity is one far less of overt rebellion than of an extraordinary endurance, its anthem the Sorrow Song. "They that walked in darkness sang songs in the olden days—Sorrow Songs—for they were weary at heart," wrote W.E.B. Du Bois. They sang "weird old songs in which the soul of the black slave spoke to men."[24]

Odd, then, that, searching for an image to emphasize the massive material reality of slavery in Virginia, "eternally present . . . cannot be removed," insusceptible to political resolution, to "*vain juggling legislative conceits*," Thomas Roderick Dew should have settled on a most powerful symbol of black African sovereignty that, in its embodiment of sheer implacable determination, reunited Nat Turner, as it were, with those of his fellows who had deprecated his impossibilist, failed attempt to change slavery's tyrannical regime.[25] Memnon.[26]

Memnon? Pausânias, the second-century (CE) Greek geographer, writes in his *Description of Greece*, "At Thebes in Egypt, when you have crossed the Nile . . . you come to a seated image which gives out a sound. Most people name it Memnon; for they say that Memnon marched from Ethiopia to Egypt and onward as far as Susa. . . . This image Cambyses cut in two; and now the part from the head to the middle of the body is thrown down; but the rest of it remains seated, and every day at sunrise it reverberates."[27]

Sedet eternumque sedebit?[28] Why did Memnon haunt Thomas Roderick Dew? What was the sound made by the broken, thrown-down statue of an Ethiopian warrior-king when touched by the rising sun, every day, day after day? Perhaps it was a sound of sorrow, the song of the black slave's soul calling out to men. But Pausânias says it was like "the breaking of the string of a lute or lyre." Perhaps it was a future echo of a different sublation, the sound of a regime changing. Perhaps the two are one.[29]

6

Revulsions of Capital: Virginia, 1829–32

> Who could have anticipated, that the bloody horrors of the Southampton massacre, instead of suggesting plans for stricter discipline, would give birth to schemes of emancipation?
>
> —BENJAMIN WATKINS LEIGH (1832)

> These doctrines, whenever announced in debate, have a tendency to disorganize and unhinge the condition of society, and to produce uncertainty and alarm; to create revulsions of capital; to cause the land of Old Virginia, and real source of wealth, to be abandoned; and her white wealthy population to flee the state, and seek an asylum in a land where they will be protected in the fruits of their industry.
>
> —THOMAS RODERICK DEW (1832)

> The nineteenth century is the century that enthroned the commodity.
>
> —IAN BAUCOM (2005)

To Thomas Ruffin Gray, as we have seen, the landscape on which Nat Turner's rebellion erupted was "calm and peaceful."[1] But in fact it was not. Most immediately, for two years the northeastern Carolina/southeastern Virginia border region had been dogged by rumors of plots, outside "agitators," and insurrection scares.[2] Meantime, measured diachronically in statewide political and economic aggregates, white Virginia was ever-more deeply enmeshed in churning political conflict. By the 1820s, forty years of white migration into Trans-Allegheny Virginia had given the state's politics a sectional cast that pitted a western "peasantry"—newly settled, predominantly nonslaveholding, and underrepresented—against the long-settled east, where "aristocratic" planter elites, heavily invested in slave labor for better than 150 years, enjoyed an establishment's political ascendancy.[3] Intrasectional antipathies complemented the geographic, particularly in the eastern region of the state where clamorous white mercantile and artisanal interests rubbed up against planter preeminence.[4] Both species of strain could be traced to the gradual decomposition of a hierarchical and premodern polity, built on uneven accumulations of land and slaves, under the persistent battering of commercial capitalism.[5] Though recognizably a specific instance of a much more general phenomenon,[6] this decomposition's actual expression was quite singular: the atrophy in the half century following the Revolution of freehold in land as the principal expression of the ideal of propertied independence central to agrarian Virginia's republican self-perception, and the key to the state's post-Revolutionary political and legal structures, and its replacement by the idealization of productive labor. In the case of the merchant, artisan, and yeoman (peasant) farmer the validating labor was their own—the self-possessed, self-disposing labor of the free contracting individual; in the case of slaveholders, the labor that validated their civic identity was that of their slaves.

Turner's rebellion, then, took place amidst regional black restlessness at the prospect of seemingly endless enslavement, and regional white discord over the relationship between land, labor, and political representation. In the rebellion's aftermath, that white discord became a more profound rupture in the politics of slavery itself, driving a bitterly divided House of Delegates to entertain the possibility of gradual emancipation. From that rupture there emerged a new political and economic equilibrium, centered not on propertied hierarchy but on property's commoditization, notably—as Thomas Roderick Dew would argue in his commentary on Virginia's emancipation debate—commodified labor.[7] In the case of self-possessed white labor, commoditization meant increased circulation: in the region's limited free labor market, in competition with enslaved labor for work, or in migration elsewhere. In the case of enslaved labor, commoditization meant more or less the same—although with the additional essential condition attached that the laborer lacked self-possession, and hence any degree of command over circulatory outcomes. But this did not mean there was no change in the *terms* of possession. A new discourse of explanation and justification no longer harnessed slavery to custom (in the shape of common law property claims), or to positive municipal law, or to paternal stewardship, but instead represented it as a quid pro quo between, as it were, creditor master and perpetually indebted slave—"the price of subsistence" as Nathaniel Beverley Tucker succinctly put it.[8] Slavery became transactional—modern—albeit the transaction could never be closed, because it turned on a debt that could never be paid off.[9]

Creditors of course will tend to seek the best return on their advances. So when Virginia slaveholders, uneasy at their labor's insurgent inclinations, found their investment in subsistence could earn better returns elsewhere than were available in their own agricultural economy, they began to send their labor, via enforced migration or the domestic slave trade, deeper into the maw of American slavery—Alabama, Mississippi, Louisiana, Texas. Slaveholders' revulsion at their own human capital for its disloyalty became a more discriminating revulsion in political economy's classic sense—a redistribution of capital in the direction of greater opportunity.[10] The Cotton Kingdom was the phantasmagoric extension of Atlantic capitalism's market for slave labor.[11] Once subsistence was priced in an extensive market, capital worked its alchemic logic and distributed priced people according to the returns their distribution could earn.

I. THE LAY OF THE LAND

Virginia's eastern and western sections meet more or less at the Blue Ridge Mountains. In the antebellum agrarian economy, planters, plantations, cash crop monoculture, and the slave labor that sustained it lay overwhelmingly to the mountains' east. The west's economy, in contrast, was predominantly one of slave-free, diversified (though largely pastoral) family farming. Both geography and human ecology were, however, a little more complicated. Between the Blue Ridge and the Chesapeake the terrain consisted of fertile upland plateau known as the Piedmont (literally foothills) settled largely in the eighteenth century, giving way at the falls of the rivers to the Tidewater, a flat riverine plain where the original seventeenth-century Virginia colony had been seated. With the exception of Norfolk, at the mouth of the Chesapeake, Virginia's major eastern towns (such as they were)—Richmond, Petersburg, Fredericksburg—all sat on the fall line. By 1830, slaves outnumbered whites in both Piedmont and Tidewater regions, particularly along the state's border with North Carolina. Eastern Virginia's towns, meanwhile, supported merchants, manufacturers, and a white artisan class far less invested in slavery than the cash-cropping agriculturalists of the surrounding countryside. Townsmen were generally estranged from the planter elites that dominated the region. Eastern Virginia in 1830 was "a complex, discordant society characterized by sometimes similar, sometimes dissimilar interests between urban and rural elites, and by more deep-rooted class rifts between democratic white artisans and aristocratic white planters."[12] What eastern planters sought from the state government, simply put, was security: security as slaveholders from the antipathies of nonslaveholders and the discontents of their slaves; security as men of wealth from the demands of others on that wealth.[13] The more planters felt outnumbered in the state ("a most respectable minority" confronted by "a bare majority")[14] the more stubbornly they relied on institutionalized maldistribution of political power to preserve their ascendancy.

The western section of the state had its own variety. Cradled between the Blue Ridge and the Allegheny Mountains lay the fertile Shenandoah Valley region, on its way to becoming a third concentration of slave-based agriculture, but less numerous and much less dense than either Tidewater or Piedmont, and lacking the deep historical roots that had made African slavery a central and essential component of white life in eastern Virginia. The northeastern Shenandoah Valley abutted the Potomac River; at its southwestern end the valley dissolved into a region of mountains and forests adjoining Kentucky and Tennessee. To its west lay the vast Trans-Allegheny region of mountains and upland plateau. Bounded on its western border by Ohio and to the north by Pennsylvania, this section would eventually become the state of West Virginia. Although pockets of slavery were to be found in both the southwest mountains and scattered across the western Trans-Allegheny region, as in Kanawha County's mining industry, neither had any major concentrations of slaveholders. What the west sought from Virginia's government was substantial infusions of capital in the shape of investment in transportation and communications improvements that would facilitate the commercial development of its diversified farming sector. Repeated frustration in this quest for improvements was the principal thorn that spurred western politicians to seek a distribution of representation and a definition of suffrage "fairer" to their section.[15]

Alison Freehling describes Virginia in 1830 not as one state but three: a "Southside" Tidewater and Piedmont of tobacco-plantation slavery and cash-crop farming; a west that had far more in common with the yeoman agriculture of free-soil Ohio and Pennsylvania; and a third Virginia she calls a "half-way house" (more accurately an assortment of half-way houses—the valley, the towns, certain eastern rural districts) between the two extremes, where some whites embraced slavery while their artisanal and enterprising neighbors regarded it with suspicion and hostility.[16] Amid this fractious mélange of white societies, Virginia's 1776 Constitution seemed an increasingly antique imposition of institutionalized homogeneity: a system of county-based representation without regard for geographical extent or population, and a freehold suffrage that in practice perpetuated the ascendancy of a "rural gentry" of Tidewater slaveholders and their Piedmont counterparts over everyone else. Unsurprisingly, as the other sections of the state gained population and developed their own distinct interests, and as the state's economy became more varied, this constitutional containment vessel was called increasingly into question, the instrument of "an odious landed aristocracy."[17]

But there was more to it than that. Though the constitution's endorsement of freehold suffrage betokened no departure from colonial practice, the resonance of "freeholder" had changed markedly in the epoch of the American Revolution. Well prior to the Revolution, the Virginia House of Burgesses had expanded on the common-law definition of freeholder—a tenant in possession of a life estate—by establishing that enfranchisement extended to any "person or persons" possessed of "an estate of freehold, or other greater estate, in one hundred acres of land, at least" if unimproved, "or twenty five acres with a house and plantation" if improved and occupied, or tenanted, or "any houses, lands, or tenements, lying and being in any city or town, laid out and established by act of assembly" whereof "such person be a freeholder, in any house or lot, or a house, and part of a lot"; that estates possessed fractionally were required to speak with one voice, unless the estate were extensive enough to allow each joint tenant a qualifying possession; and that freeholders might vote in every county in which they enjoyed a qualifying possession.[18] These were the terms of enfranchisement recognized in the 1776 constitution. But the "sole possession" that had qualified the colonial freeholder was not undivided dominion. At common law, the possession of land was a matter of tenure—tenancy—and tenure was never unqualified. "Although each tenant possessed their own individual relation to the land—an estate—with its distinct rights and privileges, these rights were not exclusive. Other tenants, too, of both superior and inferior status, might possess their own rights to the same parcel of land."[19] And ultimately, all land was held of the crown.

In place of this "feudal" conception of possession, revolutionary Virginia—Thomas Jefferson in particular—substituted an "allodial" theory of absolute private ownership. Allodial possession was embodied in two bills enacted in 1779, governing the disposition of vacant lands and settling title to western lands; by revisions to the law of inheritance enacted in 1785 that abolished primogeniture and entail; and by the Manumission Act of 1782, which, in authorizing private manumission of slaves, confirmed the absolute property rights of the slaves' owners.[20] The allodial revolution meant that the freeholders whose economic independence was supposed to underpin republican governance were to enjoy a peculiarly unencumbered authority over the disposition of the assets that materially guaranteed their independence. Unfortunately, the consequences were fatal to the ideal. Freeholder republicanism was hollowed out by commerce. "Freeholders once possessed of absolute control over their land proved unable to retain it. Personal debt proliferated and, correspondingly, mortgages and liens on estates grew more abundant."[21] The capital demands of commercial agriculture were one drain on unencumbered estate; speculation another. Landed independence proved evanescent in an agrarian political economy that had robbed land of its peculiar political distinctiveness as property and rendered it "a mere form of capital," simply one more component in a common stream of market exchanges in which "chance and avarice," not stewardship, ruled.[22]

Given land's precarity, what was to be the fate of the freehold qualification as the key to Virginia's republican polity? What form of manhood suffrage might replace the freeholder? And what might follow from so fundamental an alteration to the state's political institutions? These were the questions that the several white Virginias debated with each other, with increasing vigor, during the early decades of the nineteenth century.[23] Though multivocal, theirs was, obviously, a monochromatic debate. Nat Turner's brusque intervention lent the conversation—though indirectly, through proxies—a new coloration and a new direction. The several Virginias abandoned their attempts to shoehorn multiple economies into a single polity; they began instead openly to debate the merits of one economy in particular, the slaveholders' economy, and the ethics of African enslavement itself.

Arrestingly, the outcome was not, even gradually, an end to slavery; rather, the reverse. As free labor, in the form of white male self-possession, moved to the center of political debates over representation and enfranchisement, slaves were involuntarily annexed to the politics of civic status to qualify *their* possessors too. No longer mediated by land, the ownership of slaves—property in services perpetually owing—became the basis for planters' civic identity and membership in an increasingly

Jacksonian republican polity.[24] Simultaneously, however, slaves' labor power joined white labor as a circulating commodity: in their case, a capitalized investment—literally human capital—seeking a return. The discourse of political economy in Virginia would at first conflate, then differentiate, the slave's two abstracted bodies—the political and the economic. The main reason for the differentiation was the intervention of the slave's third body: the real, material, threatening body of the self-possessed rebel.

II. A CONSTITUTIONAL CONVENTION, 1829–30

Turner's rebellion occurred nineteen months after the Virginia Constitutional Convention of 1829–30 amended the state's suffrage qualifications and the basis for apportionment of representation, and sixteen months after the new state constitution was ratified. By now we know enough about Turner's rebellion to know that it was not in any obvious sense "caused" by the constitutional convention or its reforms, or by their approval.[25] The rebellion was, however, the direct cause of the convention's sequel, or second act, the emancipation debate that dominated the first weeks of the 1831–32 session of the newly apportioned House of Delegates. To that extent, Turner's rebellion and the two phases of antebellum Virginia's public appraisal of the consequences of slavery were intimately entangled.[26]

The 1829 constitutional convention was the culmination of years of agitation for reform of the suffrage and representation provisions of the revolutionary constitution of 1776.[27] For forty years, representatives of Virginia's Tidewater counties had resisted all but the most marginal alterations to the distribution of power designed at that time.[28] County-based representation initially granted the state's long-settled Tidewater region close to a majority of the House of Delegates (71 of 149 seats).[29] By 1815 the number of representatives seated in the House of Delegates had increased by 50, to 199, largely as a result of the organization of new counties to the west of the Alleghenies. Measured purely by the growth and distribution of the white population, by the 1820s Virginia's "center" had moved westward to the districts either side of the Blue Ridge.[30] But the division of existing counties within the Tidewater had increased its total number of representatives too, to 75. The Tidewater's plurality of counties ensured it would remain by far the best-represented region, normally able to control the General Assembly through alliances with like-minded representatives from the southern Piedmont.[31]

That control appeared to slip a little in 1828. Having ignored—or fought off—the calls that issued from the west in 1816 and again in 1825 for a state convention to consider suffrage reform and a reapportionment of the legislature,[32] the General Assembly finally agreed to allow a referendum on the issue. Participation, of course, was defined by existing freehold suffrage laws, but the convention still gained the approval of 57 percent of those voting (21,896 in favor, 16,632 against). Voting was sectional—Tidewater freeholders were largely opposed, westerners overwhelmingly in favor, the Piedmont split between its northwest and its southeast—but countervailing minorities appeared in both the west and the east; the far southwest's slaveholders voted against calling a convention while urban freeholders in the Tidewater showed up in favor.[33] Having at last obtained their convention, however, reformers saw it organized on a basis that favored their opponents: freeholders would elect four delegates from each of the state's twenty-four senate districts, which were apportioned according to the distribution of the white population in 1810, and hence left uncounted twenty years of population growth in the west.[34]

Among the elected delegates were many who had been, or would become, men of national prominence: former presidents Madison and Monroe; future president John Tyler; Chief Justice John Marshall; future associate justice Philip Barbour; John Tyler's future secretary of state, Abel Upshur; past, present and future U.S. representatives and senators—John S. Barbour, John Randolph, Littleton Tazewell, James Trezvant, Benjamin Watkins Leigh. Monroe was elected to preside over the convention, Madison to preside over its key committee, on the Legislative Department of Government. These national notables were joined by the state's incumbent governor, William Giles, and a number of current General Assembly politicians, men like Philip Doddridge and Chapman Johnson. Unsurprisingly a substantial number of delegates, as many as 75 percent, were lawyers.[35] Like their contemporaries elsewhere in the South, however, the convention's lawyers had in many cases grown beyond one-time commitments to the decentralized localism—the rule and institutions of vicinage, of attachment to land and place and community—to which the ideal of freeholder democracy belonged. "The younger generation of delegates" oriented to reform, "represented an increasingly professionalized group who were less likely to have read law under the tutelage of the local country magistrate." Like many of the elder notables present at the convention, their intellectual attachments were supralocal; their goal, "a centralized polity that would encourage a diver-

FIGURE 6.1. *Virginia Convention of 1829–30*, by George Catlin. Reproduced by permission of the Virginia Museum of History and Culture.

sified political economy open to social mobility and the pursuit of wealth"; their means, a democratic conception of civic membership that extended rights—notably in this specific instance the right to be represented and to vote for representatives—to any individual "whose consent and allegiance to the state expressed their necessary social affiliation, irrespective of any property holdings or tangible attachment to a specific community." In appearance far more inclusive than the landed property qualification of the freehold, it is important to note that this democracy was also both more intermittent and less participatory, more private in its exercise than public. "It emphasized the virtues of political expression through the occasional right to vote rather than through the more demanding and ordinary responsibilities of local office. . . . Unlike the elaborate mechanisms designed to balance self-interest and civic duty in the republic, advocates of democracy believed that citizens would be vested in a polity simply by their desire to participate in it."[36]

The objective of the convention's democracy advocates was simple enough: white basis apportionment and white manhood suffrage; that is, replacement of the existing county-based system that made representation a function of the jurisdictionally equal units into which terrain was divided for purposes of decentralized local government with a system that made representation accord with the actual distribution and concentration of population, and that enfranchised all white adult males. These had been the reform goals since 1815. They were met with a variety of responses: no change; "federal basis" apportionment, that is white population plus three-fifths of slaves counted as "other persons" (disparaged by its opponents as the "black basis");[37] "mixed basis" apportionment—white population plus an additional allowance for slaves counted as taxable property (again disparaged as the "black basis," also "the money basis");[38] and maintenance of property qualifications on suffrage. In Madison's Committee on the Legislative Department, proponents of the white basis and white manhood suffrage prevailed,[39] but once on the convention floor the committee report was fiercely resisted by mixed basis advocates, led by Benjamin Watkins Leigh and Abel Upshur, who advocated the explicit representation of white wealth against "numbers alone."[40] Wealth, Upshur confirmed, meant slaves—"a peculiar interest . . . a great, and important, and leading interest" in Virginia east of the Blue Ridge: "almost the whole productive labor" of the section."[41] Although the existence of slavery as institution might be regretted as a "moral *and political* evil,"[42] the east required that wealth in slaves be represented in legislative apportionment and in suffrage definitions to forestall a legislature apportioned and elected by "King Numbers,"[43] and the taxes it would inevitably levy on the wealth of the east.[44] Already 30 percent of state revenues derived from taxation on slave property. The prospect of additional mulcting of planters to finance the west's demands for road and canal construction could not be tolerated.[45]

From the moment of the introduction of the report on the Legislative Department of Government, early in its proceedings, the convention was deadlocked, "engaged . . . in a contest for power."[46] Meeting as a committee of the whole, for more than a month delegates debated the report in successive lengthy speeches, alternating pro and con, without concession on either side of the issue. Proponents of white manhood rule repeatedly proclaimed it a natural right, the realization of an original principle of government. Opponents decried it as "wild" abstraction, "metaphysical subtlety," mere "theory."[47] Government was entirely conventional, its only proper test practical utility.[48] It had no original principles. "The principles of Government are those principles only, which the people who form the Government choose to *adopt and apply to themselves*."[49] The single principle eastern slaveholders chose to adopt and apply was protection of their property. "All we ask is a Representation of those interests which we hold and which [you] do not."[50] They let it be known, with increasing emphasis, that the only alternative was division of the state.[51]

Once mixed basis apportionment had become the preferred response to white basis, population—not land—was confirmed as the criterion for representation on *both* sides of the argument.[52] On the mixed basis side, of course, this was population, in large part, held as property: "Representation to slaves, and political power to their masters."[53] White basis proponents stressed the novelty of this objective. Those "demanding representation for this species of property . . . are demanding a new thing, and are proceeding on a principle never before recognized in the Colony or State."[54] They were demanding a "negro Senate," a "negro House of Delegates."[55] For their part, mixed basis proponents professed to see little difference, whether from the perspective of "*political economy*," or capacity for self-government, between the propertyless white "peasantry" and "day-labourers" of the west and the enslaved agricultural laborers of the east.[56] Each was bereft of self-direction, dependent on others. If the one was to be included in calculations of apportionment, so must the other.[57]

After two weeks of debate, midway through November, the deadlock bred an attempt to compromise on the part of white basis proponents, who sought the abandonment of mixed basis by its advocates in return for apportionment on the basis of "qualified voters"—a refinement of white basis representation that would count only those enjoying the right of suffrage for reapportionment purposes (white adult males), rather than the entire white population.[58] Supporters of the compromise also embraced a suffrage property qualification, "real or personal," substantial enough to protect all forms of property from the propertyless. That is, they accepted the argument for the equivalence of "those who perform menial services—the day-labourers, the cultivators of land which they do not own, [who] are in the Eastern districts, principally slaves [and] in the Western districts, are chiefly white persons," by bowing to the exclusion of the latter from the suffrage, thereby rendering "the ratio of qualified voters, to the whole white population . . . greater in the East than in the West" and increasing its relative representation.[59]

The compromise was refused.[60] The committee of the whole then formally rejected mixed basis apportionment, whereupon its advocates immediately proposed federal basis apportionment in its stead. This too was rejected, much to the annoyance of the eastern delegates, who disputed the representativeness of the "bare majority" in the convention and accused it of a refusal to compromise with their "most respectable minority."[61] At this point the committee of the whole agreed to lay the subject of apportionment aside and to take up that part of the report on the legislative department dealing with the suffrage. When, in late November, the convention returned to apportionment, advocates of the three competing positions—white basis, mixed basis, and federal basis—haggled, increasingly acrimoniously, for the better part of three weeks, over different combinations and compromises (a white basis house, a federal or mixed basis senate) before settling on a modified county-basis legislature apportioned according to the white population as counted in the 1820 federal census, with no provision for future reapportionment.[62] This meant the legislature would remain, as before, in the hands of Tidewater and Piedmont slaveholders for as long as further reapportionment could be resisted, and assuming no significant intrasectional rifts to upset the status quo.

Whether significant rifts might indeed occur would depend on who were to be recognized as voters, and the extent to which distinctions of class or interest rather than civic solidarity governed their behavior. In this matter a memorial from nonfreeholder citizens of the city of Richmond, introduced in the second week of the convention, effectively summarized what was at stake. Nonfreeholders were "a very large part, probably a majority, of male citizens of mature age." Among them "not a few possess land: many, though not proprietors, are yet cultivators of the soil; others are engaged in avocations of a different nature . . . requiring as much intelligence, and as fixed a residence, as agricultural pursuits." Yet they had been "passed by, like aliens or slaves, as if destitute of interest, or unworthy of a voice, in measures involving their future political destiny," because they did not own the requisite "certain portion of land" that carried with it enjoyment of the suffrage. The freehold qualification, it had been said in reply, was minimal, easily met. But this was not so. "The thousands expelled from the polls too well attest the severity of its operation." For persons engaged in other than agricultural pursuits to be compelled to invest in unproductive landed property in order to be admitted to vote "is to subject them, over and above the original cost . . . to an annual tax, equivalent to the profits they might have derived from the capital thus unprofitably expended." Exclusion was also said to be *expedient*: "It is said, yield them this right, and they will abuse it: property, that is, landed property, will be rendered insecure, or at least overburthened, by those who possess it not. . . . The alarm is sounded too, of danger from large manufacturing institutions, where one corrupt individual may sway the corrupt votes of thousands." But all such apprehensions were groundless. "The generality of mankind, doubtless, desire to become owners of property: left free to reap the fruit of their labours, they will seek to acquire it honestly. It can never be their interest to overburthen, or render precarious, what they themselves desire to enjoy in peace."[63]

Expressing "with full force their degraded condition," the petitioners denounced freehold suffrage as contrary to their "rightful equality," ordained by nature and proclaimed in the Virginia Declaration of Rights. Condemned for seeking merely "an abstract right, whose privation occasions no practical injury," they replied that suffrage restriction created "an odious distinction between members of the same community; robs of all share, in the enactment of the laws, a large portion of the citizens bound by them, and whose blood and treasure are pledged to maintain them, and vests in a favored class, not in consideration of their public services, but of their private possessions, the highest of all privileges." The petitioners would not "submit to a degrading regulation which takes from them, on the supposition of mental inferiority or moral depravity, all share in the Government under which they live." They would not "yield to pretensions of political superiority founded on the possession of a bit of land, of whatever dimensions." The privilege they claimed was "theirs as of right." They were under no obligation to justify their claim, other than "that it is their own":

> If we are sincerely republican, we must give our confidence to the principles we profess. We have been taught by our fathers, that all power is vested in, and derived from the people; not the freeholders: that the majority of the community, in whom abides the physical force, have also the political right of creating and remoulding at will, their civil institutions. Nor can this right be any where more safely deposited. . . . To deny to the great body of the people all share in the Government; on suspicion that they may deprive others of their property, to rob them, in advance of their rights; to look to a privileged order as the fountain and depository of all power; is to depart from the fundamental maxims, to destroy the

> chief beauty, the characteristic feature, indeed, of Republican Government. Nor is the danger of abuse thereby diminished, but greatly augmented. No community can exist, no representative body be formed, in which some one division of persons or section of country, or some two or more combined, may not preponderate and oppress the rest. The east may be more powerful than the west, the lowlanders than the highlanders, the agricultural than the commercial or manufacturing classes. To give all power, or an undue share, to one, is obviously not to remedy but to ensure the evil. Its safest check, its best corrective, is found in a general admission of all upon a footing of equality.[64]

Western white basis proponents embraced the arguments of the Richmond petitioners against freehold suffrage in their own arguments for white manhood suffrage. Freehold suffrage was an unnatural, odious restriction imposed by the English king Charles II to punish the freemen of the Virginia colony for Nathaniel Bacon's popular rebellion.[65] Freeholders were nothing more than a privileged caste, their suffrage clear evidence of decades of misrule, a "long denial of justice to thousands of citizens" whose enfranchisement was essential to the state's political and economic fortunes.[66] Just as population had eclipsed land in the apportionment debate, in other words, so, when the convention turned to suffrage, population eclipsed land here too. Not only prosperity but safety for all lay in numbers, not in restriction. The Richmond petitioners had pointedly emphasized that "in the hour of danger . . . no invidious distinctions" were drawn between freeholder and nonfreeholder. "The muster rolls have undergone no scrutiny, no comparison with the land books, with a view to expunge those who have been struck from the ranks of freemen."[67] From the west too came arguments that white manhood suffrage was essential to underpin "the united exertions of [the] white population" whenever necessity should demand.[68] "Suffrage extension was essential not only to augment white population" but also "crucial to the state's domestic security."[69]

Opponents of suffrage extension tried, but without success, to represent the freehold—"lasting ownership of the soil"—as the acme of attachment to the community. No aristocracy, freeholders were the "chosen people of God . . . the cultivators of the soil . . . the middling farmers . . . the yeomanry . . . the bone and sinew of our country . . . men of moderate desires [who] have to labor for their subsistence."[70] Yet, as in the apportionment debate, though population trumped land it did so without handing the advantage to reformers, for they too bowed before certain sacred restrictions. "For obvious reasons, by almost universal consent, women and children, aliens and slaves, are excluded," the Richmond petitioners had observed. "It were useless to discuss the propriety of a rule that scarcely admits of diversity of opinion. What is concurred in by those who constitute the society, the body politic, must be taken to be right." Just not, they lamely concluded, in their own case: "The exclusion of these classes for reasons peculiarly applicable to them, is no argument for excluding others to whom no one of these reasons applies."[71] And what of paupers, goaded Abel Upshur and others.[72] What of convicts?[73] What of free blacks?[74]

Once again the convention deadlocked. After two days of debate, a white manhood suffrage amendment to the committee report was defeated, quickly followed by a white manhood citizenship suffrage amendment. Benjamin Watkins Leigh—with John Randolph, the most reluctant to cede a landed property basis for the suffrage—then moved a modestly expanded landed freehold suffrage, but his arguments for the merits of the freehold qualification, like those of others on his side of the debate, conflated real property with personal property.[75] The freeholder had been enfranchised *because* the freeholder was a slaveholder.[76] After Leigh's amendment, too, was defeated, the convention (still in committee of the whole) began, slowly and argumentatively, to inch toward approval of the addition of a taxpayer basis to the freehold suffrage. Taxable property, rather than landed property per se, became the criterion for suffrage expansion. As Charles Mercer of Loudoun County put it, "Other property is as essential as land. If this principle be true, what becomes of the foundation of the argument, which rests on the durability of land? The right is not founded on the land, but the relation in which the proprietor stands to it. And so it is with other capital. It is the relation of the proprietor to it; as it is between the freeholder and the soil. Personal property is an essential ingredient in the wealth of the country, and the title to it is as good, as that of the land-owner to the land."[77] Of course, as William Fitzhugh would note, "All property is not assessed; but only horses and negroes."[78]

The eventual result was not, therefore, the white manhood suffrage sought by western delegates, but a reformulation of property qualifications. Alongside those already enfranchised, who were qualified by acreage, the suffrage was extended to include every white male citizen, resident of the Commonwealth, aged at least twenty-one, and assessed (if due), who was "possessed, or whose tenant . . . is possessed, of an estate of freehold in land of the value of twenty-five dollars"; also such citizens "possessed, as tenant in common, joint tenant or parcener [joint heir] of an interest in or share of land, and having an estate of freehold therein, such interest or share being of the value of twenty-five dollars"; also such citizens "entitled to a reversion or vested remainder in fee, expectant on an estate for life or lives, in land of the value of fifty dollars";[79] also such citizens "who shall own and be himself in actual occupation of a leasehold estate, with the evidence of title recorded two months before he shall offer to vote, of a term originally not less than five years, of the annual value or rent of twenty dollars"; and finally, also any citizen "who for twelve months next preceding has been a house-keeper and head of a family within the county, city, town, borough or election district where he may offer to vote, *and shall have been assessed with a part of the revenue of the Commonwealth within the preceding year, and actually paid the same.*" Persons of unsound mind, persons convicted of "infamous" offences, paupers, and noncommissioned officers, soldiers, seamen, and marines in the service of the United States were excluded.[80]

As Christopher Curtis has argued, the significance of the reformulation lies first in its clear adoption of "a commodity conception of land" in place of land's former embodiment of attachment to place and community, and second in its recognition of self-possessed productive labor—assessed house-keepers and heads of family, or in other words the Richmond petitioners and their ilk—as another property interest worthy of enfranchisement.[81] The two innovations went together, in that each depended on the restatement of its subject as capital: by expressing landed property qualifications in dollar values rather than physical acreage, the convention accepted land as capital;[82] by embracing self-possessed productive labor as property, it too became a form of capital. As Curtis puts it, "Property remained the litmus. It continued to serve as the principal means of expressing the permanent attachment to the community necessary for the exercise of political rights. But it was a particular understanding of property, one that emphasized its economic qualities as productive capital," an understanding that allowed an equivalence to emerge between the productive capacity of labor and the productive capacity of land, and for the ownership of productive property in whatever form to become "the litmus of civic attachment."[83]

And emerging from that same equivalence one can detect a further form of ownership of productive capacity claiming recognition within the body politic: slave ownership as such.[84] Early in its proceedings, we have seen, Abel Upshur had told the convention that eastern slaveholdings represented "an interest of imposing magnitude" in a statement that in part equated property in slaves with wealth and resisted white basis apportionment for the "oppressive and unequal taxation" to which it rendered slaveholders' wealth vulnerable. Here was a conventional argument "that property should possess an influence in Government."[85] But Upshur's case for that influence was in equal part not conventional at all. Slaves were not simply "an interest of imposing magnitude" to the eastern districts of the state, but to the state as a whole. As nearly the whole productive labor of the east, slaves represented "the whole productive labour of one half of the *Commonwealth*." It made no difference "whether a certain amount of labour is brought into the common stock, by four hundred thousand slaves, or four hundred thousand freemen" because the increase "is the same to the aggregate wealth." For Upshur, then, the product of white free labor was "of no more importance to the general welfare, than the same product from the labour of slaves." Both expressed the same quantum of value added. And, Upshur pointed out, slaves were taxed on the value their labor added to aggregate wealth no less than for the wealth they represented as property in the hands of their owners: "You not only tax our slaves as property, but you also tax *their labour*. . . . The farmer who derives his income from the labour of slaves, pays a tax for those slaves, considered as property. With that income so derived, he purchases a carriage, or a horse, and these again are taxed. You first tax the slave who makes the money, and then you tax the article which the money procures."[86]

Upshur, in short, claimed slave labor was another form of productive capacity—capital—deserving civic recognition, albeit labor that qualified not self-possessed laborers, but others, the owners of those laborers: "*Our* property, so far as slaves are concerned, is *peculiar*; because it is of imposing magnitude; because it affords almost a full half of the productive labour of the State; because it is exposed to peculiar impositions, and therefore to peculiar hazards; and because it is the interest of the whole Commonwealth, that its power should not be taken away."[87] Recognizing the claim for what it was—a basis for enfranchisement founded not simply on the ownership of property (which he rejected) but on the ownership of slaves (which he despised)—Philip Doddridge answered: "What would the citizen of another state think, or how would he feel, at the sight of an hundred wretches exposed to sale . . . if in addition to the usual commendations of the auctioneer to encourage bidders, he should hear him tell them, that if they should purchase his goods, they would instantly become Sovereigns in this free land."[88]

Arguments at Virginia's constitutional convention suggested, then, a refounding of state government on the basis of the contributions made by different "interests"—different forms of productive capacity—to the general welfare. The state's predominantly agricultural economy furnished the measure of productive land, expressed in capital values rather than freehold acreages; the state's mercantile and manufacturing economy furnished the measure of productive labor, expressed in the capacity of the self-possessed producer to pay taxes as a house-keeper, or as a head of a family.[89] As to the state's owners of slave labor, their bid for inclusion—indeed primacy—in the calculus of contributions to the Commonwealth's general welfare was heard and accommodated, indirectly in the limitations imposed on white basis reapportionment, and directly in the adoption of taxpayer suffrage. Theirs, indeed, was the largest bid of all, for as Upshur stressed, they claimed to hold in their hands "the whole productive labour of one half of the Commonwealth." The question in the wake of the convention was whether slave owners would gain a more decisive accommodation of their interest's "imposing magnitude"; whether it would indeed be recognized as an "interest of the *whole* Commonwealth."[90]

III. ENTR'ACTE: NORFOLK, 1829–32

In 1827, some two years before the commencement of the Virginia Constitutional Convention, the U.S. Navy Department commissioned Loammi Baldwin the younger, of Boston—the early republic's leading civil engineer—to design and supervise the construction of a dry dock at the Norfolk Navy Yard on the southern branch of the Elizabeth River adjoining that part of the town of Portsmouth known as Gosport, adjacent to the city of Norfolk, Virginia. The Norfolk Dry Dock project was one of the most important engineering projects to be undertaken in America during the prerailroad era. Begun in November 1827 the dock was completed, at a cost of $950,000, in March 1834. It was one of two dry docks undergoing simultaneous construction as part of the same Navy Department commission, the other sited at the Charlestown Navy Yard in Boston. Dividing his time and energies between summers in Charlestown and winters in Norfolk, Baldwin oversaw both projects. He regarded the docks as "the two great works of his life."[91]

Identical in conception and appearance, the docks were both constructed of finely hammered granite.[92] But the cost of the Norfolk dock exceeded that of Charlestown by more than $265,000, the excess being

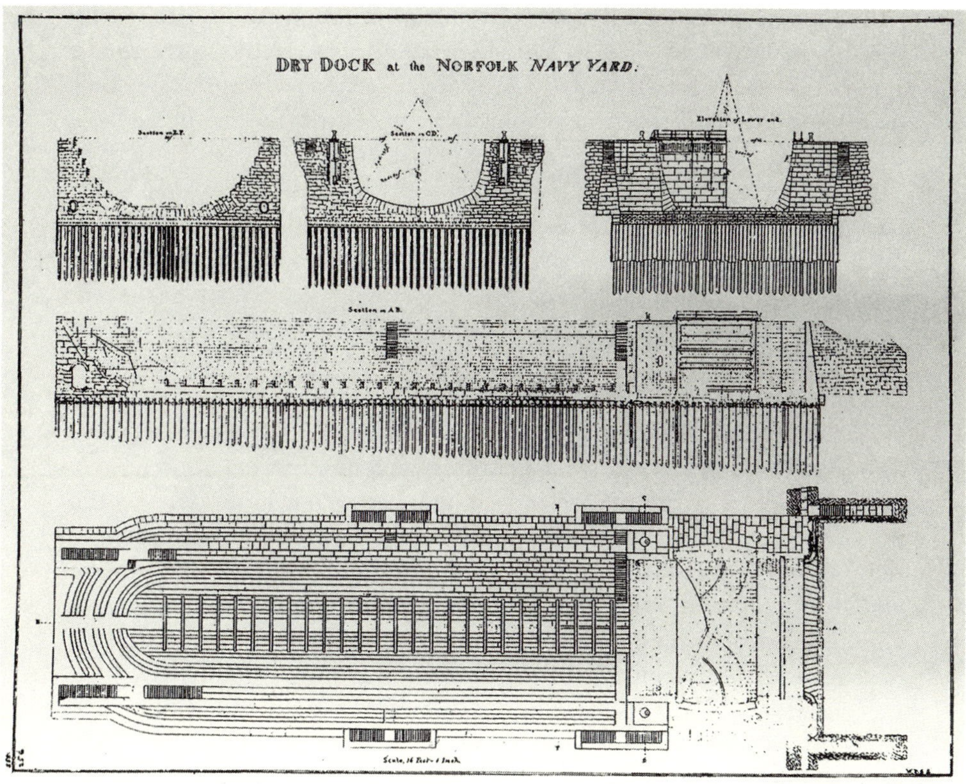

FIGURE 6.2. *Dry Dock at the Norfolk Navy Yard* (Construction Drawing and Cross Sections) 1827–33. Courtesy of Marcus W. Robbins. Photograph by Christopher Tomlins.

due, according to Baldwin's biographer, "to the extra price of both stone and labor, the stone having been sent from the North as well as most of the skilled labor."[93] Baldwin could do little about the cost of materials. So in an attempt to control his costs, he engaged in extensive employment of hired slave labor in the skilled work of stone hammering.[94] Baldwin's resort to slave labor proved controversial. The controversy provides a vivid illustration of the processes commodifying both free and slave labor in Virginia at the time of the Turner Rebellion, as well as of the conflicts that divided whites on display in the constitutional convention and that would divide them far more profoundly during the emancipation debate.[95]

The use of hired slaves was not unusual in the general work of the Norfolk Navy Yard.[96] And as Linda Upham-Bornstein has noted in her account of the Norfolk Dry Dock affair, hired slaves were quite commonly used on construction projects and in local industry in the Norfolk area in the 1820s, as indeed they were in other urban centers in Virginia: their use would increase dramatically over the next thirty years, particularly in Richmond.[97] Resort to hired slave labor during the dry dock's construction nevertheless provoked local opposition. In part this was due to the sheer scale of slave hiring on the project. During the early work of excavation, the project employed as many as two hundred slaves.[98] By September 1831, when the project was well into the construction phase, a petition denouncing the employment of slaves on the project claimed that a majority of the total work force—three hundred of five hundred—were slaves, many of them strangers hired from country slaveholders.[99] What in particular drove the controversy, however, was the use of slaves in skilled work. During the construction phase, a substantial number of the slaves on the dock were employed as common laborers "as tenders whom the masons, & stone cutters, & others occupied in various departments of labour . . . making mortar &c."[100] More than half of the hired slaves, however, were employed as stone hammerers. This was a matter of local concern because, as Upham-Bornstein observes, "slave hiring thrust white workers into competition with skilled slaves for essential jobs."[101]

The first hint of the troubles this would cause Baldwin came in a letter dated January 23, 1830, from Commodore John Rodgers, president of the Navy Board in Washington. Rodgers informed Baldwin that the secretary of the navy had received protests "from a number of persons, complaining of their being excluded from all participation in stone work upon the dock building under your direction."[102] The most detailed protest came from nine "stone masons and residents of the Town of Portsmouth, sent on from Pennsylvania expressly for the U.S. Hospital at this place, and recently discharged . . . with every *necessary* recommendation from our late architect as competent and *skillful* workmen," complaining that their applications for employment on the dry dock had been refused "in consequence of the subordinate officers hiring negroes by the year under the immediate cognizance of the chief engineer, and placing them at stone cutting for which they are entirely incompetent, to the injury of *we the undersigned* who are men of families." Such practices, if not checked, "must ultimately *subserve* the mechanical interest of this place." They were "detrimental to the labouring interest of the community, and subversive to every principle of equality."[103]

Baldwin took the complaints seriously and replied at considerable length. His reply defended the character of his subordinate officers—Henry Singleton, the project superintendent, a "well known and respected" local man, and Samuel Johnson, formerly superintendent "of the department of hammering Granite" at the Massachusetts State Prison at Charlestown and immediate supervisor of stone hammering at the dock.[104] He corrected the petitioners' claim that slaves were being hired by the year. They were in fact being hired by the day and could be dismissed for any reason or no reason. The bulk of Baldwin's reply, however, concentrated almost entirely on the economics of the project.

To Baldwin, labor was a fungible commodity. Its price was what mattered, not whether the labor bought came enslaved or free (or, for that matter, with dependents). Based on his experience with Negro convicts at the Charlestown prison, Johnson had advised Baldwin "that the blacks could be employed to great profit in hammering stone for the Dock at Norfolk." Baldwin had been skeptical, "thinking that all our hammering and dressing of stone must be done by whites." But he had decided "to try the experiment" and on arrival in Norfolk had directed Singleton to hire slaves to work under Johnson's instruction and supervision at hammering stone. "The result promises to be highly satisfactory, and so far from feeling any doubts, I fully believe, that for the rough hammering we can have it done for less than one half of what it costs by whites." As Johnson had advised, based on his Massachusetts experience, "the physical power of the blacks, who have been accustomed to hard work from infancy, especially in their wrists and arms, qualify them for coming immediately into the use of the heavy stone hammer, without suffering much fatigue, while a white man requires several weeks of practice before he can work without fatiguing his arms or making his hands sore." Two of the white stonemasons from the hospital had been employed on hammering. Both had complained of the severity of the work, neither could keep pace with the blacks, one was clearly incompetent and would likely be dismissed. Not surprisingly in view of this, Baldwin dismissed the white artisans' petition as a self-serving attempt to restrict labor market competition. Indeed, proud of the savings he was effecting he suggested that his management of the project offered Virginians (and the federal government) a valuable object lesson in the productive capacities and comparative advantages of slave labor:

> It was from an extreme desire to lessen the great expense of this branch of the work, that I adopted the plan of employing the blacks. The experiment is now going on, and I really feel great pride in the prospect and belief that the result will be a very considerable saving to the Government.
>
> I can easily imagine that the complainants should feel mortified to see the blacks of Virginia employed as handicraft men, at about one third the price they would demand; but I think it quite as important to this State, where slaves constitute so great a portion of the labourers, that Virginians should learn how the blacks may be made so much more valuable than has been hitherto thought, as it is to Pennsylvania, that some dozen of her citizens who happen to be left adrift here, should try, in the manner these "Stone masons" have done, to force themselves into a work where they are not yet wanted.

Baldwin added that he had been keeping detailed records of his "experiment" and would furnish the results.[105]

After considering Baldwin's defense of his employment practices, the Navy Department wrote to the complainant stonecutters indicating that an inquiry had been held and that employment of slaves by the chief engineer had been approved. The complainants then established a committee "on behalf of the stone cutters and other mechanicks residing in this vicinity," which composed a second protest couched not as an attack on Baldwin's management of the dry dock project, or on the general propriety of using slave labor, but as an exposé of nefarious slave hiring practices by Baldwin's subordinates. By charging that the dry dock project's subordinate officers were enriching themselves at public expense, the complainants could restate their complaint that giving the work of citizens to inferiors who were neither white nor free degraded white craftsmen, while representing it as a protest against the corrupt character of the slave labor in question, and as an attack on profiteering, rather than as a challenge to Baldwin or to the Navy Department.[106]

The new complaint was referred to James Barron, commandant of the navy yard. Once again Baldwin was invited to respond. Transmitted on April 27, Baldwin's response was lengthy and, like the mechanics' charges, voluminously documented. Once more Baldwin defended the character and reputation of his subordinates. Once more he ridiculed the complainants' charges of unjust and unfair treatment, which he dismissed as "for the most part ridiculous, fake & malicious." As in his response to the original complaint, however, the guts of Baldwin's answer consisted of a broad-ranging and emphatic defense of the economic efficiency of slave labor. "I must make a statement concerning slave labour," Baldwin told Barron "for upon that point hinges the whole matter." What followed was a report on the comparative productivity and economy of white and black labor "in this new trade," based on records Baldwin had instructed Johnson to keep. "This was begun before I knew of any complaint existing anywhere about blacks being employed. It was intended solely for my own gratification & the following little table exhibits the result. The *first* column shows the names of the workmen; the *second* shows by similar letters that the stones hammered are similar. The *third* the length of the stone; the *fourth* the square feet of face or fine hammering; the *fifth* the square feet of rough hammering; the *sixth* the number of days work on each stone; the *seventh* the wages per day; and the *eighth* column shows the actual cost of hammering" (see Table 6.1, page 158).

Baldwin's table proved to his own complete satisfaction "the great economy of employing slaves."[107] By comparing the average cost of hammering the same variety of stone it was clear that black hammerers did the same work at somewhere between half and three-quarters the cost of whites.[108]

Baldwin's "geometric" proof of the economic rationality of industrial slavery was accompanied by responses from the subordinate officials of the dry dock who had been attacked by the mechanics, together with testimonials from men prominent in the local community attesting to their honesty and casting aspersions on the complainants.[109] The responses of the subordinates were rather more cautious than Baldwin's, no doubt because they did not enjoy his social and institutional authority vis-à-vis the Navy Department and had to live in closer proximity than he to the mechanics. Samuel Johnson, for example, wrote that Baldwin had decided to employ blacks on the dry dock well before Johnson had become involved in the project and that he had merely been responsible for hiring. In this he had been directed to consult with Singleton, "as Mr. Singleton lived here and was better acquainted with hiring and employing black labourers."[110] In turn, Singleton claimed—somewhat disingenuously—that slaves had never been employed in the place of white mechanics, but only as laborers and only paid as laborers (62 cents per day for their masters, and 10 cents per day for themselves). "Some of them have been put to rough hammering of stone, which is a work to which almost all labourers, whether stone cutters or not are competent. Some white labourers are engaged in the same work, and both

Table 6.1. Loammi Baldwin's "geometric" proof of the economic rationality of industrial slavery

1	2	3	4	5	6	7	8
WHITES						**$**	**$**
J. Tinney	b	4.0	8.4	52.2	6.0	2.00	12.00
C. Allen	a	4.9	13.0	55.5	8.0	do.	16.00
S. Walker	b	4.0	8.4	52.2	6.5	do.	13.00
E. Richardson	g	2.3	7.3	32.1	6.0	do.	12.00
C. Shattuck	f	4.7	9.6	57.2	7.5	do.	15.00
E. Curtis	b	4.0	8.4	52.2	6.0	do.	12.00
T. Kingman	a	4.9	13.0	55.5	10.0	do.	20.00
C. Allen	e	4.3	8.10	54.1	6.5	do.	13.00
R. Doll	f	4.7	9.7	57.2	7.0	do.	14.00
R. Powers	g	2.3	7.3	31.2	13.0	1.75	22.75
F. Kirk	c	6.0	12.6	70.8	41.25	1.50	61.87
W. Frederick	c	6.0	12.6	70.8}			
do.	c	6.0	12.6	70.8}	43.0	2.00	86.00
do.	e	4.3	8.11	54.1}			
do.	d	2.9	8.10	25.6}			
E. Colburn	g	2.3	7.3	32.1	6.5	2.00	13.00
BLACKS							
W. Brooks	b	4.0	8.4	52.2	10.0	0.72	7.20
I. Wilson	a	4.9	13.0	57.2	12.0	do.	8.64
B. Sparrow	d	2.10	9.0	37.11	12.0	do.	8.64
J. Sparrow	e	4.3	8.10	54.1	10.5	do.	7.56
C. Portlash	b	4.0	8.4	52.2	13.0	do.	9.36
W. Cooper	f	4.7	9.6	52.2	16.0	do.	11.52
D. Carr	e	4.3	8.10	54.1	15.0	do.	10.80

classes of labourers agreeably to the direction of Col. Baldwin." Singleton also maintained that local residents had pressed an initially reluctant Baldwin to use slaves on the works, that in the navy yard slave hiring long antedated the dry dock project, and that local artisans themselves used slaves in the navy yard as "helpers."[111]

Baldwin's rejoinder appears to have satisfied Commodore Barron, whose investigation proceeded no further. Still, accusations of bias against white workers continued to circulate, taken up during the course of the next few months by stonemasons who had been brought from New England to work on the dock.[112] The lack of any response to these intermittent complaints eventually resulted the following summer in the revival of the previous year's story of corruption and profiteering, this time in the form of an anonymous letter directed at the end of July 1831 to President Andrew Jackson. Signed "a true Jackson man," the letter leveled accusations at the entire hierarchy superintending the dry dock project, from Johnson and Singleton, to Baldwin's deputy Alexander Parris, to Baldwin himself as enabler. All in one way or another were "shaving government out of all they can." All were permitted by Baldwin to hire slaves by the year, put them to work on the dock, and pocket their wages. "The poor mechanic that is at work there is now afraid to say anything if he opens his mouth about the misconduct and they hear of it his services is no longer wanted so we are compelled to hush our mouths or have our families to want," the letter concluded. "I hope you will have thing better arranged and have them more curtailed in their hiring of negroes."[113]

Jackson referred the letter to Levi Woodbury, secretary of the navy, who in turn referred it to Commodore Lewis Warrington, Barron's replacement as commandant of the Norfolk Navy Yard, with instructions to hold yet another investigation. Warrington wrote to Baldwin on August 11 to inform him of the new investigation. Two days later Singleton also wrote to tell Baldwin that, as he put it, "there has been more writing about the dock," and that as a result "we have had a little more of the old work to do."[114] The defense, as before, was one of efficiency. Slaves were hired because they completed the work just as fast as whites, and at far lower cost. "I have kept an account, by the request of Col. Baldwin, of the white and black men's work" Johnson wrote, "and have ascertained there is a saving of more than 50 percent by employing blacks to hammer stone. After 2 or 3 months practice they will average nearly as much work as the white men, particularly the rough heavy work, and their wages is not half as much as is paid to the White Stone Cutters." The blacks hired to the dock were "good faithful hands" whose work had resulted in a considerable saving to the government.[115] Singleton, meanwhile, once more, recruited local notables—"some of the most influential Jackson men of Norfolk and Portsmouth"—to write letters attesting to his probity and damning his "base, envious and malignant accusers."[116]

At this point the dispute over the employment of slaves on the dry dock was overtaken by the Turner Rebellion. Singleton wrote to Baldwin on August 26, informing him that an insurrection had occurred in Southampton County and that a number of whites had been murdered. Less than fifty miles from Jerusalem, and with a slave (3,756) and free colored (928) population almost as large as its white population (5130), not to mention the large number of slaves hired in from the surrounding countryside, Norfolk panicked. The mayor and council assembled the militia, called for local volunteers, and petitioned the navy yard and the garrison at Fortress Monroe for federal troops. Apparently fearing that the dry dock controversy would now get completely out of hand, Singleton told Baldwin he was "anxious that you should know our situation as respects the blacks."[117] The following week he wrote again, twice, that "the excitement in consequence of the insurrection among the blacks has not yet subsided," and that Norfolk remained in a "state of alarm," its white population fearing "an insurrection of the blacks every moment."[118]

On September 7 Singleton had better news for Baldwin. The alarm was subsiding. "I hope you will not be afraid to come among this blackish community again. We are healthy and have no pestilential fevers among us, and was it not for the envious scribblers we should have nothing to call our attention from the progress of this great work and its speedy completion." Baldwin was reassured. "I am happy to learn that tranquility is restored among the blacks. From your last letter and one from Mr. Campbell of the 4th I was extremely anxious about the conduct of the negroes. Though you as well as Mr. Campbell expressed little or no apprehension, still the fact of several of Mr. Drummond's men having been apprehended, and others strongly suspected, I feared some dreadful operations might have been commenced. Your letter relieves me entirely."[119]

Relief proved temporary. By the middle of September the long and acrimonious dispute over the use of slave labor on the dry dock had become central to Norfolk's response to the Turner Rebellion.

On September 21 Singleton wrote to warn Baldwin that the mechanics and laborers of the dry dock had joined forces with those of the navy yard to petition the secretary of the navy to have all slave laborers discharged from public works. "I have thought it best to provide for the change so that in case of the removal of the black hammerers, we should have white men to do the rough work, and in view of this I have placed as hammerers 9 men at 1.$ per day as above stated, which I hope will meet your approbation." Singleton blamed "a few low and noisey characters" for keeping up "the negro excitement."[120] Three days later, Singleton reported that the mechanics' campaign had gained widespread local support. Their petition had circulated far beyond the navy yard's work force. It had been signed by 492 persons, including numbers of "persons owning slaves or hiring them in the public works as well as non-slave owners and other citizens." Worse, it had been endorsed on September 17 by a "large and respectable" gathering of Portsmouth residents, who had also extended the scope of the mechanics' campaign to the employment of free blacks, resolving that, no less than slaves, "the employment of . . . free negroes upon the public works in this neighbourhood, to the exclusion of many worthy and industrious white citizens, is unjust & impolitic and ought not to be tolerated." Amongst those taking a prominent role in the September 17 meeting were not a few of the local notables who had previously spoken in condemnation of the very mechanics in whose support they were now arrayed.[121] As Upham-Bornstein notes, "Prior to the Turner rebellion . . . the dispute over the utilization of Black workers at the dry dock generally followed class lines. The complaining mechanics were largely propertyless individuals, few of whom owned slaves and none of whom held positions of political or economic power. Those who supported the dry dock managers tended to be men of power, position, and property." In the wake of the revolt, "themes of race and whiteness" became uppermost in the controversy.[122] "We deprecate the bad effects of bringing the Black people, conspicuously in large bodies, into competition with white people" the mechanics wrote. "It produces too much prejudice on the one hand & too much encroachment on the other. We therefore recommend the discharge of the Blacks." The petition, says Upham-Bornstein, "presumed the baneful effects of allowing blacks to compete with whites in the labor market." Yet even as the petitioners stressed "the salutary effects of replacing black workers with white ones,"[123] they did so in language that quite noticeably parroted Baldwin's. Long gone was any mention of the respect due "men of families," or the principle of white equality. Absent too were claims of white labor's racial superiority over black. Instead their case was made in the language of efficiency. They could work just as hard as slaves: "The preference of Black labourers has arisen from an idea that they are *better* to labour than the whites, but this is contradicted by the fact that white Mechanics, labouring here, are as efficient in standing fatigue, as those perhaps of any other place, & for the same reason white labourers are equally adequate to labour."[124]

Initially, Baldwin responded to the reports of renewed petitioning with his usual stubborn defense of the dry dock project's management.

Thus, in a letter of September 27 to Secretary of the Navy Levi Woodbury he warned of the serious consequences of acceding to the mechanics' demands that blacks be removed from employment on the dry dock. They had "performed most capable service, & indeed, at ordinary labour they equalled, & even, surpassed the white labourers." As hammerers, too, all had become very useful, some acquiring considerable skill at the job. "Indeed a few have become excellent workmen, & are equal to some of the whites who receive more than double their wages. To supply their place by teaching white men to perform the same work would occasion great delay & to supply good white hammerers, would not only cause delay, but a great additional expense." Baldwin claimed he had originally held "strong prejudices against the blacks as labourers," but had been won over. "From the little gratuity of 10 cents a day allowed for themselves, they labour as cheerfully, & generally do more work than the white labourers. In the hot summer months, their employment is almost indispensable, as they endure the heat & preserve their health much better than whites." He warned Woodbury of the effects of heeding the mechanics' petition on "public works of every kind, in the slave states." Writing to Singleton the same day, Baldwin expressed the hope that the government would ignore the petition. "So important are our blacks to us now, especially the stone hammerers, that it would be almost folly to discharge them & I do not believe the Secretary will pay any attention to it."[125]

Still, the turn of events in Norfolk—in particular, perhaps, the appearance on the side of their enemies of the local dignitaries whom the project's managers had previously regarded as political allies—added a note of resignation to Baldwin's voice. "I regret to hear the excitement about the negroes is still kept up. I have no doubt there are bad spirits enough at work in Portsmouth & vicinity to turn the blacks against the whites in the Dock & Navy Yards, if they cannot get them turned out of the work."[126] By the beginning of October he appears to have concluded that the situation was beyond rescue. Answering Singleton's account of how Portsmouth's respectables had hastily swung behind the mechanics at the meeting on September 17, Baldwin wondered aloud why "your Virginians, who are generally so loud about the principles of *free trade* . . . make such a stir about any man or public officer, employing whom they please to work for them." However, he "perceive[d] the meeting was a very respectable one," and therefore wished it to be known, should anything further transpire, that "I care very little about the continuance of the slaves on the Dock." Baldwin, though, laced resignation with anger. "I do wish . . . people would mind their own business & let us attend to ours. This is the fourth attempt to incroach upon our affairs, & we have had more vexation and trouble by the muddling interference of others, then in all the business I have ever done. God grant I may get out of it this coming year."[127]

Baldwin's last word on the subject came in a letter sent to Singleton two weeks later. The Navy Department had made no final decision on the employment of slaves on the dry dock and tensions were still acute in Norfolk; Singleton himself had been forced to sign the mechanics' petition. Baldwin expressed his sorrow "to learn that such an unhappy temper exists among the white population, relative to the blacks. Your signing the petition was certainly judicious, under the circumstances in which you were placed." The whole affair had been "trouble and vexation enough," and in the short term, at least, "the best way is to list & yield with the best grace we can, to the temper & pressure of the times, over which we can have no controul." Yet Baldwin was also hopeful that in due course control of the issue would be taken from the mechanics, that Portsmouth's slaveholders would regain the initiative in local politics, and that all, eventually, would be well:

> I cannot but think . . . the great excitement is only temporary, & your sensible, discreet, & honest neighbours, ought to be careful how they lend their aid & countenance to the wild, & malevolent passion of their more thoughtless, scheming, fellow citizens. Whether the blacks are dismissed or not, I care not; But I would ask anyone who owns slaves & receives in any way the profit of his toil, if it would not be quite rational that he should give up all his own blacks & discharge them, before he asks the Government, & his neighbour, to discharge those they employ. Why should not 20, 50, or 100 blacks be employed in the Navy Yard, as well as in the manufactory of a private citizen? Why should not Mr Herron, Mr Drummond, Mr Murray &c be required to discharge their 10 or 20 blacks employed in their manufactories, as well as Com. Warrington, those in the Navy Yard? Besides what is to be the future condition of the slaves? For my own part, I believe, that in case the blacks are now dismissed, in the course of two or three years, complaints will be made by the very petitioners to have negroes employed again.[128]

Table 6.2. Norfolk Dry Dock, Gosport, Virginia: employment of slaves, May 1830–October 1832

	May 1830	May 1831	September 1831	November 1831	February 1832	May 1832	August 1832	October 1832
Black labor	56	136	98	92	87	87	89	78
Total labor	212	397	352	359	357	341	319	261
% black	26	34	28	26	24	26	28	30

Baldwin's expectations were borne out by events. The Navy Department took no action on the mechanics' petition,[129] and his confidence that the petitioners' demands for an end to the employment of slave labor would eventually be countermanded in a resurgence of slaveholder authority proved well founded.[130] Though in the aftermath of the rebellion the employment of slaves as hammerers and laborers on the dry dock dipped from approximately one-third to one-quarter total labor, in the aftermath of the emancipation debate their numbers recovered to levels comparable to those prevailing in the first half of 1831 (see Table 6.2).[131]

Ten years after, the alienated voices of white mechanics could still be heard in the Norfolk Navy Yard complaining about the employment of blacks. Fifteen years after, in 1847, it was the turn of white journeymen house carpenters, bitter at the use of black labor to break their strike. Twenty years after, in 1851, one finds Norfolk and Portsmouth's white artisans mounting yet another appeal, this to their fellows "throughout Virginia," for concerted action to protect free white labor from encroachment. As in the months before the Turner Rebellion, however, in 1851 mechanic interests collided "with those of wealthy, influential slaveholders" opposed to attempts to restrict black employment. And again, as before, slaveholders' authority was decisive. The only difference, perhaps, was that for a short period in the immediate aftermath of the Turner Rebellion slaveholders had of necessity been extremely circumspect in the manner in which they went about defending their interests against local antislavery and negrophobia. Twenty years later they were less constrained. When Norfolk and Portsmouth artisans petitioned the General Assembly to give whites "the exclusive privilege of the mechanic arts," their petition was not listened to with respect and with a show of support. It was rejected out of hand, and with contempt.[132]

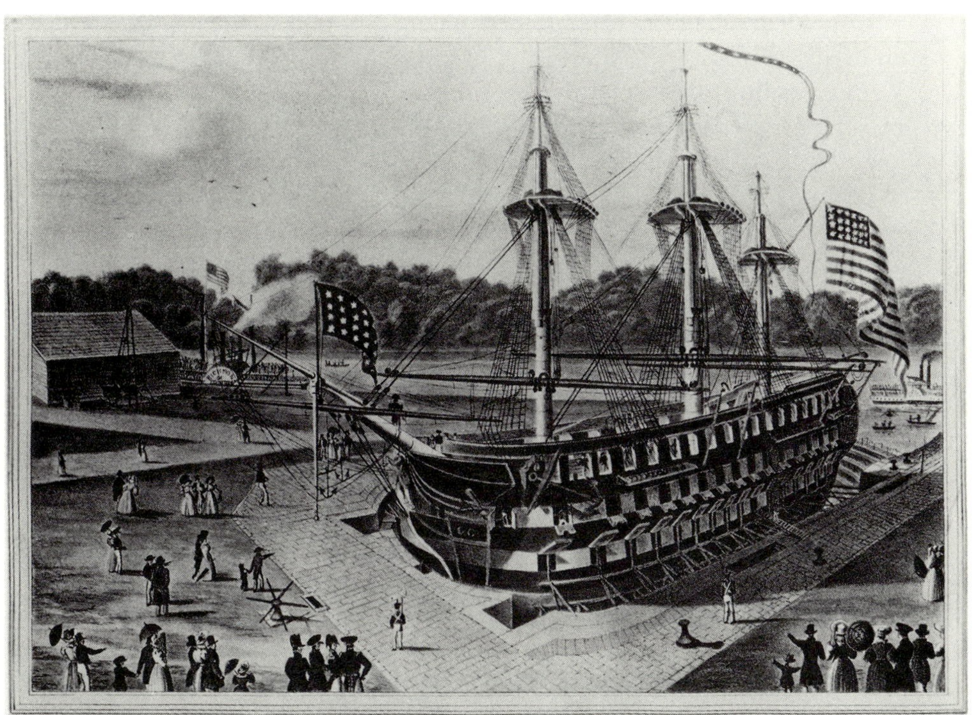

FIGURE 6.3. USS *Delaware*, first ship in the Norfolk Navy Yard Dry Dock (1833). Lithograph by Childs and Tranum, Philadelphia, after an original drawing by Joseph Goldsborough Bruff. Reproduced by permission of Navy Art Collection, Naval History and Heritage Command.

IV. THE VIRGINIA SLAVERY DEBATE, 1831–32

The Virginia General Assembly convened in Richmond on December 5, 1831, a bleak Monday. Much of that day, and the next, was given over to organizing the House, but on Tuesday the sixth delegates paused to receive Governor John Floyd's annual message. It was no doubt a somber moment. Unsurprisingly, Floyd devoted his message to "the crisis in which your country is placed" by "occurrences of a grave and distressing character . . . new, unexpected and heretofore unknown to the state." He meant, of course, Turner's rebellion. But that was by no means all he meant. Floyd's "crisis" was a compound of the rebellion, "great subjects" left unresolved from the previous legislative session, and "the unpleasant aspect of our Federal Relations." His message—his ambitions for the session to come—encompassed all three.[133]

John Floyd was from Montgomery County in southwest Virginia, and an owner of slaves. He was also a surgeon, a brigadier-general in the Virginia militia, a former member of the House of Delegates, and of the U.S. House of Representatives, and a figure in federal politics, in which he had originally been identified with the nationalist, modernizing strain of democratic republicanism associated with John C. Calhoun.[134] Floyd maintained his connections with Calhoun, whom he followed into zealous concern for state sovereignty and opposition to Andrew Jackson. He was elected governor of Virginia in February 1830 as the candidate "of the old line politicians of the eastern countries."[135] He served one twelve-month term under the 1776 constitution, and in February 1831 was unanimously reelected by the General Assembly to a three-year term as provided by the new constitution.[136]

Floyd's first annual message to the General Assembly as governor, the previous December, had been delivered in a flush of anticipation attending the new state constitution. Virginia had "exhibited to the world another grand spectacle, of a nation's changing its fundamental law without discord or difficulty, directed alone by reason." To the legislators assembled for the first time under the new constitution belonged "the task of giving the first impulse to the Government." Floyd left no doubt where that impulse should be directed: to "our internal condition . . . intercommunication between distant parts of the Commonwealth," to a unification of those dwelling below the fall line with those above it, and with those "residing beyond the mountains," that would extend to all the state's inhabitants "those facilities which open every market to . . . industry and enterprise." Here were matters of absolute economic necessity that in realization, happily, would prove entirely beneficial to the state as a political community:

> While this state of things is suffered to continue, the resources of the State admit of but partial development. Lands of inexhaustible fertility remain unreclaimed, and the country is deprived of much of its efficiency. What is the inducement to reclaim the forest or cultivate the earth, if the means of obtaining remuneration for one's labour is denied? . . . When, in connection with this, the improvement of the State is regarded as the sure means of producing unity of feeling, and harmonious action between all parts of the community, its importance cannot be questioned, or its benefits be matters of speculation.[137]

FIGURE 6.4. *John Floyd*, twenty-fifth governor of Virginia, 1830–34, by William Garl Browne Jr. Reproduced by permission of the Library of Virginia.

Floyd was well aware, of course, that improvement of the state was in fact an issue productive not at all of unity among the legislators to whom his message was addressed, but rather of division. Opposition to taxation of eastern slaveholders to underwrite western transportation projects had been the main reason the state's constitutional convention had been unable to cohere on more than a modest alteration of existing sectional apportionment. But even as he acknowledged postconvention dissatisfactions—"the one [side] in having lost more than was hoped; the other, in having gained less than was desired"—Floyd majestically swept caviling aside with grand claims of mutual economic benefit: "That argument, which, in opposition to a judicious system of improvements, is made to rest upon the inequality of contribution, either real or supposed, to be made by the different portions of the State, appears to me to fail utterly in its object. It opposes the only means which can ever bring about that equality of contribution to the public chest, which it seeks so earnestly to establish. Let markets be opened for the agricultural products of any country, and *instantly* the subjects of taxation will become common to it, and all other countries similarly circumstanced."[138] There followed a formidably detailed list of works for the legislators' attention—roads, canals, railroads, river improvements (notably to the James River, "the natural channel . . . the shortest, and might be the easiest, cheapest and most certain route, through which the inexhaustible abundance, produced from the rich soils of the western States, could find its way to the Atlantic")[139]—all accompanied by Floyd's pointed observation that where private enterprise was found wanting, the obligation fell on Virginia's government to attend to the need, and that "in this Government, there is no want of Constitutional power over this subject."[140]

The Floyd preoccupied in December 1830 by the task of uniting the state after a bruising and divisive convention behind a grand scheme of government investment in economic growth that would revive the state's economy and make Virginia a player in the race for the west was, a year later, a Floyd reelected to an unprecedented three-year term, hence an executive actually able to plan with some sense of continuity, yet required to contemplate the impact on his plans of events completely beyond his control. On the one hand Virginia confronted the distant threat of an overreaching "Federal power" antagonistic to state sovereignty, author of an oppressive tariff and of outlandish schemes to distribute the surplus revenues it generated among the states. "No scheme could be devised more ruinous to us." On the other, far more immediate, it had suffered "the relentless fury of assassins and murderers . . . a banditti of slaves . . . deluded fanatics."[141]

Though personally consumed by the quotidian rivalries and spats of federal politics, Floyd could actually do little about "our federal relations." As an identified opponent of Jackson he had no influence in the administration. All Virginia could do was complain "through our members in Congress and by legislative resolves," and be vigilant "against the evils of a system not only unconstitutional, but unjust, oppressive and ruinous."[142] This aspect of Virginia's congealing crisis was relegated to third in importance in his message. Floyd had been mulling the impact of the banditti, on the other hand, since the moment the rebellion occurred—and not just as a question of public order, but as a matter of both considerable economic significance, and political opportunity.

From the moment of its occurrence the rebellion had been bound in Floyd's mind to his ambitions for Virginia's renewal. In a letter of September 2 devoted largely to reviewing "the military view of the subject," Floyd had allowed a quite different thought to interject itself: "What the effect of this insurrection is to be upon the commercial credit of the state, upon individual credit, is a point of view not at all pleasant, to say nothing upon interest upon loans for the state itself, should she ever wish to borrow."[143] If long-term investment in capital projects was to become a reality, Floyd knew, the state *would* wish to borrow—*already* wished to borrow—and for some considerable time into the future.[144] His next clear thought on the matter, more deliberately composed, appears in a letter of November 19 to James Hamilton Jr., governor of South Carolina. Reviewing his plans for his December message to the legislature, Floyd announced he had decided to make only brief mention of the rebellion—"a very careless history of it, as it appeared to the public"—but that he was resolved to recommend to the legislature "to substitute the surplus revenue in our Treasury for slaves, to work for a time upon our Rail Roads etc etc and these sent out of the country, preparatory, or rather as the first step to emancipation."[145] No doubt aware that for the past several weeks memorials had been appearing in Virginia newspapers advocating emancipation and colonization—the latest published only four days previously in the Richmond *Enquirer*, proposing meetings in December in all counties on their respective court days "to call the attention of the ensuing Legislature to the subject of the bond and free coloured population of this State, and to urge upon them the necessity of devising some means by which the blacks may be removed beyond our borders, and by which the number of slaves may be gradually diminished"[146]—Floyd seemed ready to take a lead in the matter by proposing a scheme for eventual emancipation and deportation of Virginia's slaves that would weaken his eastern opponents and in the interim have the happy consequence of procuring a state-funded labor force for his program of internal improvements.

Floyd evidently gave considerable thought to his emancipation plan. His diary entry for November 21 records his determination that "before I leave this Government, I will have contrived to have a law passed gradually abolishing slavery in this State, or at all events to begin the work by prohibiting slavery on the West side of the Blue Ridge Mountains."[147] When it came to his annual message, however, Floyd held back from public avowal of state-funded gradual abolition. The proposal, he had told Hamilton, would require tender and cautious management. Floyd had decided on caution. He would indeed try to use the rebellion to advance his overall agenda, but indirectly, working through others. Hence, so far as commentary on slavery was concerned, Floyd's message emphasized only security. He asked the legislature to give its early attention to "revision of all the laws intended to preserve, in due subordination, the slave population of our state," to silencing black preachers, to policing "inflammatory papers and pamphlets, brought here by the agents and emissaries from other States," and to the design of measures to remove free people of color from the state.[148] "My message was well received," he noted on December 6.[149] Although the observation is soon followed by complaints that the General Assembly seemed moribund, Floyd would subsequently note, with satisfaction, two developments. First, on December 16, that "some of the members begin to talk of a loan for improving the State in Railroads"; and second, on December 26, that "the question of the gradual abolition of slavery begins to be mooted."[150]

The first of these hoped-for straws-in-the-wind spoke to the central thrust of Floyd's December 6 message, which, after traversing the rebellion, had moved on, with great vigor, to reemphasize the theme of the previous year, that the state's future depended on improving transportation and communication between east and west, and on finding the means to fund the projects this would require. In this aspect, quite unmistakably, Floyd took the "melancholy subject" of the rebellion, which had "filled the country with affliction, and . . . mourning," and deployed it in support of his campaign for economic development, as a call to action. Virginia's crisis demanded a turn from "a listless course of inadequate legislation" to "energy and decision," not on the subject of abolition but internal improvements:[151]

> You are now called upon by every consideration which can be presented to the representatives of a free people, to take such measures, as will revive the declining hopes of the country, invigorate her weakened energies, and ensure her repose. With ample means within your reach; constitutional power sufficient to effectuate every good; with generous and indulgent constituents, you cannot fail to put in operation such a system of measures, as will lead to a high degree of prosperity, and secure the future grandeur of the Commonwealth.

There followed, as in 1830, the same long list of projects—the same roads, canals, railroads, and river improvements—that would unite the state both topographically and politically behind the pursuit of commercial advantage. Purposefully, Floyd heightened his emphasis on state borrowing, on "the fostering care of the government" in raising funds for the construction of public works, and on direct state expenditure. He reported a treasury surplus of $106,000, 20 percent larger than the previous fiscal year.[152]

The second straw was no less welcome than the first. Floyd knew from the convention debates that vested slaveholding interests did not share his view that the state's economic future was tied to pansectional pursuit of commerce and were deeply suspicious of the public works and government debt that would be required to make it a reality. To avoid jeopardizing his economic program by antagonizing slaveholders sensitive to attacks on their property rights (and whose representatives had supported him for governor in 1830 and 1831), Floyd had abstained from public advocacy of gradual abolition. Privately, however, he saw gradual abolition as a necessary complement to commercial prosperity. The convention had shown how the east's slavery obstructed the west's development. The "fine soil capable of producing much to increase the exports of the State," like "the wealth of our mountains," was "doomed to remain inactive and unknown, contributing nothing to the comfort or improvement of our commerce."[153] Though the east's members in the legislature had no wish to discuss gradual abolition, "it must come if I can influence my friends in the Assembly to bring it on."[154] Aroused public interest in expelling Virginia's African population offered a rare opportunity to weaken the sectional interests that stood athwart Floyd's grand plan for the Commonwealth's economic advancement. "I will not rest until slavery is abolished in Virginia."[155]

Members had begun to talk about slavery primarily because public pressure on the issue, of which signs had been plentiful since October, had become explicit by mid-December, in the shape of petitions turning up in Richmond from all parts of the state. Between early December 1831 and late February 1832, some thirty-three petitions arrived, signed by more than two thousand citizens in twenty-seven different counties, mostly in the Tidewater and Piedmont.[156] Citizens demanded the removal from the state of free people of color (all petitions), state purchase of "a few hundred" slaves annually and their removal (approximately 40 percent of the petitions), and an end to slavery (approximately 15 percent).[157] Eva Sheppard Wolf's analysis of the petitions shows that although many were composed individually, the majority conformed to one of three formulaic texts.[158] With the exception of the petition from the Quaker Yearly Meeting of Charles City County, one of the earliest to arrive, none was couched in language that condemned slavery as a breach of moral or political ideals or sought its end as such. Petitioners might use the language of "evil" to describe the consequences of slavery, but their concern was, as Wolf emphasizes, overwhelmingly slavery's social and economic consequences for themselves, notably the presence of people of color.[159] Of the "template" petitions, those signing demands for state purchase and removal of slaves identified themselves as slaveholders seeking, for reasons of "patriotism, self interest, and our own happiness" a remedy against the "appalling and increasing evil" of black population growth. Their language was of a blight to be expunged, a "fatal, paralyzing, destroying mischief" that had to be removed—"the unhappy and degraded race of Africans, whose presence deforms our land"—if Virginians were to enjoy "peace and happiness, quiet and prosperity."[160] Those who concentrated their ire on free people of color condemned them as a grotesque oddity, "neither free men nor Slaves." Being neither one nor the other they were "of necessity, degraded, profligate, vicious, turbulent, and discontented." They did not belong. Their existence was "incompatible with the tranquility of society."[161]

As the petitions arrived in Richmond they were referred to a select committee created by the House of Delegates to consider and report on "so much of the governor's message as relates to the insurrectionary movements of the slaves, and the removal of the free persons of colour beyond the limits of the commonwealth."[162] The earliest petitions to arrive all concentrated on the removal of free persons of color and occasioned no controversy. On December 14, however, William H. Roane of Hanover introduced two petitions, one from slaveowners of Hanover County seeking state purchase and removal of slaves, the other from the Society of Friends of Charles City County seeking gradual emancipation of all slaves. After extended debate whether emancipation in any form—whether state-funded and partial, or gradual but comprehensive—was within the select committee's terms of reference, a majority of the House voted to refer both petitions to the select committee, thereby explicitly widening the committee's terms of inquiry to the future of slavery in the state.[163] "Is there one man in Virginia, who does not lament that there was ever a slave in the state?" the committee's chairman, William Brodnax of Dinwiddie, asked the House, speaking in favor of referral; "who considers the decay of our prosperity, and the retrograde movement of this once flourishing Commonwealth, who does not attribute them to the pregnant cause of slavery." Did anyone doubt slavery was an evil, that the cost of production by slave labor was far greater than by white labor? Others once burdened by slavery—New York, Pennsylvania—had met the matter boldly and were reaping the benefits. The committee should be enabled "to weigh the whole subject."[164] Petitions continued to arrive in a steady stream, and on December 20 the Richmond *Enquirer* enjoined the legislature not to rise "without ordering the police of the State on wise and secure principles."[165] On January 7 it encouraged the select committee not to content itself simply with "getting rid of the free people of color" but to address "the greatest evil. . . . 'Something must be done.'"[166] On January 9, Floyd noted that "members begin to talk of debating the question of gradually emancipating the Slaves of Virginia"; the next day he added "the slave question increases."[167]

The issue was indeed joined in the House of Delegates on January 10. William Osborne Goode, of Mecklenburg, who had led the opposition to receiving the Charles City County petition, sought an explanation for the failure of the select committee to report back to the House. Brodnax replied that the committee was delayed by its work not only on the removal of people of color but also on gradual emancipation. Goode declared his opposition to the "dangerous" course on which the committee was embarked, and the following day (January 11) moved that it be discharged from any further consideration of "manumission of persons held in servitude under the existing laws of this commonwealth" on the grounds that legislation on the matter was "not expedient."[168] Thomas Jefferson Randolph, of Albemarle, then moved to amend Goode's motion to instruct the committee to report on the expediency of polling all qualified voters on "the propriety of providing by law" as follows:

> that the children of all female slaves who may be born in this state on or after the fourth day of July, 1840, shall become the property of the commonwealth, the males at the age of twenty-one years, and females at the age of eighteen, if detained by their owners within the limits of Virginia, until they shall respectively arrive at the ages aforesaid; to be hired out until the nett sum arising therefrom shall be sufficient to defray the expense of their removal beyond the limits of the United States.[169]

The substance of Randolph's proposal was generally compatible with the ideas Floyd had outlined the previous November in his letter to Hamilton. It also resembled the proposal, well-known to the Commonwealth, that the eponymous Randolph's grandfather had offered seven years earlier, itself expanding on a plan first mooted in 1779 and described in his *Notes on the State of Virginia*.

> [The] way in which it can be done . . . is, by emancipating the after-born, leaving them, on due compensation, with their mothers, until their services are worth their maintenance, and then putting them to industrious occupations, until a proper age for deportation. . . . The estimated value of the new-born infant is so low, (say twelve dollars and fifty cents,) that it would probably be yielded by the owner gratis . . . leaving only the expense of nourishment while with the mother, and of transportation. . . . [This] would carry off the increase of every year, and the old stock would die off in the ordinary course of nature, lessening from the commencement until its final disappearance. In this way no violation of private right is proposed. Voluntary surrenders would probably come in as fast as the means to be provided for their care would be competent to it. Looking at my own State only, and I presume not to speak for the others, I verily believe that this surrender of property would not amount to more, annually, than half our present direct taxes, to be continued fully about twenty or twenty-five years, and then gradually diminishing for as many more until their final extinction; and even this half tax would not be paid in cash, but by the delivery of an object which they have never yet known or counted as part of their property; and those not possessing the object will be called on for nothing.[170]

The essential difference was that Randolph's proposal was silent on the question whether or not Commonwealth assumption of ownership of the mature *postnati* would be accompanied by compensation for their owners.[171]

Once Randolph had moved his amendment, "incidental debate" ensued.[172] Goode declared he considered it necessary "to arrest a misguided and pernicious course of legislation" that contemplated confiscation of citizens' property, a matter on which the legislature had no right to act, or even consider. Discussion was already ongoing in the press, and openly in favor of abolition. The effects on the value of slave property would be disastrous. Slaves themselves—"an active and intelligent class"—would redouble their "murderous acts" in the hope of forcing the legislature into emancipation.[173] Samuel Moore, of the Valley county of Rockbridge and another select committee member, responded with a well-prepared and extended attack on slavery as destructive of virtue and morality in both white and black populations, of the white agricultural work ethic, of the agricultural economy, and of Republican liberty. He recommended "a vigorous effort to send them from among us."[174] Phillip Bolling, of Buckingham in the western Piedmont, deplored slavery's pernicious effects on the white population: "It drives from us the laboring man—the honest industrious poor. . . . The small freeholders." It put slaveholders in bondage to merchants and creditors. Slavery had become a threat to the public good, a nuisance that had to be abated.[175] Randolph rose, finally, to defend his amendment not "as a fire-brand thrown into this House" but as a means to put the question "quietly off from our consideration to that of the people" whether emancipation should be considered by the legislature. Still, he could not resist invoking "the dark, the appalling, the despairing future" that awaited a Virginia indifferent to "irremediable evil."[176]

At the conclusion of this initial exchange, James Gholson, of Brunswick, another opponent of the Charles City County petition and also a member of Brodnax's select committee, moved to carry the matter over to the next day. Floyd noted that hopes were rising among his "young friends" in the legislature that the House might be brought to debate emancipation.[177] And indeed, in its deliberations on January 12 whether to take up Goode's motion of discharge—and hence, also, Randolph's amendment—the House discovered that it was already in the midst of a substantive exchange on the merits of emancipation.[178] The subject already broached, the House bowed to the inevitable and voted 116–7 to take up the motion of discharge, and the accompanying substitute. The expediency of gradual emancipation was thus fully on the floor. "The slave party have produced the very debate they wished to avoid," chortled Floyd, "and too, have entered upon it with open doors."[179]

Floyd's sense of triumph over the eastern interests that had obstructed his internal improvements program proved both short sighted and exceedingly short lived. Within two weeks alarm had replaced celebration. Within three, the grand agenda to solve Virginia's crisis proclaimed in his December 6 message was in ruins.

Predictably, the pivot on which the debate turned was the proposition that "the children of all female slaves who may be born in this state on or after the fourth day of July, 1840, shall become the property of the commonwealth." From the first, the slave party treated the idea as uncompensated confiscation, which of course it deprecated. Opening January 12's debate on the question whether to take up Goode's motion of discharge, James Gholson ridiculed "*new-light* politicians" who would sever the ligament of property that bound society together; who discoursed learnedly on how property "*in futuro*" was not property "in '*posse*.'" To the simple people of Brunswick, for whom he spoke, "the owner of land had a reasonable right to its annual profits; the owner of orchards, to their annual fruits; the owner of brood mares, to their product; and the owner of female slaves, to their *increase*"—increase to which they owed much of their wealth. Children were a return on a slaveholder's investment in their parents. Answering Bolling's appeal to public safety, Gholson denied that slavery posed any threat to the peace. The alarm and excitement attending the Southampton insurrection had subsided; Turner was dead; "society is restored to its ordinary current and repose," threatened only by northern "demons and devils." Virginia's slaves were "as happy a laboring class as exists upon the habitable globe," their condition far superior to "the serfs and laboring poor of Europe" and to "the servants to the North of us," their demeanor "contented, peaceful and harmless:"

> Gentlemen in the heat of their own intemperance, and by the aid of their own disturbed and distempered fancies, raise spirits and spectres at pleasure—gaze at them with horror, and then set about to shew their skill in the office of exorcism. These spirits and spectres, they call "necessity," "self-preservation," "public safety." The exorcism is the simple process of taking *eighty* or *one hundred millions of private property for public use, without compensation.*

In the name of an imagined insecurity, Gholson concluded, Randolph's proposal would do incalculable damage to eastern interests—an outcome hardly in the interests of the west, in that without eastern taxes its desired internal improvements would be rendered impossible. Slaves were the east's marketable "capital stock," realizable for "the discharge of our just obligations." They were "nearly all our wealth." Adoption of legislation unfriendly to slavery would result in the expulsion of Virginia from the interstate slave trade, which would destroy the east's economy:

> Our slaves constitute the largest portion of our wealth, and by their value, regulate the price of nearly all the property we possess. Their value . . . is regulated by the demand for it in the western markets, and any measures that should close those markets against us, would essentially impair our wealth and prosperity. . . . Should the substitute now under consideration be adopted, it

> would not only confiscate property hereafter, but in my best judgment, would, in less than ten months, diminish the value of the existing slave property of this State, by the amount of twenty-five millions of dollars.[180]

Emancipationists defended Randolph's proposal as moderate, democratic—in that it proposed first to test voter opinion on the question—and essential to the revival of the Commonwealth's fortunes in the face of "the multiplied and desolating evils of slavery." They also persisted in tying internal improvements to the slavery debate by arguing that improvements were not just a sectional western interest but would be the savior of the eastern economy by "drawing the produce of Middle and Western Virginia to the market towns of the East."[181] Their unity, however, was tested by William Brodnax, chair of the select committee, who, while joining the chorus that "something must be done," self-consciously adopted the political persona of "the moderate man" to criticize both sides of the debate for their impetuous extremism, and offered up a distinct scheme, not of gradual emancipation but of population control. Brodnax would deport annually 6,000 Africans from Virginia at state expense, "commencing, of course, with our free persons of color," which he calculated to be equivalent to the annual increase of the entire African population, free and enslaved. "By a removal then of 6,000 annually from the territory of Virginia, the capital stock would at the least be kept stationary, if not reduced—while our white population would be increasing at an accelerated pace." The result would be to rid Virginia entirely of its free people of color—the population on which his committee had been directed originally to deliberate—and to "dissipate our danger, dispel our apprehensions, and greatly diminish most of the embarrassments and evils attendant on slavery." Brodnax proclaimed himself no friend of slavery. Slavery was "*an evil*, and a transcendent evil . . . a mildew which has blighted in its course every region it has touched, from the creation of the world."[182] But in this he was hardly unique. No one had yet spoken of slavery as a good.[183] More important was Brodnax's axiomatic refusal to countenance any scheme to alleviate the effects of slavery that either weakened the security, or value, of private property, or took any slave without consent or explicit provision for "ample" compensation.[184] Three days later (January 16) Brodnax reported to the House that the select committee had come to the conclusion "that it is inexpedient for the present to make any legislative enactments for the abolition of slavery."[185]

Brodnax's attempt to steer the debate back toward free people of color and away from slavery, toward expulsion of an undesired population and away from expropriation of slaveholders' property, was resisted by emancipationist delegates. Charles Faulkner, of Berkeley, rose to underline their refusal to accept absolute rights in slave property. Turning the slave party's deprecation of natural rights in the state convention against it, Faulkner proposed his own test of "practical utility."[186] Property was "the creature of civil society." Slaves were held not as of natural or divine right "but solely by virtue of the acquiescence and consent of the society in which [slaveholders] live." As long as "that property" did not endanger social order it would be "tolerated." But once ascertained to threaten society "from that moment, the right by which they hold their property is gone. . . . The condition upon which they were permitted to hold it is violated—their right ceases." Faulkner recognized slaveholders enjoyed legal claims to their property, by dint of the state's "positive enactments," but law was trumped by "the public safety." Nor did slaveholders enjoy any irrevocable right to compensation: the community was not required to pay for property "removed or destroyed because it is a nuisance and found injurious to that society." Society could not be required to suffer "that the slave-holder may continue to gather his *crop* of human flesh." Randolph's proposal, which allowed slaveholders the present use of their property, was sufficient compensation.[187] "This is a fine talented young gentleman," Floyd wrote of Faulkner's speech.[188]

At this point in the debate, three positions had been articulated: the slave party had defended the east's investment in slave capital and resisted any form of action to vacate their property rights without compensation. Emancipationists had argued that slaveholders' property rights must yield to the interests of society at large, which was no longer served by slavery. And William Brodnax, with some success, had attempted to divert attention from emancipation to population control.[189] No one had yet defended slavery as such, although some in the slave party were coming close to doing so.[190] Finally, everything had occurred in the shadow of the pending select committee report.

Once the committee had reported, on January 16, against any further consideration of abolition, its opinion displaced the debate over the original Goode resolution (to discharge the committee from considering emancipation petitions) and Randolph's amendment to it. Each distinct faction then attempted to seize hold of the committee resolution. Archibald Bryce, of Goochland, moved to add a preamble to the report endorsing the removal of free people of color, as Brodnax had personally recommended. He was unsuccessful.[191] James Gholson spoke in favor of continuing debate on the original Goode resolution rather than debating the committee resolution. This was defeated by a floor vote, 60–62, which confirmed that the committee resolution was indeed now before the House.[192] William Preston, of Montgomery, a nephew of Governor John Floyd, then moved to amend the committee resolution by striking the word "inexpedient" in favor of "expedient," thus reversing the tenor of the committee resolution. The question thus became whether "legislative enactments for the abolition of slavery" were or were not expedient.[193] In support of his amendment Preston reemphasized the critique of slave party property claims already offered by Faulkner. To preserve Virginia from the "appalling consequences" of rapidly increasing numbers of blacks that, thanks to Turner, could no longer be sold to the southwest ("the line which God and nature has drawn between us [lies] in their color"), encroachment on the outrageous claims by the slave party to all slave property, both existing and unborn, claims "*superior to all law and above all necessity*," was inevitable and essential. "We attack that property because it is dangerous—we attack it because it is subversive of the well being of society—we attack it on principles of necessity and policy—we wish to remove the danger from the East, and to prevent its existence in the West."[194]

Slave party rhetoric elevated as well. Alexander Knox, of Mecklenburg, rose to condemn "the wild and revolutionary measures sought to be imposed on the people of this Commonwealth," the work of fanatics, demagogues, and agrarians. And for the first time during the debate, slavery was defended uncompromisingly as a positive good. Slavery was no "crying evil," no "cormorant preying upon the vitals of the body politic." Slavery, rather, was the foundation of the Commonwealth's "high and elevated character." Historically, moreover, slavery had been proven "indispensably requisite in order to preserve the forms of a Republican government. . . . From the very inherent nature of society, it has and will continue to exist." Such was human circumstance, "distinction between him who drives, and him who rides within the coach" was inevitable: the one must lend his services to accommodate the other. Should "deluded fanaticism" force emancipation on the east, "the bonds of this Confederacy must be dissolved."[195] John Thompson Brown, of the town of Petersburg, spoke out too in slavery's defense. Slavery was neither criminal nor immoral. "In what code of ethics, human or divine, is it written that slavery is an offence of so odious a character than no circumstances can palliate it—no necessity excuse it? Whence is derived the authority for saying that it is a sin, so very foul and monstrous, that Virginia is bound to pluck it from her bosom, though her life's blood should gush after it?" Christ who came into the world to reprove sin, had not reproved slavery. Leave slavery be and eventually it would abolish itself in Virginia by exporting itself to the lower South where it was more profitable.[196] William Goode would later repeat the same argument. "The superior usefulness of the slaves in the south will constitute an effectual demand, which will remove them from our limits. We shall send them from our state, because it will be our interest to do so."[197] The interstate slave trade would abolish slavery in Virginia.[198]

As positions on both sides of the debate on the committee resolution became more intransigent, Randolph attempted an intervention to reestablish his proposal as a line of compromise. "I do not concur in the abstract opinions of the West. I cannot concur with the hopeless ultra absolutism of the South." The proposal he had advanced was silent, it was true, on compensation for slave property. But this did not mean no compensation was intended. "The resolution does not prescribe the condition upon which [slave property] shall become the property of the commonwealth." The question would be for the legislature to decide. "Whether by the surrender of such portions as are not removed within the time specified—whether by payment for it at birth, at its full value, or at a reduced average, or such portions of it at this age, as the funds of the commonwealth would justify . . . [whether] to be left with the masters of their mothers until their services shall have paid the expense of rearing." Any of these provisions was possible, or any other "that the wisdom of this house should direct." In a speech marked by frequent interjections, however, Randolph was also determined to address his every critic, not least those whose claims of absolute rights in slave property were founded on an entirely commercialized conception of slavery:

> The gentleman [John Thompson Brown, of Petersburg] has spoken of the increase of the female slaves being a part of the profit. . . . It may be questioned, how far it is desirable to foster and encourage this branch of profit. It is a practice, and an increasing practice in parts of Virginia, to rear slaves for market. How can an honourable mind, a patriot, and a lover of his country, bear to see this ancient dominion . . . converted into one grand menagerie where men are to be reared for market like oxen for the shambles. . . . He has compared slave property to a capital in money. I wish it were money, sir, or anything else than what it is. It is not money, it is

> labour; it is the labour which produces that, of which money is the representative. The interest on money is 4 to 6 per cent. The hires of male slaves is about 15 per cent, upon their value: in ten years or less, you have returned your principal with interest. Thus it is with much of the $100,000,000 of property, the loss of which the gentleman has so eloquently depicted as ruining the country.[199]

"Nothing now is talked of or creates any interest but the debate on the abolition of slavery," Governor Floyd noted in his diary that day, adding, hopefully, "All is well."[200]

But all was not well. The following day another of Floyd's nephews, James McDowell, of Rockbridge, took to the floor to reiterate the "abstract opinions of the West" that the right of private property must yield to the right of society to be secure.

> The rights of private property and of personal security exist under every government, but they are not equal. Security is the primary purpose for which men enter into government; property, beyond a sufficiency for natural wants, is only a secondary purpose. It is because private property ministers to the uses and comforts and enjoyments of persons that it is sanctioned by law, and it is for these ends and these only that it is sanctioned. To these ends, therefore, must it be kept constantly subordinate, constantly conformed. When it loses its utility—when it no longer contributes to the personal benefits and wants of its holder in any equal degree with the expense or the risk or the danger of keeping it—much more—when it jeopards [*sic*] the security of the public—when this is the case, then the original purpose for which it is authorized is lost; its character of property, in the just and beneficial sense of it, is gone, and it may be regulated, without private injustice, in any manner which the general good of the community, by whose laws it was licensed, may require.[201]

McDowell was answered the next day, at considerable length, by James Dandridge Halyburton, of New Kent, in a speech that followed the trend begun by Alexander Knox, in which, rather than treat slavery as an unfortunate fact of life, slave party advocates turned instead to increasingly strenuous justification.[202] Floyd's diary suddenly became a succession of increasingly anxious entries: the debate was "engendering bad and party feelings" and displaying "erratic tendencies" (January 21); "the slave part of the state . . . must not be hurt," simply "held in check"

(January 23); the tone of the debate had become angry—"It is not good that it should be so" (January 24).[203]

That same day, January 24, Goode, of Mecklenburg, repeated earlier slave party warning that passage of an act of emancipation would mean "a division of this great Commonwealth."[204] There followed the next day a motion calling for indefinite postponement of further debate.[205] This was defeated (60–71), but so, immediately after, was the Preston amendment to the select committee resolution (58–73).[206] Bryce then revived his preamble, which was adopted as an amendment to the committee resolution (67–60), and the amended resolution was then adopted (65–58). "The debate is stopped," noted Floyd.[207] But that was not all: "The members from the South side of the James River talk of making a proposition to divide the State by the Blue Ridge Mountains."[208] Talk continued, but no proposal was formulated. The sequel, however, was disaster for Floyd's hopes for vigorous prosecution of internal improvements—the cause that had led the governor to put his weight behind the gradual abolition initiative in the first place. On February 3 the House considered, and approved without a division, a resolution "that the best interests of the Commonwealth demand the immediate commencement and rigorous prosecution of a line of commercial intercourse by such mode or modes as may be deemed most eligible, uniting the navigable waters of the Ohio with the tide-water of the James River." The House then rejected (57–67) the accompanying resolution "that this measure is appropriately a State work, and that it ought to be executed under the direction of the Government, by funds to be provided upon the faith and credit of the Commonwealth."[209] Of the 124 representatives present and voting on February 3, 115 had recorded votes on all four of the January 25 resolutions. Thirty-eight of those voting for Commonwealth funding on February 3 had voted as a bloc on all four January 25 resolutions; 45 of those voting against Commonwealth funding had also voted as a bloc on all four January 25 resolutions to exactly the opposite effect.[210] Floyd's diary for February 3 noted despondently that the bill had been defeated by "the members on the East side of the Blue Ridge Mountains . . . saying they had no interest in such improvements and in revenge for the debate on the negro subject of abolition."[211]

A further expression of eastern disaffection appeared the following day, February 4, in the shape of a long letter "To the People of Virginia" written by Benjamin Watkins Leigh under the pseudonym "Appomatox" and published in the Richmond *Enquirer*.[212] Mocking Turner as a hallucinating impostor and his rebellion as "a mere scene of massacre" perpetrated by a gang of drunkards and cowards, easily dispersed, Leigh expressed studied incredulity that the House of Delegates should now seriously be debating not stricter discipline and security but abolition. An "unmanly" panic had been whipped up by the press mouthing "the slang of the English newspapers . . . that *something must be done*," and the House had allowed itself to be manipulated into a discussion of the "violent abrogation of the rights of slave property," the "general demoralization of the master race," and the encouragement of "the slave race." Hinting that agitators unnamed would like nothing better than to see another insurrection to hasten their schemes, Leigh warned that in fact it was their solution—gradual abolition—that would result in "general servile war."[213]

Leigh's tract appeared after the House debate had wound down, but while Richmond newspapers were still in the midst of reporting verbatim the speeches of its first few days. In manner and composition, apart from the absence of the spoken debate's florid parliamentary niceties, the letter did not differ materially from those speeches; appearing among them, the letter gave Leigh all the appearance of an active participant. Nor did it differ much in content. The substance of Leigh's letter broke no new ground. Written in late January, however, the letter noticeably had much in common with the pugnacious and increasingly unapologetic tone that eastern Virginia's defenders of slavery had adopted during the second week of the debate. "The evils of slavery have been displayed in this debate . . . in my opinion those evils have been exaggerated, too, in a manner which sober reason must forever condemn." Slavery produced not tyranny in the master and moral depravity in the slave but mutual affection between them, tempered by "the ordinary duties of police, intended to keep our slaves out of mischief and in due subordination."[214] Slaveholders did not live in fear of their slaves but in harmony with them; their role was pastoral, the exercise of a providential, Christian care. "*Necessity*, it has been argued, imperiously dictates abolition and deportation. On the contrary, we lie under an invincible necessity to keep them here, and to hold them in subjection; a necessity imposed upon us by Providence. For I firmly believe, that it was a dispensation of Providence which sent them hither; it is the dispensation of Providence that here they shall remain; and Providence, in its own good time, will dispose of them and us according to its wisdom."[215] How interesting, that Benjamin Watkins Leigh's deprecation of Nat Turner's evil hallucination should be grounded on an answering dispensationalist hallucination all his own.

But though Leigh's letter broke little new ground it did underline some of the abolition debate's most important points. First, it stressed that the single most important attribute of slave property was its status as both labor and capital. So far as returns on labor were concerned, "the owners of slaves must bear the charge of rearing the young, tending the sick, and maintaining the diseased, the decrepid and the aged." The charge was necessarily met "out of the profits of the labor of such as are in the vigor of youth or manhood." The slave-owner's opportunity for gain lay in whatever surplus accrued from the profits of the slave's labor over the costs of maintenance. But "very frequently" in fact, gain was to be had only from "the increase of their slave property." Leigh therefore underlined the fundamental *economic* importance to the slaveholder of retaining rights of possession over the increase in population so that he could earn a return on slave property as capital. Second, in addition to the normal defense of the principle of property rights in slaves from an uncompensated assumption by the Commonwealth in the name of necessity, Leigh criticized the proposal's efficiency. "There is not a man that ever bestowed a thought upon such subjects, who does not know, that property of any kind in the hands of the public, is worse managed and more unprofitable, than property of the like kind in the hands of individuals; and slave property let out to hire under the management of public agents, having no other interest than to enhance to the utmost, the expenses of their agency, will be peculiarly unproductive." One could be sure that the "nett profits" would never suffice to defray the costs of transporting the emancipated slave population out of the state. And indeed the same fate awaited all the schemes of gradual emancipation, transportation, and colonization floated by the state's "abolitionist" interests: all were in violation of "the known elements of political economy."[216]

Leigh's letter signaled new trouble for Governor Floyd, for it was written not simply as a general defense of the position of the eastern slaveholders whose obstruction of his internal improvement proposals had moved the governor into the gradual emancipation column, but specifically to rally "the people of eastern and southern Virginia" in the forthcoming April elections against "all projects for abolition, present or prospective, or for the *liberation of slaves* by colonization," so putting the bung in the bottle indefinitely.[217] Floyd responded rather as he had when the emancipation issue had first arisen the previous November, but more emphatically: he resiled from taking any open position himself, and instead put the matter in other hands. By mid-February, Floyd seems to have been either discouraged or exhausted (or both) by Virginia's internal affairs. For much of the next five weeks Floyd was ill; for the rest of 1832 his diary contains little other than observations on federal politics. Nothing further of the General Assembly session warrants mention.[218]

The hands into which Floyd shoveled the whole mess—the aftermath of Turner's rebellion, the divisive debate over slavery and gradual abolition, Virginia's suffering economy and sectional discord over internal improvements—were those of Thomas Roderick Dew. Plainly Floyd was not seeking an immediate political solution, for Dew was no General Assembly crony but a professor (of history, metaphysics, and political law) at the College of William and Mary in Williamsburg, fifty miles southeast of Richmond.[219] Apparently in search of assistance in recouping his losses, Floyd had latched on to another "young friend" (Dew was thirty years old in 1832, to Floyd's forty-nine) who might help him distance himself from the disaster the debate had dealt his attempts to tackle the state's crisis.[220]

Dew responded, as any academic would, by writing an essay. Entitled "Abolition of Negro Slavery," it appeared in the *American Quarterly Review* for September 1832, where it occupied a significant seventy-six pages.[221] Publication in the *Quarterly*, which was based in Philadelphia, meant Dew's essay would reach a national audience of intellectual elites. Hence it served in large part as a considered response to the agitated discussion of slavery and abolition that had occupied the northeastern as well as the Virginia press in the months after the Turner rebellion. But the *Quarterly* had edited Dew's manuscript substantially, omitting "one whole division of the subject, treating of the origin and progress of slavery" and suppressing (Dew's word) other "minor portions."[222] Meanwhile, Dew himself continued to add to the essay, so that by December it had grown into a 130-page pamphlet. It was published as such in Richmond a few days after Dew's thirtieth birthday under the new title, *Review of the Debate in the Virginia Legislature of 1831 and 1832*.[223]

The pamphlet would make Dew famous as one of the first Southern intellectuals to expound in detail the idea that slavery was neither a moral nor an economic "evil" but a positive good.[224] It did so by grounding an extended critique of the House of Delegates' debate, and the various proposals for gradual emancipation and colonization of Virginia's black population that the debate had spawned, on a stadialist history of human development in general and of servile labor forms in particular. To these elements Dew added a pointed analysis of the basis on which sectional discord within the state might be ameliorated

FIGURE 6.5. *Portrait of Thomas Roderick Dew (1802–1846)*, professor of history, metaphysics, and political law, College of William & Mary, and president of the College, 1836–46, by William Garl Browne Jr. Reproduced by permission of Muscarelle Museum of Art, College of William & Mary.

by common pursuit of comparative economic advantage.[225] His conclusion—the strategic importance of internal improvements—amply repaid Floyd's hopes in turning to him. At the same time, Dew developed a comparative efficiency argument for slavery that, like Loammi Baldwin's more or less contemporaneous defense of his Norfolk Dry Dock employment practices, restated labor as such as a fungible, homogenous commodity. Purely as a matter of political economy, the argument went, it mattered little what form labor took.[226] The slave form was culturally and climatically rather than economically or civically determined. It was a creature of the agricultural stage of human development, and primarily of the plantation.

This notwithstanding, economics furnished the main argument *against* any form of abolition, namely the catastrophic loss of invested capital that it would necessarily entail. For even were slavery the calamitous evil its legislative opponents depicted, still Virginia could not be rid of it without causing the state terminal economic damage. "The physician will not order the spreading cancer to be extirpated although it will eventually cause the death of his patient, because he would thereby hasten the fatal issue." Happily, Dew could show the metaphor was inapt. Slavery was no cancer: "All those dreadful calamities which the false prophets of our day are pointing to, will never in all probability occur."[227]

V. THE CONFESSIONS OF THOMAS RODERICK DEW

"In looking to the texture of the population of our country, there is nothing so well calculated to arrest the attention of the observer as the existence of Negro slavery throughout a large portion of the confederacy. A race of people differing from us in colour and in habits, and vastly inferior in the scale of civilization, have been increasing and spreading, 'growing with our growth and strengthening with our strength,' until they have become intertwined and intertwisted with every fibre of society." Dew's opening sentences created the empirical baseline for what would follow. His subject in general was "the elastic and powerful spring of population." His particular concern was the conditions of coexistence of two races, "living together as master and servant," culturally distinct yet—an echo of Hegel's dialectic—"interwisted."[228] Could they be separated by returning "the black . . . to his African home"? Could they, alternatively, be united in civility and equality, the black "liberated from his thraldom"?[229] These were the questions that the Virginia legislature had taken on itself to consider in the wake of Turner's rebellion. Dew was in no doubt that the legislature had been both precipitate and unequal to the task. The rebellion had been a shocking but singular interruption to Virginia's customary "tranquillity and repose," its legislative aftermath a moment "when reason was almost banished from the mind." The House of Delegates had been full of "young and inexperienced" men. Delay would have allowed the selection of the "*grave* and *reverend* seniors . . . required for the settlement of a question of such magnitude." But the legislature had "boldly set aside all prudential questions . . . and openly and publicly debated the subject before the world." Dew assailed the outcome—"wild and intemperate" proposals for abolition and emancipation, founded on "false principles and assumptions of the most vicious and alarming kind; subversive of the rights of property and the order and tranquillity of society," portending "the most . . . ruinous consequences." He would demonstrate the total impracticality of every proposed plan of emancipation and deportation, and as well the total impossibility of any emancipation that permitted freed slaves to remain in the state, an idea "utterly subversive of the interests, security, and happiness, of both the blacks and whites, and consequently hostile to every principle of expediency, morality, and religion."[230] Plans for abolition were "puerile conceits." Slavery in Virginia was "eternally present and cannot be removed."[231]

The principal weight in Dew's argument was contemporary, founded on the demography and political economy of slavery as it existed in Virginia. This was preceded in the pamphlet, however, by the long section (nearly one-third of the whole) that the *American Quarterly Review* had cut out, Dew's discourse on the "Origin of Slavery and its Effects on the Progress of Civilization."[232] Here Dew marshaled arguments to dispose of the contention that slavery was "unnatural and horrible." On the contrary, slavery was divinely authorized; it was usual and ordinary; it had been and remained the condition of "by far the largest portion of the human race."[233] But Dew did not rest his case on the Bible, or on unsubstantiated claims about contemporary Eastern Europe, or Asia, or Africa. Rather, his method was classically stadialist, in the Scottish eighteenth-century tradition.[234] Describing successive historical stages of human development—hunter/gatherer, pastoral, agricultural, and urban/commercial—Dew focused on the effects across time of four legal-institutional conditions productive of servile labor (Dew did not distinguish slavery from serfdom or other forms of involuntary labor rent): the laws of war, habits of property, propensity to trade, and criminal punishment. His objective was to demonstrate "that slavery is inevitable in the progress of society, from its first and most savage state to the last and most refined."[235]

Those in humanity's original hunter/gatherer state had no developed habit of property, hence no propensity to accumulate. Their warfare was simple slaughter, motivated by revenge. Habits of property developed only as the savage hunter/gatherer stage was succeeded by pastoral, and particularly sedentary agricultural civilization.[236] Property bred an interest in its further accumulation, and that interest prevailed over the primitive impulse to vengeance. Slavery hence emerged as a diminution of "the cruelties of war," as victors found it in their interest "to make slaves of [their] captives, rather than put them to death."[237] Dew had no difficulty in finding extensive authority in the law of nations to support his argument.[238] He carefully distinguished Blackstone, who denied any right to enslave captives, as an isolated opinion based on an unrealistic understanding both of slavery and of war.[239]

Property having emerged from the progress of civilization to the stage of agriculture, Dew turned to an examination of the history of property. Initially, "there was, in fact, but one kind of property, and that consisted of land." In the absence of strong government, the will to accumulate ensured that landed property became concentrated in the hands of "a few," who thereby became despotic rulers over "the many." In Europe this meant allodial proprietorship was displaced in favor of feudal.[240] "The people of those days could find no employment except on the land, and consequently were entirely dependent on the landlords, subject to their caprices and whims, paid according to their pleasure, and entirely under their control; in fine, they were *slaves complete*."[241] So matters had continued until Europe began to move into the fourth and most advanced stage of human development—commerce, attended by the development of manufactures and the rise of cities. This, and this alone, had meant the end of slavery in Europe. The lesson for Virginia was that for as long as Virginia remained predominantly a plantation agriculture economy, it would do no good to emancipate its slaves because they would simply fall back into slavery.[242] The culture of the economy itself dictated that outcome.

Dew's third condition, propensity to trade, was founded explicitly on Adam Smith's observation of the human disposition "to truck, barter, and exchange one thing for another."[243] Trade—of oneself, of others (such as one's children)—to satisfy a debt or in exchange for subsistence was common throughout the world, ancient and modern. "In China . . . the common mode is to mortgage themselves with a condition of redemption."[244] Once again, Blackstone—who argued there could be no quid pro quo to selling oneself into slavery, hence no validity to the sale—was distinguished. "Again—Blackstone alludes to that pure state of slavery where, a man's life, liberty, and property, are at the mercy of his master. That is far from being the condition of slavery now. In most parts of the world the slave is carefully protected in life, limb and even in a moderate share of liberty, by the policy of the laws; and his nourishment and subsistence are positively enjoined."[245] Formally free laborers enjoyed no such legal guarantee: "He is subjected to all the hardships and degradation of the slave and derives none of the advantages." Were they only able to find buyers, Dew did not doubt that the incidence of free laborers' self-sale into slavery would increase significantly. "The capitalist in Great-Britain, could not afford to purchase the operative and treat him as we do the slave."[246]

Last of all, Dew pointed to imprisonment as slavery. Penal servitude, common throughout the nation, was as much a form of slavery as bound agricultural labor.[247] Dew also observed that penal servitude was a common punishment for insolvency, once again linking slavery to transactions and consequential debt.[248]

Far from an evil, Dew concluded from his survey, slavery had been an engine of development, "perhaps the principal means for impelling forward the civilization of mankind." It had mitigated the cruelties of warfare; it had enabled the development first of pastoralism, and then, decisively, of sedentary agriculture. "Hunting can never support slavery. Agriculture first suggests the notion of servitude, and, as often happens in the politico-economical world, the effect becomes in turn a powerful operating cause." Slavery tamed the hunter/gatherer, eradicated his habitual indolence and sloth, his improvidence and carelessness, and rendered him fit for labor. It also released women from the desperate drudgery that was a mark of hunter/gatherer life: "The labor of the slave . . . becomes a substitute for that of the woman."[249]

The final stage in Dew's historical inquiry was devoted to the origin of Negro slavery in the United States. The Atlantic slave trade had begun in the mid-fifteenth century; slaves had been introduced to Virginia in 1620, a century after their appearance in the Caribbean; the trade had been fanned by the region's "fertile soil and extensive territory, its sparse population and warm climate so congenial to the African constitution."[250] Dew considered but rejected arguments that the Atlantic slave trade had been beneficial—that it had saved many lives from African wars, spread civilization by conducting large numbers of Africans into the presence of whites, and improved their physical condition by introducing them to a climate more congenial even than their own. Though one might excuse it, the trade had wrought injustice. But the injustice was not the doing of Americans, who had continually sought its cessation, only to be overruled by the British. They had taken steps to ban the trade as soon as they were able. In this

Virginia had taken the lead, and "therefore, *especially*, has nothing to reproach herself with."[251]

The purpose of the historical first third of Dew's pamphlet was to normalize slavery as a condition of human labor, while excepting the United States in general and Virginia in particular from responsibility for the introduction of Negro slavery to the Americas. In normalizing slavery, Dew's stadial account of its "origin and progress" also situated the conditions for its eventual disappearance *outside* the realm of politics and law: "something else is requisite to convert slavery into freedom, than the mere enunciation of abstract truths, divested of all adventitious circumstances and relations." It had been precisely such a regime of enunciation that, Dew argued, had been on display in the House of Delegates debate.[252] His objective in the next part of the pamphlet was to demonstrate conclusively the impotence of wishful thinking in the face of political economy's clear-eyed empirical truths.

The effects of projects of emancipation and deportation advocated during the legislative debate were, Dew observed, amenable to analysis by "the most rigid and accurate calculations." The 1830 census counted Virginia's slave population at 470,000. Dew attributed to each slave an average capital value of $200, producing a total capitalization of slave labor of $94,000,000 as of 1830, or $100,000,000 as of 1832.[253] The assessed value of all lands and improvements (houses) in the state was $206,000,000.[254] Slaves hence constituted one-third of the state's accumulated wealth. More than that, they constituted the laboring population that earned all invested capital (slave and nonslave) its return, hence maintaining its value. Remove the slaves "and you pull down the atlas that upholds the whole system."[255] Advocates of emancipation and deportation proposed to avoid such a sudden shock by commencing emancipation at levels that would simply remove the increase of the black population. Their goal was to alter the demographic balance between the two populations to a level at which the number of blacks would seem harmless. Dew estimated that increase at 6,000 per annum.[256] Valuing the 6,000 at $200 per capita and allowing a transportation cost of $30 per capita, the cost of gradual emancipation and removal became $1,380,000 per annum. Dew pronounced this cost unsustainable.[257] In any case, Virginia was already exporting some 6,000 slaves per annum. "Virginia is in fact a *negro* raising state for other states; she produces enough for her own supply and six thousand for sale." By entering the market to purchase 6,000 slaves per annum for emancipation and deportation the state government would simply redirect the flow of slaves already available for purchase, abating "this efflux, which is now so salutary to the state, and such an abundant source of wealth," and which in fact had been on the increase since the rebellion, accompanied by rising prices for Virginia slaves, and instead incurring for the state a deadweight capital loss.[258]

Proponents of emancipation and deportation argued that investment in the expulsion of slave labor was not a deadweight loss because it would encourage the immigration and substitution of free labor, which they claimed was "infinitely superior . . . in every point of view."[259] Dew discounted the possibility that the minimalist project of removing the increase in the black population could have any incentive effects on white immigration—"If we are too proud to work in a field with fifty negro men this year, we shall surely be no more disposed to do it next year, because one negro, the increase of the fifty, has been sent to Liberia." He also argued that white labor was not more efficient—not, at least, when working in association with black.[260] But his main objection was that "the spring of population" would defeat any attempt to alter the balance between the white and black populations through gradual emancipation and expulsion. "Government entering into the market with individuals, would elevate the price of slaves beyond their natural value, and consequently the raising of them would become an object of primary importance throughout the whole state." Everything Dew knew about the political economy of slavery in Virginia convinced him that increased demand for slaves—whatever the source—would be met by increased supply: "Slaves in Virginia multiply more rapidly than in most of the Southern States;—the Virginians can raise cheaper than they can buy; in fact it is one of their greatest sources of profit." Meanwhile, fiscal imposition of the costs of gradual emancipation and expulsion on the white population would diminish its wealth and encourage its emigration.[261] The unintended and undesired consequence would be an increase in the black population and a decrease in the white: "*uno avulso non deficit alter*," Dew solemnly intoned.[262]

Proponents had attempted to avoid the crushing cost of gradual emancipation and expulsion by imposing it on the slaves themselves, requiring them to cover the cost of their own expulsion by taking them into state ownership on maturity and requiring that they work for hire, administered by the state, until the cost of expulsion had been met. Dew denounced the idea as a confiscation of slave property, "convert[ing] the fee simple possession of this kind of property into an estate for years"; a destruction of the slave's realizable capital value (for no one would buy a slave destined to be assumed by the state); an uncompensated imposition of the costs of rearing on the slaveholder; a reliance for the recovery of the cost of expulsion on the superintendence of government, that "most miserable of all managers"; and an arbitrary and destabilizing division of enslaved youth into *ante-* and *post-nati* that would simply breed more rebellions among those destined to remain in slavery. "All of these plans merit nothing more than the appellation of *vain juggling legislative conceits*, unworthy of a wise statesman and a moral man. If our slaves are ever to be sent away in any systematic manner, *humanity* demands that they should be carried in families."[263] Worst of all was that variation on gradual emancipation that deemed property a social creation, held subject to society's right to abate as a nuisance any property that endangered the general good. The object of government, Dew responded, was the protection of property not its abatement. "No government can exist which does not conform to the state of property." Here lay the gravest threat of all, a threat to all property, calculated to "disorganize and unhinge the condition of society . . . to produce uncertainty and alarm . . . to create revulsions of capital," that would imperil the entire economy. "The ruin of the farmer will draw down ruin upon the mechanic, the merchant, the sailor, and the manufacturer."[264]

Dew then turned from gradual emancipation and deportation to the necessary condition of deportation, successful colonization of the expelled population. His argument was simple: successful colonization required immense expenditure, a viable environment, and a population capable of absorbing enormous hardship. None of these conditions was met by the proposals to repatriate Virginia's African population. Adding settlement costs to transportation costs, Dew arrived at an estimate of $200 per capita, making the annual cost of removing 6000 slaves $2,400,000, an expenditure "sufficient to destroy the entire value of the whole property of Virginia."[265] Proponents had suggested seeking the aid of the federal government in a general scheme to abate American slavery, but the effect of federal involvement would be no different than the effect of state involvement: government purchase of slaves would simply drive up demand, increase price, and invigorate the spring of population. "Emigration has rarely checked the increase of population, by directly lessening its number—it can only do it by the abstraction of capital and by paralyzing the spring of population,—and then it blights and withers the prosperity of the land." In any case, to seek the aid of the federal government would fatally compromise Virginia's position within the Union.[266]

Deportation proven to be wholly impracticable, what of emancipation without deportation? No one, Dew argued, supported any such course, "so fraught with danger and mischief both to the whites and blacks."[267] Virginia's slaves were utterly unfit for freedom among the white population. Referencing James Mill, Dew pronounced his measure of fitness to be the capacity to engage voluntarily in labor sufficient to "the supply of the fund of . . . necessaries and conveniences." The example of free people of color—"worthless and indolent . . . *drones* and *pests*" —was sufficient to establish that freed slaves could not meet the necessary standard:

> Much was said in the legislature of Virginia about superiority of free labor over slave, and perhaps under certain circumstances this might be true; but in the present instance, the question is between *the relative amounts of labor that may be obtained from slaves before and after their emancipation*. [In the United States] it is well known to everybody that slave labor is vastly more efficient and productive, than the labor of free blacks.[268]

The same had already been proven by the experience of the Caribbean, notably Saint-Domingue, which for forty years had recorded a continuous and precipitous decline in the production of sugar, coffee, and cotton.[269] Freed slaves simply had no propensity to accumulate. Nor was the unfitness of bound black labor for freedom a question merely of racial incapacity: Polish peasants freed by the 1791 constitution had become "degraded and wretched beings" who, "instead of hoarding the small surplus of their absolute necessaries, are almost universally *accustomed to expend* it in . . . schnaps." The same was true of the serfs freed in the eastern Baltic province of Livonia.[270] The "prematurely liberated" bound laborer was, for Dew, a monster, "a human form" endowed by its creator—the naïve legislator—"with all the physical capabilities of man, and with the thews and sinews of a giant," but completely lacking in moral sense. "He finds too late that he has only created a more than mortal power of doing mischief, and himself recoils from the monster he has made."[271]

What then was to be done? Dew's answer was . . . nothing. Even were slavery to be admitted an injustice, and an economic calamity, its precipitate elimination would produce more of both, to the detriment of both master and slave. Better, then, to accept the responsibility thrust on the slaveholder, "entailed upon us by no fault of ours."[272] But Dew denied that slavery was in fact either injustice or calamity. First, slavery was sanctioned by both Old Testament and New.[273] Second, slavery was assuredly a republican institution for "the perfect spirit of equality" it created among whites. "Color alone is here the badge of distinction, the true mark of aristocracy, and all who are white are equal in spite of the variety of occupation." The responsibilities of aristocracy—management, control—instilled in masters both humanity and virtue, which in turn inspired loyalty and happiness in their slaves. "A merrier being does not exist on the face of the globe, than the negro slave of the United States."[274] Third, slavery, in its proper place, properly directed, was in no way inferior to free labor. The efficiency of free labor depended on its propensity to accumulate. The English had learned to accumulate, the Irish far less so, the Spanish and Italians not at all. "In southern countries, idleness is very apt to predominate, even under the most favorable circumstances, over the desire to accumulate."[275] In southern staple-producing countries slave labor was more efficient than free. This had been proven by the Saint-Domingue experiment, and also by the history of the southern mainland colonies, which had far exceeded in wealth and productivity those of the north. The only reason the north was now gaining in wealth over the south was not that slave labor was ruining the south, but that the federal government, with its protective tariff, was systematically ruining slave labor.[276]

Slavery's comparative advantage in southern climes meant that, ruinous federal policies notwithstanding, slavery had a long-term future in the United States. "We very much doubt even whether slave labor be not best for all southern agricultural countries."[277] Dew thought Virginia "too far north" to expect slavery to exist there indefinitely.[278] And indeed, although the black population was growing, the majority white population had begun to grow faster, increasing in proportion its power and security. But at least in the short term, Virginia's comparative demography was more ambiguous, because although the state's white population had been growing faster it had also been emigrating westward in large numbers. Dew recognized this as an important economic problem. Black migration occurred principally through the agency of the internal slave trade. "This emigration becomes an advantage to the state, and does not check the black population as much as at first view we should imagine, because," as he had already explained, "it furnishes every inducement to the master to attend to his negroes, to encourage building, and to cause the greatest possible number to be raised."[279] Through sale on the market the slaveholder received back the capital invested in the slave, while the spring of black population growth created an equivalent to take the place of the departed. In the case of white emigration, in contrast, the state lost both a laborer, usually in the prime of life, and the capital invested in the laborer by his family in the form of rearing and education, and was thus doubly impoverished by the migrant's departure. Dew placed particular emphasis on the state's capital loss from emigration, estimating that a young educated man could generate income of two thousand to three thousand dollars per annum, the equivalent of ten common laborers. Unable to ascertain annual white emigration, but venturing that it was no less than three thousand persons per annum, Dew pronounced the loss to the state to be the equivalent of twelve thousand "*mere laborers*." The effect of the loss of productive citizens and capital was to obstruct the accumulation of wealth and the increase of white population, leaving little of value behind "but *lands*, *negroes*, and *houses*."[280]

Because white population growth was increasing at a more rapid rate than black, even in the eastern section of the state, Dew was prepared to treat white emigration as a serious but not fatal problem. And in the long term he identified two countervailing factors that would decisively check white emigration and the loss of capital and population it meant, and encourage the eventual demise of slavery in the state: first, the filling up of vacant western territory; and second, "the completion of such a system of internal improvement in Virginia, as will administer to the multiplied wants of her people, and take off the surplus produce of the interior of the state to the great market of the world."[281] Of these, it was internal improvement, "the great *panacea*, by which most of the ills which now weigh down the state may be removed, and health and activity communicated to every department of industry," that in Dew's mind was decisive.[282] Internal improvement—the completion of west-east arteries connecting the Ohio to the James Rivers—would bring about the final crucial shift in Virginia's political economy, from agriculture to commerce, that stadial political economy predicted. For the eastern region of the state it would mean the rise of cities and manufactures, the immigration of free labor, a corresponding increase in the density of population and the division of labor, growing urban demand for local foodstuffs, a breakdown of plantation agriculture in favor of truck farming, and a consequent decline in demand for enslaved agricultural labor. For the west it would mean the opening of markets and the substitution of commercial arable for subsistence pastoral agriculture.

The rise of manufactures and commerce, and a change in tillage, east and west—here was "the *true ground* for *unity* of *action*." Emancipation was at best an irrelevance, at worst a fatal impediment to economic prosperity. The state faced a simple choice between productive and unproductive capital investment. "Where is the state to get the money from, to cut canals and rail roads through her territory, and send out thousands besides to Africa?" Virginians should reject the foolish prattling of politicians and wait patiently while the historical logic of political economy unfolded. "Time and internal improvement will cure all our ills."[283]

Dew's *Review of the Debate* has been described as a decisive reorientation of Southern proslavery arguments, "from the defense of a necessary evil to the assertion of a positive good."[284] This is, if not incorrect, somewhat beside the point.[285] It is of course entirely appropriate to conclude from an examination of the language of the *Review* that Dew was himself "proslavery," and that he thought slavery a positive good.[286] But neither was really at issue in the *Review*. In Virginia, the rhetoric of positive good had already made itself apparent in the course of the emancipation debate. Rather, Dew was applying a mode of analysis in which he was well versed to a contentious contemporary issue. Using that mode of analysis his objective was to demonstrate the profound and damaging error of imagining that legislative politics was the realm in which divisions over slavery should be addressed or could be resolved. Government—"that most miserable of all managers"—should abstain from interventions in economic activity because its actions would always result in consequences unanticipated by their advocates.[287] Whether in the short or the long term, economic outcomes were driven by very different forces than political decision making: in the short term, they were driven by self-interest and "the spring of population"; in the long term, by the gradual accumulation of social and institutional change that conformed to the classic conjectural human progression, from the "savage" society of hunting and gathering, to pastoral and then sedentary agriculture, to commerce. In the long term, it seems clear, Dew thought slavery in Virginia would wither away because Virginia would eventually make the transition from an agricultural to a commercial stage of development. Dew thought it in the state's economic interests to make that transition. But the transition should not be hurried "by the helping hand of government."[288] And for as long as Virginia remained engaged in plantation agriculture, the comparative advantage of slave over free labor would ensure that the state's economy would remain committed to slavery. "The time for emancipation has not yet arrived, and perhaps it never will." Attempts forcibly to change this state of affairs by improvident and wasteful legislative plans could have only the ruinous effect of destroying "more than half of Virginia's wealth."[289]

VI. CIRCULATIONS OF LABOR

Thomas Roderick Dew's *Review of the Debate* drew a line under the Virginia House of Delegates' argument over gradual abolition by answering conclusively the question left hanging by the state convention two years earlier. The convention's slanted reapportionment and suffrage compromises had guaranteed slaveholders sufficient political resources to protect their interest, and the slave party had used them to wrestle the postrebellion bid for gradual emancipation to a standstill. But the damage had been severe—east and west both deeply embittered,[290] the state brought to the very edge of dissolution, the governor's improvements scheme destroyed. Here was no foundation on which those who held in their hands a full half of Virginia's "productive labour" might hope to see their particular interest acknowledged an "interest of the whole Commonwealth."[291] Dew provided the way back: his *Review* unreservedly endorsed internal improvements as the means to knit the battered sections together again and set the Commonwealth on a new path to wealth and prosperity; slavery, meanwhile, stood endorsed just as unreservedly as an interest of the whole, not a liability but the source of Virginia's comparative advantage for as long as it remained a predominantly agricultural state. "All the sources of wealth and departments of industry, all the great interests of society, are really interwoven with one another," Dew wrote. They formed "an indissoluble chain," such that "a blow at any part quickly vibrates through the whole length—the destruction of one interest involves another."[292] Slave emancipation was "at war with the true interests of Virginia, in every quarter—in the west as well as the east." Emancipation was economic suicide. Instead let east and west "steadily unite in pushing forward a vigorous system of internal improvement."[293]

Unite they did. After the halting commitments and studied displays of legislative indifference of the 1820s and early 1830s, "Virginians worked feverishly to modernize their economy through large investments in canals, railroads, and banks."[294] But the pattern of development did not bridge the state's sectionalism. Improvement projects were localized, managed by private corporations, and funded locally—even capital-hungry railroads—by private subscription. The result was a complete absence of "system." Localities with capital to draw on prospered, but major interregional projects withered on the vine, unable to promise tangible local benefit or surmount local competition, hence unable to attract capital investment.[295] When, in the mid-1830s, the state government finally began to overcome the legislature's reluctance to invest directly in internal improvements, it was able to do so only by pandering to local interests. State funding did not mean planned development for projects local capital would not touch: instead it was logrolled through the legislature, distributed haphazardly across competing projects and competing modes of transportation, "schemes of purely local character, some of them are wholly impracticable, and others such as by their construction would inflict injury upon interests already in existence."[296] By 1860, largely by deficit finance, the state had invested $40 million in internal improvements, 80 percent ($32 million) in the previous fifteen years, the remainder mostly between 1834 and 1845.[297] Yet it had no central trunk railroad, or water transportation network connecting east and west, Ohio and James rivers, to show for it. Instead, nearly 70 percent of the state's funds had been expended on projects east of the Blue Ridge, and more than half of the remainder (18 percent) in the Valley. State funding of improvements in the Trans-Allegheny west lagged badly behind the rest of the state.[298]

The absence of unity meant antagonism toward the slave party continued to fester. But it had no further legislative expression. To that considerable extent, Dew's other main purposes, the declaration that slavery was an interest of the whole and, more important, that it was an *economic* interest, beyond politics, were substantially achieved. As important, however, was the direction to Virginia slavery imparted by the specificities of his economic analysis of slavery: human capital, commodified labor, shorn of customary or paternal obligation, expressible as a return on investment that might be realized either through work, or, just as rationally, sale. Six thousand per annum was Dew's figure for slaves "rais[ed] for other states," earning $2.4 million—not an insignificant figure, given that the state's total nonhuman exports in 1829 had amounted to less than $3.8 million, and equal to its balance of payments deficit for that year.[299] Others had different figures at their fingertips. During the legislative debate, William Preston, of Montgomery, had claimed the number of slaves forced annually into interstate commerce was 8,500. Henry Berry thought it was 9,500. Campbell, of Brooke, had suggested two-thirds of an annual increase he estimated at 16,000 were sold out of state, or approximately 10,700; Marshall, of Fauquier, thought more than 108,000 had left Virginia during the depressed 1820s, or 10,800 per annum.[300] Randolph, of Albemarle, also had figures—like Preston he thought it was 8,500 a year, and indeed had been for twenty years. Virginians had become addicted to the returns they could earn by selling their slaves; Randolph spoke, with feeling, of the "increasing practice in parts of Virginia, to rear slaves for market."[301]

What were the numbers? Using the federal census it is possible roughly to estimate the increase in population one might anticipate from census to census, and to compare this figure with the actual increase in population.[302] This method suggests that between 1820 and 1830 approximately 7,600 slaves per year were sold or sent out of the state.[303] Between 1830 and 1840 this figure jumps to more than 11,800, before falling back to 8,900 in the 1840s and 8,250 in the 1850s. There is no reason at all to suppose annual figures were uniform across each decade; nevertheless Dew's figure of 6,000 in 1832 is conservative, given the average for the previous decade and the slope of a rising demand curve, corresponding to the rapid extension of cotton cultivation in the states of the southwest, which peaked between 1835 and 1836 as cotton prices doubled between 1830 and 1835. Forced slave migration might well have reached 25,000 per year at the 1830s peak, when Virginia slave prices hit $1,100, before falling off rapidly with the collapse of cotton prices in the late 1830s. A slow recovery in cotton prices began in the mid-1840s and continued for fifteen years, during which it is likely that the bulk of the 1840–1860 interstate slave sales occurred, at prices rising from $500 to $1200, albeit at lower volumes than during the mid-1830s, no doubt because Virginia's own staple crop prices were rising at the same time, which had certainly not been the case in the 1820s and 1830s.[304]

The movements of slaves, when correlated with staple prices, slave prices, and land values in states of origin and reception, suggests that although his estimate was conservative, in 1832 Thomas Roderick Dew knew well of what he wrote. Slave labor had been completely commodified.[305] Slaveholders chose to realize the full value of their embodied capital when the return on it as capital exceeded its anticipated rate of return as labor—or in other words when price movements meant Virginia's agricultural economy lost its comparative advantage vis-à-vis adjacent agricultural economies. What white labor could do on its own behalf—circulate in search of advantage—was done to black labor by slaveholders for their own benefit. It was not done en masse because, as Philip Doddridge had bitterly remarked back in 1829, slaves made their owners sovereigns, and because Virginia slaveholders could still scratch a living, and in the 1840s and 1850s rather more than a living, from their own land. But it was done easily enough to prove Dew's point, and the doing of it earned slaveholders considerable returns.

CONCLUSION

Like Thomas Ruffin Gray, Thomas Roderick Dew and his fellow slave party travelers went to some considerable trouble to pronounce Turner's rebellion an aberration, the event itself "trifling and farcical," the fears attending it but a passing phase, "of short, *very short* duration."[306] The market behavior of Virginia slaveholders in the 1830s seemed to prove them right. The number of slaves they forced into circulation increased from 17 percent of total population in the 1820s to 25 percent in the 1830s before falling back toward 17 percent over the next two decades, suggesting a heightened propensity to sell in the wake of the rebellion. But this was no panic selling—it actually represented a net decrease in Virginia's contribution to the total number of slaves in interregional motion, one that arrested the secular growth of the slave population, but did not put it into decline. Rather, in selling into a rising market, Virginia's slaveholders were engaged in a rational realization of returns on their invested capital.

Still, before accepting as gospel the slave party's elaborate contempt for the Turner Rebellion, we should also consider the words of John Thompson Brown, of the Town of Petersburg, on the seventh day of the emancipation debate. Brown was one of those who downplayed the rebellion, but he did so less out of bravado than fear of the consequences of allowing the rebellion to turn Virginia away from the slavery that was its lifeblood, and on which he and those like him depended for a living. He reminded the House of Delegates that Virginia's slaves were "the net proceeds of the labor of our ancestors and ourselves, [from] the foundation of the colony at James Town, to the present moment." They had taken the soil, he said, and cultivated it, and invested the proceeds—$100,000,000—in slaves.

> It now forms our capital stock. It is the sum total of the hard earnings of successive generations, during the long and toilsome lapse of more than two hundred years. We derive our subsistence from the labour of our slaves, precisely in the same manner that we would live on the interest of our money if the one hundred millions had been invested in bank stock. From the annual products

> of their labour, we obtain the necessaries of life, and have a surplus of more than four millions for exportation.

One can hear Brown's voice quaver as he contemplated the possibility that a rebellious slave might actually induce a majority of his fellows to reconsider their toleration of his investment. "Take from us these slaves without compensation," he pleaded, "and what have we left?"[307] At that moment, perhaps, his revulsion at the prospect—his fear of what the future might bring—was all too real.

EPILOGUE

Demonic Ambiguities

> If one looks upon history as a text, then one can say of it what a recent author has said of literary texts—namely, that the past has left in them images comparable to those registered by a light-sensitive plate. "The future alone possesses developers strong enough to reveal the image in all its details. Many pages in Marivaux or Rousseau contain a mysterious meaning which the first readers of these texts could not fully have deciphered." (Monglond; N15a,1.) The historical method is a philological method based on the book of life. "Read what was never written," runs a line in Hofmannsthal. The reader one should think of here is the true historian.
>
> —WALTER BENJAMIN (1940)

To fashion a meditative end for this speculative history, let us begin with three observations, each a fragment torn from a longer text.

> I, James Rochelle, Clerk of the County Court of Southampton in the State of Virginia, do hereby certify, that Jeremiah Cobb, Thomas Pretlow, James W. Parker, Carr Bowers, Samuel B. Hines, and Orris A. Browne, esqr's are acting Justices of the Peace, in and for the County aforsesaid, and were members of the Court which convened at Jerusalem, on Saturday the 5th day of November, 1831, for the trial of Nat *alias* Nat Turner, a negro slave, late the property of Putnam Moore, deceased, who was tried and convicted, as an insurgent in the late insurrection in the county of Southampton aforesaid, and that full faith and credit are due, and ought to be given to their acts as Justices of the peace aforesaid.[1]

> The fate of our times is characterized by rationalization and intellectualization and, above all, by the "disenchantment of the world." . . . Nothing is gained by yearning and tarrying alone, and we shall act differently. We shall set to work and meet the "demands of the day," in human relations as well as in our vocation.

This, however, is plain and simple, if each finds and obeys the demon who holds the fibers of his very life.[2]

Schuld (consider the demonic ambiguity of this word).[3]

Here in this epilogue, the task I have set myself is to conjoin, in one constellation, the three texts from which these observations have been ripped, and ourselves as readers of texts, and thereby attempt to provide my story with meaning and purpose. The first text is *The Confessions of Nat Turner*, with which we have become very familiar over the course of this book. The second is Max Weber's famous lecture "Science as a Vocation," delivered November 7, 1917, in Munich, on the eve of the Russian revolution. The third is Walter Benjamin's abbreviated fragment "Capitalism as Religion," written in 1921, unpublished in his lifetime. In this epilogue the second and third texts become prisms from the future, as we are ourselves. They, and we, refract and enliven the first, and so reveal its image.[4] They are as unlike each other as each is unlike *The Confessions*, except in one regard—the glance each casts at the demonic. Though brief, these glances are of significance if we are to assess the final meaning of the "full faith and credit" held due the decision of the Southampton County Court to convict Nat Turner of fomenting "insurrection," and order that he hang.[5]

Like guilt and debt, the dual meanings of *Schuld* that, for Walter Benjamin, confirm that capitalism is a parasite on Christianity, the conjunction of faith and credit has its own demonic ambiguity, simultaneously sacralizing (faith) and secularizing (credit) the processes and penalties of the law.[6] Max Weber's austere pronouncement of the world's calculability, its "disenchantment," partakes deliberately of the same ambiguities, naming "science" (secular knowledge) a "vocation" (religious calling) that exists at the crossroads of *Geist* (spirit) and *Geld* (cash). "As Max Weber sees it," Michael Löwy and Robert Sayre tell us, "capitalism was born with the spread of merchants' account books, that is, with the rational calculation of possessions and duties (*l'avoir* and *le devoir*), of receipts and expenses. The ethos of modern industrial capitalism is *Rechenhaftigkeit*, the spirit of rational calculation."[7] In "Science as a Vocation," according to Thomas Kemple, Weber's purpose was to comprehend the passing of charismatic inspiration consequential on modernity's assumption of Rechenhaftigkeit, and to contemplate on what terms it might reappear. They would be terms, Weber said, of engagement: a matter not of "watching and waiting" but of "acting and working." But to know the meaning of that engagement, the truth of its terms of reenchantment, one would first have to pay one's debts to the demon "who holds the fibers of his very life."[8]

In Christianity as inspiration, in capitalism as parasite, in law as accountability, we will find that the juxtaposition of all the demonic ambiguities fuses them together in a structure of overwhelming simultaneity, a structure that is both economic and juridical, both moral and psychological, both profane and sacral.[9] They form a phantasmagoria, a congealed armature, "dialectics at a standstill."[10] Turner's rebellion both underscores that fusion and renders it momentarily legible. We have already encountered the demonic in chapter 3, at the crossroads of faith and ethics, in Turner's invisible decision to act. We have seen that to precipitate the event Turner had to shed the garb of the lonely knight of faith, cease his watching and waiting, and enter on the field of engagement, of action and work, the profane world of persuasion, which is also the ethico-legal world of guilt.[11] So doing, he acquired his own demonic ambiguity, for persuasion is indebting. But, in its orthogonal eruption out of the continuum of history, Turner's rebellion instantiated the event's decisive temporal discontinuities. In its extremity, it was a rupture in the armature's "myth and dream-work," its endless Rechenhaftigkeit.[12] For at its center lay a "precious but tasteless seed"[13]—Turner's answer to the retributive tribunal's charge: "*Not guilty*; saying to his counsel, that he did not feel so."[14]

What does it mean that Turner did not feel guilty?

I. CAPITALISM AS RELIGION

Nat Turner's trial, we have seen, took place on November 5, 1831, before a bench of ten magistrates, Jeremiah Cobb, Esquire, presiding.[15] The case report that Thomas Ruffin Gray wrote includes what purports to be the statement Cobb made in sentencing Turner to hang. Cobb accuses Turner of depriving Southampton County "of many of our most valuable citizens," of forcing them (and his deceased black comrades) "from Time to Eternity." Perhaps infuriated by Turner's plea, Cobb labels him "borne down by this load of guilt." In the climactic "acts" of the court, for which its clerk, James Rochelle, will demand of the world "full faith and credit," Cobb sentences Turner to an emphatic death—"hung by the neck until you are dead! dead! dead"—but just as emphatically he sentences Turner to everlasting guilt: "The blood of all cries aloud, and calls upon you, as the author of their misfortune."[16]

In commentary on Walter Benjamin's "Capitalism as Religion," the late Werner Hamacher annexes the fragment to the ancient Greek equation of time with guilt that Benjamin discusses in contemporary notes on the concept of history, in which he calls guilt "the highest category" of world history:[17]

> Every world-historical moment is indebted and indebting. Cause and effect can never be decisive categories for the structure of world history, because they cannot determine any totality. . . . It is a mistake of the rationalistic conception of history to view any historical totality (that is, a state of the world) as cause or effect. A state of the world is, however, always guilty with regard to some later one.[18]

How is "Capitalism as Religion" related to this "guilt-history"? Hamacher explains: "If the task of a critique of history can only be satisfied by a critique of guilt-history"—history's highest category—"then the privileged object of this critique must be Christianity."[19] Why? The reason is to be found in another of Benjamin's essays, "Fate and Character," published in 1921. "An order whose sole intrinsic concepts are misfortune and guilt, and within which there is no conceivable path of liberation . . . cannot be religious, no matter how the misunderstood concept of guilt appears to suggest the contrary."[20] But Christianity is precisely the religion of guilt. Or rather, Christianity is "the religion of *guilt-economy*." Here is the first demonic ambiguity, followed closely by a second. Christianity is the religion of *guilt-economy* just as capitalism is "the system of a deterministic *debt-religion*."[21]

Benjamin's text-fragment attributes a religious form to capitalism.[22] This is not the Weberian contention that capitalism is "a formation *conditioned* by religion." Rather, Benjamin argues that in purporting to allay "the same anxieties, torments, and disturbances" that (so-called) religions address, capitalism is in itself "an essentially religious phenomenon."[23] Specifically, Benjamin identifies capitalism as a parasite on religion, an emanation of Reformed Christianity that, "by exploiting the 'demonic ambiguity' of its culpabalizing *and* indebting power," takes control of its host to such an extent that the history of Reformed Christianity eventually becomes entirely the history of its parasite.[24]

As religion, capitalism has three features, all of which are extremes. First, it is "purely cultic," which means it is bereft of a theology. "In capitalism, things have a meaning only in their relationship to the cult" (for example, "valuable citizens").[25] Second, it is unending, incessant, celebrated "*sans [t]rêve et sans merci*. . . . There is no day that is not a feast day."[26] Third, "the cult makes guilt pervasive."[27] Capitalism, says Hamacher, is "a structure of belief and behavior, of law and economy," that organizes "the guilt- and debt-nexus of the living." It is "a system for the attribution of guilt as well as debt, just as all pagan cult-religions that precede it . . . just as Christianity that goes along and identifies with it."[28] Religious form and economic form become homologous. They fuse in a mutual production, accumulation, articulation, and universalization of guilt:

> Capitalism is probably the first instance of a cult that creates guilt, not atonement. In this respect, this religious system is caught up in the headlong rush of a larger movement. A vast sense of guilt that is unable to find relief seizes on the cult, not to atone for this guilt but to make it universal, to hammer it into the conscious mind, so as once and for all to include God in the system of guilt and thereby awaken in Him an interest in the process of atonement.[29]

The "vast sense of guilt" by which the cult of capitalism is seized, and which it universalizes, even to the inclusion of God, can be found represented in, for example, the Westminster Confession of Faith (1647):

> Man, by his fall into a state of sin, hath wholly lost all ability of will to any spiritual good accompanying salvation; so as a natural man, being altogether averse from that good, and dead in sin, is not able by his own strength, to convert himself, or to prepare himself thereunto.[30]

By God's immutable purpose, before the foundation of the world, some were predestined "out of His mere free grace and love, without any foresight of faith or good works" to everlasting life. As for the rest, "God was pleased, according to the unsearchable counsel of His own will . . . to ordain them to dishonor and wrath for their sin."[31]

How, we might ask (this was Max Weber's question), did the isolated and desperate individuals created by Reformed Christianity produce the social organization of capitalism? Precisely by their acceptance of the accompanying conception that the world existed solely "to serve the self-glorification of *God*" and that God "willed the social achievement of the Christian, *because* it was his will that the social structure of life should accord with his commands and be organized in such a way as to achieve this purpose."[32] The principal representation of Christian obedience?

Pursuit of a calling, the purposeful asceticism of which also served as the means "to strive for the subjective certainty of one's election and justification in daily struggle."[33] Unlike Nat Turner's joyful, ecstatic realization of his perfection, the Reformed Christian must struggle constantly against soul-corroding doubt.[34] Hence the "vast sense of guilt."[35] And rather than taking a mere "interest" in the believer's attempts to expiate sin, God becomes implicated in bearing the entire guilt/debt-burden. Both the Geneva Bible (1576, 1599) and the King James Bible (1611) have Christ teach the multitude to plead with God that he "forgive us our debts,"[36] that He take on His shoulders all the deficits of the world:

> The nature of the religious movement which is capitalism entails endurance right to the end, to the point where God, too, finally takes on the entire burden of guilt, to the point where the universe has been taken over by that despair which is actually its secret *hope*. Capitalism is entirely without precedent, in that it is a religion which offers not the reform of existence but its complete destruction. It is the expansion of despair, until despair becomes a religious state of the world in the hope that this will lead to salvation.[37]

Capitalism as cultic religion promises redemption but cannot deliver because the redeemer himself is irredeemably guilty. "God Himself has fallen from Himself."[38]

Benjamin's remorseless text finds no resolution to the ever-intensifying agony of guilt and despair that capitalism produces. It cannot be reformed from within. The most trenchant argument for capitalism's "reform" available—Marx's claim for the transfiguration of its most advanced stage into socialism—becomes simply more of the same: "The capitalism that refuses to change course becomes socialism by means of the simple and compound interest that are functions of *Schuld* [debt]."[39] Nor, given its universality, can there exist a position outside the cult from which to renounce the cult. Instead it holds out (endures) "right to the end."[40]

Hamacher argues that, at the extremity of the despair it engenders, in the finality of its destruction of all existence, the cult necessarily annihilates itself as well. "The 'utter guilt' of capital's divinity is thus the ultimate moment of a jump back to its origin where it becomes . . . the 'not' of guilt. At the origin, the law of retribution does not rule, but that of guilt's annihilation."[41] Annihilation is the orthogonal instant of justice that overwhelms capitalism's *durée* of despair. "It comes about not as reform or reformation, but as the true revolution eliminating at every moment the traces of the guilt-system. The nothing of this counter-history is time itself as the time to come."[42] To make his claim, Hamacher draws on another of Benjamin's unpublished fragments, "The Meaning of Time in the Moral Universe," also written in 1921.[43] Here (as in "Fate and Character") we encounter law: it is "the tendency to retribution," as such clearly a component in the cult of endless guilt. It exists in a world apart (sharply set off) from the moral universe of the fragment's title. Like the cult, retribution is endless, "fundamentally indifferent to the passage of time . . . it remains in force for centuries without dilution." Retribution even imposes, in a profoundly heathen way, on the Last Judgment, which it takes to be "the date when all postponements are ended and all retribution is allowed free rein." But in the moral universe forgiveness battles against the durée of retribution, and enlists time as its ally. For in the moral universe time "is not the lonely calm of fear but the tempestuous storm of forgiveness which precedes the onrush of the Last Judgment":

> This storm is not only the voice in which the evildoer's cry of terror is drowned; it is also the hand that obliterates the traces of his misdeeds, even if it must lay waste to the world in the process. As the purifying hurricane speeds ahead of the thunder and lightning, God's fury roars through history in the storm of forgiveness, in order to sweep away everything that would be consumed forever in the lightning bolts of divine wrath.[44]

Samuel Weber offers a less cathartic, less hopeful, interpretation of "Capitalism as Religion" than Werner Hamacher. As all-pervasive cult, capitalism completely overwhelms the phenomenological and theological world that existed prior to its emergence, putting in its place a new knowledge, knowledge only of itself, knowledge of *die Bilanz* (the bottom line). It seizes on a specific material practice—commerce's mode of calculus (Rechenhaftigkeit)—and renders it utterly ubiquitous. "All that is conceivable is continuation of the cult itself."[45] Bilanz is the knot that ties the faith of the individual worshipper to the cult's "salient trait," the interest-bearing function of money. (This, the capacity of money to price itself, and hence endlessly generate more of itself from itself, is what identifies capitalism in Benjamin's text, rather than the production of surplus value.)[46] "It is possible, indeed inevitable," says Weber, for capitalism "to 'hold out until the end' once that 'end' is determined as the bottom line, for each bottom line ends one balance sheet and begins another. The process is in principle infinite and yet immanent."[47]

Yet, like Hamacher (although in very different fashion), Weber is unwilling to leave us entirely entangled in the durée of despair. It became Benjamin's objective, most notably in *Das Passagenwerk* (*The Arcades Project*), to render visible, in the riot of material images that he called phantasmagoria, "the hidden framework" *die Armature* of commodity culture "that allows things to be seen, displayed, exhibited, desired, purchased, and consumed—but which itself remains generally unnoticed."[48] Rendering the framework legible renders the space it delimits, the space of the commodity and of commodity exchange, liable to alteration, its "layout" and that which is "laid-out" within it appearing in "the unstable dynamics of an ongoing relation: the lay of the land." The lay of the land can of course be stabilized, but there is nothing *in* it (as opposed to in the framework *surrounding* it) that imposes a particular stability.[49]

To use so apparently abstruse an engagement in the philosophy of history as an interpretive prism on empirical events is not without risk.[50] Still, in Turner's confession—its first part at least—and in the Southampton County Court's response to Turner we are dealing with philosophies of history quite as much as with historical events. Hence, resort to one species of messianic philosophy of history to help unravel another may be worthwhile.

With this in mind, consider first the philosophy manifest in Turner's utterly fractile statement that *he did not feel guilty*. Saidiya Hartman has drawn to our attention law's ruthless annexation of the African American, whether slave or freed, to guilt/debt. The self haltingly realized by the African American is entirely supplanted by a self imposed by law—a self of criminality and obligation.[51] Here (in Hamacher's terms) Turner is refusing that burden, stating that he is the *not* of the "load of guilt" that the court insists he bear for the dispatch of "valuable citizens" from "Time to Eternity." In the first part of the *Confessions* he has explicitly located the self of faith he has fashioned for himself far beyond the universalized guilt/debt nexus in which the court (with its cultic insistence that its acts be worshipped and credited) is so plainly embedded. To the court's demand that he humbly accept its retribution he has "nothing more to say."[52]

How can he stand beyond that nexus, which, we have seen, Benjamin appears to hold inescapable—a perfect fusion of the economic and the juridical with the moral and the psychological?[53] Consider the terms of Turner's decision to act: "I heard a loud noise in the heavens and the Spirit *instantly* appeared to me and said the Serpent was loosened and Christ had laid down the yoke he had born for the sins of men, *and that I should take it on and fight against the Serpent*."[54] In Christian eschatology the final battle against Satan immediately precedes the Last Judgment, when all forms of existence known hitherto are annihilated,[55] when "whosoever . . . not found written in the book of life [is] cast into the lake of fire," leaving only pure origin and end, "Alpha and Omega": God's eternal, forgiving, reign over man.[56] In Benjaminian terms, God's final abandonment of His burden of guilt (laying down the yoke) signifies Hamacher's "jump back" to origin—a distinct representation of the "not" of guilt—and the end of the time of retribution in the tempest of Messianic forgiveness and judgment. The parallel between the two representations of extremity is remarkable:

> If [liberation] is neither possible within the guilt-relations of the capital religion nor without them, then it is possible in a place—and only here—where these relations have reached an extreme that belongs neither to these relations themselves nor to their outside. The possibility of liberation from guilt can thus only be located at the very extreme of guilt. This extreme would be the outer- and innermost limit upon which guilt is no longer itself and yet is nothing other than itself, where it is—as guilt—freed of itself.[57]

Consider, finally, "decision" itself, which for Benjamin is an index of human freedom in the realm of faith, freedom without the "demonic," which is to say "creaturely," ambiguity of the Hegelian universal's moral choice: "Only the decision, not the choice, is inscribed in the book of life. For choice is natural and can even belong to the elements; decision is transcendent."[58] In the demonic material life-world of Southampton County's commodified slavery, Turner did not possess choice. In the metaphysical world of his own faith—pondering, eventually finding, and ultimately realizing his purpose—decision became his. Is this why Gray seems so fascinated by "the decision of his character," by Turner's "natural intelligence and quickness of apprehension . . . surpassed by few men I have ever seen"?[59] Turner realizes his vocation is decision—to fight against the Serpent, whether it be Satan or parasite. No wonder one can sense stark truth in Gray's famous wince: "I looked on him and my blood curdled in my veins."[60] Why does his blood curdle? It curdles because he has seen Turner, really seen him, for the first time. He has looked on Turner and has encountered the Real; or what is the same thing, his own lack gazing back at him.[61] "It is a dreadful thing to be in relationship with the gods really present. Painful and unexpected consequences may ensue."[62]

II. SCIENCE AS A VOCATION

Nat Turner's purpose in revealing his life story was to open others' eyes to the sacred space and time in which they lived and would die. Thomas Ruffin Gray's purpose in compositing *The Confessions of Nat Turner* was to pay down his debts by trading on the notoriety of the Southampton County "insurrection." But there was more to his labor than money-making. Gray coveted the role of authoritative commentator on Turner's rebellion, and on his capture and condemnation. He effected that role by overwriting Turner's revelation with a competing—and, necessarily, under the circumstances, commanding—theory of the events and their cause that determinedly "made sense" out of what had happened. He took an empirical *blur*—darkness and light, heat and dust, elation and panic, excitement and terror, alcohol and blood, confusion, chaos—and methodically *organized* it. His account is a rational empirical *accounting*, blow-by-blow, step-by-step, of innocent whites killed and guilty blacks captured. Gray sought to make the blur knowable, and knowable *as a slave rebellion*, by turning forty-eight hours of action into a particular kind of secular knowledge—*Also, an Authentic Account of the Whole Insurrection*.[63] A balance sheet.

The rational and empirical second half of the confession repudiates the metaphysics of the first part, restoring earthly temporal and spatial order and providing explanation. Turner is exposed to view as "a gloomy fanatic . . . bewildered, and overwrought." Here was no methodical adversary, says Gray, no systematic plan, no widespread conspiracy, no revenge for a (deniable but comprehensible) tally of oppressions and injustices, no inherent systemic failure. The explanation why a "calm and peaceful" society was suddenly torn apart by "woe and death" is sheer chance—the random visitation on valuable citizens of the primitive irrationality of a lone maniac's confounded mind. The proper response, hence, is not panic or self-questioning but redoubled reliance on precisely the positivist rationality on display in the pamphlet. Gray's account "is calculated . . . to demonstrate the policy of our laws in restraint of this class of our population" and to recommend "that they are strictly and rigidly enforced."[64]

From a Weberian perspective, the purpose and the achievement of Gray's pamphlet is "disenchantment." The trope is the theme of Max Weber's "Science as a Vocation" and one of the best known of his observations of modernity. "The fate of our times is characterized by rationalization and intellectualization and, above all, by the 'disenchantment of the world.'"[65] Rationalization and intellectualization were the products of scientific thinking—"our common fate and . . . our common goal." Their practical meaning was not that humanity had, per se, acquired "an increased and general knowledge" of the conditions under which it lived, but that if it so wished it *could* acquire that knowledge "at any time." This momentous alteration in humanity's circumstances meant that "there are no mysterious incalculable forces that come into play . . . one can, in principle, master all things by calculation." Calculability had disenchanted the world. "One need no longer have recourse to magical means in order to master or implore the spirits. . . . Technical means and calculations perform the service."[66]

Weber's stance was not normative. Disenchantment was not to be welcomed, or regretted. It was simply the way of the world, the slow substitution of one onto-epistemological reality for another. In Gray's case, in contrast, normativity stood uppermost—the crushing of fanaticism beneath the ordered rationality of empirical explanation and positive law was a social good. It was the framework reestablished, the lay of the land restabilized, the blood-curdling Real tidied away.

Gray had allies in the enterprise of orderliness: the justices of the Southampton County Court, who likewise contrasted their "justice" to Turner's "fanaticism";[67] other commentators;[68] and the agencies of the state, not least Governor John Floyd. Floyd's letters and diary entries for late August and September 1831 are full of the bustle and relay of brisk executive command. Information is received, "men, arms, ammunition, etc." ordered into action: "Captain Randolph with a fine troop of cavalry and Captain John B. Richardson with light artillery [and] one thousand stand of arms," along with "two companies of Infantry from Norfolk and Portsmouth."[69] Floyd never displays the least doubt that the insurrection will be crushed—his biggest concern is the "wretched and abominable" state constitution, which keeps putting "vain and foolish ceremony" in his way. "I must first require advice of Council, and then disregard it, if I please." By early September, Floyd's diary entries recording the disposition of his forces have become routine, interspersed with remarks on the stream of sentencing records arriving from Southampton for gubernatorial approval and comments on his own health.[70]

But on September 7, momentarily alarmed by a report of insubordination amongst "negroes" in Northampton and Accomack, a tired and feverish Floyd allows himself to wonder whether "this insurrection in Southampton is to lead to much more disastrous consequences than is at this time apprehended by anybody." What he has on his mind may be as much revealed by a letter written five days earlier as by unsubstantiated rumors of renewed revolt. We have already encountered this letter, but it is worth drawing attention to it again: "What the effect of this insurrection is to be upon the commercial credit of the state, upon individual credit, is a point of view not all pleasant, to say nothing upon interest upon loans for the state itself, should she ever wish to borrow."[71]

Southampton's county court would in due course seek credit for its rational juridical action. Floyd's epistolary anxiety grants us a glimpse of credit's vaster workings. Credit underpinned all of the state's valuable citizens. It underpinned the state itself. Could the faith of creditors in the value of citizens and state falter just because of a ragged bunch of rebellious slaves and their crazed prophet-leader? Could the lay of the land be so destabilized?[72]

In Floyd's rush of anxiety we can actually see all the demonic ambiguities—faith and credit, guilt and debt, the economic, the juridical, the moral, and the psychological—collapsing in on each other, fusing in one august, deeply threatening, simultaneity: a monad.[73] Marx's theogeny of capital disinters its meaning.[74] "The public debt becomes one of the most powerful levers of primitive accumulation. As with the stroke of an enchanter's wand, it endows unproductive money with the power of creation, and thus turns it into capital." Hence "public credit becomes the *credo* of capital. . . . Lack of faith in the national debt takes the place of the sin against the Holy Ghost, for which there is no forgiveness."[75] Barren money becomes fertile, as Hamacher remarks, in "a sacramental process of indebting that endows capital with productivity . . . a generative process within God Himself."[76]

> The mechanics of debt—of "advanced" or "credited" money—compose the process by which value transforms itself into surplus value—which is what defines value as value to begin with. This transformation is the process of a god's genesis out of something that is not—a theogeny out of self-incurred debts. And more precisely, it is a theogeny out of credit, a credit that is itself drawn from unpaid labor, exploitation, colonization, theft and murder, legalized under the laws of the privileged.[77]

Such was Governor Floyd's disquiet that he was moved to emphasize the peace, the "*profound* peace," that Virginia's dragoons, and infantry, and artillery, and its thousand stand of arms, had restored to Southampton County.[78] The "unpaid labor, exploitation, colonization, theft and murder, legalized under the laws of the privileged" that constituted the state's guarantee of capital's bottom line would continue undisturbed.[79] "What . . . would be thought" were it to appear otherwise?[80] Credit's demands—and the demand for credit—held Floyd's life in its grip, and Virginia's.[81]

CONCLUSION: THE THREAT OF STONE

We have seen that Southampton's local difficulties prompted the Virginia legislature to debate the possibility of eradicating slavery from the state by gradual emancipation, and that the debate provoked Thomas Roderick Dew to write his lengthy critique of the case for eradication from the impeccably disenchanted perspective of political economy. Dew thought the very idea of debating abolition imprudent, but "in its zeal for discussion" the legislature had ignored prudence. Well and good. "The seal has now been broken."[82]

Like Thomas Ruffin Gray, only more so, Thomas Roderick Dew sought to bring order of a particular kind to the chaos of divergent opinion, to enlist "the empire of reason" to quell proposals he labeled products of "excitement and apprehension." The calculus of political economy showed the abolition of slavery in Virginia to be unimaginable, an impossibility: "Every plan of emancipation and deportation which we can possibly conceive, is *totally* impracticable." Without slavery the state would be ruined. "Virginia will be a desert."[83]

There are odd but interesting conjunctions between the disenchanted world of Thomas Roderick Dew's political economy and the sacred space and time in which Nat Turner dwelled. Both Dew and Turner "spoke out" on matters they judged of immense importance, but only after the removal of a seal.[84] Both were preoccupied with numbers that they invested with crucial significance. (Some of their numbers were the same.)[85] Both remarked on how difficult it was "to fall upon any definite plan which can for a moment command . . . approbation."[86]

For Dew, the difficulty was decisive: there was simply no calculable means to abolish slavery in Virginia that could preserve the state from "the blighting hand of Providence"—the revulsion of capital that would "render our soil barren and our labor unproductive."[87] Slavery was

Virginia's destiny. In contrast, Turner and his comrades confronted difficulty, formulated a plan, and put it into effect. In two senses the failure of their plan seems to prove Dew right. First, failure was undoubtedly "an unerring symptom of the difficulty and impracticability of the whole."[88] Second, it furnished decisive evidence that slaves were indeed too valuable to surrender. As state law provided, the rebellious slaves condemned to death were all valued by the Southampton County Court. The mean value of the thirty condemned was $377. Dew valued the entire Virginia slave population as of the 1830 census at $94 million, the average slave being worth in his estimation only $200.[89] The Southampton rebels were well above his undervalued average. Had all been executed they would have cost the state $11,310, more than 10 percent of its precious treasury surplus,[90] only adding to the fiscal anxieties of Governor Floyd.

In Dew's calculus of Virginia slavery we see one of the workings of the chattel principle—"the property principle, the bill of sale principle," the principle of the priced person.[91] But the very existence of these priced people frustrated Dew's rationality. As his political economy of property rights in priced people remorselessly shot down solution after solution, plan after plan, Dew's tone, oddly, became more frantic than triumphal. "All of these plans merit nothing more than the appellation of *vain juggling legislative conceits*, unworthy of a wise statesman." At times Dew was not so much defending slavery as defining paralysis. He appears to desire an answer for Virginia's "great difficulty," its self-proclaimed, self-pitying, ordeal-by-bondage, yet his rationality deprives him. And so he vents. "All these puerile conceits fall far short of surmounting the great difficulty which, like Memnon, is eternally present and cannot be removed."[92]

Eternally present. Cannot be removed. Guilt/debt, faith/credit, the economic, the juridical, the moral, the psychological: fused in eternal immobility. Turner's decision to act—to hack into slavery's monadic ineffability, to blast it out of the continuum of history—stands in world-historical contrast to Dew's rationalist rigor mortis. In decision lies fulfillment.[93]

For Herman Melville, chronicler of the antebellum republic's increasingly troubled *herrenvolk* psyche, Memnon was an immense rock, "menacingly impending," that seemed like nothing so much as an enormous tombstone looming over the lay of the land.[94] Pierre—he of the ambiguities—"squeezed himself into the narrow space between the earth and overhanging boulder," and, lying prostrate in the embrace of what he calls the Terror Stone for an orthogonal, eternal, instant, he tempts demonic Fate. "If invisible devils do titter at us when we most nobly strive; if Life be a cheating dream . . . if Duty's self be but a bugbear, and all things are allowable and unpunishable to man;—then do thou, Mute Massiveness, fall on me! Ages thou hast waited."[95] Nothing happens. The stone does not move. "Modernity exists under the sign of absence."[96]

Augustus Toplady, Charles and John Wesley, Nikolaus Ludwig, Count von Zinzendorf, Jonathan Edwards, countless others then and since—all had sought spiritual comfort in the unclosed cleft, the side wound of Jesus. The irreligious Thomas Ruffin Gray had not; not, that is, until the very end of his life, when he met head on his fear of death.[97] And Pierre? For him, if he did, no comfort was there to be found. Eventually, "Pierre crawled forth . . . and went his moody way."[98] Melville, says Stephen Hartnett, was recording the historical degeneration of onetime Protestant glories into antebellum "capitalist hubbub," with its "endless ambiguity," its pell-mell greed, its deep and permanent solicitude for nothing but the bottom line. Such was the Bethlehem toward which Pierre slouched.[99]

Nor would there be any comfort in the cleft for Thomas Roderick Dew. Probably, like Gray (at least until Gray's final moments), he did not feel the need. Dew was a prig, Michael O'Brien tells us, morally inert. He had sold his mortal soul to political economy, and it had granted him its secular salvation, its complaisant certainties, its Mephistophelean promise of an unlimited prosperity for which, in return, nothing would be required but time (and internal improvements).[100]

But the Memnon that Dew's facile display of learning had summoned from the shades of antiquity—this Memnon was not so mute, so impassive, so unmoving. This Memnon lived. It vibrated. This Memnon might crush him.[101]

"All the sources of wealth and departments of industry, all the great interests of society, are really interwoven with one another," we have seen Dew write. They formed "an indissoluble chain," such that "a blow at any part quickly vibrates through the whole length—the destruction of one interest involves another."[102] In the form of Nat Turner, body of Christ, the broken, thrown-down statue of the Ethiopian warrior-king had taken to its feet. It had struck a blow at the indissoluble chain.

"As with all that appears exceptional . . . the imaginary life of statues has its own laws."[103]

The image was not Dew's to control. Instead, in its orthogonal instant, Turner's rebellion had pieced together "what history has broken to bits."[104] It had loosed the threat that lay within the stone,[105] the lives that, by defending their enslavement, Dew had ensured would remain present and unremoved; lives "silent and strong, biding their time,"[106] the fiber of Dew's own life twisting in their grip. That is why Memnon would haunt Thomas Roderick Dew. Despite his priggishness, perhaps, he could sense the bad ending to come:[107]

> The master's room was wide open. The master's room was brightly lit, and the master was there very calm . . . and our men stopped . . . he was the master . . . I went in.
>
> It's you, he said to me, very calmly . . .
>
> It was I, it was indeed me, I said to him, the good slave, the faithful slave, the slavish slave . . .
>
> and suddenly his eyes were two cockroaches frightened on a rainy day . . .
>
> I struck, the blood spurted:
>
> that's the only baptism I remember today.[108]

We who are readers of texts, who are historians, if we are to read as true historians, we must always be ready to read what was never written.[109] Always.

ACKNOWLEDGMENTS

I cannot now remember what first stirred my curiosity about Nat Turner. Suffice it to say, he has been somewhere in the back of my mind for many, many years. I did not write about him until the early 1990s, and then only indirectly (that essay, revised, now forms part of chapter 6 in this book), but in the wake of my last book, *Freedom Bound* (2010), I decided that it was time to attempt to take him on. After *Freedom Bound*, which ambitiously addresses close to a half millennium of Anglo-American history, I told myself to try something I thought would be more precise, more focused. As it turned out, I soon found myself writing about God.

No book would ever be written without the assistance of others, both friends and strangers, willing to add to their own burdens in order to lighten that of the author. It is an enormous pleasure to acknowledge all those who have helped make *In the Matter of Nat Turner* possible. Catherine Fisk, James Martel, Kunal Parker, Anat Rosenberg, Lena Salaymeh, Bryan Wagner, and Barbara Welke all read complete drafts of the manuscript at different moments in its evolution, and offered advice, criticism, and encouragement. Jim Sidbury read the near-final draft as well as the first. Jim has been a source of wisdom and support ever since I decided that I would try to write a book about Nat Turner. Two anonymous readers for Princeton University Press added to the harvest of advice. Fredrika Teute provided an early stimulus. Jon Butler generously shared some research notes.

Eric Crahan, my editor at Princeton, expressed keen interest when I first mentioned the book to him, and his enthusiasm never flagged. It has been a pleasure to renew a working relationship with Eric that began years ago at Cambridge University Press. Others at Princeton University Press have been equally supportive. Pamela Weidman and Thalia Leaf brought cheerful energy and commitment to the demanding process of making my manuscript ready for production. Jack Rummel was a patient and thoughtful copy editor. Tobiah Waldron took charge of the index. Nathan Carr, Pamela Schnitter, and Brigid Ackerman oversaw production and design.

Among the tasks that ready a manuscript for production, one that usually occurs quite late in the process is that of obtaining permissions for the use of copyrighted materials that are not or may not be governed by criteria of "fair use," such as artistic epigraphs, or that are used as illustrations. Many people helped me with this task in one form or another, by smoothing the path to obtaining this or that illustration, or by simply answering questions and directing me to the help I sought. I have never met any of the following, but I should like to thank them all for their assistance: Michael Barnes; Tracie Butler; Federico Campagna; Michael Carlisle; Mike Caulo; Ruth Dennis; Graham Dozier; Melvin C. Farrington; Carrie Feldman; Laura Fogarty; Gerald Gaidmore; Kealy Gordon; Diane Grossé; Garmon Gruffudd; Tomislav Ljevar; Jeff Mangum; Carter Manley; Jeff Moen; Susan Munro; Christina Rentz; Mark Richardson; Marcus Robbins; Laure Schlink; Alexandra Styron; Michele von Ebers; Claire Weatherhead; and Stephanie B. Williams.

Since I began this work, friends and colleagues at a number of institutions, and at academic meetings across the world, have generously taken the time to discuss elements of the book with me as it took shape in the form of a series of research papers. I persisted in describing those papers (to myself as well as to my interlocutors) as "experiments" rather than proto-chapters because that is how I thought of them. I felt that as long as I could call my work experimental I had a license to "speculate" in the constructive fashion that I have tried hard to carry over into the book. I tried out some rudimentary first thoughts in early 2011 on participants in UC Irvine Law School's "in progress" workshop, and also at the New Projects Workshop of the Program in Law and Public Affairs at Princeton. Those first thoughts became a paper entitled "Demonic Ambiguities: Enchantment and Disenchantment in Nathaniel Turner's Virginia," first delivered at the Conference on the New History of American Capitalism at Harvard University (November 2011) and as a History Faculty Lecture at Melbourne University the following month. It was later discussed at the second biennial Law As . . . Symposium, held at UC Irvine (March 2012), at the 2012 Law & Society Association Annual Meeting in Hawai'i (June 2012), and at the conference Markets, Law, and Ethics, 1300–1850, held at the University of Sheffield (June 2012). A second paper, soon followed, "Debt, Death, and Redemption: Toward a Soterial-Legal History of the Turner Rebellion." It became a keynote address at the United Kingdom Socio-Legal Studies Association Conference, Exploring the Legal in Socio-Legal Studies, held at the London School of Economics and Political Science (September 2012), and again at the Australian and New Zealand Law and History Society's Annual Meeting, University of Technology Sydney (December 2012). It was also discussed at New World(s) of Faith: Religion and Law in Historical Perspective, 1500–2000, a conference held at the University of Pennsylvania Law School (June 2013); at a meeting of the Network for Interdisciplinary Studies of Law at the University of New South Wales Law School in Sydney (August 2013); and at faculty seminars for the Miller Center for Historical Studies, University of Maryland, College Park (December 2012), the Department of History, University of California San Diego (January 2013), and the Department of History, Queen Mary, University of London (May 2014). I unleashed "The Turner Rebellion: A Project for Legal History," on my future colleagues at Berkeley Law in January 2013, and followed up with "Styron's Nat" at the Association for the Study of Law, Culture, and the Humanities Annual Meeting in London (March 2013). "Styron's Nat" was also discussed at the University of Minnesota Law School's Legal History Workshop (April 2013); the Law & Society Association Annual Meeting in Boston (May 2013); at Law Faculty seminars at Australian National University (August 2013) and the University of Colorado School of Law, Boulder (October 2013); at the Australian and New Zealand Law and History Society Annual Meeting at the University of Otago, Dunedin, Aotearoa/New Zealand (December 2013); and at the Fifth Berg International Conference, The Arts in Legal History, held at the Buchmann Faculty of Law, Tel Aviv University (June 2014). "*The Confessions of Nat Turner*: Paratextual Cadences," first saw light of day at the Conference Law, History, Culture: Reading Sources, held at the Faculty of Law, University of Technology Sydney (July 2013). It was followed by "Revulsions of Capital: The Political Law of Slavery in the Epoch of the Turner Rebellion, Virginia, 1829–1832," first presented at the Center for the Study of Law and Society, Berkeley (September 2014), and then at the Elizabeth Battelle Clark Workshop, Boston University School of Law (October 2014); the 2014 Annual Meeting of the American Society for Legal History in Denver, Colorado (November 2014); the Huntington Library (November 2014); and the Australian and New Zealand Law and History Society Annual Meeting at the University of New England, Coffs Harbour (December 2014). "The Work of Death: Massacre and Retribution in Southampton County, Virginia, August 1831" was discussed by faculty workshops at Stanford Law School and at Berkeley Law (both September 2015), and at the University of Kent, Canterbury, UK (June 2016). It was also given as a keynote address to the North American Labor History Conference,

Wayne State University, Detroit, Michigan (October 2015); as a public lecture to the Buchmann Faculty of Law, Tel Aviv University (May 2016); and as a paper presented at the Law, Literature, and the Humanities Association of Australasia Annual Meeting in Sydney (December 2015), and the "Cruel and Unusual" Research Symposium on Legal Violence at Concordia University, Montreal (April 2016). Finally, "'The Guilt of Fragile Sovereigns': Tyranny, Intrigue, and Martyrdom in an Unchanging Regime (Virginia, 1829–32)" was discussed by the Settler Colonialism Working Group, Tel Aviv University, and by a legal cultures research colloquium at the Radzyner School of Law, Interdisciplinary Center (IDC) Herzliya, Israel (both in May 2016). To all of the organizers of all these events, and to all of those in attendance who asked questions and offered critical comments, I am deeply grateful.

As this roster of research papers suggests, many elements of *In the Matter of Nat Turner* have appeared in earlier formulations as published articles, or as chapters or essays in edited collections. Although some of these earlier publications correlate roughly with this book's chapters, it is fairer to say both that their influence is scattered throughout the book, and at the same time that the book's chapters are substantially more considered presentations of the ideas first advanced somewhat piecemeal in the earlier publications. With these provisos in mind, research for the prologue first appeared in "Styron's Nat: or, The Metaphysics of Presence," *Critical Analysis of Law* 2, no. 2 (2015): 383–96, and reappears here with thanks to *CAL*. Research for chapter 1 first appeared in "*The Confessions of Nat Turner*: A Paratextual Analysis," *law&history* 1 (2014): 1–28, and (in revised form) in "Looking for Law in *The Confessions of Nat Turner*," in Marianne Constable, Leti Volpp, and Bryan Wagner, editors, *Looking for Law in All the Wrong Places: Justice Beyond and Between* (New York: Fordham University Press, 2019), 225–45. I am grateful to *law&history* and to Fordham University Press, respectively, for the opportunity to reuse work that they first published. Elements of chapter 2 first appeared in "Debt, Death, and Redemption: Toward a Soterial-Legal History of the Turner Rebellion," in David Cowan and Daniel Wincott, editors, *Exploring the Legal in Socio-Legal Studies* (London: Palgrave-Macmillan, 2016), 35–56. I am grateful for the opportunity to reuse work that first appeared under Palgrave MacMillan's imprint. A curtailed version of chapter 4 appeared as "The Work of Death: Massacre and Retribution in Southampton County, Virginia, August 1831," in Joshua Nichols and Amy Swiffen, editors, *Legal Violence and the Limits of the Law: Cruel and Unusual* (Abingdon, UK: Routledge, 2017), 92–107. That work is reproduced here by permission of Informa UK Limited through PLSclear. Seeds of chapter 5 are to be found in "'The Guilt of Fragile Sovereigns': Tyranny, Intrigue, and Martyrdom in an Unchanging Regime (Virginia, 1829–32)," *Critical Analysis of Law* 3, no. 2 (2016): 286–305. Thanks once again to *CAL*, and to Norm Spaulding, for that initial opportunity to think about "regime change." A substantially curtailed version of chapter 6 appeared as "Revulsions of Capital: The Political Economy of Slavery in the Epoch of the Turner Rebellion, Virginia, 1829–1832," in Sven Beckert and Christine Desan, editors, *American Capitalism: New Histories* (New York: Columbia University Press, 2018), 195–217. That work is reused here with permission of Columbia University Press. The approach taken in the book's epilogue was first tried out in "Demonic Ambiguities: Enchantment and Disenchantment in Nat Turner's Virginia," *UC Irvine Law Review* 4, no. 1 (March 2014): 175–202. My thanks to the law review for its attention and editing work on that occasion. That essay was subsequently reprinted in Simon Middleton and James Shaw, editors, *Market Ethics and Practices, c.1300–1850* (London: Routledge, 2017), 87–106. I am grateful for the opportunity to reuse that work here. Finally, research that originally appeared under the title "In Nat Turner's Shadow: Reflections on the Norfolk Dry Dock Affair of 1830–1831," *Labor History* 33, no. 4 (fall 1992): 494–518, is the basis for part III of chapter 6. That work is reused here by permission of Taylor & Francis Ltd, www.tandfonline.com.

Reader response theory teaches authors that readers are active participants in literary works, creating their own meanings through their own interpretations of the texts they encounter. I have always thought of epigraphs as an author's way of leaving the reader clues to the author's intentions in a work. Here, from the very first pages of this book, I have used epigraphs closely related to the book's content to try to establish the book's tone, and to indicate to the reader how I hope its words will be received. Many are taken from the King James Bible, and those require no further identification here. Details of the remainder follow. The opening quotation from Walter Benjamin (1923) is from "The Task of the Translator," originally published in *Charles Baudelaire, "Tableaux parisiens": Deutsche Übertragung mit einem Vorwort über die Aufgabe des Übersetzers, von Walter Benjamin* (Heidelberg: Verlag von Richard Weissbach, 1923), in Walter Benjamin, *Illuminations*, edited and with an introduction by Hannah Arendt, Harry Zohn translator (New York: Schocken Books, 1968), 69–82, 70. The epigraph to the preface is from Thomas Wolfe, *Look Homeward, Angel* (New York: Charles Scribner's Sons, 1929), 3. The epigraph to the prologue is from William Styron, "Afterword to the Vintage Edition: Nat Turner Revisited," in William Styron, *The Confessions of Nat Turner* (New York: Vintage International, 1993), 435, and is used here by permission of William Styron's estate. The epigraph to chapter 1 is from Thomas Carlyle, *Past and Present* (London: Chapman and Hall, 1872), 208–9. The first epigraph to chapter 2 is from Ann Griffiths, Hymn II Verse 3 (English translation), in H. A. Hodges, *Flame in the Mountains: William Pantycelyn, Ann Griffiths and the Welsh Hymn* (Talybont: Y Lolfa, 2017), and is used here by permission of Y Lolfa. The second epigraph to chapter 2 is from Phillis Wheatley, "On The Death Of The Rev. Mr. George Whitefield, 1770," in *Poems on Various Subjects, Religious and Moral, by Phillis Wheatley, Negro Servant to Mr. John Wheatley, of Boston, in New England* (London: Printed for A. Bell, Bookseller, Aldgate; and sold by Messrs. Cox and Berry, King Street, Boston, 1773), 23. The epigraph to chapter 3 is from Alain Badiou, *Polemics* (London: Verso, 2011), 8, and is used here by permission of Verso. The epigraph to chapter 4, part 1 is from Joseph Holmes, "Interview of June 17, 1937," Image 199 of *Federal Writers' Project: Slave Narrative Project, Vol. 1, Alabama, Aarons-Young* (Created/Published 1936–37), Source Collection: Federal Writer's Project, U.S. Work Projects Administration (USWPA) http://hdl.loc.gov/loc.mss/mesn.010 (last accessed February 22, 2019) Library of Congress. The epigraph to chapter 4, part 2, is from John Sergeant Wise, *The End of an Era* (Boston and New York: Houghton, Mifflin and Company, 1899), 44. The epigraph to chapter 4, part 3 is from "A Discussion: The Uses of History in Fiction: Ralph Ellison, William Styron, Robert Penn Warren, C. Vann Woodward (moderator)," *Southern Literary Journal* 1, no. 2 (spring 1969): 82. The epigraph to chapter 4, part 5 is from Gilles Deleuze, *Francis Bacon: The Logic of Sensation*, translated and with an introduction by Daniel W. Smith (Minneapolis: University of Minnesota Press, 2003), 21, and is used here by permission of the University of Minnesota Press. *Francis Bacon: The Logic of Sensation* was published in French as *Francis Bacon: Logique de la sensation* Copyright 2002. Les Éditions du Seuil. A first edition of this work was published in 1981 by Éditions de la Différence. English translation copyright Continuum International Publishing Group Ltd. The epigraph to chapter 4, part 6 is from Franz Kafka, *In the Penal Colony*, Ian Johnston translator (New Delhi: Kartindo Books, 2013), 2. The epigraph to chapter 5 is from Thomas Roderick Dew, *Review of the Debate in the Virginia Legislature of 1831 and 1832* (Richmond: Printer by T. W. White, opposite the Bell Tavern, 1832), 64. The first epigraph to chapter 6 is from Benjamin Watkins Leigh, *The Letter of Appomatox to the People of Virginia: Exhibiting a Connected View of the Recent Proceedings in the House of Delegates, on the Subject of the Abolition of Slavery: And a Succinct Account of the Doctrines Broached by the Friends of Abolition, in Debate: And the Mischievous Tendency of those Proceedings and Doctrines* (Richmond: Thomas W. White, Printer, 1832), 7. The second epigraph to chapter 6 is from Thomas Roderick Dew, *Review of the Debate*, 68. The third epigraph to chapter 6 is from Ian Baucom, *Specters of the Atlantic: Finance Capital, Slavery, and the Philosophy of History* (Durham, NC: Duke University Press, 2005), 17. The epigraph to the Epilogue is from Walter Benjamin, "The Dialectical Image," in "Paralipomena to 'On the Concept of History,'" written in 1940, in Howard Eiland and Michael W. Jennings, editors, *Walter Benjamin: Selected Writings, Volume 4, 1938–1940* (Cambridge, MA: Harvard University Press, 2003), 405. The verses by Vic Chesnutt that appear as epigraphs to parts I and II, and the words of the titles of the three parts of this book, are all taken from the composition *Glossolalia*, words by Vic Chesnutt, music by Jeff Mangum. Copyright © 2007 by Ghetto Bells Music and Unknown Publisher. All Rights for Ghetto Bells Music Administered by BMG Rights Management (US) LLC. All Rights Reserved. Used by Permission. Reprinted by Permission of Hal Leonard LLC. The epigraph to part III is from Søren Kierkegaard, *Fear and Trembling: Dialectical Lyric*, C. Stephen Evans and Sylvia Walsh, editors (Cambridge: Cambridge University Press, 2006), 101, originally published in Danish as *Frygt og Bæven: Dialektisk Lyrik* (Copenhagen: C. A. Reitzel, 1843), Sylvia Walsh translator.

The reproduction of the cover of William Styron's *The Confessions of Nat Turner* (1st ed., 1967) appears by permission of Penguin/Random House. The reproduction of the title page of Thomas Ruffin Gray's *The Confessions of Nat Turner* (1st ed., 1831), is from Special Collections, Swem Library, College of William & Mary, to whom I am grateful for their generosity. The photograph of Nat Turner's Bible is by Michael Barnes of the Smithsonian Institution. It appears by permission of the National Museum of African American History and Culture. The reproduction of the woodcut entitled "Horrid Massacre in Virginia" comes from the Photo, Prints and Drawings Collection of the Library of Congress (Digital Collections). It can be found at https://www.loc.gov/item/98510363/. The photograph of the Virginia State Capitol (engraving by Fermer Sears and Co. after the painting by William Goodacre, published on November 1, 1831, by I. T. Hinton & Strupkin & Marshall of London), and the photograph of George Catlin's painting of the Virginia State Convention (1829–30) are both from the Virginia Museum of History

& Culture, and appear by permission of the Museum. The construction drawing of the Dry Dock at the Norfolk Navy Yard was made available for reproduction by Marcus W. Robbins, to whom I am grateful for his generous assistance. It can be found at http://www.usgwarchives.net/va/portsmouth/shipyard/Drydock1.pdf. The reproduction of the USS *Delaware* in the Norfolk Navy Yard Dry Dock (lithograph by Childs and Tranum, Philadelphia, after an original drawing by Joseph Goldsborough Bruff) is from the Navy Art Collection, Naval History and Heritage Command, and appears by permission of the Navy Art Collection. The reproduction of William Garl Browne Jr.'s painting of John Floyd, twenty-fifth governor of Virginia (1830–34), is from The Library of Virginia and appears by permission of the Library. The reproduction of William Garl Browne Jr.'s painting of Thomas Roderick Dew, professor of history, metaphysics, and political law at the College of William & Mary, and later president of the college (1836–46), is from the Muscarelle Museum of Art, College of William & Mary, and appears by permission of the Museum.

I close these acknowledgments with two people, one of whom I never knew personally, the other I have known since 1978. The first is the late Anthony Kaye. When I discovered early in my own work that Tony Kaye was also pursuing Nat Turner I wrote to him to introduce myself. He generously welcomed me to the "murky waters" of Cabin Pond. We exchanged occasional messages, and papers, but never met, and seemed to be going in different directions. My work on Turner had taken its soterial (salvific) course early on, very different from what I took to be Tony's original interest in extending his work on neighborhoods (first described in *Joining Places*) and his newer research on the influence that he thought Old Testament descriptions of warfare had had on Turner's conception of his rebellion. I was saddened by the news of Tony's death in May 2017. Then, on reading Greg Downs's obituary in the *Journal of the Civil War Era*, I learned our paths toward Nat Turner had begun to converge in at least some respects. It sorrows me that I will not have a chance to read Tony's book about the man who fascinated both of us, or to hear what he thought of mine.

The second person is my wife, Ann, to whom this book is dedicated. When I told her I had decided to write a book about Nat Turner she was not surprised, for she remembered my interest in him from twenty years before. That is why this book is for her. We have managed to love and care for each other for more than forty years, bumps notwithstanding. This is the best token that I have to offer.

NOTES

PREFACE

1. Symbolic of "Nat Turner" as involuntary enigma, it is not even clear whether "Nat Turner" is what he called himself, or what others called him. The name "Nat" seems indisputable from the available archive, but as a diminutive it reproduces the intentionally derogatory aspects of slaveholder practices in naming and addressing adult African Americans. Would Nat Turner wish to be perpetually insulted by those of us trying to remember him? Henry Highland Garnet pointedly referred to him as "Nathaniel Turner" in his 1843 "Address to the Slaves of the United States." See Henry Highland Garnet, *A Memorial Discourse* (Philadelphia: J. M. Wilson, 1865), 50. Frederick Douglass also used "Nathaniel Turner" in order to avoid the infantilization implicit in the diminutive form. See, for example, Frederick Douglass, "The Slaves' Right to Revolt," in John W. Blassingame, editor, *The Frederick Douglass Papers* (New Haven: Yale University Press, 1982), 2:131. Turner's African American contemporaries used "Nat" but often countered its infantilizing connotations by adding honorifics: "Captain Nat," or "General Nat," or "Ol' Prophet Nat." The attributed surname, "Turner," meanwhile, is not a patronymic but the surname of the slaveholder into whose possession the person who came to be known as "Nat Turner" was born. It is quite possible that among local whites he was known as "Turner's Nat." On naming, see Kenneth S. Greenberg, "Name, Face, Body," in Kenneth S. Greenberg, editor, *Nat Turner: A Slave Rebellion in History and Memory* (New York: Oxford University Press, 2003), 3–23, at 10; and "Nat Turner in Print and on Film," in Jeff Forret and Christine E. Sears, editors, *New Directions in Slavery Studies: Commodification, Community, and Comparison* (Baton Rouge: Louisiana State University Press, 2015), 78.

   In this book I have chosen, albeit somewhat reluctantly, to use "Nat Turner" to identify the person in question, believing this is how the vast majority of potential readers can best identify him. My practice has been to use "Turner" rather than "Nat" wherever possible. Like Garnet and Douglass, I think that the diminutive first name is more disrespectful than the attributed surname, the latter's provenance notwithstanding.
2. Despite its notoriety, fifty years on one can still detect the influence of Styron's *Confessions* both in historical literature and in popular culture—for example, in Nate Parker's *The Birth of a Nation* (Fox Searchlight Pictures, 2016).
3. My emphasis. My invitation is a Benjaminian invitation, which is hardly surprising for this is a Benjaminian book. The particulars of the invitation may best be explained thus: "Every present day is determined by the images that are synchronic with it: each 'now' is the now of a particular recognizability. In it, truth is charged to the bursting point with time. . . . It is not that what is past casts its light on what is present, or what is present its light on what is past; rather, image is that wherein what has been comes together in a flash with the now to form a constellation. In other words: image is dialectics at a standstill. For while the relation of the present to the past is purely temporal, the relation of what-has-been to the now is dialectical: not temporal in nature but figural [*bildlich*]. Only dialectical images are genuinely historical. . . . The image that

is read—which is to say, the image in the now of its recognizability—bears to the highest degree the imprint of the perilous critical moment on which all reading is founded." Walter Benjamin, *The Arcades Project*, Howard Eiland and Kevin McLaughlin, translators (Cambridge, MA: Harvard University Press, 1999), 462–63. See also Walter Benjamin, "Eduard Fuchs, Collector and Historian," in Howard Eiland and Michael W. Jennings, editors, *Walter Benjamin: Selected Writings, Volume 3, 1935-1938* (Cambridge, MA: Harvard University Press, 2002), 260–71. For a classic commentary on "dialectics at a standstill," see Rolf Tiedemann, "Dialectics at a Standstill: Approaches to the *Passagen-Werk*," in Benjamin, *The Arcades Project*, 929–44.

4. Scot French, *The Rebellious Slave: Nat Turner in American Memory* (Boston: Houghton Mifflin Company, 2004), 274–77. See also Tony Horwitz, "Untrue Confessions: Is Most of What We Know about the Rebel Slave Nat Turner Wrong?" *New Yorker* 75 (December 13, 1999), 80–89 at 88–89.
5. John Blassingame, *The Slave Community: Plantation Life in the Antebellum South* (New York: Oxford University Press, 1979), xi–xii. See also John Blassingame, editor, *Slave Testimony: Two Centuries of Letters, Speeches, Interviews, and Autobiographies* (Baton Rouge: Louisiana State University Press, 1977). For a summary of the arguments over sources described here, see Bryan Wagner, *The Tar Baby: A Global History* (Princeton: Princeton University Press, 2018), 1–19.
6. Fredric Jameson writes that history is "an absent cause . . . inaccessible to us except in textual form," that "our approach to it and to the Real itself necessarily passes through its prior textualization, its narrativization." Fredric Jameson, *The Political Unconscious: Narrative as a Socially Symbolic Act* (Ithaca: Cornell University Press, 1981), 35. Jameson's "Real" here invokes "the Real" of Jacques Lacan, "that which 'resists symbolization absolutely'" (35). See Slavoj Žižek, *How to Read Lacan* (New York: W. W. Norton, 2007), 57–78. See also below, note 18.
7. French, *The Rebellious Slave*, 277.
8. See David F. Allmendinger Jr., *Nat Turner and the Rising in Southampton County* (Baltimore: The Johns Hopkins University Press, 2014), 1–8, 242–57.
9. Robert A. Orsi, *History and Presence* (Cambridge, MA: Harvard University Press, 2016), 38, 58. See, for example, Burton Mack, "Introduction: Religion and Ritual," in Robert G. Hammerton-Kelly, editor, *Violent Origins: Walter Burkert, René Girard, and Jonathan Z. Smith on Ritual Killing and Cultural Formation* (Stanford: Stanford University Press, 1987), 4: "All three understand religion as a social phenomenon and wish to clarify the role of religion in the formation of society and culture. Each is an empiricist, seeking to give an account of religious behavior in terms provided by the human sciences; none invokes the mystique of the Sacred in order to explain the attractiveness of religion. For all, religion arises in relation to some human activity fundamental to social life, and for each of them religion in all its manifestations is essentially a human construction." This has been the way of the world at least since Durkheim, although we should not blame Durkheim for that. See Émile Durkheim, *The Elementary Forms of Religious Life*, Karen E. Fields, translator (1912; reprint New York: The Free Press, 1995).
10. As a skeptic of modernist reductions, I find myself in the company of Karl Löwith: "More intelligent than the superior vision of philosophers and theologians is the common sense of the natural man and the uncommon sense of the Christian believer. Neither pretends to discern on the canvas of human history the purpose of God or of the historical process itself. They rather seek to set men free from the world's oppressive history by suggesting an attitude, either of skepticism or of faith, which is rooted in an experience certainly nurtured by history but detached from and surpassing it, and thus enabling man to endure it with mature resignation or with faithful expectation. Religious faith is so little at variance with skepticism that both are rather united by their common opposition to the presumption of a settled knowledge. . . . A

man who lives by thought must have his skepticism—literally a passion for search—which may end in upholding the question as question or in answering it by transcending his doubt through faith. The skeptic and the believer have a common cause against the easy reading of history and its meaning." Karl Löwith, *Meaning in History* (Chicago: University of Chicago Press, 1949), v–vi.

11. Randolph Ferguson Scully, *Religion and the Making of Nat Turner's Virginia: Baptist Community and Conflict, 1740–1840* (Charlottesville: University of Virginia Press, 2008), 218.
12. Michael Gomez, *Exchanging Our Country Marks: The Transformation of African Identities in the Colonial and Antebellum South* (Chapel Hill: University of North Carolina Press, 1998), 257. The idiom of the onto-epistemology that I explore here, particularly in chapter 2, is the idiom of Christian faith grounded in a profound understanding of the Bible. My objective is "to work from inside the experience of those who have encountered sacred presences outward toward the environment within which these experiences have their destiny." Orsi, *History and Presence*, 62. For a distinct but no less valuable approach—a modernism that nevertheless manages to elide reductionism—see Ann Taves, *Revelatory Events: Three Case Studies of the Emergence of New Spiritual Paths* (Princeton: Princeton University Press, 2016).
13. See above, text at note 9. Patrick H. Breen, *The Land Shall Be Deluged in Blood: A New History of the Nat Turner Revolt* (New York: Oxford University Press, 2015), 5, stresses not "resistance" but the dismay of most of Southampton County's slaves at news of rebellion. At the level of ideology (psychology), Anthony Kaye stresses the inadequacies of agency/resistance as a quintessentially liberal explanation of the motivation of enslaved persons. See Anthony E. Kaye, "The Problem of Autonomy: Toward a Postliberal History," in Forret and Sears, editors, *New Directions in Slavery Studies*, 150–75. See also Ashley Byock, "Dark Matters: Race and the Antebellum Logic of Decorporation," *Symploke* 24, no. 1–2 (2016): 47–63. For an exceptionally well-documented case study of a contemporary occurrence in which religion/violence challenges an emergent nineteenth-century liberal problematic of human motivation, a case study full of uncanny parallels and connections—of faith and death, of rationalist superordinate investigation of illogical subaltern "fanaticism"—see Michel Foucault, editor, *I Pierre Rivière, having slaughtered my mother, my sister, and my brother . . . A Case of Parricide in the 19th Century*, Frank Jellinek, translator (Lincoln: University of Nebraska Press, 1982).
14. Compare Ranajit Guha, "The Prose of Counter-Insurgency," in Ranajit Guha and Gayatri Chakravorty Spivak, editors, *Selected Subaltern Studies* (Oxford: Oxford University Press, 1988), 78–84.
15. Slavoj Žižek, *In Defense of Lost Causes* (London: Verso, 2017), 485. And see below, chapter 3, note 3.
16. Allmendinger, *Rising*, 166–98, 281–85, supplies the most detailed account of patterns of recruitment, abstention, and exit during Turner's rebellion. On other outcomes, see, for example, below, chapter 3, note 23. On the phenomenon of opportunistic microviolence (settling scores) in situations of polarized macrolevel conflict, see Stathis N. Kalyvas, *The Logic of Violence in Civil War* (Cambridge: Cambridge University Press, 2006), 14, 388–90.
17. Walter Benjamin identifies the task of translation to be "finding the particular intention toward the target language which produces in that language the echo of the original." Walter Benjamin, "The Task of the Translator," Harry Zohn, translator, in Marcus Bullock and Michael W. Jennings, editors, *Walter Benjamin, Selected Writings, Volume 1, 1913-1926* (Cambridge, MA: Harvard University Press, 1996), 258. The words *intention* and *echo* signify the problematic distance between original language and target language. As to intention, "We must draw a distinction in the concept of 'intention' between what is meant and the way of meaning it" (257). What is meant in each language is identical. Their ways of meaning, however, are entirely distinct. The

task of translation consists, then "in relating the distinctive ways of meaning in different languages to one another, and secondly and correlatively, in bringing out what is ultimately 'meant'—signified—by these different but related ways of meaning." Samuel Weber, *Benjamin's -abilities* (Cambridge: Harvard University Press, 2008), 71.

Turner's languages of faith (for himself) and action (for others), we may argue, express identical meanings, but their ways of meaning are quite different. Translation between original and target produces only the "echo" of the original, for two reasons. First, the "essential quality" of the original "is not communication or the imparting of information"—at least not with the idea of being translated in mind. Hence translation is itself neither a subordinate nor a dependent activity, focused on the transmission of preexisting content, but a form of composition in itself, focused on the original's "translatability," its potential not to endure as such, but to be realized anew (*Benjamin, Selected Writings, Volume 1*, 253, 254, 262; see, generally, Weber, *Benjamin's -abilities*, 53–94). Second, and as this suggests, translation does not signify the original but something different, the afterlife of the original. Translation signifies a historical relationship in which the original takes its leave, and is transformed in translation.

18. Through Jacques Lacan one can express the concept supplement/excess in the formula $1+1+a$. The first part of the formula, $1+1$, denotes an objectively antagonistic pair—in our case slaves and slaveholders—standing in a form of equilibrium, or harmony. Without the supplement, *a* (which Lacan calls *objet petit a*, standing for *autre* or other) the antagonism of the pair will remain latent and their equilibrium intact, which is how Thomas Ruffin Gray expressed their relationship prior to the rebellion in the original *Confessions*, at 4: "Every thing upon the surface of society wore a calm and peaceful aspect . . . not one note of preparation was heard to warn the devoted inhabitants of woe and death." The role of *objet petit a* is double—it stands for a disavowal of antagonism between 1 and 1, the contention that without *a* there would be none; and simultaneously it is the alien other (*autre*) that stands *for* the antagonism, whose addition negates the equilibrium amongst those who would otherwise be simply "devoted inhabitants" (Gray, at 4). As Slavoj Žižek puts it in *Living in the End Times* (London: Verso, 2011), 136, using class struggle as his referent: "If we had only the two classes, $1+1$, without the supplement, then we would get not pure class antagonism but, on the contrary, class peace: the two classes complementing each other in a harmonious Whole." It is *objet petit a*, the element that "displaces the 'purity' of the . . . struggle"—in our case the person Nat Turner and his Christian religiosity—that precipitates struggle. We can see Turner confirmed in the role of *objet petit a* in the very emphasis on his exceptionalism that suffuses *both* Gray's pamphlet (Turner is a Satanic fanatic) *and* slaveholder ideology's structural "harmony" between paternal slaveholder obligation and the due subordination of the enslaved, which is slavery's equivalent of class peace. Turner is the *autre* of Gray's pamphlet, both central to and textually expelled beyond the limits of the very event that as *autre* he has precipitated.

We should note that for Lacan, *objet petit a* is untranslatable, which means that precipitation as such has no necessary or sufficient (instrumental) connection to what the precipitant actually *is* in itself. Thus, *objet petit a* can be, objectively, entirely involuntary in its relation to $1+1$, as it is in Žižek's example (where *objet petit a* is "the Jew"). Žižek explains it (in the 1996 film *Love Thy Symptom As Thyself*) as "the remainder of the Real that sets in motion the symbolic movement of interpretation, a hole at the center of the symbolic order, the mere appearance of some secret to be explained [or] interpreted."

19. Ben Brewster, "Glossary," in Louis Althusser, *For Marx*, Ben Brewster, translator (London: Allen Lane, 1969), 252–53. See also Stewart Motha, *Archiving Sovereignty: Law, History, Violence* (Ann Arbor: University of Michigan Press, 2018), 39.

20. On "evental site" and "event," see below, chapter 3, notes 5 and 8, and accompanying text. As explained there, my "theory" of the event is informed primarily by Alain Badiou. See Alain Badiou, *Being and Event*, Oliver Feltham, translator (London: Bloomsbury Academic, 2013); Alain Badiou, *Logics of Worlds: Being and Event, 2*, Alberto Toscano, translator (London: Bloomsbury Academic, 2013). See also Ian Baucom, *Specters of the Atlantic: Finance Capital, Slavery, and the Philosophy of History* (Durham, NC: Duke University Press, 2005), 119–23. For discussions of the event as a concept in historical analysis that are far less philosophical in orientation, see William H. Sewell Jr., *Logics of History: Social Theory and Social Transformation* (Chicago: University of Chicago Press, 2005), notably 197–270; Robin Wagner-Pacifici, *What Is an Event?* (Chicago: University of Chicago Press, 2017).
21. Mark Juergensmeyer, *Terror in the Mind of God: The Global Rise of Religious Violence* (Berkeley: University of California Press, 2000), 218.
22. On the relationship between political economy, conjectural history, and providentialism, see Mary Poovey, *A History of the Modern Fact: Problems of Knowledge in the Sciences of Wealth and Society* (Chicago: University of Chicago Press, 1998), 214–306. On the transition from classical political economy to market reasoning and class division in antebellum America, see Jeffrey Sklansky, *The Soul's Economy: Market Society and Selfhood in American Thought, 1820-1920* (Chapel Hill: University of North Carolina Press, 2002), 14–15, 31, 72–103. See also Jeffrey Sklansky, "The Elusive Sovereign: New Intellectual and Social Histories of Capitalism," *Modern Intellectual History* 9, no. 1 (2012): 233–48; Jordy Rosenberg, *Critical Enthusiasm: Capital Accumulation and the Transformation of Religious Passion* (New York: Oxford University Press, 2011).
23. *The Confessions of Nat Turner, the Leader of the Late Insurrection in Southampton, Va. As fully and voluntarily made to Thomas R. Gray, in the prison where he was confined, and acknowledged by him to be such when read before the Court of Southampton; with the certificate, under seal of the Court convened at Jerusalem, Nov. 5, 1831, for his trial. Also, An Authentic Account of the Whole Insurrection, With Lists of the Whites who were Murdered, And of the Negroes Brought before the Court of Southampton, and there Sentenced, &c.* (Baltimore: Lucas & Deaver, 1831), 7.
24. Teresa Brennan, *History After Lacan* (Abingdon, UK: Routledge, 1993), 33. Some might profess (for good or ill) to detect in my "speculative history" a fragment of the "speculative realism" described by Graham Harman in his *Speculative Realism: An Introduction* (Cambridge: Polity Press, 2018). Although I do not wish to commit myself, I will say that I am very much in sympathy with Harman's accent on the adjectival component of his description: speculative realism is *speculative*, he tells us, "in the sense that unlike the commonsensical realisms of yesteryear [its proponents] reach conclusions that seem counterintuitive or even downright strange" (5). History is a realist practice, in my view, but not commonsensically so. The historian must always be open to conclusions that are "counterintuitive or even downright strange."
25. Karl Löwith writes: "It is the privilege of theology and philosophy, as contrasted with the sciences, to ask questions that cannot be answered on the basis of empirical knowledge. All the ultimate questions concerning first and last things are of this character; they remain significant because no answer can silence them. They signify a fundamental quest; for there would be no search for the meaning of history if its meaning were manifest in historical events. It is the very absence of meaning in the events themselves that motivates the quest." Löwith, *Meaning in History*, 3–4.

PROLOGUE: WHAT'S PAST?

1. William Styron, *The Confessions of Nat Turner* (New York: Random House, 1967). In the course of Styron's self-representation as the character "Stingo" in *Sophie's Choice* he allows himself to identify *Confessions* as his best work. See John Kenny Crane, *The Root*

of All Evil: The Thematic Unity of William Styron's Fiction (Columbia: University of South Carolina Press, 1984), 6.

2. *The Confessions of Nat Turner* . . . (Baltimore: Lucas & Deaver, print., 1831). For the full title see above, Preface note 23.
3. William Styron, "Afterword to the Vintage Edition: Nat Turner Revisited," in William Styron, *The Confessions of Nat Turner* (New York: Vintage International, 1993), 441. "Nat Turner Revisited" was first published in *American Heritage Magazine* 43, no. 6 (October 1992): 64–73. All references to Styron's *Confessions* are to the 1993 Vintage edition.
4. William Styron in "The Uses of History in Fiction: Ralph Ellison, William Styron, Robert Penn Warren, C. Vann Woodward, moderator," *Southern Literary Journal* 1, no. 2 (spring 1969): 82; Styron, "Afterword," 441–42; William Styron, "More Confessions," in Mark C. Carnes, editor, *Novel History: Historians and Novelists Confront America's Past (and Each Other)* (New York: Simon & Schuster, 2001), 222. Styron's excoriation of Turner as fanatic takes its cue from Thomas Ruffin Gray, who describes Turner as "a gloomy fanatic." Gray, *Confessions*, 4. Gray's usage (which stresses Turner's religious enthusiasm) exemplifies what Joel Olson calls "the pejorative tradition" in which fanaticism is represented as a pathology (a monomania) rather than an expression of total commitment. "The basic limitation of the pejorative tradition is that it fails to recognize zealotry as a political strategy to achieve one's 'absolute ends.'" Joel Olson, "The Freshness of Fanaticism: The Abolitionist Defense of Zealotry," *Perspectives on Politics* 5, no. 4 (2007): 688. See, generally, Alberto Toscano, *Fanaticism: On the Uses of an Idea* (London: Verso, 2010). But note also the racial specificity of the label "fanatic" in the American case. As Jon-Christian Suggs argues, "From antebellum America to this century" black passion has been prototypically defined "as demonic, as unnatural, or as inhuman and limbic, as appetite only." Jon-Christian Suggs, *Whispered Consolations: Law and Narrative in African-American Life* (Ann Arbor: University of Michigan Press, 2000), 94.
5. "Interview with William Styron," in Greenberg, editor, *Nat Turner*, 214–27, at 222. Styron's belief that, as a creative writer, he was free to take complete control of Turner is manifest from the outset. See below, text at note 48.
6. Styron, *Confessions*, 257.
7. Styron, "Afterword," 442.
8. *Ibid.*, 441.
9. *Ibid.*, 442.
10. *Ibid.*, 442.
11. Robert K. Morris and Irving Malin, "Vision and Value: The Achievement of William Styron," in Robert K. Morris with Irving Malin, editors, *The Achievement of William Styron* (Athens, GA: University of Georgia Press, 1981), 11–13; Robert K. Morris, "Interviews with William Styron," in Morris with Malin, *Achievement*, 29–69, at 56–57, 59–60.
12. George Plimpton, "A Shared Ordeal: Interview with William Styron," *New York Times* (October 8, 1967), in Melvin J. Friedman and Irving Malin, *William Styron's* The Confessions of Nat Turner: *A Critical Handbook* (Belmont, CA: Wadsworth, 1970), 36–42, at 42.
13. *Ibid.*, 42.
14. Styron, *Confessions*, 426, 428.
15. Styron, "Afterword," 446–47. Years later, because the relationship between the characters of Nat Turner and Margaret Whitehead proved highly controversial, Styron would seek to minimize it. "The allegation is that I made Nat Turner a victim of runaway lust for this young girl. In reality, a careful reading of the book will show that the relationship, which takes about 18 pages in a 400-page book [actually 30], was really very tentative. It was basically a relationship in which she was a little southern

tease, playing the role of the little southern vamp; that he was, himself, more a victim of her than the other way around. This idea of the connection between the two has been completely distorted and twisted out of all reality." See "Interview" in Greenberg, editor, *Nat Turner*, 222. For an earlier and much stronger statement, see R.W.B. Lewis and C. Vann Woodward, "Slavery in the First Person: Interview with William Styron," *Yale Alumni Magazine* (November 1967), in Friedman and Malin, *Critical Handbook*, 51–58, at 55.

16. Styron, "Afterword," 441–42.
17. William Styron, "This Quiet Dust," *Harper's Magazine* 230, no. 1379 (April 1965): 135–46, at 138; Styron, "Afterword," 442.
18. William Styron, "Author's Note," in Styron, *Confessions*, xi.
19. Styron, "This Quiet Dust," 138 (emphasis in original). Mary Strine observes, "In its most inclusive sense, the novel constitutes a sociopsychological exploration into the causes and consequences of racial violence as a primary impediment—past and present—to the realization of community in the United States." Mary Strine, "The Confessions of Nat Turner: Styron's 'Meditation on History' as Historical Act," *Quarterly Journal of Speech* 64, no. 3 (1978): 253.
20. On "the Negro" as construct, see Cedric J. Robinson, *Black Marxism, The Making of the Black Radical Tradition* (Chapel Hill: University of North Carolina Press, 2000), 81–82; Robin D. G. Kelley, "Foreword," in Robinson, *Black Marxism*, xiii–xiv.
21. Styron, "Author's Note," xi (emphasis in original). See above, text at notes 3–5, 8. As Harry D. Amis put it in 1978, "Styron . . . committed the error of assigning his own moral and ethical values to another people's hero." Harry D. Amis, "History as Self-Serving Myth: Another Look at Styron's *The Confessions of Nat Turner*," *College Language Association Journal* 22, no. 2 (1978): 146.
22. Fanny Söderbäck, "Being in the Present: Derrida and Irigaray on the Metaphysics of Presence," *Journal of Speculative Philosophy* 27, no. 3 (2013): 254.
23. *Ibid.*, 253, 255–56.
24. *Ibid.*, 254.
25. Robert W. Gordon, "'Critical Legal Histories Revisited': A Response," *Law & Social Inquiry* 37, no. 1 (winter 2012): 200–215, at 200. Historians of the last half century have adopted the proverbial first line of L. P. Hartley's novel *The Go-Between* (London: Hamish Hamilton, 1953)—"The past is a foreign country: they do things differently there"—virtually as a motto, acknowledging that history has become, very largely, a contextualizing discipline, a discipline that fetishizes thick description, contingency, and complexity.
26. Kunal M. Parker, *Common Law, History, and Democracy in America: Legal Thought Before Modernism* (Cambridge: Cambridge University Press, 2011), 5, 7.
27. Söderbäck argues that Luce Irigaray offers an ontology of presence that, in place of Derrida's deconstruction of "selfsame being," reclaims "the present" by casting it in temporal-relational terms, "an account of presence injected with aliveness." She continues: "If the [metaphysical] tradition has separated everlasting presence from time, and if the latter has been conceived as a line leading from the past into the future, it seems that the task would be not only to bring presence back from an eternal beyond, but also to reinscribe the present into the very structure of time (without giving it the priority that it has been given in the tradition) . . . as it unfolds 'here and now.'" Söderbäck, "Being in the Present," 256. Irigaray's enlivened temporal-relational present, or *being-with*, is predicated on an ontology of sexuate difference. Here I argue that historical presence is a temporal-relational condition of difference (between past and here-and-now) that can similarly be thought of as an enlivening *being-with*. See below, notes 28–29, and text at notes 132–44, 164–67.

28. Christopher Tomlins, "The Strait Gate: The Past, History, and Legal Scholarship," *Law, Culture and the Humanities* 5 (February 2009): 11–42, and "After Critical Legal History: Scope, Scale, Structure," *Annual Review of Law and Social Science* 8 (2012): 31–68.
29. "The true image of the past flits by. The past can be seized only as an image which flashes up at the moment of its recognizability, and is never seen again. . . . For it is an irretrievable image of the past which threatens to disappear in any present that does not recognize itself as intended in that image." Walter Benjamin, "On the Concept of History," in Howard Eiland and Michael W. Jennings, editors, *Walter Benjamin: Selected Writings, Volume 4: 1938–1940* (Cambridge, MA: Harvard University Press, 2003), 390–91.
30. On the perpetual postponement of the meaning of "Nat Turner," see William L. Andrews, *To Tell a Free Story: The First Century of Afro-American Autobiography, 1760–1865* (Urbana: University of Illinois Press, 1986), 77: "We should not think of Nat Turner as a historical personage or as a character created by Gray or Turner, but as a product of the dynamics of the text itself." See, generally, Jeffrey Mehlman, "The 'Floating Signifier': From Lévi-Strauss to Lacan," *Yale French Studies* 48 (1972): 10–37. Andrews offers a substantial reconsideration of "perpetual postponement" in William L. Andrews, "*The Confessions of Nat Turner*: Memoir of a Martyr or Testament of a Terrorist?" in Vincent L. Wimbush, editor, *Theorizing Scriptures: New Critical Orientations to a Cultural Phenomenon* (New Brunswick, NJ: Rutgers University Press, 2008), 79–87.
31. William Cooper Nell, *The Colored Patriots of the American Revolution, With Sketches of Several Distinguished Colored Persons: To Which Is Added a Brief Survey of the Conditions and Prospects of Colored Americans* (Boston: R. F. Wallcut, 1855); Martin R. Delany, *Blake; or, The Huts of America*, Floyd J. Miller, editor (Boston: Beacon Press, 1970), first published serially in *The Weekly Anglo-African* (January–July 1859, November 1861–May 1862); Sharon Ewell Foster, *The Resurrection of Nat Turner: Part One, The Witnesses* and *Part 2, The Testimony* (New York: Howard Books, 2011 and 2012); Kyle Baker, *Nat Turner* (New York: Abrams Comicarts, 2008); Nate Parker, director, *The Birth of a Nation* (Fox Searchlight Pictures, 2016); Nathan Alan Davis, *Nat Turner in Jerusalem* (New York: Samuel French, 2017). On Nell and Delany (and Frederick Douglass, and Harriet Beecher Stowe, and Harriet Jacobs) and the assimilation of Nat Turner to the antebellum "literature of resistance," see Manisha Sinha, *The Slave's Cause: A History of Abolition* (New Haven: Yale University Press, 2016), 450–60; Vincent Harding, *There Is a River: The Black Struggle for Freedom in America* (New York: Harcourt Brace, 1981), 101–5, 308. The assimilation ran deep. Ahmed White notes that at the funeral of Lee Tisdale, an African American steel worker fatally wounded in the Memorial Day Massacre (Republic Steel, 30 May 1937, Chicago), the eulogy (reported in the *Chicago Defender*) likened Tisdale to Nat Turner. Just as Turner "gave his life so that his people might be freed from the shackles of slavery," so Tisdale had given his life "that all workers might be freed from industrial slavery." See Ahmed White, *The Last Great Strike: Little Steel, the CIO, and the Struggle for Labor Rights in New Deal America* (Oakland: University of California Press, 2016), 145. See also, generally, French, *The Rebellious Slave*, 65–282.
32. As Avery Gordon puts it, "Haunting describes how that which appears to be not there is often a seething presence, acting on and often meddling with taken-for-granted realities. . . . The ghost or the apparition is one form by which something lost, or barely visible, or seemingly not there to our supposedly well-trained eyes, makes itself known or apparent to us, in its own way." Avery F. Gordon, *Ghostly Matters: Haunting and the Sociological Imagination* (Minneapolis: University of Minnesota Press, 2008), 8. And see Jacques Derrida, *Specters of Marx: The State of the Debt, the Work of Mourning, and the New International*, Peggy Kamuf, translator (New York: Routledge, 1994); Christopher Tomlins, "Be Operational or Disappear: Thoughts on a Present Discontent," *Annual Review of Law and Social Science*, 12 (2016), 1–23; Orsi, *History and Presence*, 70–71.

33. James L. W. West III, *William Styron, A Life* (New York: Random House, 1998), 20, 62–63, 77, 79–147.
34. *Ibid.*, 173–75, 203–4, 300–301, 310–12. See, generally, Jane Flanders, "William Styron's Southern Myth," in Morris with Malin, *Achievement*, 106–23; Frederick J. Hoffman, "William Styron: The Metaphysical Hurt," in Friedman and Malin, *Critical Handbook*, 126–41; Samuel Coale, "Styron's Disguises: A Provisional Rebel in Christian Masquerade," in Harold Bloom, editor, *William Styron's Sophie's Choice: Modern Critical Interpretations* (Philadelphia: Chelsea House Publishers, 2002), 11–19.
35. *Set This House on Fire* (1960), on which work began in the early 1950s; *The Confessions of Nat Turner* (1967), and *Sophie's Choice* (1976).
36. Flanders, "Southern Myth," 106–7.
37. See, e.g., Richard Foster, "An Orgy of Commerce: William Styron's *Set This House on Fire*," *Critique* 3, no. 3 (summer 1960): 59–70.
38. West, *William Styron*, 55–56, 183.
39. *Ibid.*, 220–23.
40. *Ibid.*, 222.
41. *Ibid.*, 317.
42. Styron, "This Quiet Dust," 135, 136.
43. West, *William Styron*, 315.
44. *Ibid.*, 316. Styron's use of Baldwin as a model for Turner was publicly acknowledged and commended by Baldwin, but only implicitly by Styron. See West, *William Styron*, 336–37; "Interview" in Greenberg, editor, *Nat Turner*, 218–19; French, *The Rebellious Slave*, 240.
45. Styron, "This Quiet Dust," 138–39.
46. Raymond A. Sokolov, "Into the Mind of Nat Turner," *Newsweek* (October 16, 1967), in Friedman and Malin, *Critical Handbook*, 42–50, at 44; Plimpton, "A Shared Ordeal," 37; "The Uses of History in Fiction," 82. Given Styron's insouciant approach to research, one cannot help noting the lazy trickle of little errors that mark his trail in "This Quiet Dust," 139–40: for example, that Turner was thirty-one years old at the time of the rebellion (thirty); that Turner "was purchased and sold several times" (once); that he became a Baptist preacher (Methodist); that he began his rebellion with five others (six), and so on.
47. "The Uses of History in Fiction," 82.
48. *Ibid.*, 83.
49. Whether Camus's novel actually exemplifies existentialism is highly debatable. The point is, Styron identified it as such. On Styron's limited understanding of existentialism, see Roy Arthur Swanson, "William Styron's Clown Show," in Friedman and Malin, *Critical Handbook*, 149–64, at 155–56.
50. Stanley M. Elkins, *Slavery: A Problem in American Institutional and Intellectual Life* (Chicago: University of Chicago Press, 1959). Other scholarly research on slavery that had a noticeable impact on Styron's *Confessions* includes Ulrich Bonnell Phillips, *Life and Labor in the Old South* (Boston: Little, Brown and Company, 1929) and Frank Tannenbaum, *Slave and Citizen: The Negro in the Americas* (New York: Knopf, 1947). For further details of Styron's secondary reading, see West, *William Styron*, 339–42.
51. Erik H. Erikson, *Young Man Luther: A Study in Psychoanalysis and History* (New York: W. W. Norton, 1958).
52. Plimpton, "A Shared Ordeal," 36–37.
53. Elkins, *Slavery*, 128–30. The influence of *Slavery* on Styron's *Confessions* is clear, although his characterization of the book's place in the historiography of slavery is singular: "I think the most influential book for me, in putting together *Nat Turner*, was Stanley Elkins's book *Slavery*. It's a work that has been a subject of great dispute and of course has had much criticism descend on it. But for me it was a seminal book because it

discussed the whole historiography of slavery in a way I had never understood before. He showed how the argument about slavery had fluctuated from apology to its opposite. He showed how slavery was portrayed on the one hand by Ulrich B. Phillips as a benevolent system, and how another historian such as Kenneth Stampp tried to portray it as an unremittingly vicious institution. *The great virtue of Elkins' book was to try to calm the waters and to examine slavery far more objectively*." "Interview," in Greenberg, editor, *Nat Turner*, 219 (emphasis added).

54. Styron, *Confessions*, 27, 57, 97, 169.
55. Erikson, *Young Man Luther*, 14. In a *New York Review of Books* essay that criticized Herbert Aptheker's *American Negro Slave Revolts* for exaggerating African American slaves' propensity to rebel, Styron turned to Elkins to contrast Turner, "a literate preacher and a slave of the Upper South, [who] lived outside the thralldom of organized plantation slavery," with "the many millions of other slaves, reduced to the status of children, illiterate, tranquillized, totally defenseless, ciphers and ants, [who] could only accept their existence or be damned, and be damned anyway, like the victims of a concentration camp." William Styron, "Overcome," *The New York Review of Books* 1, no. 3 (September 26, 1963), available at http://www.nybooks.com/articles/archives/1963/sep/26/overcome/ (last accessed February 22, 2019), at paragraph 5. Styron would later tell R.W.B. Lewis and C. Vann Woodward that Turner was "a unique slave . . . *one of the few slaves in history who achieved identity*." Lewis and Woodward, "Slavery in the First Person," 53 (emphasis added). Compare Ta-Nehisi Coates, *Between the World and Me* (New York: Spiegel & Grau, 2015), 69 ("Slavery is not an indefinable mass of flesh").
56. Styron, *Confessions*, 246–47.
57. *Ibid.*, 117 (emphasis added), 252–53.
58. Erikson, *Young Man Luther*, 41–42.
59. Styron's daughter, Alexandra, describes her father's fiction as "closely autobiographical" populated by narrators "usually defined by the same qualities—Southern orientation, literary bent, sexual longing, deep ambivalence toward the enticements of power—that also preoccupied their creator." Alexandra Styron, *Reading My Father: A Memoir* (New York: Scribner, 2011), 159.
60. In a 2001 commentary on Styron's *Confessions*, Eugene Genovese argues (controversially) that Styron's mad rapist Will [Francis] "could, in fact, have been the Nat Turner of the historical record." He continues: "By splitting revolutionary personality into these two discrete parts—the ruthlessly sane and the cold-bloodedly insane—Styron was able to represent the two warring souls of the historical Nat Turner: the one a single-minded murderous fanatic whose moral sense and very humanity have been crushed by years of brutal treatment; the other an admirable man who, notwithstanding the destruction he wreaks, retains his humanity." Eugene D. Genovese, "William Styron's *The Confessions of Nat Turner*: A Meditation on Evil, Redemption, and History," in Carnes, editor, *Novel History*, 209–20, at 211.
61. Styron, *Confessions*, 340, 367, 372.
62. *Ibid.*, 10, 413–17, 423; Styron, "This Quiet Dust," 146.
63. Erikson, *Young Man Luther*, 260 (emphasis in original).
64. Styron, *Confessions*, 428. And see Flanders, "William Styron's Southern Myth," 120–21.
65. Erikson, *Young Man Luther*, 260–61, quoting Erik H. Erikson, *Childhood and Society* (New York: W. W. Norton, 1953), 268. See also Erik Homburger Erikson, "The Problem of Ego Identity," *Journal of the American Psychoanalytic Association* 4, no. 1 (1956): 56–121.
66. James M. Mellard, "This *Un*quiet Dust: The Problem of History in Styron's *The Confessions of Nat Turner*," *Mississippi Quarterly* 36, no. 4 (fall 1983): 525–43, at 537–38, 543.

67. In "This Quiet Dust," at 138, Styron describes Gray's *Confessions* as a "transcript" that "in all major respects . . . seems completely honest and reliable." However, after the controversy over Styron's *Confessions* was broached by Herbert Aptheker, who pointed to numerous discrepancies between Gray's *Confessions* and the novel, Styron scoffed that Aptheker was naïvely accepting "as gospel truth . . . the probity of a Southern white lawyer." Styron now argued that "the *accuracy* of the 'Confessions,' the overall fidelity to the circumstances of Nat's life and career" should indeed be doubted. "The entire pedantic, impossibly elevated and formal tone of the 'Confessions' makes me believe that they were *not* recorded with 'little or no variation' from Nat's words, as Gray states in his prologue, and so how much during that tense encounter was subtly bent and twisted by the interrogator? Gray was a man of his time, a Southern racist, and as a functionary of the Commonwealth [*sic*] it may well have been to his advantage . . . to distort many things that the helpless prisoner told him, to add things, to leave things out." See "Truth and Nat Turner: An Exchange," *The Nation* (April 22, 1968), 543–47, at 546.
68. See above, text at notes 3–5, 8. Even as, in 1992, he continued to disparage Gray's *Confessions* as "incoherent," Styron insisted on this one completely clear conclusion, even labeling it: "*The fact*: he was a person of conspicuous ghastliness." Styron, "Afterword," 441 (emphasis added), 452. See also Mary Kemp Davis, *Nat Turner Before the Bar of Judgment: Fictional Treatments of the Southampton Slave Insurrection* (Baton Rouge: Louisiana State University Press, 1999), 244, and generally 234–70.
69. Gray, *Confessions*, 4, 19.
70. Gray was known as "a scoffer at religion." Thomas C. Parramore, *Southampton County, Virginia* (Charlottesville: University Press of Virginia, 1978), 120 (quoting an obituary in the *Norfolk and Portsmouth Herald*, 27 August 1845). See also Thomas C. Parramore, "Covenant in Jerusalem," in Greenberg, editor, *Nat Turner*, 75.
71. "Old Testament vengeance . . . plainly animated Nat." Styron, "Afterword," 442.
72. *Ibid.*, 441. Jordy Rosenberg helpfully defines enthusiasm as "the passionate experience of unmediated communion with God . . . the capacity of individual subjects to know and understand the divine order." Rosenberg, *Critical Enthusiasm*, 6.
73. These are the motives that Styron's answer to Aptheker hints Gray has missed, distorted, or left out. See above, note 67.
74. See e.g. Styron, *Confessions*, 328–30, 335, 360–61. And note Genovese's comment: "Styron ennobles the historical Nat Turner by giving him qualities he may have possessed but the empirical record does not reveal: rational motivation, concrete objectives, a definite strategy, and tactics that required 'timing and coordination'—qualities the most diligent historians have found no evidence of." Genovese, "Evil, Redemption, and History," 210.
75. Morris, "Interviews with William Styron," 38.
76. Styron, *Confessions*, 95–105; Plimpton, "A Shared Ordeal," 41. Styron's attack on the legal system is concentrated in *Confessions,* Part I "Judgment Day," centering on the ambiguous and deceptive role played (in the novel) by Thomas R. Gray.
77. Plimpton, "A Shared Ordeal," 41.
78. See above, text at notes 60–64.
79. Lewis and Woodward, "Slavery in the First Person," 54. See also Plimpton, "A Shared Ordeal," 42: "One must remember that he is a religious fanatic. And the book, as you can tell, is a sort of religious parable and a story of exculpation. The last words of the book are the last words of the Bible, the last words of the Book of Revelation. I mean, without revelation, the book doesn't make sense. It should be apparent that the book expresses the idea of Old Testament savagery and revenge redeemed by New Testament charity and brotherhood—affirmation. It's in there somewhere, *hoped* for, lurking in the terrible story" (emphasis in original).

80. Lewis and Woodward, "Slavery in the First Person," 54.
81. Gray, *Confessions*, 9–11.
82. See, generally, Jonathan Edwards, *A History of the Work of Redemption*, transcribed and edited by John F. Wilson, volume 9 of *The Works of Jonathan Edwards* (New Haven: Yale University Press, 1989). On the relationship between Edwards's millenarian eschatology and Turner's see below, chapter 2, text at notes 152–98. Just as inexplicable is Styron's claim that his recourse to imagery from the Book of Revelation was "my own invention, of course," given that Revelation's apocalyptic eschatology is such a clear component of Turner's postmillennial hermeneutics. Styron's claim is made in Lewis and Woodward, "Slavery in the First Person," 54.
83. On this particular matter, Genovese is far more astute: "Styron presents Nat Turner as a prophet and 'an avenging Old Testament angel.' Simultaneously he presents him as ultimately in submission to Jesus' call for forgiveness and redemption. The agnostic Styron here moves from a questionable separation of the Old from the New Testament—a piece of theological juggling liberal theologians love to indulge in—to an orthodox affirmation of Jesus' assurance that He has come to fulfill, not overthrow, the Law. For if the God of the Old Testament is a God of Wrath and 'a jealous God,' He is also the first person of a triune God that includes a Jesus whose nature is inseparable from that of the Father. Recall that Jesus, the God of love, displayed that very wrath and asserted His own 'jealous' nature when He drove the money changers from the Temple and, more tellingly, consigned those who blaspheme against the Holy Ghost to everlasting damnation. Father and Son alike declare wrath and redemption inseparable from justice, as well as from confession and atonement." Genovese, "Evil, Redemption, and History," 217.
84. See William Styron, *This Quiet Dust and Other Writings* (New York: Vintage International, 1993), 3–4.
85. Styron, "This Quiet Dust," 141.
86. *Ibid.*, 144.
87. *Ibid.*, 145.
88. *Ibid.*, 145.
89. *Ibid.*, 144–45.
90. *Ibid.*, 145.
91. *Ibid.*, 135. The verses read as follows: "You mought be rich as cream / And drive you coach and four-horse team, / But you can't keep de world from moverin' round / Nor Nat Turner from gainin' ground. / And you name it mought be Caesar sure. / And got you cannon can shoot a mile or more, / but you can't keep de world from moverin' round / Nor Nat Turner from gainin' ground." See also Albert Murray, "A Troublesome Property," *The New Leader* (December 4, 1967), 18–21, in John B. Duff and Peter M. Mitchell, editors, *The Nat Turner Rebellion: The Historical Event and the Modern Controversy* (New York: Harper & Row, 1971), 174–80, at 176, 178, referencing "The Nat Turner Southern Negro school children used to celebrate in pageants during Negro History week" and "the Nat Turner of Negro folklore." See also Ralph Ellison in "The Uses of History in Fiction," 62–65, 68, discussing American written history ("as 'official' as any produced in any communist country") and American fiction—"they're both artificial; both are forms of literature"—with their origins in the tall tale; contrasting both with "a stream of history" that exists "in the Negro part of the country and in the Southern part of the country . . . which is still as tightly connected with folklore and the oral tradition as official history is with the tall tale," of which historians, and historical novelists, had taken no notice; and calling for "a full American history" that specifically included the latter. See generally French, *The Rebellious Slave*, 135–214. By 1992, Styron was grudgingly acknowledging the existence of Turner in an African-American historical tradition. See Styron, "Afterword," 452–53.

92. "About Nat Turner—of whose departed flesh-and-blood self so little is known, or ever will be known—I cared to discover only so much as my instinct as a novelist told me to care." Styron, *This Quiet Dust*, 7.
93. Exceptions were Wilfrid Sheed, "The Slave Who Became a Man," *The New York Times* (October 8, 1967), and Richard Gilman, "Nat Turner Revisited," *The New Republic* (April 27, 1968), both in Friedman and Malin, *Critical Handbook*, 59–63, 104–11, and particularly Stanley Kauffmann, "Styron's Unwritten Novel," *The Hudson Review* 20, no. 4 (winter 1967): 675–80.
94. An important exception was John Hope Franklin in the *Chicago Sunday Sun Times* Book Week (October 8, 1967) 1, 11.
95. C. Vann Woodward, "Confessions of a Rebel: 1831," *The New Republic* (October 7, 1967), 25–28, at 25. Styron's other frontline professional defender, Eugene Genovese, was equally forthright: "The novel is historically sound. Styron takes liberties with fact, as every novelist does, but he does not do violence to the historical record." Eugene D. Genovese, "The Nat Turner Case," *The New York Review of Books* (September 12, 1968), available at http://www.nybooks.com/articles/archives/1968/sep/12/the-nat-turner-case/ paragraph 7 (last accessed February 22, 2019).
96. Professor of African World History and, in 1969, founding chairman of the Department of Black and Puerto Rican Studies at Hunter College of the City University of New York; Carter G. Woodson Distinguished Visiting Professor of African History at Cornell University's Africana Studies and Research Center; in 1968 cofounder (with the Black Caucus of the African Studies Association) of the African Heritage Studies Association. http://en.wikipedia.org/wiki/John_Henrik_Clarke (last accessed February 22, 2019).
97. John Henrik Clarke, "Introduction," in John Henrik Clarke, editor, *William Styron's Nat Turner: Ten Black Writers Respond* (Boston: Beacon Press, 1968), vii.
98. See Loyle Hairston, "William Styron's Nat Turner—Rogue-Nigger," and Charles V. Hamilton, "Our Nat Turner and William Styron's Creation," both in Clarke, editor, *Ten Black Writers*, 66–72, 73–78.
99. Genovese, "The Nat Turner Case," paragraph 2, paragraph 40. For a second critical review of *Ten Black Writers*, see Martin Duberman, "Historical Fictions," *The New York Times* (August 11, 1968), in Friedman and Malin, *Critical Handbook*, 112–16. For Duberman, like Woodward and Genovese, Styron's *Confessions* was "superlative history" (112).
100. Genovese, "The Nat Turner Case," paragraph 23, pargraph 39. In "Historical Fictions," at 114, Duberman likewise commented that "Blacks are entitled to their version of Turner . . . but let them not pretend that [their version is] incontestably validated by the historical evidence." Given that Duberman had just described Styron's *Confessions* as "the most subtle, multifaceted view of antebellum Virginia, its institution of slavery and the effects of that institution on both slaves and masters, available in any single volume" (112), one must conclude he believed any black version of Turner would be inferior to Styron's portrayal.
101. Genovese, "The Nat Turner Case," paragraph 25.
102. See, for example, Styron, "Afterword," 449; "Interview" in Greenberg, editor, *Nat Turner*, 221–22. Herbert Aptheker, "Truth and Nat Turner: An Exchange," *The Nation* (April 22, 1968), 543–44. Styron's animus recalls his May 1952 declaration that *his* Nat Turner would not be "a Great Leader of the Masses—as the stupid, vicious Jackass of a Communist writer might make him out." See above, text at note 39.
103. West, *William Styron*, 369.
104. *Ibid.*, 368–69.
105. *Ibid.*, 376. In *Newsweek*, Raymond Sokolov claimed that 200,000 copies had been printed by release day. Sokolov, "Mind of Nat Turner," 43.

106. West, *William Styron*, 382–83, 396–98.
107. See above, note 37. A careful analysis of the framing, commercial presentation, marketing, and reception of Styron's *Confessions* appears in Albert E. Stone, *The Return of Nat Turner: History, Literature, and Cultural Politics in Sixties America* (Athens: University of Georgia Press, 1992), 1–176. See also French, *The Rebellious Slave*, 242–50.
108. Norman Mailer, *Advertisements for Myself* (Cambridge: Harvard University Press, 1992), 464.
109. Shaun O'Connell, "Styron's Nat Turner . . ." *The Nation* (October 16, 1967), 374.
110. Philip Rahv, "Through the Midst of Jerusalem," *The New York Review of Books* 9, no. 7 (October 26, 1967), available at http://www.nybooks.com/articles/archives/1967/oct/26/through-the-midst-of-jerusalem/ (last accessed February 22, 2019), paragraph 3, paragraph 5.
111. Vincent Harding, "You've Taken My Nat And Gone," in Clarke, editor, *Ten Black Writers*, 23–33. As Harding explains, his title is taken from Langston Hughes's 1949 poem, "Note on Commercial Theater": You've taken my blues and gone—/ You sing 'em on Broadway / And you sing 'em in Hollywood Bowl, / And you mixed 'em up with symphonies / And you fixed 'em / So they don't sound like me. / Yep, you done taken my blues and gone. / You also took my spirituals and gone. / You put me in MACBETH and CARMEN JONES / And all kinds of SWING MIKADOS / And in everything but what's about me—/ But someday somebody'll / Stand up and talk about me, / And write about me—/ Black and beautiful—/ And sing about me, / And put on plays about me! / I reckon it'll be / Me myself! / Yes, it'll be me.
112. Styron, "Author's Note," xi (emphasis in original).
113. *Ibid.*, xi.
114. See Melvin J. Friedman, "*The Confessions of Nat Turner*: The Convergence of 'Nonfiction Novel' and 'Meditation on History,'" *Journal of Popular Culture* 1, no. 2 (fall 1967): 166–75, at 170–71. On Proustian "actualization" see also Tomlins, "The Strait Gate," 15–19.
115. "I've never really been able to figure out just what I meant by it." William Styron (1968), quoted by Charles Joyner, "Styron's Choice: A Meditation on History, Literature, and Moral Imperatives," in Greenberg, editor, *Nat Turner*, 179–213, at 192.
116. Herbert Aptheker, ". . . A Note on the History," *The Nation* (October 16, 1967), 375–76; Aptheker, "Exchange," 543.
117. For example, "Seldom has a novel based on history hewed so close to basic evidence" and "I know as much as anybody about slavery in the South in 1831," both in Robert Taylor, "The Contentions of William Styron: The Novelist Responds to Critics of 'Nat Turner,'" *Boston Sunday Globe* (April 20, 1969), 6, 12. On occasion, Styron adopted the persona of an authoritative scholar, first assumed in his 1963 *New York Review of Books* critique of Aptheker's reissued *American Negro Slave Revolts* (see above, note 55). Thus, responding to questions about Aptheker's criticism of his book, Styron told the *New York Times* that Herbert Aptheker was a person "for whom neither I nor anyone else in the field of history has any respect," and that Aptheker's writings did not "convince me or any other responsible historian." See John Leo, "Some Negroes Accuse Styron of Distorting Nat Turner's Life," *New York Times*, (February 20, 1968), 34.
118. For example, William Styron, "William Styron Replies," *The Nation* (April 22, 1968), 544–47, at 545: "In writing *The Confessions of Nat Turner* I at no time pretended that my narrative was an exact transcription of historical events, had perfect accuracy been my aim I would have written a work of history rather than a novel, one of the advantages of which is its ability to allow a certain free play to the imagination."
119. West, *William Styron*, 393.
120. Styron first cites Lukács in his reply to Aptheker in *The Nation* (see above, note 118), and subsequently refers to the same passages in virtually every explanation of what

he intended to accomplish as the author of *Confessions*. See, for example, "The Uses of History in Fiction," 65–67; "Afterword," 440–41; "More Confessions," 224. Interestingly, later in his reply to Aptheker, at 546, Styron insists on the tyranny of fact in answering charges that he had failed to acknowledge Turner's wife: "There is not a shred of contemporary evidence—not a hint, not a single statement either in the original "Confessions" or in the few newspaper accounts—to show that Nat Turner had a wife." Unfortunately for Styron, his statement was erroneous. See, for example, the Richmond *Constitutional Whig* (September 26, 1831), in Henry Irving Tragle, *The Southampton Slave Revolt of 1831: A Compilation of Source Material* (Amherst: University of Massachusetts Press, 1971), 90–99, at 92.

121. "William Styron Replies," 545; "The Uses of History in Fiction," 65.
122. "The Uses of History in Fiction," 67. See also 75 ("facts *per se* are preposterous. They are like the fuzz that collects at the top of dirty closets. They don't really mean anything.")
123. Georg Lukács, *The Historical Novel*, Hannah and Stanley Mitchell, translators (London: Merlin Press, 1962), 162.
124. *Ibid.*, 166–67: "Mere fidelity to the individual facts of history" without a properly historical conception of the whole "is utterly valueless." But "this whole in the novel is the reflection of other facts of life. What matters in the novel is fidelity in the reproduction of the material foundations of the life of a given period, its manners and the feelings and thoughts deriving from these."
125. Styron's defensiveness on the matter could on occasion be very revealing: "The novelist should not (in fact, must not) be very careful. It is his right and privilege to substitute imagination for facts. . . . That I did ignore or even willfully avoid certain information which may have been available to me is true. Also, had I been entirely meticulous, I should not have implied . . . that I examined every source of fact and data. There obviously existed material which, had I been something more of a scrounger, I might not have wanted to skip. However, I don't see much importance in all of this. . . . A historical novel is in actual flight from facts and the restrictions of pure data, and . . . the better the novel is—so long as it does not seriously compromise the historical record—the less likely it will show itself to be cluttered by the detritus of fact." Styron, *This Quiet Dust*, 7.
126. Styron, "Afterword," 440–41.
127. *Ibid.*, 454.
128. Lewis and Woodward, "Slavery in the First Person," 52–53.
129. Genovese, "The Nat Turner Case," paragraph 4, paragraph 7; Styron, *This Quiet Dust*, 6.
130. Seymour L. Gross and Eileen Bender, "History, Politics, and Literature: The Myth of Nat Turner," *American Quarterly* 23, no. 4 (October 1971): 487–518, at 506; Styron, "Afterword," 452–53.
131. Styron, "Afterword," 453.
132. Styron, "This Quiet Dust," 146. And compare Styron, "Afterword," 455. See also Morris and Malin, "Vision and Value," 11; Strine, "*Confessions*," 250–53.
133. West, *William Styron*, 234.
134. Emily Dickinson, *The Single Hound: Poems of a Lifetime*, #74 (Boston: Little, Brown, and Company, 1914), 81.
135. Styron, "This Quiet Dust," 146.
136. William Faulkner, *Requiem for a Nun* (New York: Vintage International, 2012), 73.
137. Woodward, "Confessions," 25; Lewis and Woodward, "Slavery in the First Person," 52; "The Uses of History in Fiction," 59, 77–78.
138. Genovese, "The Nat Turner Case"; Genovese, "Evil, Redemption, and History."
139. Lukács, *The Historical Novel*, 70.

140. Walter Benjamin, "Literary History and the Study of Literature," in Michael W. Jennings, Howard Eiland, and Gary Smith, editors, *Walter Benjamin: Selected Writings, Volume 2, Part 2, 1931-1934* (Cambridge, MA: Harvard University Press, 1999), 459–65, at 464.
141. Michael W. Jennings, *Dialectical Images: Walter Benjamin's Theory of Literary Criticism* (Ithaca, NY: Cornell University Press, 1987), 40.
142. Lukács, *The Historical Novel*, 42, 43: "What matters therefore in the historical novel is not the re-telling of great historical events, but the poetic awakening of the people who figured in those events. What matters is that we should re-experience the social and human motives which led men to think, feel and act just as they did in historical reality." And again, "The historical novel therefore has to *demonstrate* by *artistic* means that historical circumstances and characters existed in precisely such and such a way" (emphasis in original).
143. Benjamin, *The Arcades Project*, 391 (emphasis in original).
144. West, *William Styron*, 336, 343. See also George Core, "*The Confessions of Nat Turner* and the Burden of the Past," in Morris with Malin, *Achievement*, 206–22, at 221–22. One is reminded of Benjamin's injunction that the researcher "abandon the calm, contemplative attitude toward his object in order to become conscious of the critical constellation in which precisely this fragment of the past finds itself with this present. 'The truth will not run away from us'—this statement by Gottfried Keller indicates exactly that point in historicism's image of history where the image is pierced by historical materialism. For it is an irretrievable image of the past which threatens to disappear in any present that does not recognize itself as intimated in that image." Benjamin, "Eduard Fuchs," 262.
145. Plimpton, "A Shared Ordeal," 41. But see also Horwitz, "Untrue Confessions," 83: "Styron publicly drew parallels between the black rage of the sixties and that of Nat Turner in 1831. He appeared on the cover of *Newsweek*, which quoted provocative passages from the novel and noted that both Turner and H. Rap Brown were 'coolly hell-bent after Whitey.'"
146. "The Uses of History in Fiction," 71.
147. Styron, *This Quiet Dust*, 7, 8.
148. Styron, "Afterword," 439, 454.
149. "Interview," in Greenberg, editor, *Nat Turner*, 227.
150. See above, Preface note 3, and accompanying text.'
151. "Interview," in Greenberg, editor, *Nat Turner*, 227; Anthony Stewart, "William Turner-GrayStyron, Novelist(s): Reactivating State Power in *The Confessions of Nat Turner*," *Studies in the Novel* 27, no. 2 (summer 1995): 177, 181–82.
152. Styron, "More Confessions," 225.
153. Benjamin, *The Arcades Project*, 463; Benjamin, "Eduard Fuchs," 262.
154. "Styron ennobles the historical Nat Turner." Genovese, "Evil, Redemption, and History," 210.
155. Genovese, "The Nat Turner Case," paragraph 9. As Vincent Harding stressed, the refusal to understand Turner's religious persona was one of Styron's greatest failings. See Harding, "You've Taken My Nat," 24–31.
156. See, for example, Kenneth Stampp, *The Peculiar Institution: Slavery in the Ante-Bellum South* (New York: Vintage Books, 1956), 132–34.
157. "Nat Turner led a slave revolt under extremely difficult conditions and deserves an honored place in our history." Genovese, "The Nat Turner Case," paragraph 11.
158. For important exceptions, see the essays collected in Greenberg, editor, *Nat Turner*, and the careful studies by Allmendinger, *Rising*; and Breen, *Deluged in Blood*.
159. Stampp, *Peculiar Institution*, 132, 133. More recently, in *What Hath God Wrought: The Transformation of America, 1815-1848* (New York: Oxford University Press, 2007), at 324,

Daniel Walker Howe reads Turner more or less entirely through Styron's eyes, as an agent of "Old Testament vengeance."

160. Genovese, "Evil, Redemption, and History," 210–11; see also "The Nat Turner Case," paragraph 11 ("a general who on the day before he marches does not know where he is marching to.").
161. Arna Bontemps, "Introduction to the 1968 Edition," in Arna Bontemps, *Black Thunder: Gabriel's Revolt: Virginia, 1800* (Boston: Beacon Press, 1992), xxvi, xxvii.
162. See, for example, Eric J. Sundquist, *To Wake the Nations: Race in the Making of American Literature* (Cambridge, MA: Harvard University Press, 1993), 36–83.
163. Styron, "Truth and Nat Turner," 546.
164. Benjamin, "On the Concept of History," 391 (emphasis added).
165. Walter Benjamin, "Dear Teddie," in "Exchange with Theodor W. Adorno on 'The Paris of the Second Empire in Baudelaire,'" in Eiland and Jennings, editors, *Walter Benjamin: Selected Writings, Volume 4*, 99–115, at 108.
166. Benjamin, "On the Concept of History," 390, 391.
167. "Exchange with Adorno," 108.
168. One wonders why. The answer may lie in another of Benjamin's essays, his exquisite "Observations on the Works of Nikolai Leskov." The essay quietly notes how modernity is marked by the loss in value of experience, a form of intelligibility the communication of which is the essence of storytelling. It registers that loss in the proliferation of media that displace experience in favor of "information"—a completely distinct form of intelligibility—first of all, notably, the book. "The earliest indication of a process whose end is the decline of storytelling," Benjamin writes, "is the rise of the novel." And for the novelist, novels must be sold; intelligibility must be commodified. Walter Benjamin, "The Storyteller: Observations on the Works of Nikolai Leskov," in Eiland and Jennings, editors, *Walter Benjamin: Selected Writings, Volume 3*, 143–66, at 146.

    Styron had wanted to tell Turner's story ever since he had been a boy. But he also grew up wanting to be "a writer." The writer divorced Turner's story from experience. This was what enraged African American intellectuals. The story gestated instead in Styron's mind, to be inscribed eventually in a book that was very successfully sold. Nevertheless, in the course of the divorcing, the gestating, the inscribing, and the selling, the story acquired another point, even though Styron himself never successfully articulated it: the "long moment indistinguishable" that stitched past and now together.

CHAPTER 1: *CONFESSIONS*: OF TEXT AND PARATEXT

1. One free black—Billy Artis—joined Turner's band and died in the aftermath of the massacre. Four others were arraigned as participants, and tried, but only one convicted—Berry Newsom. He was hanged.
2. The events of August 22 and 23, their context, and their aftermath, are ably recounted in two recent histories: Allmendinger, *Rising*, and Breen, *Deluged in Blood*.
3. *The Confessions of Nat Turner* . . . (Baltimore: Lucas & Deaver, print., 1831), 3, 3–4, 7, 18. In this chapter, all references to the pamphlet are to the original 1831 edition.
4. Parramore, *Southampton County*, 111–12; Kenneth S. Greenberg, "The Confessions of Nat Turner: Text and Context," in Kenneth S. Greenberg, editor, *The Confessions of Nat Turner and Related Documents* (Boston: Bedford St. Martin's, 1996), 1–35, at 8; Tragle, *Southampton Slave Revolt*, 279, 327. *The Liberator* (December 17, 1831) reported that the Baltimore printing alone was an edition of 50,000 copies.
5. David F. Allmendinger Jr., "The Construction of *The Confessions of Nat Turner*," in Greenberg, editor, *Nat Turner*, 24–42, at 40.

6. See, for example, Herbert Aptheker, *Nat Turner's Slave Rebellion* (Mineola, NY: Dover, 2006); Stephen B. Oates, *The Fires of Jubilee: Nat Turner's Fierce Rebellion* (New York: Harper & Row, 1975); Greenberg, editor, *Nat Turner*; Anthony Santoro, "The Prophet in His Own Words: Nat Turner's Biblical Construction," *Virginia Magazine of History and Biography* 116, no. 2 (2008): 114–49; Daniel S. Fabricant, "Thomas R. Gray and William Styron: Finally a Critical Look at the 1831 *Confessions of Nat Turner*," *American Journal of Legal History* 37, no. 3 (July 1993): 332–61.
7. Michael Johnson, "Denmark Vesey and His Co-Conspirators," *William and Mary Quarterly*, 3d Ser., 58, no. 4 (October 2001): 915–76. The books in question were Douglas R. Egerton, *He Shall Go Out Free: The Lives of Denmark Vesey* (Madison, WI: Madison House, 1999); David Robertson, *Denmark Vesey* (New York: Knopf, 1999); and Edward A. Pearson, editor, *Designs against Charleston: The Trial Record of the Denmark Vesey Slave Conspiracy of 1822* (Chapel Hill: University of North Carolina Press, 1999). The full title of the *Official Report* is: *An Official Report of the Trials of Sundry Negroes, charged with an attempt to Raise an Insurrection in the state of South Carolina: preceded by an Introduction and Narrative; and in an appendix, a report of the trials of Four White Persons, on indictments for attempting to excite the slave to insurrection. Prepared and Published at the request of the Court. By Lionel H. Kennedy & Thomas Parker, Members of the Charleston Bar, and the Presiding Magistrates of the Court* (Charleston: Printed by James R. Schenck, 23, Broad-Street. 1822).
8. Johnson, "Denmark Vesey," 915–16, 934, 971. Johnson's critique was answered by the three historians in question, and its significance discussed by five others, with a final response from Johnson: See Edward A. Pearson, "Trials And Errors: Denmark Vesey and His Historians," 137–42; Douglas R. Egerton, "Forgetting Denmark Vesey; Or, Oliver Stone Meets Richard Wade," 143–52; David Robertson, "Inconsistent Contextualism: The Hermeneutics of Michael Johnson," 153–58; Philip D. Morgan, "Conspiracy Scares," 159–66; Thomas J. Davis, "Conspiracy And Credibility: Look Who's Talking, about What—Law Talk and Loose Talk," 167–74; Winthrop D. Jordan, "The Charleston Hurricane of 1822; Or, the Law's Rampage," 175–78; James Sidbury, "Plausible Stories and Varnished Truths," 179–84; Robert L. Paquette, "Jacobins of the Lowcountry: The Vesey Plot On Trial," 185–92; Michael P. Johnson, "Reading Evidence," 193–202, all in "*Forum*: The Making of a Slave Conspiracy," *William and Mary Quarterly*, 3d Ser., 59, no. 1 (January 2002): 135–202. In 2017, Douglas Egerton and Robert Paquette published *The Denmark Vesey Affair: A Documentary History* (Gainesville: University Press of Florida, 2017), which, they argued (at xxii–xxiv), fully answered Johnson's doubts that an authentic conspiracy had existed. No "smoking gun" was forthcoming, but the *Documentary History* includes correspondence of white Charleston residents relaying reports that confessions from some condemned participants had been heard by white ministers while visiting them in jail. See, for example, Mary Lamboll Beach to Elizabeth Gilchrist (5 July 1822; 15 July 1822), in *Documentary History*, 373–77, 392–93. See also Robert L. Paquette and Douglas R. Egerton, "Of Facts and Fables: New Light on the Denmark Vesey Affair," *South Carolina Historical Magazine* 105, no. 1 (2004): 8–48.
9. Parramore, *Southampton County*, 105–7, 119–20; Greenberg, "Text and Context," 8–10.
10. *Confessions*, 18. The questions Gray acknowledges asking during Turner's narrative are explicitly identified as such in the course of the narrative statement that the pamphlet attributes to Turner.
11. Commentary on the pamphlet in the Richmond *Enquirer* (November 25, 1831) identified "one defect—we mean its style. The confession of the culprit is given, as it were, from his own lips—(and when read to him, he admitted its statements to be correct)—but the language is far superior to what Nat Turner could have employed—Portions of it are even eloquently and classically expressed.—This is calculated to cast some shade of doubt over the authenticity of the narrative, and to give the Bandit a

character for intelligence which he does not deserve, and ought not to have received.—In all other respects, the confession appears to be faithful and true." The *Enquirer*'s desire to undermine Turner's "character for intelligence" is reminiscent of Thomas Jefferson's dismissal of Phillis Wheatley's poetry in his *Notes on the State of Virginia* (New York: W. W. Norton, 1982), 140.

12. Sundquist, *To Wake the Nations*, 80. The standard for corroboration—notably whether rumor, hearsay, or third-party reportage could be accorded evidentiary weight—was debated by Johnson and the historians of the Vesey Conspiracy he criticized. See Egerton, "Forgetting Denmark Vesey," 145, 148–49; Robertson, "Inconsistent Contextualism," 154–55, 156. See also Paquette, "Jacobins of the Lowcountry," 188–90, 192. Johnson replied in, "Reading Evidence," 195–96.
13. *Confessions*, 3–5, 18–20.
14. French, *The Rebellious Slave*, 51. Both Allmendinger, *Rising*; and Breen, *Deluged in Blood*, conform to this pattern.
15. Sundquist, *To Wake the Nations*, 10, 37, and generally 36–83.
16. Jeannine Marie DeLombard, *In the Shadow of the Gallows: Race, Crime, and American Civic Identity* (Philadelphia: University of Pennsylvania Press, 2012), 164–83. On the confessing subjects of execution sermons and gallows literature, and their successors, see David Dowd Hall, *Worlds of Wonder, Days of Judgment: Popular Religious Belief in Early New England* (New York: Alfred A. Knopf, 1989), 178–86; Daniel A. Cohen, *Pillars of Salt, Monuments of Grace: New England Crime Literature and the Origins of American Popular Culture, 1674-1860* (Amherst: University of Massachusetts Press, 1993); Karen Halttunen, *Murder Most Foul: The Killer and the American Gothic Imagination* (Cambridge, MA: Harvard University Press, 1998). On the antebellum slave narrative, see John Sekora and Darwin T. Turner, *The Art of Slave Narrative: Original Essays in Criticism and Theory* (Macomb, IL: Western Illinois University, 1982); Charles T. Davis and Henry Louis Gates Jr., editors, *The Slave's Narrative* (Oxford: Oxford University Press, 1985); Marion Wilson Starling, *The Slave Narrative: Its Place in American History* (Washington, DC: Howard University Press, 1988).
17. Jacques Derrida, *Of Grammatology* (Baltimore: The Johns Hopkins University Press, 1974), 158.
18. "Il n'ya pas de hors-texte" is often translated as "there is nothing outside the text," but actually means "there is no outside-text," which is rather different.
19. Andrews, "*Nat Turner*," 79–87, at 81.
20. Laura Thiemann Scales, "Narrative Revolutions in Nat Turner and Joseph Smith," *American Literary History* 24, no. 2 (2012): 205–33, at 209–11, 215.
21. *Ibid.*, 216. The play of "sacred" and "gothic" tropes in popular crime literature is a key component of Halttunen's analysis in *Murder Most Foul.* For a further, probing account of their presence and interaction in *The Confessions*, see Stephen Howard Browne, "'This Unparalleled and Inhuman Massacre': The Gothic, the Sacred, and the Meaning of Nat Turner," *Rhetoric and Public Affairs* 3, no. 3 (fall 2000): 309–31. Browne ably disentangles "two distinctive and competing discourses" in *The Confessions*, the one representing violence "as the fated consequence of divine will" (310), the other stressing human depravity. Unfortunately, Browne's commitment to the interpretive capacities of genre overcomes careful and detailed attention to the text itself. Nor can one have confidence in Browne's understanding of the historical circumstances and effects of Turner's rebellion.
22. John Mac Kilgore, "Nat Turner and the Work of Enthusiasm," *Publications of the Modern Language Association of America* [*PMLA*] 130, no. 5 (2015): 1347–62, at 1355, 1358.
23. Caleb Smith, *The Oracle and the Curse: A Poetics of Justice from the Revolution to the Civil War* (Cambridge, MA: Harvard University Press, 2013), 157.
24. *Ibid.*, 157.

25. *Ibid.*, 161, 160–63.
26. See Gérard Genette, "Introduction to the Paratext," *New Literary History* 22, no. 2 (spring 1991): 261–72. I am grateful to Levi Cooper for introducing me to Genette's work.
27. This is not to say the pamphlet's epitext is not worth interrogating. Indeed, as the works cited in note 6, above, indicate, the pamphlet has enjoyed a long and controversial history of reception, review, and commentary, early in its life generating an oppositional tradition of apocrypha and literary embellishment, and later scholarly critique. For an account, see French, *The Rebellious Slave*. For comparable "paratextual" studies of antebellum slave narratives, see John Sekora, "Black Message/White Envelope: Genre, Authenticity, and Authority in the Antebellum Slave Narrative," *Callalloo* 32 (summer 1987): 482–515; James Olney, "'I Was Born': Slave Narratives: Their Status as Autobiography and as Literature," in Davis and Gates, editors, *The Slave's Narrative*, 148–75, particularly 152–53.
28. The statement of copyright reads as follows:

> DISTRICT OF COLUMBIA, TO WIT:
>
> *Be it remembered*, That on this tenth day of November, Anno Domini, eighteen hundred and thirty-one, Thomas R. Gray of the said District, deposited in this office the title of a book, which is in the words as following :
>
> "The Confessions of Nat Turner, the leader of the late insurrection in Southampton, Virginia, as fully and voluntarily made to Thomas R. Gray, in the prison where he was confined, and acknowledged by him to be such when read before the Court of Southampton; with the certificate, under seal, of the Court convened at Jerusalem, November 5, 1831, for his trial. Also, an authentic account of the whole insurrection, with lists of the whites who were murdered, and of the negroes brought before the Court of Southampton, and there sentenced, &c. the right whereof he claims as proprietor, in conformity with an Act of Congress, entitled "An act to amend the several acts respecting Copy Rights."
>
> EDMUND J. LEE, Clerk of the District.
> In testimony that the above is a true copy, from the record of the District Court for the District of Columbia, I, Edmund I. Lee, the Clerk thereof, have hereunto set my hand and affixed the seal of my office, this 10th day of November, 1831.
>
> (Seal.)
>
> Edmund J. Lee, C.D.C.

29. The justices' statement of certification reads as follows:

> We the undersigned, members of the Court convened at Jerusalem, on Saturday, the 5th day of Nov. 1831, for the trial of Nat, *alias* Nat Turner, a negro slave, late the property of Putnam Moore, deceased, do hereby certify, that the confessions of Nat, to Thomas R. Gray, was read to him in our presence, and that Nat acknowledged the same to be full, free, and voluntary; and that furthermore, when called upon by the presiding Magistrate of the Court, to state if he had any thing to say, why sentence of death should not be passed upon him, replied he had nothing further than he had communicated to Mr. Gray. Given under our hands and seals at Jerusalem, this 5th day of November, 1831.

JEREMIAH COBB, [*Seal.*]
THOMAS PRETLOW, [*Seal.*]
JAMES W. PARKER, [*Seal.*]
CARR BOWERS, [*Seal.*]
SAMUEL B. HINES, [*Seal.*]
ORRIS A. BROWNE, [*Seal.*]

30. The clerk of court's statement of certification reads as follows:

State of Virginia, Southampton County, to wit:

I, James Rochelle, Clerk of the County Court of Southampton in the State of Virginia, do hereby certify, that Jeremiah Cobb, Thomas Pretlow, James W. Parker, Carr Bowers, Samuel B. Hines, and Orris A. Browne, esqr's are acting Justices of the Peace, in and for the County aforesaid, and were members of the Court which convened at Jerusalem, on Saturday the 5th day of November, 1831, for the trial of Nat *alias* Nat Turner, a negro slave, late the property of Putnam Moore, deceased, who was tried and convicted, as an insurgent in the late insurrection in the county of Southampton aforesaid, and that full faith and credit are due, and ought to be given to their acts as Justices of the peace aforesaid.

[Seal.] In testimony whereof, I have hereunto set my hand and caused the seal of the Court aforesaid, to be affixed this 5th day of November, 1831.

JAMES ROCHELLE, C. S. C. C.

31. On truthfulness in avowal (confession), see Michel Foucault, *Wrong-Doing, Truth-Telling: The Function of Avowal in Justice*, Fabienne Brion and Bernard E. Harcourt, editors, Stephen W. Sawyer, translator (Chicago: University of Chicago Press, 2014), 92–93, 200–202. Foucault writes, "It seems to me that one of the most fundamental traits of Christianity is that it ties the individual to the obligation to search within himself for the truth of what he is. . . . To decipher it as a condition of salvation, and to make it manifest to someone else . . . is a very different kind of obligation of truth from the one that ties the individual to a dogma, text, or teaching." (92).

The title's use of the plural, *Confessions*, is noteworthy. It is not uncommon to find the plural form used to describe the autobiographical apologia of a single individual. The most famous example, of course, is *The Confessions of St. Augustine of Hippo*. Still, the criminal confessions of individuals were far more commonly entitled "Confession" (as the interior title of Turner's confession narrative within the pamphlet is entitled). Of fifteen (nonduplicate) titles explicitly including the word *Confessions* in Shaw & Shoemaker's *Early American Imprints* (1801–19), only two are attributable to single individuals, only one of which is a criminal confession. Of 81 (nonduplicate) titles explicitly including the word *Confession* in the same source, 39 are attributable to single individuals, of which 29 are criminal confessions. See also below, note 38.

In *Wrong-Doing, Truth-Telling*, Foucault develops both the relationship between Christianity's spiritual "veridiction of the self" (94) and the function of avowal by the subject of law in criminal justice, and their unassimilability one to the other. The use of the plural in *The Confessions of Nat Turner* seems, then, to hint at a process with dual and distinct emphases, one that is juridical (presumptively Gray's purpose) and one that is sacramental (Turner's).

32. See, for example, the Richmond *Enquirer* (August 30, 1831) citing a letter from Jerusalem dated August 24: "A fanatic preacher by the name of Nat Turner . . . was at the bottom of this infernal brigandage. . . . The ringleader." In Tragle, *Southampton Slave Revolt*, 44, 45; trial of Davy, late the property of Elizabeth Turner, 2d day of September, 1831, in Tragle, 185–89, at 188.
33. See above, note 29. The full court numbered ten justices. Did four justices refuse to certify, or was a majority (quorum) that included the presiding magistrate enough for Gray, hurrying to be off to Richmond? Patrick Breen has observed that "three of the four men who did not sign the affidavit left the bench immediately following Turner's trial," which suggests that the four were unavailable. Breen, *Deluged in Blood*, 174.
34. Taken individually, neither certificate does the whole work of certification to which the singular "certificate" in the pamphlet's title alludes. Rather, the reader encounters an accumulation of certifications that collectively (a) attest to the circumstances to which the title alludes (the justices' certificate) and (b) require credence for the justices' acts as justices of the peace, including the certification just granted (the clerk's certificate). Gray himself merges the two certificates by referring to them (page 4) as "one stamp of truth and sincerity."
35. Thus, there is no reference on the title page to a preface authored by Thomas Ruffin Gray.
36. Notably of white escapees unknown to Turner, including one "concealed for protection by a slave of the family." *Confessions*, 19.
37. The pamphlet is rich in signatures: the copyright, the two certificates, and the preface are all signed. But the confession is not signed. Nor is the trial report.
38. Gray's copyright was granted in accordance with the terms of the federal "act to amend the several acts respecting copyrights" enacted by the 21st Congress, February 3, 1831. Section 1 of the act provides "that from and after the passing of this act, any person or persons, being a citizen or citizens of the United States, or resident therein, who shall be the author or authors of any book or books, map, chart, or musical composition, which may be now made or composed, and not printed and published, or shall hereafter be made or composed, or who shall invent, design, etch, engrave, work, or cause to be engraved, etched, or worked from his own design, any print or engraving, and the executors, administrators, or legal assigns of such person or persons, shall have the sole right and liberty of printing, reprinting, publishing, and vending such book or books, map, chart, musical composition, print, cut, or engraving, in whole or in part, for the term of twenty-eight years from the time of recording the title thereof, in the manner hereinafter directed." Section 3 of the act introduces a distinction between "author" and "proprietor." Section 4 of the act provides that either an "author" or a "proprietor" may have the benefit of the act by depositing "a printed copy of the title of such book, or books, map, chart, musical composition, print, cut, or engraving, in the clerk's office of the district court of the district wherein the author or proprietor shall reside," the clerk being "directed and required to record the same thereof forthwith, in a book to be kept for that purpose." The purpose of the distinction between author and proprietor is to allow a person who has ownership of a work but is not the author of the work, or not the sole author of the work, to have the benefit of the act in the manner and form directed by section 4. As we have seen (above, note 28), Gray obtains copyright in the manner and form directed, but as "proprietor" not "author."
39. *Confessions*, 3–5. See also Browne, "'This Unparalleled and Inhuman Massacre,'" 317–23.

40. The relevant gubernatorial instruction was transmitted from the Executive Department of the Government of Virginia to the Clerks of the County Courts of Southampton, Isle of Wight, Nansemond, Sussex, and Prince George Counties on September 26, 1831 (that is, after many of the Southampton trials had taken place), as follows: "Sir: I am instructed by the Governor to request that upon the trial of such slaves as may be condemned in the County Court of ____________ the utmost accuracy may be observed in taking down and certifying the evidence to this Department. It is important that the evidence be taken verbatim as given in Court and that it be so certified." The instructions were issued pursuant to Virginia's statute of January 15, 1801, "An Act to empower the governor to transport slaves condemned, when it shall be deemed expedient," which provided that the governor, "with the advice of Council," might proceed to sell any slave "under sentence of death, for conspiracy, insurrection, or other crimes" to any person or persons for carriage out of the United States," and requiring that "in all cases where any slave or slaves shall be tried and convicted for any crime which may affect life, the court before whom such trials shall be had, shall cause the testimony for and against every such slave to be entered of record, and a copy of the whole proceedings to be transmitted forthwith to the executive." *Statutes at Large of Virginia, from October Session 1792, to December Session 1806, Inclusive*, Samuel Shepherd, editor, 3 volumes (Richmond: Printed by Samuel Shepherd, 1835), 2:279–80. And see Philip J. Schwarz, "The Transportation of Slaves from Virginia, 1801-1865," *Slavery and Abolition* 7, no. 3 (1986): 215–40. The purpose of the statute was to allow commutation of slaves convicted of capital crimes to sale for transportation outside the state in order to save the Commonwealth the cost of compensating their owners out of the public fisc.
41. Note that the steady accumulation of date/place stamps conveys powerfully the impression that the entire manuscript—not just the confession—was complete and in final draft on November 5.
42. The previous five are: title, copyright, preface, justices' certificate, clerk's certificate.
43. The succession of date/place stamps effectively "notarize" each component of the pamphlet.
44. *Confessions*, 18. Gray's "certain death" statement contrasts with that of the examining magistrate James Trezvant at Turner's trial that at the preliminary examination of Turner on October 31 "the prisoner . . . was in confinement but no threats or promises were held out to him to make any disclosures." On the significance of this contrast see Fabricant, "A Critical Look," 348.
45. The narrative reads, "And my father and mother strengthened me in this my first impression, saying in my presence, I was intended for some great purpose, which they had always thought from certain marks on my head and breast—" at which point Gray self-consciously breaks in "[a parcel of excrescences which I believe are not at all uncommon, particularly among negroes, as I have seen several with the same. In this case he has either cut them off or they have nearly disappeared]" before the narrative resumes "—My grand mother, who was very religious, and to whom I was much attached—" and so forth. *Confessions*, 7.
46. The narrative reads, "All my time, not devoted to my master's service, was spent either in prayer, or in making experiments in casting different things in moulds made of earth, in attempting to make paper, gunpowder, and many other experiments, that although I could not perfect, yet convinced me of its practicability if I had the means." Gray adds an asterisk at the end of the sentence and footnotes the statement as follows: "When questioned as to the manner of manufacturing those different articles, he was found well informed on the subject."
47. Both interrogatories are wrapped into the text of the narrative as interruptions. Thus on page 9: "As I was praying one day at my plough, the spirit spoke to me, saying,

'Seek ye the kingdom of Heaven and all things shall be added unto you.' *Question*—what do you mean by the Spirit. *Ans.* The Spirit that spoke to the prophets in former days—and I was greatly astonished" and so forth. On page 11: "I heard a loud noise in the heavens, and the Spirit instantly appeared to me and said the Serpent was loosened, and Christ had laid down the yoke he had borne for the sins of men, and that I should take it on and fight against the Serpent, for the time was fast approaching when the first should be last and the last should be first. *Ques.* Do you not find yourself mistaken now? *Ans.* Was not Christ crucified. And by signs in the heavens that it would make known to me when I should commence the great work" and so forth.

48. "Knowing the influence I had obtained over the minds of my fellow servants (not by the means of conjuring and such like tricks—for to them I always spoke of such things with contempt) but . . ."
49. The paragraph reads as follows:

> Since the commencement of 1830, I had been living with Mr. Joseph Travis, who was to me a kind master, and placed the greatest confidence in me; in fact, I had no cause to complain of his treatment to me. On Saturday evening, the 20th of August, it was agreed between Henry, Hark and myself, to prepare a dinner the next day for the men we expected, and then to concert a plan, as we had not yet determined on any. Hark, on the following morning, brought a pig, and Henry brandy, and being joined by Sam, Nelson, Will and Jack, they prepared in the woods a dinner, where, about three o'clock, I joined them.
>
> *Q.* Why were you so backward in joining them.
>
> *A.* The same reason that had caused me not to mix with them for years before.

50. *Confessions*, 7–8.
51. The reintroduction of dashes occurs on pages 14–15, where they appear in three distinct clumps, intermingled with complete, fully punctuated, and syntactically correct sentences.
52. *Confessions*, 12–13.
53. *Ibid.*, 9.
54. *Ibid.*, 11 (emphasis added). On compression in Christian temporality as "a visible sign that, according to God's will, the Final Judgment is imminent, that the world is about to end," see Reinhart Koselleck, *Futures Past: On the Semantics of Historical Time*, Keith Tribe, translator (New York: Columbia University Press, 2004), 11, 12; Dennis E. Johnson, *Triumph of the Lamb: A Commentary on Revelation* (Phillipsburg, NJ: P&R Publishing, 2001), 277.
55. DeLombard is also intrigued by the pamphlet's multiple temporal resonances, but does not distinguish between the different rhythms of its two parts. Rather, "Gray's Turner is the embodiment of the temporal mashup that has become the hallmark of modernity." DeLombard, *In the Shadow of the Gallows*, 177.
56. Anthony Santoro likewise describes the *Confessions* as "a schizophrenic text." Santoro, "The Prophet in His Own Words," 116. See also Browne, "'This Unparalleled and Inhuman Massacre,'" 311, 313, 317, 328. And see above, note 31.
57. Notably of the first skirmish between Turner's party and white militia. *Confessions*, 15–16. See also Breen, *Deluged in Blood*, 177–78. In his concluding commentary Gray adds, "There were two [whites] whom they thought they left dead on the field at Mr. Parker's, but were only stunned by the blows of their guns, as they did not take time to re-load when they charged on them." *Confessions*, 19.
58. Care in composition suggests that this is the section in which Gray was most invested, with which he was most familiar, and for which he was best prepared.
59. Allmendinger, "Construction," 24–42.

60. Tragle, *Southampton Slave Revolt*, 177–221, 229–44.
61. *The Constitutional Whig*, Richmond, Virginia. (September 26, 1831), in Tragle, *Southampton Slave Revolt*, 90–99. Allmendinger, "Construction," 31–36.
62. Fabricant "A Critical Look," 338–40, 344–46.
63. "Much of what Gray knew before [his meetings with Turner] found its way into *The Confessions of Nat Turner*." Allmendinger, "Construction," 37. See, generally, Allmendinger, *Rising*, 216–53; Henry Irving Tragle, "Styron and His Sources," *Massachusetts Review* 11, no. 12 (winter 1970): 135–53. Note that in syntax and grammar, Gray's self-identified interventions in the first half are correct, unlike the text into which they intrude, but like the text of the second half.

    What is at issue here is not whether the second half of the confession is an accurate account of what happened on August 21 and 22, 1831, but how that account was composed, and to what extent the manner of its composition differs from the first half's account of Turner's life and motivations. Analysis of variation in the composition of the confession permits one to determine how and to what extent it may be used as historical evidence relevant to the Turner Rebellion and to the intellectual persona of Nat Turner.
64. See above, prologue, notes 69–70 and accompanying text.
65. *Confessions*, 12. See trial of Jack a negro man slave the property of William Reese decsd., 3d day of September, 1831, in Tragle, *Southampton Slave Revolt*, 195–96, at 196. See also 198 (Gray was the court-appointed counsel for Jack [Reese]).
66. It is also the only interrogatory that is not an interruption, wrapped into the text. Situated at the conclusion of the preceding cleanly written paragraph it signifies the emergence of the confession narrative's second author, and with that emergence less of a need to ask questions.
67. *Confessions*, 18.
68. *Ibid.*, 20.
69. *Ibid.*, 20. See, generally, Fabricant, "A Critical Look," 343–44.
70. This is the position taken by the novelist Sharon Ewell Foster in *The Resurrection of Nat Turner*. In his commentary on Michael Johnson's analysis of the Vesey Conspiracy, Philip Morgan cautions us that a locality's white notables were certainly capable of endless duplicity when alarmed by the possibility of slave resistance. See Morgan, "Conspiracy Scares," 159–66, at 163. But although one cannot completely discount the possibility that indeed Gray did make the whole thing up, the structural analysis that discloses the multiplicity of component parts in the pamphlet suggests fabrication is highly unlikely. Had Gray made the whole thing up, the document would have been more uniform, less complex, in its composition. Gray's only other known publication—a pedestrian pamphlet published in February 1834 to rebut public charges (unrelated to the Turner Rebellion) leveled by Southampton County magistrate Dr. Orris Browne that Gray was "entirely destitute of honor or honesty"—does not display much authorial talent. One may agree wholeheartedly with the self-evaluation he offered there, "I possess an ordinary share of intelligence" (8), and conclude that in *The Confessions* it was principally exposure to his extraordinary interlocutor that caused him to exceed his capacities. See Thomas Ruffin Gray, *To the Public* (February 14, 1834), Virginia State Library, Richmond. My thanks to Alfred L. Brophy for sharing his copy with me.

    Could Gray have forged the certifications of the six justices and the clerk of court endorsing the account he would publish? Had he done so his fledgling legal career (he had been admitted only eight months earlier), which was his only real source of income, would have been over. Perhaps, then, the justices, the clerk, and Gray all conspired to fabricate the pamphlet. But so wide a conspiracy would carry substantial risks of discovery, particularly in light of gubernatorial instructions to furnish a properly certified record. Unlike the Vesey affair, the Southampton event was an actual occurrence. The opportunity for local notables to concoct a narrative to frame Nat Turner seems vanishingly small. See also Allmendinger, *Rising*, 249–50.

71. County court proceedings were not routinely reported, except occasionally (and briefly) in local newspapers. The same applied to most state trial courts. State appellate court decision were reported, but reports remained nominate, taken in longhand or using phonetic shorthand, throughout the nineteenth century. The first nonprivate, non-nominate reports to appear were those of the U.S. Supreme Court, in 1874. In substance, Gray's trial report, largely devoid of procedural technicality, resembles a newspaper report of a local case of great notoriety.
72. The report of Trezvant's testimony in the trial record does not suggest any major discrepancy between that testimony and the tenor of the confession narrative. Trezvant's testimony appears as reported speech recorded and abbreviated by the clerk of court, complete with Trezvant's own prejudicial glosses on what the committing magistrates' examination had revealed: "He [Turner] gave a long account of the motives which lead him finally to commence the bloody scenes which took place—that he pretended [*sic*] to have had intimations by signs and omens from God that he should embark in the desperate attempt—That his comrades and even he were impressed with a belief that he could by the imposition of his hands [*sic*] cure disease—That he related a particular instance, in which it was believed that he had in that manner effected a cure upon one of his comrades, and that he went on to detail a medley of incoherent [*sic*] and confused [*sic*] opinions about his communications with God, his command [*sic*] over the clouds &c. &c. which he had been entertaining as far back as 1826." See Tragle, *Southampton Slave Revolt*, 222 (with minor corrections from the original clerk's record, Southampton County Court *Minute Book* (November 5, 1831), 122–23.) Each of Trezvant's evaluative statements [marked *sic* above] imposes Trezvant's own subjective characterization on a statement or event also reported in the confession narrative recorded by Gray. Thus, see below, chapter 2, note 78, and accompanying text [signs and omens]; note 68 and accompanying text [cure disease/cure a comrade]; notes 26–79 and accompanying text [communications with God]; note 52 and accompanying text [command over the clouds].
73. See Tomlins, "After Critical Legal History," 42. It is worth emphasizing the difference between this approach and poststructural emphases on textual plasticity, and on the contingency and indeterminacy of language.
74. Sundquist, *To Wake the Nations*, 37.
75. Tragle, *Southampton Slave Revolt*, 223. With minimal variation the same formulaic clerical statement summarizes every capital sentence handed down during the trials occasioned by the rebellion.
76. Smith, *Oracle*, 161, 162, 163.
77. *Ibid.*, 161.
78. *Confessions*, 7 (emphasis added).
79. Marie Maclean, "Pretexts and Paratexts: The Art of the Peripheral," *New Literary History* 22, no. 2 (spring 1991): 273–79; and see Genette, "Introduction to the Paratext," 261.
80. Michel Serres, *Statues: Le Seconde Livre des Fondations* (Paris: Editions F. Bourin, 1987), 90, in Maclean, "Pretexts and Paratexts," 273 (Maclean's translation).

CHAPTER 2: READING LUKE IN SOUTHAMPTON COUNTY

1. Charles F. Irons, *The Origins of Proslavery Christianity: White and Black Evangelicals in Colonial and Antebellum Virginia* (Chapel Hill: The University of North Carolina Press, 2008), 147.
2. Smith, *Oracle*, 164–65.
3. Daniel Walker Howe, *What Hath God Wrought: The Transformation of America, 1815-1848* (New York: Oxford University Press, 2007), 324, citing Isaiah 61:1–2. For Styron, see above, prologue notes 12, 71, and 79, and accompanying text. For his part, also without evidence, Stephen Oates holds Turner beholden to the Old Testament in general and Ezekiel in particular. Oates, *Fires of Jubilee*, 26, 35–36, 54, 69, 87. Gerald Mullin, too, finds "magnificent Old Testament visions" at the heart of Turner's rebellion. They "transfigured him and sustained his movement," and supplied its crucial "sacred dimension." Gerald W. Mullin, *Flight and Rebellion: Slave Resistance in Eighteenth Century Virginia* (New York: Oxford University Press, 1975), 160. Mullin convinced Lawrence Levine, who in any case was himself already fully persuaded of the "Old Testament bias" of slave religion. See Lawrence W. Levine, *Black Culture and Black Consciousness: Afro-American Folk Thought from Slavery to Freedom* (1977; reprint New York: Oxford University Press: 2007), 50, 75. See also Breen, *Deluged in Blood*, 146.
4. Sundquist, *To Wake the Nations*, 49, 76–77, 81. On the significance of religion in slave rebellion, see James Sidbury, "Reading, Revelation, and Rebellion: The Textual Communities of Gabriel, Denmark Vesey, and Nat Turner," in Greenberg, editor, *Nat Turner*, 119–33, and generally, *Ploughshares into Swords: Race, Rebellion, and Identity in Gabriel's Virginia, 1730-1810* (Cambridge: Cambridge University Press, 1997). Sundquist seems to me to display too great a desire to secularize Turner's religiosity, suggesting that it provided a medium within which might be conveyed an (implicitly more acceptable) "ideological message" of "revolutionary democracy" (49, 81).
5. Sundquist, *To Wake the Nations*, 73. The scripture with which Turner was acquainted was that of the King James Bible. See Object Number 2011.28, "Bible Belonging to Nat Turner," Collection of the Smithsonian National Museum of African American History and Culture (figure 2.1 this volume). On the ubiquity of the King James Version in America "from early in the colonial period until deep into the twentieth century," see Mark A. Noll, *In the Beginning Was the Word: The Bible in American Public Life, 1492-1783* (New York: Oxford University Press, 2016), 17.

   Noll gives particular emphasis to "personal Biblicism" in African American reception of evangelical revivalism, describing an intense "Bible-only faith" unmediated by inherited Christian structures. In the first narratives of the black autobiographical tradition, personal Biblicism "slipped easily into public anti-slavery," but for the most part it appeared to lack an explicit politics: "For African Americans [revivalist personal Biblicism] established a tradition of biblical practice that functioned with almost no opportunity for exercising power in public" (231, and see generally 207–34). Compare Peter P. Hinks, *To Awaken My Afflicted Brethren: David Walker and the Problem of Antebellum Slave Resistance* (University Park: Pennsylvania State University Press, 1997), 232–33. See also below, note 110. In response to Noll, I wish to stress two observations that I believe are central to any attempt to understand Turner. One I have already mentioned (above, preface, text at note 12), Michael Gomez's essential point that Nat Turner was a Christian, "inspired by God," by "Christian faith and the Bible." Gomez, *Exchanging Our Country Marks*, 257. The second is Cedric Robinson's no less essential point that the "African tradition that grounded collective resistance by Blacks to slavery and colonial imperialism" focused "on the structures of the mind. Its epistemology granted supremacy to metaphysics, not the material. . . . [To] mind, metaphysics, ideology, consciousness." Robinson, *Black Marxism*, 169.

6. Sundquist, *To Wake the Nations*, 70.
7. Turner's fondness for Luke has not been much remarked, but has also been noted in Allmendinger, *Rising*, 14–20, 248.
8. On the organization of the New Testament and the unity of Luke and Acts, see Darrell L. Bock, *A Theology of Luke and Acts: Biblical Theology of the New Testament* (Grand Rapids, MI: Zondervan, 2012), 27, 55–61; Charles H. H. Scobie, "A Canonical Approach to Interpreting Luke: The Journey Motif as a Hermeneutical Key," in Craig B. Bartholomew et al., editors, *Reading Luke: Interpretation, Reflection, Formation* (Grand Rapids, MI: Zondervan, 2005), 327–49.
9. Bock, *Theology*, 27, 177–78; Charles H. Talbert, *Reading Luke: A Literary and Theological Commentary on the Third Gospel* (Macon, GA: Smyth & Helwys, 2002), 4.
10. On the influence of typology in American biblical culture see, generally, Eran Shalev, *American Zion: The Old Testament as a Political Text from the Revolution to the Civil War* (New Haven: Yale University Press, 2013), 6–7, 9, 19, 43, 85. Shalev, however, concentrates on typology as a mode of incorporation of Old Testament narrative and imagery. American biblicism "was profoundly focused on the Old Testament" (101). Turner's typology in contrast is focused on the New Testament, manifesting the influence of evangelical Christianity's turn over the previous century to the New Testament and to the fulfillment of God's providential plan for the redemption of humanity. On typology in this idiom, see below, text at notes 173–76. Shalev notes the growing dominance of the New Testament over the Old in public discourse during the course of the nineteenth century, particularly after 1820 (102, 148, 157, 165–68).
11. Hans Conzelmann, *The Theology of St. Luke*, Geoffrey Buswell, translator (New York: Harper and Row, 1961), 173. See also F. Scott Spencer, "Preparing the Way of the Lord: Introducing and Interpreting Luke's Narrative," in Bartholomew et al., editors, *Reading Luke*, 104–24, at 116–17.
12. Bock, *Theology*, 152.
13. *Ibid.*, 160, 161, 253–54.
14. Luke 4:14, 16–20; Bock, *Theology*, 161, 162. We should note Nazareth's reaction to Jesus's preaching his mission: "And all they in the synagogue, when they heard these things, were filled with wrath, / And rose up, and thrust him out of the city, and led him unto the brow of the hill whereon their city was built, that they might cast him down headlong." Luke 4:28–29.
15. I am grateful to Kellen Funk for this observation. Aurelius Ambrosius (St. Ambrose) Bishop of Milan (ca. 340–397 CE) observed of Luke's Gospel, "This Gospel is represented fittingly by the calf, because it begins with priests and ends with the Calf who, having taken upon himself the sins of all, was sacrificed for the life of the whole world. . . . He is both Calf and Priest. He is the Priest because he is our Propitiator. We have him as an advocate with the Father. He is the Calf because he redeemed us with his own blood." Ambrose, *Exposition of the Gospel of Luke*, 1.4.7, in Arthur A. Just Jr., editor, *Ancient Christian Commentary on Scripture: New Testament, III: Luke* (Downer's Grove, IL: InterVarsity Press, 2003), 2.
16. *Confessions*, 8–9, 10. On the characteristics of ascetic Protestantism, see Max Weber, "The Protestant Ethic and the 'Spirit' of Capitalism," in Peter Baehr and Gordon C. Wells, editors, *The Protestant Ethic and the "Spirit" of Capitalism and Other Writings* (New York: Penguin, 2002). Turner's self-description might be thought Calvinist [for example, Weber comments (74) on "the striking frequency of the warnings, especially in English Puritan literature, against placing any trust in the help and friendship of men"], but it is clearly leavened by the eighteenth-century evangelical pietism of Methodism and the Baptist movement, on which see further below. Turner specifically disclaims any interest in "conjuring" or the ways of the trickster—"I always spoke of such things with contempt" (9)—but he does claim to possess special knowledge ("superior

judgment") such that, as a child, "the negroes in the neighborhood, even at this early period of my life . . . would often carry me with them when they were going on any roguery, to plan for them" (8). Early in his narrative Turner also displays acquaintance with, and some fascination for, what may best be described as "almanac" knowledge, such as "casting different things in moulds made of earth . . . attempting to make paper, gunpowder, and many other experiments" (8), and later knowledge of "the elements, the revolution of the planets, the operation of tides, and changes of the seasons" (10), as well as hieroglyphic characters, numbers, and astrological signs—"the forms of men in different attitudes" (10). And see below, note 65. In all these respects the general knowledge claims Turner makes and the sources on which he appears to draw roughly parallel those characteristic of his contemporary visionary, Joseph Smith. See Richard Lyman Bushman, *Joseph Smith: Rough Stone Rolling, A Cultural Biography of Mormonism's Founder* (New York: Vintage, 2007), 30–83, and D. Michael Quinn, *Early Mormonism and the Magic World View*, Revised and Enlarged (Salt Lake City: Signature Books, 1998), 1–236, and illustrations, 320–21. See also John L. Brooke, *The Refiner's Fire: The Making of Mormon Cosmology, 1644-1844* (Cambridge: Cambridge University Press, 1994), particularly 278–84. It is also entirely possible that Turner's reference to "hieroglyphic characters" (10) references the symbols used in late-eighteenth-century hieroglyphic bibles used to introduce children to Bible and general reading, a subject to which he makes indirect reference in recounting how, "whenever an opportunity occurred of looking at a book, when the school children were getting their lessons, I would find many things that the fertility of my own imagination had depicted to me before" (8). On hieroglyphic bibles, see Shalev, *American Zion*, 110–11.

It is important to note that the circuits of religious and secular knowledge were by no means distinct in the early republic. For example, the New England Tract Society (predecessor of the American Tract Society) began publishing an annual *Christian Almanack* in 1821. The *Almanack* "carried information about religious tract work collected from the [society's] auxiliaries, as well as the usual calendars and meteorological data." Publication was continued by the American Tract Society (founded 1825 in a merger of the New England Tract Society and the New York Tract Society and dedicated to the aggressive dissemination of evangelical Christian literature throughout the expanding United States). By 1830 the *Christian Almanack* was being published "in twenty-one different geographical editions." The Almanack was but one fragment of the immense volume of religious literature circulated in the early republic, particularly between 1829 and 1833, by nondenominational national and regional societies (the American Bible Society, the American Tract Society, the American Sunday School Union) committed to the idea of "general supply"—that is, a universal circulation by sale or gift of evangelical literature. The American Tract Society, for example, relied on distribution through auxiliary societies and other local groups fed by regional depositories. In the mid-1820s the ATS had depositories in Richmond and Norfolk, as well as in other parts of Virginia. See David Paul Nord, *Faith in Reading: Religious Publishing and the Birth of Mass Media in America* (New York: Oxford University Press, 2004), 55, 76–80, 85–86, 93–94; *The American Tract Society Documents, 1824-1925* (New York: Arno Press, 1972), 174. See generally, Nathan O. Hatch, *The Democratization of American Christianity* (New Haven: Yale University Press, 1989), 141–46; Albert Raboteau, *Slave Religion: The "Invisible Institution" in the Antebellum South* (New York: Oxford University Press, 2004), 153–54.

17. *Confessions*, 8 (emphasis added). Turner returns to the same memory at 9, which suggests it made a significant impression on him.
18. *Confessions*, 9. On the crucial importance of the calling to ascetic Protestantism, see Weber, "Protestant Ethic," 28–36, 77–87.

19. Gray held Turner "warped and perverted by the influence of early impressions." *Confessions*, 18–19. In *Rising*, at 13, Allmendinger writes, "The germ of rebellion . . . had formed by his twenty-first year."
20. An unsigned letter to the Richmond *Enquirer* (dated November 1, 1831) that Allmendinger attributes to Southampton County attorney William C. Parker (who would be named Turner's trial counsel), reports that in his preliminary examination before Southampton magistrates James W. Parker and James Trezvant on October 31, 1831, Turner indicated that his life's motivation had been a search for "superior righteousness." The letter continued: "It was not until rather more than a year ago that the idea of emancipating the blacks entered his mind." Richmond *Enquirer* (November 8, 1831), in Tragle, *Southampton Slave Revolt*, 137; Allmendinger, *Rising*, 243. See also *The Norfolk Herald* (November 4, 1831), in Tragle, 135: "He says the idea of an insurrection never crossed his mind until a few months before he started with it."
21. "Having arrived to man's estate," *Confessions*, 9. Turner gave himself a precise date of birth—October 2, 1800. If arrival "to man's estate" can be taken to indicate he had turned twenty-one, this suggests Turner's religiosity began to intensify around 1821. See also below, note 182 and accompanying text.
22. *Confessions*, 9. Turner's account of his youthful religiosity prior to this moment hints at self-reproach for his immaturity and superficiality, indeed artifice: "To a mind like mine, restless, inquisitive and observant of every thing that was passing, it is easy to suppose that religion was the subject to which it would be directed, and although this subject principally occupied my thoughts—there was nothing that I saw or heard of to which my attention was not directed. . . . Growing up among [the negroes in the neighborhood], with [their] confidence in my superior judgment, and when this, in their opinions, was perfected by Divine inspiration, from the circumstances already alluded to in my infancy, and which belief was ever afterwards zealously inculcated by the austerity of my life and manners, which became the subject of remark by white and black.—Having soon discovered to be great, I must appear so, and therefore studiously avoided mixing in society, and wrapped myself in mystery . . ." (8–9).
23. However Matthew frequently uses "kingdom of heaven" interchangeably with "kingdom of God" whereas the phrase "kingdom of heaven" does not occur in Luke at all.

    Bock comments, "Luke's kingdom comes in two phases, 'already' and 'not yet.' It has been inaugurated,' but it is not yet 'consummated.' The kingdom is present but not all its promises have come." Bock, *Theology*, 143; see also 389–405; Talbert, *Reading Luke*, 109–10. For commentary that stresses the deep eschatological tension between the kingdom's simultaneous presence and deferral, see Conzelmann, *Theology of St. Luke*, 13–17. Conzelmann's interpretation of Luke turns on the proposition that Luke takes his fundamental task to be to explain the delay of the Parousia (second coming) that Christ's disciples had anticipated would follow almost immediately upon the Passion and Resurrection. The problem of deferral, says Conzelmann, is not one that can be solved by a profane historical concept of "development" from one stage to the next. Rather, Luke "confronts the problem of the interval by interpreting his own period afresh . . . the treatment of his main problem is the result of coming to grips with his own situation." This is a problem of salvation history, which is determined by two factors: "*(a)* The period of Jesus and the period of the Church are represented as two distinct but systematically related epochs. Thus the view of Jesus as a historical phenomenon gains positive theological meaning." It is not determined by a profane (Conzelmann says "Greek") conception of history, "which aims to instruct." Rather it arises "from the problem of the existence of the Church in a continuing period of time. In order to be able to set out clearly in the person of Jesus a salvation which is *timeless* [emphasis added] his period must be distinguished from the present period. The church understands her present existence by recognizing that period as the authentic manifestation of salvation and thereby is enabled to understand not only her present but her future existence. And on the other hand, she comes to understand the nature of her Lord by looking back to his historical existence. *In other words, Luke is confronted by the situation in which the Church finds herself by the delay of the Parousia and her existence in secular history*" [emphasis added]. But this is not all, a second factor bears on the problem of salvation history: "*(b)* In looking back to the past another distinction emerges even within this present, latest epoch of saving history, a distinction between the present in which the author lives and the '*arché*', the foundation period of the apostles and eye-witnesses. . . . When Jesus was alive, was the time of salvation; Satan was far away, it was a time without temptation. Since the Passion, however, Satan is present again and the disciples of Jesus are again subject to temptation. In view of this distinction, the continuity between the period of Jesus on the one hand and the period of the Church on the other has to be plainly demonstrated. The plan of [Luke's] whole historical writing serves this purpose" (Conzelmann, 13–14, 16).

Luke's history of salvation thus emerges in three stages: a "before" which is "the period of Israel"; the period of Jesus's ministry, of the Incarnation (birth, death, resurrection); and the period since Jesus's ascension. The Incarnation is a radical cleft in time, by which the time of the law has become the time of the Saviour. The time of the Saviour will end with the second coming and the Last Judgment. On earth it is a period of intense anticipation, filled with the promise of the end, and agonizing deferral. It is "the period of the *ecclesia pressa* [the persecuted church], during which the virtue of patience is required," during which it is possible "by looking back to the period of Jesus, also to look forward to the Parousia." The Parousia itself does not represent a further "stage" of salvation history but its end. "It corresponds to the other extreme, the Creation" (Conzelmann, 16–17). It can come at any moment, and there is reason to believe it is imminent: "Verily I say unto you, This generation shall not pass away, till all be fulfilled" (Luke 21:32; and see 9:27). But none knows when, but God: "Be ye therefore ready" (Luke 12:40). Once introduced to anticipation of the kingdom, the Christian is constantly confronted by the eschatological tension of the now/not yet. See Francois Hartog, *Regimes of Historicity: Presentism and Experiences of Time*, Saskia Brown, translator (New York: Columbia University Press, 2017), 60–63.

Conzelmann's hermeneutics are by no means unchallenged—for a general survey of Lukan hermeneutics, see Anthony C. Thiselton, "The Hermeneutical Dynamics of 'Reading Luke' as Interpretation, Reflection, and Formation," in Bartholomew et al., editors, *Reading Luke*, 3–52. Most important, as Bock argues, "salvation history" does not replace eschatology in Luke; it is its own eschatology. "The predominant idea in Luke-Acts is that Jesus' coming represents the inauguration and culmination of a program of promise God introduced to Israel through the covenants to Abraham and David, and the offer of a new covenant." Christ's return will complete God's plan by exercising "judgment on behalf of righteousness." Bock, *Theology*, 392, 389–405, 448. See also I. Howard Marshall, *Luke: Historian and Theologian* (Downers Grove IL: IVP Academic, 1988), 19, 77–102, 107–11, 116–56. Nonetheless, my contention in this chapter is that the temporalities that Conzelmann draws to our attention—the temporalities of salvation history and its radical cleft in time—are the temporalities within which Turner finds himself living as his search for the kingdom matures, and in which he experiences and suffers the severe eschatological tension between anticipation/deferral of the Parousia and his own (and the Church's) existence in secular history. For the implications of the latter as they pertain to Turner's particular situation

(Virginia Christianity's evangelical renewal, and racial tensions within Virginia's churches), see generally Irons, *Origins of Proslavery Christianity*, and Randolph Ferguson Scully, *Religion and the Making of Nat Turner's Virginia: Baptist Community and Conflict, 1740–1840* (Charlottesville: University of Virginia Press, 2008). See also below, note 60, and notes 157–76 and accompanying text.

24. Matthew 5:1–7:28; Luke 12:1–59; see Conzelmann, *Theology of St. Luke*, 65, 72–73; Scobie, "A Canonical Approach," 343–44.
25. Marshall, *Luke: Historian and Theologian*, 142, 143; Luke 12:21, and see also 1:51–53. See also chapter 3 notes 12–14 and accompanying text.
26. *Confessions*, 9. According to David Crump, "A feature of prayer in Luke-Acts . . . is the perception of supernatural phenomena." He continues, "Prayer is not simply man's address to God; it is also one of the ways in which individuals open themselves to God's address to them. Prayer creates a channel for discourse between heaven and earth." David Crump, *Jesus the Intercessor: Prayer and Christology in Luke-Acts* (Grand Rapids, MI: Baker Books, 1999), 116.
27. *Ibid.*, 9. Bock comments, "Luke-Acts presents God explicitly and implicitly in the words of the gospel's characters. They function as witnesses to him and his acts. God guides, predicts, directs, acts, redirects, or explains his program. Witnesses appear in situations where they are free to speak and are Spirit-enabled (Luke 1:67; 2:25; Acts 2:17). Dreams, visions, and theophanies are key means by which direction comes." Bock, *Theology*, 124.
28. *Confessions*, 9.
29. Note the profound contradiction that the believing slave faced in living up to ascetic Protestantism's demand for "absolute self-control." Weber, "Protestant Ethic," 81.
30. Turner reports being "placed under an overseer, from whom I ran away." *Confessions*, 9. This moment—which is one of stress in Turner's worldly life—follows the death (1822) of Samuel Turner (the son of Turner's original master Benjamin Turner) and the assumption of control over Samuel's affairs by his widow, Elizabeth. See Allmendinger, *Rising*, 16. (Allmendinger places Turner's absconsion in late 1823/early 1824, but this is an approximation. As he says (15), "the memoir's chronology between 1821 and 1825 is confused."
31. *Confessions*, 9.
32. *Ibid.*, 9.
33. Although, in other words, Turner has shed the superficial (indeed manipulative) religiosity of his youth (see above, note 22) for a more mature Christian *belief*, he is still bargaining with God for the returns on belief. His belief is not yet *faith*. Charles Talbert comments, "In the realm of spiritual insight—including an understanding of the religious significance of Scripture—one does not know God's will and then decide whether to do it. Rather, one wills to be obedient to God's will first and then, and only then, discerns what it is." Talbert, *Reading Luke*, 39. See also Crump, *Jesus the Intercessor*, 130, 135–36.
34. Turner remembers this as, "For he who knoweth his Master's will, and doeth it not, shall be beaten with many stripes." *Ibid.*, 9–10.
35. *Ibid.*, 9. The theme of service recurs in Luke 17:7–10, 19:10–26.
36. Luke 12:39–40. (Or as 1 Thessalonians 5:2 puts it, "The day of the Lord so cometh as a thief in the night.") He that is not ready will be chastened. Turner will no doubt also have noticed the verse previous to Luke 12:47, that "the lord of that servant" who is indifferent to his lord's will and to his return, who is faithless, "will come in a day when he looketh not for him, and at an hour when he is not aware, and will cut him in sunder, and will appoint him his portion with the unbelievers." And see Bock, *Theology*, 396: "Jesus' call here is to be faithful until the return takes place, however long it takes." The faithless servant suffers a total punishment: "Dismemberment is the most graphic way possible to express rejection." The faithless servant is "chopped beef."

37. Thus, Eric Sundquist argues that "Turner appropriates and overturns one of proslavery's favorite passages, transfiguring a text of racist subjugation into his own prophetic call to revolt. For many slaveholders Scripture was a tool of suppression; for Turner it became a tool of God's own violent chastening of the masters." *To Wake the Nations*, 59. See also Santoro, "The Prophet in His Own Words," 139.
38. As the scribes and Pharisees murmured against Christ and his disciples for consorting with publicans and sinners in God's name. See Luke 5:30, 15:2, 19:7.
39. *Confessions*, 9, 10. The "master" that Turner is serving in his narration, is not, of course, "in the world."
40. See Revelation 3:19: "As many as I love, I rebuke and chasten: be zealous therefore, and repent." The meaning here is clarified by 1 Corinthians 11:32: "When we are judged, we are chastened of the Lord, that we should not be condemned with the world." One might note that unlike his own (earthly) father, who had "made [his] escape to some other part of the country" (9), Turner returns. An Eriksonian reading of this moment would perceive it as Turner reinventing himself as his own creation. See Erikson, *Childhood and Society*. Alternatively, or in addition, by returning Turner demonstrates he can resist temptation and shows allegiance to God. See Bock, *Theology*, 105.
41. *Confessions*, 10.
42. Luke 23:45.
43. As in Revelation 1:1–3, 10–11, 19. Johnson, *Triumph of the Lamb*, 6–7.
44. Luke 3:4–5.
45. David P. Moessner, "Reading Luke's Gospel as Ancient Hellenistic Narrative: Luke's Narrative Plan of Israel's Suffering Messiah as God's Saving 'Plan' for the World," in Bartholomew et al., editors, *Reading Luke*, 140. And see Luke 9:23. Jared Hickman has argued that in fact this vision registers Turner's displeasure at "the Christian God's complicity in slavery" and his departure "from an unambiguously Christian cosmos." Hickman bases this argument on the contention that "the spiritual communications are not properly tagged, their content is not scriptural." The voice of Turner's vision "speaks not in King James English but something more like demotic Virginian." See Jared Hickman, *Black Prometheus: Race and Radicalism in the Age of Atlantic Slavery* (New York: Oxford University Press, 2017), 210, and generally 208–12. Hickman's reading of *The Confessions* is highly imaginative, but I think overall unsustainable. Here, for example, Turner's return from his absconsion is not a confrontation with the Christian God but an acknowledgment of failure to seek His kingdom; the voice of the vision speaks in clearly identifiable scriptural language; and, as we shall see, no cosmic move out from under the Christian God follows. Hickman correctly notices that Turner's account of himself is of a person undergoing wrenching intellectual transformation, but in my view he misinterprets the nature of that transformation.
46. For example, Mechal Sobel describes Turner's phrase as "this decisive revelation of the racial violence to come." Mechal Sobel, *Trabelin' On: The Slave Journey to an Afro-Baptist Faith* (Westport, CT: Greenwood, 1979), 163.
47. Johnson, *Triumph of the Lamb*, 184, 294. As Johnson explains (at 184n8), the mark of God's kingdom come is the authority that Christ grants his disciples to expel demons, "an authority rooted in the authority he would win over the prince of demons in his death and resurrection," that is, at the crucifixion. Emblematic of that authority is Christ's statement (Luke 10:18), "I beheld Satan as lightning fall from heaven."
48. Revelation 6:10–11, 7:9, 14–15. As Richard Bauckham notes, Revelation's imagery of messianic war "describes the whole process of the establishment of God's kingdom." Christ's victory at the crucifixion is decisive, but "his followers are called to continue the battle in the present" for the final victory is still to come. Richard Bauckham, *The*

Theology of the Book of Revelation (Cambridge: Cambridge University Press, 1993), 70. On the mingling of temporalities of redemption in Revelation, see Elaine Pagels, *Revelations: Visions, Prophecy, and Politics in the Book of Revelation* (New York: Viking, 2012), 16–35, and, generally, Johnson *Triumph of the Lamb*.

49. Revelation 1:14; Luke 9:29. On "darkness" see *Confessions*, 10; below, note 59, and accompanying text.

50. Leonard Lawlor, "What Happened? What Is Going to Happen? An Essay on the Experience of the Event," in Amy Swiffen and Joshua Nichols, editors, *The Ends of History: Questioning the Stakes of Historical Reason* (Abingdon, UK: Routledge, 2013), 185, 186. In "Learning Theological Interpretation from Luke," in Bartholomew et al., editors, *Reading Luke*, 55–78, Joel Green comments that "the human situation in Lukan thought was one characterized by ignorance needing correcting rather than sin needing forgiveness. . . . Ignorance for Luke is actually misunderstanding—a failure at the most profound level to grasp adequately the purpose of God. . . . The resolution of 'ignorance' is not simply 'the amassing of facts,' but a realignment with God's ancient purpose," which is the redemption of humanity, a promise "long latent" but unforgotten by God and "in the process of actualization in the present" (63–64, 71).

51. *Confessions*, 10. Turner's vision shows him to be one called on "to continue the battle" following the crucifixion until the final victory—Parousia and Last Judgment (see above, note 48, Bauckham, *Theology*, 70). He is called to commit himself, as Yolanda Pierce's work suggests, to the mighty *spiritual* struggle "that transforms a dehumanizing and degrading life into one that holds out hope and freedom. . . . To move from paralysis and servitude to possibility and freedom, from the realm of the condemned to the realm of the blessed and chosen." See Yolanda Pierce, *Hell Without Fires: Slavery, Christianity, and the Antebellum Spiritual Narrative* (Gainesville: University Press of Florida, 2005), 9.

52. *Confessions*, 10. See above, note 16 (almanac knowledge). Turner places this revelation in the year 1825.

53. *Ibid.*, 10. After the superficial religiosity of youth, and the false "bargaining" belief of early adulthood (see above, notes 22 and 33), Turner has come to true faith, with all that implies. Reception of the Holy Spirit "enables inspired interpretation of the scriptures" and "engagement in the salvific work of Christ, including his outpouring of the Holy Spirit." Green, "Learning Theological Interpretation," 70, 73.

It is important to note that throughout the first half of the narrative recorded in *The Confessions*, Turner is an active participant in his own transformation. "While the language of traditional white spiritual narratives portrays the conversion experience as one of yielding and surrender, of 'humility and dependence' [citation omitted], for the African American spiritual narrator, conversion is presented as a process of empowerment. Conversion is an active not a passive process. . . . While the grace of God is a gift to be freely given and freely received, it is the responsibility, the *active* choice on the part of the convert, to participate in this radical transformation." Pierce, *Hell Without Fires*, 30 (emphasis in original). And see below, note 151. Compare Turner's experience of sanctification with Pierce's account of the early nineteenth-century sanctification experience of George White (14–36), and the mid-century experience of Zilpha Elaw (88–110), both African American Methodists. On African American slaves' rejection of white attempts "to reduce Christianity to an ethic of pure submission," see Levine, *Black Culture and Black Consciousness*, 45. In his *African American Religions, 1500–2000: Colonialism, Democracy, and Freedom* (Cambridge: Cambridge University Press, 2015), 137, Sylvester Johnson criticizes the formulation of Africans "converting" to Christianity as a colonialist instantiation of "Christian supremacism" that is "rooted in the imagination of purities and binaries." See also

Katharine Gerbner, *Christian Slavery: Conversion and Grace in the Protestant Atlantic World* (Philadelphia: University of Pennsylvania Press, 2018), 6–12. That said, Johnson acknowledges Christianity as a tradition in which Africans could participate. "Christianity both constrained and constituted African subjectivity in ways that severely compromised the sovereign freedom of individual Africans. Yet, at times, it also clearly enabled agential tactics" (138).

54. *Confessions*, 10. One is reminded of Charles Davis and Henry Louis Gates's comment on James Gronniosaw's *A Narrative of the Most Remarkable Particulars in the Life of James Albert Ukawsaw Gronniosaw, An African Prince, as Related by Himself* (Bath: Printed by W. Gye, 1770): "The voice in the text was truly a millennial voice for the African person of letters . . . for it was that very voice of deliverance and of redemption which would signify a new order for the black." Davis and Gates, *The Slave's Narrative*, xxvii.

    It is, of course, entirely appropriate in terms of Christian eschatology that this second vision—the promise of the second coming—should follow in the wake of Turner's vision of the crucifixion. Turner's Christian purpose is being unfolded before him.

55. Revelation 1:7. See also Luke 21:27; Matthew 24:30, 26:64; Mark 13:26, 14:62. Revelation, says Johnson, "sweeps across the span of redemptive history," from the Fall to the end of time. It is a book "permeated by worship and punctuated throughout with songs of praise" in celebration of God's "redemptive triumph through the Lamb"—destruction of enemies, vindication of martyrs, "and the inauguration of the new heavens and earth." Johnson, *Triumph of the Lamb*, 21, 31.

56. Revelation 1:1–3, 10–11, 19. John is a Jewish-Christian prophet from the Roman province of Asia writing toward the end of the first century CE. Patmos was an island penal settlement in the eastern Aegean to which John had most likely been exiled. See Johnson, *Triumph of the Lamb*, 56; Bauckham, *Theology*, 2–4; Pagels, *Revelations*, 10–11.

57. *Confessions*, 10. On lights stretched across the sky see Luke 17:24 and Matthew 24:27. Only Luke's gospel names the place of Christ's crucifixion as Calvary, at 23:33. Matthew 27:33, Mark 15:22, and John 19:17, all name the place Golgotha.

58. Revelation 1:16, 1:19–20. The number seven signifies completeness. Christ's message is thus addressed to his church as a whole. Bauckham, *Theology*, 16.

59. *Confessions*, 10. Allmendinger, *Rising*, points to 1 Thessalonians 5:5, where Paul refers to children of light and darkness, but the implication of darkness remains error: "For yourselves know perfectly that the day of the Lord so cometh as a thief in the night. / For when they shall say, Peace and safety; then sudden destruction cometh upon them, as travail upon a woman with child; and they shall not escape. / But ye, brethren, are not in darkness, that that day should overtake you as a thief. / Ye are all the children of light, and the children of the day: we are not of the night, nor of darkness."

60. Revelation 2:5, 3:4. Might Turner have been drawn to Christ's condemnation of the Asian churches in Revelation by the slide of Virginia's evangelical churches toward racial hierarchy? See Scully, *Religion*, 179–91. Contra Scully, Irons, *Origins of Proslavery Christianity*, 97–132, argues that biracial Christianity flourished in 1820s Virginia. But W. Harrison Daniel notes documentary evidence of racial segregation in the churches dating from 1811. For example, "White members of the Wicomico Baptist Church erected a wooden partition inside the church building, dividing the house of worship into two sections, one for the black members and the other for the whites. It was reported that some of the blacks were distressed with this arrangement, but the partition was not removed." W. Harrison Daniel, "Virginia Baptists and the Negro in the Early Republic," *Virginia Magazine of History and Biography* 80, no. 1 (January 1972): 60. Jon Sensbach refers to "the atavistic fear" evoked in white church members by "the

implied racial leveling of integrated worship." Jon Sensbach, *A Separate Canaan: The Making of an Afro-Moravian World in North Carolina, 1763-1840* (Chapel Hill: University of North Carolina Press, 1998), 187.

61. *Confessions*, 10. What is important here, as elsewhere in the first half of *The Confessions*, is the sacred meaning Turner gives to an occurrence that might not otherwise seem extraordinary. To a slave laboring in the field the discovery of drops of blood might not be all that remarkable. As Frederick Douglass wrote of "Mr Severe," the overseer, "The field was the place to witness his cruelty and profanity. His presence made it both the field of blood and of blasphemy." Frederick Douglass, *Narrative of the Life of Frederick Douglass, An American Slave. Written by Himself* (Boston: Published at the Anti-Slavery Office, 1845), 11.
62. Luke 22:44; Revelation 7:14.
63. *Confessions*, 10. There is a fascinating resonance here between Turner's words, "forms of men in different attitudes," and Frank Kermode's, "men in certain postures of attentiveness," which Kermode uses to describe humanity in "the realm of the *kairoi*," that order of apocalyptic time in which *kairos*, the orthogonal instant, "the season, a point in time filled with significance, charged with a meaning derived from its relation to the end" (47) is ascendant over *chronos*, which signifies mere duration, unfulfilled "'passing time' or 'waiting time'—that which, according to Revelation, 'shall be no more.'" Frank Kermode, *The Sense of an Ending: Studies in the Theory of Fiction* (Oxford: Oxford University Press, 2000), 47–48, 73, 195. He continues (at 89), "In apocalypse there are two orders of time, and the earthly runs to a stop; the cry of woe to the inhabitants of the earth means the end of their time; henceforth 'time shall be no more.'"
64. See, generally, Johnson, *Triumph of the Lamb*. On blood images, see, for example, Revelation 1:5—"Jesus Christ, who is the faithful witness, and the first begotten of the dead, and the prince of the kings of the earth. Unto him that loved us, and washed us from our sins in his own blood"; Revelation 8:7—"The first angel sounded, and there followed hail and fire mingled with blood, and they were cast upon the earth."
65. Talbert, *Reading Luke*, 72–75, 200. In *A Calculating People: The Spread of Numeracy in Early America* (New York: Routledge, 1999), 165, Patricia Cline Cohen notes that "almanacs, the staple of every man's reading, began to be garnished with facts and figures in the 1810s." Turner's "hieroglyphic characters, and numbers, with the forms of men in different attitudes, portrayed in blood, and representing the figures I had seen before in the heavens" (*Confessions*, 10) might thus reference astrology's "Man of Signs" and other astrological images and tables commonly included in period almanacs. For examples, see Quinn, *Early Mormonism*, figs. 15–24. See also Hall, *Worlds of Wonder*, 7, 58–61. And see above, note 16 (almanacs and hieroglyphic bibles). Vincent Harding argues, in contrast, that this was "African imagery," but without more evidence his claims, like mine, do not rise above the suggestive. See Harding, *There Is a River*, 79.
66. *Confessions*, 10–11.
67. By postmillennialist I mean that school of Christian millenarian thought that interprets Revelation to prophesy that Christ incarnate's second coming will immediately precede the loosening of the serpent and the Last Judgment as the redemptive climax of the millennial Kingdom of God realized on earth, during which Christ has reigned spiritually but not physically; as opposed to the premillennialist school that holds that Christ's physical second coming *establishes* the millennial Kingdom of God, and the amillennialist school that holds Revelation's millennium to be entirely symbolic. See also below, note 195 and accompanying text.
68. Reports of Turner's preliminary examination before Southampton magistrates James W. Parker and James Trezvant on October 31, 1831, include references to his claims "of supernatural powers and gifts, in curing diseases." See the unsigned letter to the Richmond *Enquirer* (dated November 1, 1831) that Allmendinger attributes to

Southampton County attorney William C. Parker, in Tragle, *Southampton Slave Revolt*, 137; Allmendinger, *Rising*, 243. The healing of Etheldred Brantley (through prayer and fasting) is the only reference to any such claim in the *Confessions*. On syncretic supernaturalism in antebellum religion, see, generally, Jon Butler, *Awash in a Sea of Faith: Christianizing the American People* (Cambridge, MA: Harvard University Press, 1990), 225–56.

69. *Confessions*, 11. Daniel Crofts identifies Persons Mill Pond, behind Persons Methodist Church west of Cross Keys, as the site of the baptism. See Daniel W. Crofts, *Old Southampton: Politics and Society in a Virginia County, 1834–1869* (Charlottesville: University of Virginia Press, 1992), 9–10. Allmendinger, *Rising*, 19, identifies Etheldred T. Brantley from tax lists as "a landless young laborer [who] worked for neighboring farmers." However, an Etheldred Brantley also appears in the U.S. Federal Census for 1830 (the only entry in the entire U.S. census bearing the name Etheldred Brantley) residing in Northampton, North Carolina, in a household of eight white persons and twelve slaves. Northampton is approximately thirteen miles southeast of the farmstead of Thomas Moore, west of Cross Keys, then Turner's owner. Brantleys descended from an Etheldred Brantley born 1760 in Southampton County lived on both sides of the Virginia/North Carolina border and as far south as Mecklenburg, North Carolina. Etheldred T. Brantley appears to have been the eldest son of James Brantley (m. Tazzy Lundy 1800, possibly m. Nancy Harris 1793), and grandson of the Etheldred Brantley born in 1760. This branch of the Brantley family owned at least 11 slaves in 1789, judging from a petition disputing the administration of the estate of Etheldred's brother James filed in March of that year with the Southampton County Court sitting in Chancery. See Petition 21678901 (1789–03), Race & Slavery Petitions Project, Southampton County, VA, Digital Library on American Slavery, http://library.uncg.edu/slavery/petitions/details.aspx?pid=12852 (last accessed February 22, 2019). (I am deeply grateful to Janelle Swearingen for guiding me to this information.) Etheldred Brantley was either a landless young laborer related to a family of slave owners, or a somewhat older man who was himself a slave owner. Either way it seems unlikely, if Turner was planning race war in 1825–26, that the first person to hear of it would have been Etheldred Brantley. Much more likely, what Turner communicated to Brantley was the imminence of the second coming and the Day of Judgment.
70. Bock, *Theology*, 143–45, 159. See Luke 3:20–22.
71. *Confessions*, 11 (emphasis added). Here I take "as" to mean "in the same manner" rather than "because." Note that Turner states he was baptized "by the Spirit" (*Confessions*, 11). Of the four synoptic gospels, only Luke does not specify that Christ was baptized by John the Baptist, who according to Luke had been imprisoned by Herod. Rather Jesus "being baptized"—note the passive construction—"and praying, the heaven was opened, / And the Holy Ghost descended in a bodily shape like a dove upon him." Luke 3:21–22.
72. Matthew 27:39; Luke 18:31–33. See also above, note 14 (Nazareth's rejection of Christ).
73. John of Patmos writes (Revelation 20:1–3) "And I saw an angel come down from heaven, having the key of the bottomless pit and a great chain in his hand. / And he laid hold on the dragon, that old serpent, which is the Devil, and Satan, and bound him a thousand years, / And cast him into the bottomless pit, and shut him up, and set a seal upon him, that he should deceive the nations no more, till the thousand years should be fulfilled: and after that he must be loosed a little season."
74. *Confessions*, 11 (emphasis added). On the "loud noise in the heavens" see Revelation 1:10, 4:1, and particularly 8:6–11:15, which is Revelation's cycle of trumpets. Turner's words, "I should take it on," appear to reference the moment during the trumpet cycle, specifically between the sixth and seventh trumpets, when, Johnson notes, "the Revelation of Jesus Christ is symbolically entrusted to John, completing his

commissioning as a spokesman for the risen Lord," and heralding the final consummation of God's redemptive plan. Johnson, *Triumph of the Lamb*, 157, 162, and see generally 155–76; Bauckham, *Theology*, 81–82. Revelation draws on Matthew 24:30–31, on the moment of the second coming: "And then shall appear the sign of the Son of man in heaven: and then shall all the tribes of the earth mourn, and they shall see the Son of man coming in the clouds of heaven with power and great glory. / And he shall send his angels with a great sound of a trumpet, and they shall gather together his elect from the four winds, from one end of heaven to the other." The serpent is of course the serpent of Genesis, in the guise of which Satan brings about the fall of man, prompting Christ's assumption of the role of redeeming mediator between God and humanity. See Roland Boer, *Criticism of Heaven: On Marxism and Theology* (Chicago: Haymarket Books, 2009), 68; John Milton, *Paradise Lost*, Gordon Teskey, editor (New York: W. W. Norton, 2005), Bk. 3. In Revelation (20:7–15) the final loosening of the serpent presages the Last Judgment.

75. Luke 13:30. As he does throughout the confession, Turner combines Revelation with the synoptic gospels, largely, I have argued, Luke, but here also Matthew 19:30, 20:16; Mark 10:31. The passage in all the gospels occurs as Christ is making his way toward Jerusalem and the Passion. Thus Luke 13:22–30: "And he went through the cities and villages, teaching, and journeying toward Jerusalem. / Then said one unto him, Lord, are there few that be saved? And he said unto them, / Strive to enter in at the strait gate: for many, I say unto you, will seek to enter in, and shall not be able. . . . / And, behold, there are last which shall be first, and there are first which shall be last."

76. Condemning "the fearful, and unbelieving, and the abominable, and murderers, and whoremongers, and sorcerers, and idolaters, and all liars" to their second—which is to say eternal—death. Revelation 21:8, and see 20:13–15. On the meaning of "season," see above, note 63.

77. *Confessions*, 11. Luke 19:27. See also Matthew 22:1–14. Turner waits, as did Christ. "Christ waited for his *kairos*, refusing to anticipate the will of his father; that is what he meant when he said 'Tempt not the Lord thy God'" (Luke 4:12; Matthew 4:7). Kermode, *The Sense of an Ending*, 86.

78. 21:11: "And great earthquakes shall be in divers places, and famines, and pestilences; and fearful sights and great signs shall there be from heaven."

79. Luke 1:20, 64. The story of Zacharias appears only in Luke. Here too, Turner combines Luke and Revelation. The removal of the seal also recalls the removal of Revelation's seventh and final seal, which signifies the imminence of humanity's tribulation, the removal of the seal on the serpent, whose "loosening" signifies the imminence of the Last Judgment, and the final injunction to John, "Seal not the sayings of the prophecy of this book: for the time is at hand." See Revelation 8:1; 20:3; 22:10.

80. *Confessions*, 11. The four were the slaves Hark [Moore], Henry [Porter], Nelson [Edwards], and Sam [Francis]. One cannot discount the possibility that Turner chose four confederates in emulation of the four conquering horsemen of Revelation 6:1–8. But note also an undated and anonymous letter published in the Richmond *Enquirer*, November 8, 1831, which reported that Turner had told only two (unnamed) others, and not until April or May. See "The Bandit—Taken! Extracts of Letters" [Thomas Ruffin Gray (?), undated letter], Richmond *Enquirer*, Richmond, Virginia (November 8, 1831), in Tragle, *Southampton Slave Revolt*, 138.

81. *Confessions*, 11. Santoro suggests the possibility of disagreement among Turner and his confidants over the nature of their action—divinely ordained justice or secular revolt. Santoro, "The Prophet in His Own Words," 120–22. In his Richmond *Enquirer* letter of November 8, 1831 (see above, note 68) William C. Parker reported that he was unable to obtain from Turner an explanation how his beliefs and the apparent purpose

of the revolt [apparent, that is, to Parker] were related. "Notwithstanding I examined him closely upon this point, he alway [*sic*] seemed to mystify."

82. *Confessions*, 11.
83. *Ibid.*, 11; Luke 21:25. The second sign was the unusual appearance of the sun between August 12 and 15, at first light green, then pale yellow, then '"like a globe of silver through the thick haze.'" See Almendinger, *Rising*, 22. Following the February eclipse, when "the sun became black as sackcloth of hair" (Revelation 6:12), the dimming of the sun in August would no doubt have recalled Revelation 8:12 "the third part of the sun was smitten." Johnson notes, the first "is a preview of the final dissolution of the old created order," while the second "symbolizes providential disasters that precede the final cataclysm." Johnson, *Triumph of the Lamb*, 146.
84. *Confessions*, 11.
85. *Ibid.*, 7–8. Compare Luke 2:40, 46–47: "And the child grew, and waxed strong in spirit, filled with wisdom: and the grace of God was upon him. . . . / And it came to pass, that after three days they found him in the temple, sitting in the midst of the doctors, both hearing them, and asking them questions. / And all that heard him were astonished at his understanding and answers." The "infancy" material appears only in Luke. As I have already noted, Turner's account of himself begins before his own birth, just as Luke's account of Christ begins before *his* birth. See *Confessions*, 7; Luke 1–2. Bock writes, "Luke's presentation of Jesus begins mostly in regal and prophetic terms. . . . But Jesus' unique birth by the Spirit makes it clear that 'something more' is here. Exactly what is not explicitly clear in Luke 1–2. . . . Mary and those around her take the promise only in Messianic terms. What that 'something more' involves emerges as Luke develops his description of Jesus." Bock, *Theology*, 177. It is precisely the intimation of "something more," something then unknown, with which Turner's account of himself begins.
86. See above, text at notes 30–36. Compare Luke 4:1–13.
87. See above, text at notes 69–71.
88. Thus, Luke's account of Christ's suffering on the Mount of Olives "Saying, Father, if thou be willing, remove this cup from me: nevertheless not my will, but thine, be done. . . . / And being in an agony he prayed more earnestly: and his sweat was as it were great drops of blood falling down to the ground." Luke 22:42, 44.
89. See Bock, *Theology*, 128, 133–34; Moessner, "Reading Luke's Gospel," 149–51. An alternative (but compatible and equally plausible) interpretation of Turner's reply is that in referencing Christ's crucifixion, Turner validates his own action by situating it in relation to the central event of the entire Christian-apocalyptic history of salvation he has just described. In other words, he could not possibly have been mistaken in his convictions precisely because Christ had indeed been crucified.
90. *Confessions*, 8. On "experiments" see above, note 16.
91. *Confessions*, 9, 10, 11.
92. Craig G. Bartholomew and Robby Holt, "Prayer in/and the Drama of Redemption in Luke: Prayer and Exegetical Performance," in Bartholomew et al., editors, *Reading Luke*, 350–75, at 351, 352; Talbert, *Reading Luke*, 107–9.
93. Bartholomew and Holt, "Prayer in/and the Drama of Redemption in Luke," 351 (emphasis in original).
94. *Ibid.*, 357.
95. Crump, *Jesus the Intercessor*, 6, and see 120.
96. *Confessions*, 10–11. Crump comments, "Through prayer the individual participates in a dialogue with heaven and is allowed to discover how he or she may be involved in God's sovereign plans for the church and the world. At times this will mean the revelation of unexpected things at unexpected moments. But the challenge of genuine

prayer lies in the disciple's willingness to yield himself to whatever guidance or instruction God's answer may bring, however surprising it may be." Crump, *Jesus the Intercessor*, 239.

97. *Ibid.*, 9.
98. *Ibid.*, 10.
99. Max Turner, "Luke and the Spirit: Renewing Theological Interpretation of Biblical Pneumatology," in Bartholomew et al., editors, *Reading Luke*, 268. See also Bock, *Theology*, 211–26; David Wenham, "The Purpose of Luke-Acts: Israel's Story in the Context of the Roman Empire," in Bartholomew et al., editors, *Reading Luke*, 79–103, at 85, 94.
100. Max Turner, "Luke and the Spirit," 268.
101. By which Max Turner means "author of revelatory visions and dreams"; giver of "revelatory words or instruction or guidance"; source of "charismatic wisdom or revelatory discernment"; and inspiration for "charismatic praise . . . charismatic preaching or witness . . . or charismatic teaching." *Ibid.*, 279.
102. *Ibid.*, 268.
103. Bock, *Theology*, 212–13; Max Turner, "Luke and the Spirit," 272–73.
104. Luke, 1:15, 2:26–32.
105. Luke, 3:16–17, and see Bock, *Theology*, 213–16.
106. Bock, *Theology*, 100, 216.
107. Luke, 4:1.
108. Bock, *Theology*, 216; Luke 3:17.
109. Bock, *Theology*, 99–100, 217.
110. *Confessions*, 9. There is little on the surface of Turner's narrative, as I have described and analyzed it, to suggest the syncretic African American Christianity described in Jon Butler's survey of antebellum religious practice and belief in *Awash in a Sea of Faith*, 247–52; compare Raboteau, *Slave Religion*, 44–92. Indeed, we have already noted—see above, note 16—Turner's explicit repudiation of "conjuring and such like tricks." In other words, the central idioms of Turner's religiosity can be assimilated to a sophisticated and militant evangelical Christianity—a Euro-Christianity, in Jared Hickman's terms (Hickman, *Black Prometheus*, 210–12)—without looking further afield. But it would be foolish to deny the possible influence of non-Christian African religious practice and belief on Turner just because an evangelical Christian idiom can explain the mentalités in evidence, or the possibility that the faith Turner articulates represents a syncretic and specifically African Christianity. In her "African Signs and Spirit Writing," *Callalloo*, 19, 3 (1996), 670–89, for example, Harryette Mullen encompasses Turner in powerful arguments for "a continuum of syncretic survival of African spiritual traditions and aesthetic systems which could hide and thrive in the interstices of accepted Christian practices" (676). Turner's pneumatology does appear to have such resonances, in that in his description the Spirit appears less as a (Euro-Christian) indwelling or infilling phenomenon than as an external guide. For additional arguments emphasizing the fruitfulness of these lines of inquiry, see Jakobi Williams, "Nat Turner: The Complexity and Dynamic of His Religious Background," *Journal of Pan African Studies* 4, no. 9 (January 2012): 113–47; Sobel, *Trabelin' On*, 162; Gomez, *Exchanging Our Country Marks*, 244–90; Steven Hahn, *A Nation Under Our Feet: Black Political Struggles in the Rural South from Slavery to the Great Migration* (Cambridge, MA: Harvard University Press, 2005), 43–47.

In *There Is a River*, 80–94, Vincent Harding offers a powerful argument for the emergence in the late 1820s of a distinctive form of pan-African Christian syncretism, one that married African-inflected Christian evangelism to messianic political promise: "Divine intervention on behalf of the Ethiopian nation in America" (85).

The principle point of articulation of this explicit theology of liberation was, of course, the Methodist revolutionary David Walker. See *David Walker's Appeal to the Coloured Citizens of the World* (1829), Peter P. Hinks, editor (University Park: Pennsylvania State University Press, 2000); Hinks, *To Awaken My Afflicted Brethren*. Neither Harding nor Hinks finds evidence that *Walker's Appeal* influenced Turner, but Hinks believes the *Appeal* circulated in the Southside border region, and he shares in Harding's observation that "a certain affinity" existed between Walker and Nat Turner. See Harding, *There Is a River*, 84, 94; Hinks, *Walker's Appeal*, 169.

111. *Confessions*, 11. And see above, text at note 45 ("Whoever bears Jesus' cross and shame as faithful to the end will be rewarded with the life of heaven.")

112. Revelation, 20:3.

113. Bock, *Theology*, 75, commenting on Luke 17:11–18:8. See also, I. Howard Marshall, "Political and Eschatological Language in Luke," in Bartholomew et al., editors, *Reading Luke*, 157–77, at 164, 165. See, generally, Richard H. Brodhead, "Millennium, Prophecy, and the Energies of Social Transformation: The Case of Nat Turner," in Abbas Amanat and Magnus Bernhardsson, editors, *Imagining the End: Visions of Apocalypse from the Ancient Middle East to Modern America* (London: I. B. Tauris, 2002), 212–33.

114. See Christine Leigh Heyrman, *Southern Cross: The Beginnings of the Bible Belt* (Chapel Hill: University of North Carolina Press, 1997), 9–27; Scully, *Religion*, 19–92; Irons, *Origins of Proslavery Christianity*, 1–96. For Patrick Rael, "Turner appears not so much a figure of the revolutionary black Atlantic as a militant prophet of the Second Great Awakening." Patrick Rael, *Eighty-Eight Years: The Long Death of Slavery in the United States, 1777–1865* (Athens: University of Georgia Press, 2015), 164.

115. Oates, *Fires of Jubilee*, 8–9; Scully, *Religion*, 192; Crofts, *Old Southampton*, 8; *Confessions*, 8. On the use of Methodist homes for meetings and sermons, see John H. Wigger, *Taking Heaven by Storm: Methodism and the Rise of Popular Christianity in America* (Urbana: University of Illinois Press, 2001), 36–37.

116. See, for example, the Richmond *Enquirer* (August 30, 1831), in Tragle, *Southampton Slave Revolt*, 44, 45 ("a fanatic preacher. . . . Pretends to be a Baptist preacher"); the Richmond *Constitutional Whig* (August 29, 1831), in Tragle 53, 54 ("a preacher and a prophet" . . . "a Baptist preacher"); the Richmond *Compiler* (September 3, 1831), in Tragle 60 ("has long been a preacher"). Southampton Baptists, however, denied that Turner was a Baptist preacher or a member of any Baptist church. See the *Lynchburg Virginian* (September 15, 1831), in Tragle 80 ("This fellow is very improperly represented to be a Baptist preacher. . . . [It] is an entire mistake").

117. Of Methodism, Weber writes as follows: "According to Wesley's doctrine, which represents a logical development of the doctrine of sanctification, but is a decided departure from the orthodox version, a person reborn . . . can now, in *this* life, through the workings of grace, come to the consciousness of *perfection*, or sinlessness." Weber, "Protestant Ethic," 96 (emphasis in original). See also Heyrman, *Southern Cross*, 94 (describing the Methodist doctrine of sanctification, or sinlessness, as "second grace"); Wigger, *Taking Heaven by Storm*, 15–19.

118. Heyrman, *Southern Cross*, 153–54. The passive voice in Turner's own description of his sanctification—"from the first steps of righteousness until the last, was I made perfect" (*Confessions*, 10)—suggests the influence of John Wesley's Arminian doctrine of "prevenient," or enabling, grace, which holds that divine grace toward humanity in general *precedes* the individual human's awareness of sinfulness or impulse to seek God's grace. Those strands of Methodism associated with the itinerant revivalist George Whitefield (1714–70) rather than Wesley (1703–91) were Calvinist in orientation, notably the Countess of Huntingdon's Connexion, which had a number of African American adherents, among them Olaudah Equiano and Phillis Wheatley.

119. Turner's behavior as described in the confession might be taken to manifest Baptist as well as Methodist "prevenient" sensibility. For example, of the Baptist movement, stressing Baptist belief in "the *inward appropriation*" of Christ's work of redemption, Weber writes: "This appropriation is the result of individual *revelation*, the working of the divine spirit in the individual, and *only* in this way. It is offered to everyone and the only requirement is to wait on the spirit and not to resist its coming by sinful attachment to the world." Weber emphasizes that Baptist belief sees "the Holy Spirit working in the daily lives of the faithful . . . speak[ing] directly to the individual if he is willing to listen." Weber adds that without the inner light, "the natural man . . . remains a purely creaturely being." Weber, "Protestant Ethic," 99 (emphasis in original), 100.
120. Heyrman, *Southern Cross*, 19, 33–34, 35. On "enthusiasm," see, for example, David Hempton, *Methodism: Empire of the Spirit* (New Haven: Yale University Press, 2005), 33–41. In the half century after 1750, and particularly in the years after 1785, "evangelical Protestantism became the primary religious idiom of African Americans in Virginia." Scully, *Religion*, 39. See also Wigger, *Taking Heaven by Storm*, 127; Hempton, *Methodism*, 24–25; Sylvia R. Frey and Betty Wood, *Come Shouting to Zion: African American Protestantism in the American South and British Caribbean to 1830* (Chapel Hill: University of North Carolina Press, 1998), 118–81; Nathan O. Hatch, *The Democratization of American Christianity* (New Haven: Yale University Press, 1989), 102–13; Raboteau, *Slave Religion*, 128–50. The majority of Virginia's African American evangelicals were Baptists, but black Methodism was particularly strong in the southeastern counties (such as Southampton) bordering North Carolina (Frey and Wood, *Come Shouting to Zion*, 153; Irons, *Origins of Proslavery Christianity*, 53).
121. Ruth H. Bloch, *Visionary Republic: Millennial Themes in American Thought, 1756-1800* (Cambridge: Cambridge University Press, 1985), xiv, 134–37, 177–78, 217–18, 225–26. See also Howe, *What Hath God Wrought*, 285–327; Jeffrey Williams, *Religion and Violence in Early American Methodism: Taking the Kingdom by Force* (Bloomington: Indiana University Press, 2010), 172.
122. Ann Taves, *Fits, Traces, and Visions: Experiencing Religion and Explaining Experience from Wesley to James* (Princeton: Princeton University Press, 1999), 47–117; Wigger, *Taking Heaven by Storm*, 96–97, 104–24; Hempton, *Methodism*, 149.
123. Mark A. Noll, *The Rise of Evangelicalism: The Age of Edwards, Whitefield, and the Wesleys* (Downers Grove, IL: IVP Academic, 2003).
124. *Ibid.*, 119–20.
125. *Ibid.*, 19. For a critique of the essentializing tendencies inherent in applying the description "evangelical" to the popular religious cultures of the eighteenth-century Atlantic world, see Douglas Winiarski, *Darkness Falls on the Land of Light: Experiencing Religious Awakenings in Eighteenth-Century New England* (Chapel Hill: University of North Carolina Press, 2017), 14–17.
126. Noll, *Rise of Evangelicalism*, 63–64; Hempton, *Methodism*, 13–16; Sensbach, *A Separate Canaan*, 24–25, 41–42.
127. Noll, *Rise of Evangelicalism*, 64.
128. Frederick Dreyer, *The Genesis of Methodism* (Bethlehem: Lehigh University Press, 1999), 37–38.
129. *Ibid.*, 40–41. On "legalism" versus the spiritual radicalism of evangelical enthusiasm, see Anthony J. La Vopa, "The Philosopher and the *Schwärmer*: On the Career of a German Epithet from Luther to Kant," *Huntington Library Quarterly* 60, no. 1/2 (1997): 85–115, particularly 92–93.
130. Nikolaus Ludwig von Zinzendorf, *Ein und zwanzig Discurse über die Augspurgische Confession* . . . (n.p. [1749]), 160–61, Craig D. Atwood, translator, in Craig D. Atwood, "Understanding Zinzendorf's Blood and Wounds Theology," *Journal of Moravian History* 1

(2006): 38; Craig D. Atwood, *Community of the Cross: Moravian Piety in Colonial Bethlehem* (University Park: Pennsylvania State University Press, 2004), 48–49.

131. Craig D. Atwood, "Zinzendorf's 'Litany of the Wounds,'" *Lutheran Quarterly* 11 (1997): 189–214; Atwood, *Community of the Cross*, 95–112. Though extreme in the form of its expression, Zinzendorf's theology was entirely compatible with the general Christian emphasis "on Christ's body as a historical human body" that had "suffered pain and death for the sins of all humanity." Heather Miyano Kopelson, *Faithful Bodies: Performing Religion and Race in the Puritan Atlantic* (New York: New York University Press, 2014), 7. See, generally, Susan Juster, *Sacred Violence in Early America* (Philadelphia: University of Pennsylvania Press, 2016). Kopelson notes the "multiple meanings at different historical moments" that the body of Christ has been assigned in Christian cosmology (7), not least as metaphor for communal belonging and differentiation (7, 74–100). The meaning assigned by Zinzendorf, however, is anything but metaphorical. The suffering body of Christ is redemption and refuge materially incarnate.

132. Dreyer, *Genesis of Methodism*, 25–26, 43; Noll, *Rise of Evangelicalism*, 82–86.

133. Dreyer, *Genesis of Methodism*, 44 (emphasis in original); Noll, *Rise of Evangelicalism*, 92–95.

134. "Christ the Friend of Sinners" (Charles Wesley, 1738), in John Wesley, *A Collection of Hymns for the Use of the People Called Methodists* (London: John Mason, 1831), 34–35. During his life Charles Wesley would compose some 6,500 hymns. David Hempton writes, "It has long been recognized that the most distinctive, characteristic, and ubiquitous feature of the Methodist message, indeed of the entire Methodist revival, was its transmission by means of hymns and hymn singing." Hempton, *Methodism*, 68, and see 68–74. See also Martin V. Clarke, *British Methodist Hymnody: Theology, Heritage, and Experience* (London: Routledge, 2018). The same was true of the Moravians. See Atwood's analysis of Moravian hymnody in *Community of the Cross*, 141–48; Noll, *Rise of Evangelicalism*, 64–65. For hymnody in Congregational New England, see Rhys S. Bezzant, *Jonathan Edwards and the Church* (Oxford: Oxford University Press, 2014), 218–25. On the role of song in the Christianization of late eighteenth-century and antebellum popular culture, see Hatch, *Democratization of American Christianity*, 146–60.

135. Dreyer, *Genesis of Methodism*, 47 (emphasis in original), 71. For the persisting influence of the Moravians on English evangelicals, see Noll, *Rise of Evangelicalism*, 160.

136. Dreyer, *Genesis of Methodism*, 62, 77.

137. Hempton, *Methodism*, 25; Atwood, "Blood and Wounds Theology," 37.

138. Dreyer, *Genesis of Methodism*, 47. Dreyer argues that Wesley's "idea of faith" was derived from the Moravians, even as Wesley himself suppressed the connection (29–30, 35).

139. "O for a Thousand Tongues to Sing" (Charles Wesley, 1739), in Wesley, *A Collection of Hymns*, 7.

140. "Jesus, thy Blood and Righteousness" (Nikolaus Ludwig, Count von Zinzendorf, 1739; Translator: John Wesley), in Wesley, *A Collection of Hymns*, 186.

141. Williams, *Religion and Violence*, 17 (emphasis added).

142. *Ibid.*, 6, 17, 22, 24, 34, 39, 41.

143. Wigger, *Taking Heaven by Storm*, 104–24.

144. *Ibid.*, 19.

145. Williams, *Religion and Violence*, 1–12, 81–92, 162, and generally 69–130; Ari Kelman, *A Misplaced Massacre: Struggling over the Memory of Sand Creek* (Cambridge, MA: Harvard University Press, 2013), 8–18. See, generally, Juergensmeyer, *Terror in the Mind of God*, 159–66.

146. "Jesus the Conqueror Reigns" (Charles Wesley, 1749), in Wesley, *A Collection of Hymns*, 265.

147. Atwood, "Zinzendorf's 'Litany of the Wounds,'" 189; Atwood, "Blood and Wounds Theology," 32. See generally Atwood, *Community of the Cross*, 1–19, 203–21.

148. Atwood, "Blood and Wounds Theology," 32–33; Karl Westmeier, "Out of a Distant Past: A Challenge for Modern Missions from a Diary of Colonial New York," *Transactions of the Moravian Historical Society* 27 (1992): 74. On Moravian evangelization of Africans in the Caribbean and the American South, see Frey and Wood, *Come Shouting to Zion*, xiii, 64, 83–87; Sensbach, *A Separate Canaan*; Gerbner, *Christian Slavery*, 138–88; Vincent Brown, *The Reaper's Garden: Death and Power in the World of Atlantic Slavery* (Cambridge, MA: Harvard University Press, 2008), 205–6.
149. Sensbach, *A Separate Canaan*, 56, 76.
150. Nikolaus Ludwig, Count von Zinzendorf, *Kinder Reden*, Craig D. Atwood, translator, in Atwood, "Blood and Wounds Theology," 42–43n39.
151. Sensbach, *A Separate Canaan*, 245–49; on "blood and wounds," see 43–44. As we have seen, Atwood, *Community of the Cross*, disagrees with Sensbach's contention that blood and wounds was aberrant. On the dissemination of Moravian theology, see also Juster, *Sacred Violence*, 252–54. On the "pedagogy of conversion," see Frey and Wood, *Come Shouting to Zion*, 86; Hempton, *Methodism*, 132. Turner's account of his own achievement of grace is noticeably free of the fear and doubt of *Bußkampf* pietism.
152. "Christ the Rock of Ages" (Augustus Toplady, 1763), in Wesley, *A Collection of Hymns*, 572. And see Noll, *Rise of Evangelicalism*, 272; Atwood, *Community of the Cross*, 107–8.
153. On whom, see George M. Marsden, *Jonathan Edwards: A Life* (New Haven: Yale University Press, 2003). See also Douglas A. Sweeney, *Edwards the Exegete: Biblical Interpretation and Anglo-Protestant Culture on the Edge of the Enlightenment* (New York: Oxford University Press, 2016); Avihu Zakai, *Jonathan Edwards's Philosophy of History: The Reenchantment of the World in the Age of the Enlightenment* (Princeton: Princeton University Press, 2003).
154. Jonathan Edwards, *Religious Affections* (1754), *The Works of Jonathan Edwards*, Paul Ramsey, editor (WJE Online Vol. 2), 310, at http://edwards.yale.edu/research/browse (last accessed February 22, 2019). See also Noll, *Rise of Evangelicalism*, 78.
155. Jonathan Edwards, "Notes on the Apocalypse" (1723), in *Apocalyptic Writings*, *The Works of Jonathan Edwards*, Stephen J. Stein, editor (WJE Online Vol. 5), 102, 109, at http://edwards.yale.edu/research/browse (last accessed February 22, 2019).
156. Butler, *Awash in a Sea of Faith*, 216–18; Bloch, *Visionary Republic*, 6–21.
157. Mark Noll calls him "the greatest intellectual in the whole history of evangelicalism." Noll, *Rise of Evangelicalism*, 256. According to George Marsden, "After the American Revolution, New England Calvinism with a deep Edwardsian imprint emerged as one of the most influential movements shaping the new American voluntary religious culture." Marsden, *Jonathan Edwards*, 8, and see also 499.
158. John F. Wilson, "Editor's Introduction," in Edwards, *A History of the Work of Redemption*, 1–109, at 11, 20–25. Edwards had long intended to revise and greatly expand the thirty sermons himself, envisaging "a great work, which I call *A History of the Work of Redemption*, a body of divinity in an entire new method, being thrown into the form of an history, considering the affairs of Christian theology, as the whole of it, in each part, stands in reference to the great work of redemption by Jesus Christ." His sudden death in March 1758, the result of a smallpox inoculation, prevented him from realizing his ambition. See Marsden, *Jonathan Edwards*, 481–82, 493–94.
159. Wilson, "Editor's Introduction," 26–27. Between the Revolution and the Civil War, American editions of Edwards's *History* were published in 1782 (Boston), 1786 (New York), 1792 (Worcester, Massachusetts), 1793 (New York), 1808 (Worcester), 1830 (New York), 1832 (New York), 1839 (New York) and 1840 (New York—the last four being publications of the American Tract Society (see above, note 16).
160. Wilson, "Editor's Introduction," 82, and see 27–28. Wilson specifically contrasts the *History*'s enormous impact on popular culture to its limited influence on elite culture, where responses "were largely critical (not to say hostile)." An article in volume 52 of the London *Monthly Review* (1775), at 117–20, discussing the first (Edinburgh 1774)

edition of the *History* dismissed Edwards as "an intoxicated visionary" and "poor departed enthusiast," and his *History* as "nonsense." Wilson, "Editor's Introduction," 81, 86–87.

161. Wilson, "Editor's Introduction," 56, 82. See Marsden, *Jonathan Edwards*, 193–200, 482–89; Bezzant, *Jonathan Edwards*, 91–98.
162. Heyrman, *Southern Cross*, 78.
163. Edwards, *History*, 120–25. These hermeneutics are unambiguously Lukan. See Michael Goheen, "A Critical Examination of David Bosch's Missional Reading of Luke," and Scott W. Hahn, "Kingdom and Church in Luke-Acts: From Davidic Christology to Kingdom Ecclesiology," both in Bartholomew et al., editors, *Reading Luke*, 229–64, and 294–326.
164. Edwards, *History*, 143. In full: "From the fall of man to this day wherein we live the Work of Redemption in its effect has mainly been carried on by remarkable pourings out of the Spirit of God. Though there be a more constant influence of God's Spirit always in some degree attending his ordinances, yet the way in which the greatest things have been done towards carrying on this work always has been by remarkable pourings out of the Spirit at special seasons of mercy." Edwards specifically identified revivals with such "special seasons of mercy." Mark Noll comments, "Because of the importance of revival to evangelical consciousness, Edwards's assessment rapidly became standard." Noll, *Rise of Evangelicalism*, 138, and see 138–41; Marsden, *Jonathan Edwards*, 201; Winiarski, *Darkness Falls*, 18, 214–84.
165. Edwards, *History*, 513. See also Moessner, "Reading Luke's Gospel," 136–37, 149–51. Moessner concludes (150, 151), "in the opening of the third gospel, Jesus is presented to the Lord with a sacrifice of redemption as the firstborn of Israel (Luke 2:22–23); in the 'end,' Jesus presents himself to the Lord as a sacrifice for the redemption of Israel and all the nations." In this respect, "the Gospel of Luke can be read like no other."
166. Edwards, *History*, 513: "The work of the new creation is more excellent than the old. So it ever is, then when one thing is removed by God to make way for another, the new one excels the old: tabernacle and temple; so new covenant, new dispensation: throne of Saul and David, priesthood of Aaron and priesthood of Christ, old Jerusalem and new; so old creation and new. God has used the creation that he has made to no other purpose but to subserve to the design of this affair."
167. *Ibid.*, 130. When humanity fell "Christ immediately without further delay entered on his work and took on him that office that he had stood engaged to take on him from eternity. As soon as man ever fell, Christ the eternal Son of God clothed himself with his mediatorial character and therein presented himself before the Father. He immediately stepped in between an holy, infinite, offended majesty and offending mankind, and was accepted in his interposition; and so wrath was prevented from going forth in the full execution of that ensuing curse that man had brought on himself." See also Milton, *Paradise Lost*, Bk. 3, ll. 1–415.
168. Edwards, *History*, 130–31: "From this day forward Christ took on him the care of the church of the elect, he took here the care of fallen man in the execution of all his offices. . . . When Satan the grand enemy had conquered and overthrown man, the business of resisting and conquering him was committed to Jesus Christ. . . . He was thus appointed the captain of the Lord's hosts and captain of their salvation, and always acted as such thenceforward, and so he appeared from time to time and he will continue to act as such to the end of the world. Henceforward this lower world with all its concerns was as it were devolved upon the Son of God."
169. Wilson, "Editor's Introduction," 25, 38–40, 52–56; Marsden, *Jonathan Edwards*, 168. As we have seen, Zinzendorf also uses the language of Christ's "purchase" of humanity's redemption (see above, text at note 130). To elaborate: "We are truly paid for, as a person purchases one item from another, as one can ransom a prisoner, so we are

purchased from wrath, from judgment, from the curse, from the Fall and all ruin, from sin, death, the devil and hell through a true, alone in the treasury of God, legal and complete payment, namely 'through the blood of the one who tasted death for us all through the grace of God.'" Zinzendorf, *Berliner Reden* (Men) 8:98, in Atwood, *Community of the Cross*, 99. Zinzendorf is no Calvinist. "God in his essence is love without wrath, but humans in sin perceive God as wrathful. Christ came to reconcile the world to God, not God to the world. The creature feels its utter worthlessness and its need to be punished, but the Crucifixion stands as the assurance of forgiveness" (*ibid.*, 99). But there is some soteriological overlap here in what Atwood describes as Zinzendorf's "blend of violent imagery with joyful spirituality" in describing "the ransom of Christ for human souls lost in perdition" (99–100).

170. Wilson, "Editor's Introduction," 48–49; and see, for example, Edwards, *History*, 241–43.

171. Edwards, *History*, 176, 184, 196–98. Whenever in the Old Testament God takes material form, as, for example, the burning bush (174) and pillars of cloud and of fire (176, 184) in Exodus, or apparent human form, as in "the similitude of the Lord" that speaks with Moses, as referenced in Numbers 12:8 (196), Edwards holds that this is in fact Christ. Christ as mediator is God's material or human incarnation in the world. "Christ thus appeared time after time in the form of the nature he was afterwards to take upon him, because he now appeared on the same design and to carry on the same work that he was to appear in his nature to work out and carry on" (198). In other words, manifestations of the Godhead in the scriptural world of the Old Testament are treated as earthly manifestations of Christ prior to his initial coming incarnate "as God-man . . . the natural completion of the preparation of redemption in Israel's history." Wilson, "Editor's Introduction," 54.

172. Wilson, "Editor's Introduction," 32.

173. Bezzant, *Jonathan Edwards*, 98–106. See for example Edwards, *History*, 218: "The law was given by Moses but yet all the institutions of the Jewish worship were not given by Moses. Some were added by David, by divine direction. So this greatest of all personal types of Christ did not only perfect Joshua's work in giving Israel the possession of the promised land, but he also finished Moses' work in perfecting the instituted worship of Israel. Thus there must be a number of typical prophets, priests, and princes to complete one figure or shadow of that of which Christ was the antitype, he being the substance of all the types and shadows. Of so much more glory was Christ accounted worthy than Moses, Joshua, David, and Solomon, and all the great prophets, priests and princes, judges and saviors of the Old Testament put together." And see Wilson, "Editor's Introduction," 45–48; Marsden, *Jonathan Edwards*, 77.

174. Eric Auerbach, *Mimesis: The Representation of Reality in Western Literature*, Willard R. Trask, translator (Princeton: Princeton University Press, 1953), 73. And see Wilson, "Editor's Introduction," 43.

175. As, for example, in Edwards, *History*, 218 (quoted in note 173 above). In hermeneutic usage "antitype" does not mean "opposite" but rather that which is "shadowed forth" or represented by the "type" or "figure." See Edwards, *History*, 281. This is a literalization of pre-Reformation allegory, which John Wycliffe called "*goostly vndirstondinge*" (ghostly understanding). See Galatians 4:24 in the Wycliffite Bible (Early Version, 1382).

176. Marsden, *Jonathan Edwards*, 88–90.

177. Eric Sundquist also notes Turner's resort to typological hermeneutics, but without exploring their source. See Sundquist, *To Wake the Nations*, 73, 79.

178. See, for example, Allmendinger, *Rising*, 16: "Between 1821 and 1823, Turner had begun to take an open public role at religious gatherings in the neighborhood, exhorting and singing." Turner was widely identified as a preacher in the aftermath of the

rebellion (see above, note 116), but Thomas Ruffin Gray, denied that Turner was any kind of preacher, calling him one who merely "exhorted and sung at neighborhood meetings" and who manipulated credulous others with tales of the supernatural. See Anon. [Thomas Ruffin Gray] in the Richmond *Constitutional Whig* (September 26, 1831), in Tragle, *Southampton Slave Revolt*, 92–93. This is consistent with Gray's general desire to depict religiosity (in anyone) as fanaticism. But it is also consistent with evidence that Turner's religious leanings were predominantly Methodist. Under Baptist church rules, Turner could not have been recognized as a Baptist preacher unless granted "liberty" (licensed) by an individual church to preach—something that Southampton's Baptist churches were wary of doing in the case of their black members. See Scully, *Religion*, 175–79. The Methodists had licensed preachers too—salaried professional clergy who were itinerant on a circuit assigned by a Methodist bishop—but also a second group of self-supporting "local preachers" who "occasionally preached and otherwise ministered to the faithful in their neighborhoods," as well as local "exhorters." Turner could have considered himself (and been accepted as) a Methodist "local preacher" without any license, particularly as "in practice" the difference between preaching and exhorting "often became blurred almost beyond meaning." See Wigger, *Taking Heaven by Storm*, 29, 130–31. The character of Methodist preachers also explains some of Turner's self-presentation: his asceticism, but also in particular his appearance (in the *Confessions*) as single and celibate, notwithstanding evidence that he had a wife and at least one son. On Methodist preachers, see Heyrman, *Southern Cross*, 86–104, who comments (113–14) on Methodism's culture of "spiritual charisma" derived from celibate youthful itinerants' "embrace of 'holy poverty' and lives of extreme physical hardship and deprivation."

179. Turner could read and write from an early age. He mentions "constantly improv[ing]" his knowledge "at all opportunities" and his habit of looking at books "whenever an opportunity occurred." *Confessions*, 8.

180. *Confessions* 8, 10, and see above, notes 16 and 65. If Turner was influenced by Edwardsian ideas it was not because Edwards was a committed opponent of slavery, because he was not. See Kenneth P. Minkema and Harry S. Stout, "The Edwardsean Tradition and the Antislavery Debate, 1740–1865," *Journal of American History* 92, no. 1 (2005): 47–74 (cf. Marsden, *Jonathan Edwards*, 256–58). Still, Edwards's influence was huge, and as Minkema and Stout note, "Indians and African Americans adapted Edwardsean teachings to fit their own perspectives" (59).

181. Edwards, *History*, 324, 325. Noticeably, Edwards's description replicates the Lukan narrative of Christ as subordinate.

182. *Confessions*, 7, 8 (emphasis added), 9, 11. Few slaves knew their dates of birth. As one of the most famous wrote, "I have no accurate knowledge of my age, never having seen any authentic record containing it. By far the larger part of the slaves know as little of their ages as horses know of theirs, and it is the wish of most masters within my knowledge to keep their slaves thus ignorant. I do not remember to have ever met a slave who could tell of his birthday." Douglass, *Narrative of the Life of Frederick Douglass*, 1.

183. Wilson, "Editor's Introduction," 50, comments: "Edwards' formal topic was God's Work of Redemption, that is to say, the achievement of the redemption of the world as the greatest of God's works. Unity derived directly from the divine intention that was thought to undergird that work and make it the goal of creation—a goal possibly required by the logic of the trinitarian Godhead. This unifying factor was deeply woven into Edwards' 'history' through the central role of Christ. (He saw the Spirit active throughout the whole as well.) Further, the boundaries given to the subject—the fall of man and the last judgment—rendered it coextensive with human consciousness of historical existence." Wilson notes that Christ and the Spirit are central

throughout the *History* but that their relationship changes as one phase of the History succeed another (at 60): "The principle of explicit witness through the Spirit punctuates the earlier periods of the Old Testament. In the very first period of the Old Testament the Spirit is poured out on Enos." Infusions of the Spirit cease in the second period of the *History*, which is dominated by Christ's incarnate presence. After the resurrection "the principle of Spirit witness or presence becomes increasingly important in the third period (from the resurrection of Christ to the end of the world). There the Spirit is the great agent through whom the Work of Redemption—which Christ has finished—is developed and completed." Turner's invocations of the Spirit conform to this pattern, as the pattern itself conforms to Luke-Acts. He first identifies "the Spirit" as "that [which] spoke to the prophets in former days" (*Confessions*, 9) or in other words as that manifestation of the Godhead which enjoined explicit witness in the first of Edwards's periods. Subsequently he is himself called to witness (see above, text at notes 43 and 54–56), in conformity with his temporal location in Edwards's third period. His invocations of Christ incarnate, meanwhile, reference the Saviour on earth during his first coming, and the resumed physicality of the Saviour as the second coming approaches. *Confessions*, 9–11. Thus, in the *Confessions* Christ and the Spirit exchange places in the same rhythm as in Edwards's *History*.

184. *Confessions*, 10.
185. Edwards, *History*, 151–52. Edwards here comes remarkably close to replicating the key elements of Zinzendorf's theology of blood and wounds: the blood of the Saviour, equated with the Holy Spirit that "made the entire earth a streambed," baptizes the world; and the side wound in Christ's body, which opens his body as a refuge for his people and his church, renders the ark a type of Christ's body, "the refuge and hiding place of the church." See above, note 130 and accompanying text.
186. *Confessions*, 10; Edwards, *History*, 175–76. See also Edwards at 507—As the lower world is destroyed at the Last Judgment, Christ presents the church of the elect to God, saying "I have done all that for them which thou hast appointed me. I have perfectly cleansed them from all filthiness in my blood, and here they are in perfect holiness, shining with thy perfect image."
187. *Confessions*, 11; Edwards, *History*, 328. And compare Zinzendorf, above, text at note 150.
188. *Confessions*, 11.
189. The first approximation of the phrase that I have been able to trace is in the sixth edition of Robert Burton, *The Anatomy of Melancholy* (first published 1621; sixth edition 1652): "As Judas Maccabeus killed Apollonius with his own weapons, we arm ourselves to our own overthrows" (London: Printed for Thomas Tegg, 1845) 85. The sixth edition was the last edition of this obsessively amended and augmented work to have been corrected by its author before his death in 1640. The passage does not appear in earlier editions. Burton's reference is to 1 Maccabees 3:10–12: "Then Apollonius gathered the Gentiles together, and a great host out of Samaria, to fight against Israel. / Which thing when Judas perceived, he went forth to meet him, and so he smote him, and slew him: many also fell down slain, but the rest fled. / Wherefore Judas took their spoils, and Apollonius' sword also, and therewith he fought all his life long" (Sir Lancelot C. L. Brenton, translator, 1851). Maccabees is included in the Septuagint, but was considered apocrypha rather than canonical scripture by Protestant denominations, and was not included in many editions of the authorized English translation of the Christian Bible for the Church of England (King James Version), particularly after 1885. The original 1611 edition of the King James Bible does include the apocrypha, and 1 Maccabees 3:10–12 appears there in a translation identical to Brenton's 1851 version, save for minor differences in punctuation. But that translation bears no resemblance to Burton's gloss. *The Anatomy of Melancholy* was out

of print between 1676 and 1800, and is unlikely to have circulated in any edition among Southside Virginia farm households.

190. The *Oxford English Dictionary* lists George Marcelline, *The Triumphs of King James I* (1610); Edmund Mary Bolton's translation of *The Roman Histories of Lucius Iulius Florus from the Foundation of Rome, till Cæsar Augustus* (1619); James Mabbe's translation of Mateo Alemán, *The Rogue; or, The Life of Guzman de Alfarache* (1622); Ralph Cudworth, *The True Intellectual System of the Universe* (1678); Samuel Foote, *The Minor: A Comedy* (1760); Charles Johnstone, *The History of John Juniper, Esq* (1781), and Samuel Johnson's remarks on Congreve, in his *Prefaces, Biographical and Critical, to the Works of the English Poets* (1784). Johnson is the first of these to use the phrase in its modern form, as Turner does, i.e., to overcome an adversary "with his own weapons." All the others use an early-modern form of expression derived from the idea of a tourney—taking a turn "at" weapons. Thus, for example, Mabbe: "That he should put a full stoccado upon me, and go brag when he had done, that he had beaten a master of defence at his owne weapon." Examples of post-1850 usage recorded in the *OED* suggest the widening currency of the modern form. The examples offered are evangelical-religious, rather than secular in connotation, suggesting that the move from the early-modern "at weapons" tourney-derived version to the modern "with" had an evangelical resonance/origin. Thus Charles Kingsley, *Alton Locke, Tailor and Poet* (1850): "Try no more to meet Mammon with his own weapons, but commit your cause to Him who judges righteously"; Bram Stoker, *Dracula* (1897): "He has chosen this earth because it has been holy. Thus we defeat him with his own weapon, for we make it more holy still." Wider etymological searches beyond the *OED* also suggest an evangelical Christian connection dating from the later eighteenth century.

191. Edwards, *History*, 206 (emphasis added). As Karl Löwith writes, "The Christian meaning of history . . . consists in the most paradoxical fact that the cross, this sign of deepest ignominy, could conquer the world of the conquerors by opposing it." Löwith, *Meaning in History*, 3. Edwards's first use of the metaphor predates his *History*, appearing in his sermon "The Excellency of Christ" (1734): "It was in Christ's last sufferings, above all, that he was delivered up to the power of his enemies; and yet by these, above all, he obtained victory over his enemies. . . . When Christ's enemies came to apprehend him, he says to them, *Luke 22:53*, 'When I was daily with you in the temple, ye stretched forth no hand against me: but this is your hour and the power of darkness.' And yet it was principally by means of those sufferings, that he conquered and overthrew his enemies. Christ never so effectually bruised Satan's head, as when Satan bruised his heel. The weapon with which Christ warred against the devil, and obtained a most complete victory and glorious triumph over him, was the cross, the instrument and weapon with which he thought he had overthrown Christ, and brought on him shameful destruction. . . . In his last sufferings Christ sapped the very foundations of Satan's kingdom; he conquered his enemies in their own territories, and beat them with their own weapons; as David cut off Goliath's head with his own sword." Jonathan Edwards, *Sermons and Discourses, 1734–1738*, in *The Works of Jonathan Edwards*, M. X. Lesser and Paul Ramsay, editors (WJE Online Vol. 19), 579–80, at http://edwards.yale.edu/research/browse. It seems at least possible that Edwards adapted his usage of the phrase from *The Anatomy of Melancholy* (see above, note 189).

Edwards's reference to the cross as a weapon of Christ's enemies turned against them by Christ as a weapon of deliverance is also a reminder that in his anonymous account of the rebellion published in the Richmond *Constitutional Whig* (September 26, 1831), in Tragle, *Southampton Slave Revolt*, 92, Thomas Ruffin Gray reported the recovery of papers "given up by [Turner's] wife, under the lash," upon each of which "a crucifix and the sun is distinctly visible." Gray also reports finding numbers—6,000, 30,000,

80,000—on the same papers. It is conceivable that Turner adopted the cross as a symbol both of deliverance and of armament. As to the sun, it has two interwoven meanings in Edwards's *History*: first as a metaphor for Christ—"When Christ ascended into heaven after his passion and was solemnly installed on the throne of heaven as King of Heaven, then this sun rose in heaven, even the Lamb that is the light of the new Jerusalem" (132); second, as a metaphor for the redemptive enlightenment (gospel light) cast on the world by Christ's coming—"the light that the church enjoyed from the fall of man till Christ came was like the light which we enjoy in the night, not the light of the sun directly but as reflected from the moon and stars, which light did foreshadow Christ to come, the sun of righteousness hereafter to arise" (136). The latter usage also indirectly evokes the eclipse that Turner treated as a sign of the arrival of the moment of preparation. See also the *History* at 229, 373, and 480 for more overt eclipse analogies. As to the numbers, it is worth noting that the compound of 6×3×8 is 144, and that 144,000 happens to be the number of those in Revelation 7:3–4, "sealed the servants of our God in their foreheads," whom God will protect from what is to come, along with those already martyred for the word of God, whose robes had been "made . . . white in the blood of the Lamb" (7:14). Perhaps Turner was attempting to calculate what spiritual forces he might have at his disposal, or alternatively what the burden of redemption might be. See also Bauckham, *Theology*, 76–78.

192. Edwards, *History*, 205–6. In the authoritative 1989 edition of the *History*, used here, the latter part of the quote appears in brackets: "The last shall be first and [the first last]" indicating that in the original written text from which the edition was prepared, Edwards had not bothered to complete the well-known scriptural language, which is from Luke 13:30, and Matthew 20:16. In all the late eighteenth- and early nineteenth-century editions of the *History* that I have consulted the quotation appears in full.

193. *Confessions*, 11. Turner's slight variation—placing first/last before last/first—reproduces the order found in Matthew 19:30 and Mark 10:31.

194. The textual similarities that I point to as circumstantial evidence that Turner was familiar to some degree with Edwards's *History* could also suggest the disquieting possibility that Gray augmented the pamphlet with bits copied out of the *History* to underline Turner's fanatical "enthusiasm." That Gray was a skeptic of religion, let alone evangelical religion, is not in doubt (see above, prologue note 70). His Richmond *Constitutional Whig* (September 26, 1831) account of the rebellion includes a denunciation of blockheaded ministers whose religious passion "gives a warrant to any negro who hears . . . to do whatever he pleases provided his imagination, can make God sanction it." See Tragle, *Southampton Slave Revolt*, 92. His pamphlet was conceived as an attack on the evils of religiosity as well as an exposé of the Southampton insurrection. That said, the intricate interpolation of text with what appear to be, undeniably, intimate details of Turner's life history and circumstances would no doubt have demanded more scriptural and theological knowledge than an irreligious man possessed, and—in any case—more compositional time than Gray had available. See above, chapter 1, text at notes 3–4. For skeptical assessment of the possibility that the pamphlet was in some fashion fabricated, see also above, chapter 1, note 70 and accompanying text.

195. Eric Sundquist is also interested in Turner's millenarianism, but identifies it as premillennial, which in my view is not at all in accord with Turner's articulated eschatology. See Sundquist, *To Wake the Nations*, 73–75. Sundquist also follows Ernest Tuveson, *Redeemer Nation: The Idea of America's Millennial Role* (Chicago: University of Chicago Press, 1980), at 34, in using the term "millenarian" to mean premillennialist, and "millennial" to mean postmillennialist. Here, in contrast, I adopt the common practice of using "millenarian" as a general term denoting any variety of religious apocalypticism focused on "thousand year" beliefs, and pre- and postmillennial as specific (and distinct) categories of Christian millenarianism. See above, note 67, text at note 121.

196. Howe, *What Hath God Wrought*, 289.
197. *Ibid.*, 289. This was the complaisant antebellum Protestantism that overtook eighteenth-century Methodism. As John Wigger puts it: "As Methodists grew progressively more comfortable in American society. . . . The church simply could not be both respectable and countercultural. Eventually it did not even represent a subculture." Wigger, *Taking Heaven by Storm*, 188.
198. On which see Parramore, *Southampton County*, 68–70. Eric Foner notes Virginia was in a state of economic decline and agricultural depression throughout the 1820s. In 1830 Southampton County's assessed land value ranked 46th in the state compared with 5th at the turn of the century. Eric Foner, ed., *Nat Turner: Great Lives Observed* (Englewood Cliffs, NJ: Prentice-Hall, 1971), 2. See also Clyde A. Haulman, *Virginia and the Panic of 1819: The First Great Depression and the Commonwealth* (London: Pickering & Chatto, 2008), 137–51.
199. *Confessions*, 8 (the note of bitterness in "if I had the means" seems plain). On African American constructions of a "fugitive science," in which Turner here is an active participant, see Britt Rusert, "Delany's Comet: Fugitive Science and the Speculative Imaginary of Emancipation," *American Quarterly* 65, no. 4 (2013): 799–829.
200. *Confessions*, 8. And see above, notes 16 and 65.
201. See, for example, Edwards, *History*, 352–53, 372–74, 381–84, 387–98.
202. Revelation 6:12, in Edwards, *History*, 373, 394, 397.
203. Revelation 21:6; Edwards, *History*, 509.
204. Revelation 20:3.
205. Edwards, *History*, 488, 489, 490.
206. *Ibid.*, 490. And see 495: "How will the sight of that awful majesty terrify them, when taken in the midst of their wickedness. Then they shall see who he is, what kind of a person he is whom they have mocked and scoffed at and whose church they have been endeavoring to overthrow. . . . Their countenances shall be changed from a show of carnal mirth, haughty pride, and contempt of God's people; it shall put on a show of ghastly terror and amazement, and trembling and chattering of teeth shall seize them."
207. *Confessions*, 11 (emphasis added). I have already suggested Turner had referenced the cross, Christ's yoke, in his narrative (see above, notes 45 and 111, and accompanying text). Was he also thinking of the final, gentle words of "encouragement to burdened souls" with which Edwards concluded his extraordinary and utterly wrenching account of Christ's Passion and its meaning in the four sermons that discussed the purchase of redemption: "Come therefore, hearken to the sweet and earnest calls of Christ to your soul. Do as he invites, and as he commands you in Matthew 11:28–30, 'Come unto me, all [ye that labour and are heavy laden, and I will give you rest]. Take my yoke [upon you, and learn of me . . . and ye shall find rest unto your souls]. For my yoke is easy, [and my burden is light].'" Edwards, *History*, 343.
208. *Confessions*, 11. Did they discuss killing? On the very eve of the massacre, Turner seems to cast doubt on it, reportedly telling his comrades "that his reasons for not telling of it before, was, that the negroes had frequently attempted similar things, confided their purpose to several, and that it always leaked out." See below chapter 4, note 30 and accompanying text.
209. Edwards, *History*, 491, 503. Turner, wrote Gray, "expressed himself fully satisfied as to the impracticability of his attempt." *Confessions*, 18. We take this to mean that Turner was in effect admitting to Gray that his "rebellion" had no chance of success. But "impracticable" also carries the connotation of that which requires faith rather than works, that which cannot be achieved except by an act of God.
210. Edwards, *History*, 117, 295, 305, 331, 334, 358. For parallels with the roughly contemporary Adventist, William Miller, see Everett N. Dick, *William Miller and the Advent Crisis* (Berrien Springs, MI: Andrews University Press, 1994); Ruth Alden Doan, *The Miller Heresy: Millennialism and American Culture* (Philadelphia: Temple University Press,

1987); and generally Stephen D. O'Leary, *Arguing the Apocalypse: A Theory of Millennial Rhetoric* (New York: Oxford University Press, 1994). Gary Laderman comments that Miller's eschatology "focused more on collective images of death and the dead than on personal considerations of individual death. In Miller's plan the imminent moment of the second coming of Jesus was to be both an orgy of death and the end of death—as well as the end of history." Gary Laderman, *The Sacred Remains: American Attitudes Toward Death, 1799-1883* (New Haven: Yale University Press, 1996), 58.

211. *Confessions*, 11. Luke 19:27. See also Matthew 22:1–14.
212. *Confessions*, 7 (emphasis added). And see above, chapter 1, text at note 78.
213. Walter Benjamin, "The Meaning of Time in the Moral Universe," in Bullock and Jennings, editors, *Walter Benjamin: Selected Writings Volume 1*, 286–87. Turner's "confession" is in fact revelation, no less than that received by John of Patmos.
214. Smith, *Oracle*, 161.
215. *Confessions*, 21.
216. Smith, *Oracle*, 163.

CHAPTER 3: THE SHUDDER OF THE THOUGHT

1. See above, chapter 2, note 20; below, chapter 5, note 16. We should recall that in his anonymous letter to the Richmond *Enquirer* of November 8, 1831 (see above, chapter 2, note 68) William C. Parker reported that he was unable to obtain from Turner an explanation how his beliefs and the apparent purpose of the revolt [apparent, that is, to Parker] were related. "Notwithstanding I examined him closely upon this point, he alway [*sic*] seemed to mystify." This suggests that Turner's idiom upon examination was entirely eschatological. (See also above, chapter 1, note 72.) A second report of the examination stated, "During all the examination, he evinced great intelligence and much shrewdness of intellect, answering every question clearly and distinctly, and without confusion or prevarication. He . . . says he was actuated to do what he did, from the influence of fanaticism." Theodore Trezvant, letter to the Norfolk *American Beacon*, November 2, 1831, in Tragle, *Southampton Slave Revolt*, 132. As we have seen, Turner himself told Gray it was not insurrection but "enthusiasm" that had "terminated so fatally to many." (See above, chapter 2, text at note 212).

    Against these reports, in his anonymous letter to the Richmond *Constitutional Whig* of September 26, 1831 (see above, chapter 1, note 61) Thomas Ruffin Gray reported, "I have been credibly informed, that something like three years ago [1828], Nat received a whipping from his master [Thomas Moore], for saying that the blacks ought to be free, and that they would be free one day or other." We should note that it was about this time (May 1828, see *Confessions*, 11) that Turner first *explicitly* references Luke's language of reversal—"the first should be last and the last should be first." But he makes no mention of any whipping, nor is there any independent evidence of a whipping. We might note an otherwise unrelated story from the mid-1850s told by Henry Clay Bruce in his memoir, *The New Man: Twenty-Nine Years a Slave. Twenty-Nine Years a Free Man* (York, PA: P. Anstadt & Sons, 1895), 73: "I remember a story told on Uncle Tom Ewing, an old colored preacher, who was praying on one occasion, after the close of his sermon, in the church near Jacob Vennable's place, five miles from Brunswick [Missouri]. The old fellow got warmed up, and used the words, 'Free indeed, free from death, free from hell, free from work, free from the white folks, free from everything.' After the meeting closed, Jacob Vennable, who sat in front of the pulpit took Tom to task and threatened to have his license revoked if he ever used such language in public. Jacob Vennable was a slaveholder and considered a fair master, so I was informed by Jesse, one of his slaves, and others who were supposed to know. I heard Uncle Tom preach and pray many times after the above-described occurrence, but never heard him use the words quoted above." See also Raboteau, *Slave Religion*, 232.

2. *Confessions*, 11.
3. *Ibid.*, 11. See also above, chapter 2, note 83.

In this chapter and the next the goal is to come to an understanding of the decision Turner and his comrades reached and more or less immediately put into effect: the decision "to rise and kill all the white people." I have already described what would be initiated in St. Luke's Parish in the wake of God's reminder as "divine violence" (see above, preface, text at notes 13–15). This idea is taken from Walter Benjamin's essay "Critique of Violence." See Bullock and Jennings, editors, *Walter Benjamin: Selected Writings Volume 1*, 236–52. Divine violence is not a simple idea; a vast literature discusses what Benjamin meant to convey by it. Slavoj Žižek, for example, defends reading divine violence to signify human revolutionary violence. See, e.g., Žižek, *In Defense of Lost Causes*, 477–78; Slavoj Žižek, *Robespierre: Virtue and Terror* (London: Verso, 2007), vii–xxxix. In pointed contrast, Simon Critchley defends reading divine violence to signify what he terms "nonviolent violence," or what one might think of, importing Giorgio Agamben, as the "destituent" violence of Sorelian anarcho-syndicalism. See, e.g., Simon Critchley, *The Faith of the Faithless: Experiments in Political Theology* (London: Verso, 2014), 207–45. See also James R. Martel, *Divine Violence: Walter Benjamin and the Eschatology of Sovereignty* (Abingdon, UK: Routledge, 2012); James R. Martel, "Must the Law Be a Liar? Walter Benjamin on the Possibility of an Anarchist Form of Law," in Andreas Philippopoulos-Mihalopoulos, editor, *Routledge Research Handbook of Law and Theory* (Abingdon, UK: Routledge, 2019), 387–408. Critchley and Martel both emphasize the "bloodless" quality of divine violence in Benjamin's description, which exemplifies the idea by drawing on the story of God's judgment on Korah the Levite, and on those who stood with him against Moses and Aaron (the story can be found in full in Numbers 16:1–50). Benjamin writes, "God's judgment strikes privileged Levites, strikes them without warning, without threat, and does not stop short of annihilation. But in annihilating it also expiates, and a profound connection between the lack of bloodshed and the expiatory character of this violence is unmistakable. For blood is the symbol of mere life. . . . Mythic violence is bloody power over mere life for its own sake, divine violence pure power over all life for the sake of the living. The first demands sacrifice, the second accepts it." Benjamin, "Critique of Violence," 250. "Korah," says Critchley, "was not slaughtered by God; rather the earth opened up to engulf him with all his belongings" (216). But Critchley does not dwell on the fate of Korah's retainers (engulfed with him), or on the fate of Korah's 250 allies (burned up in divine fire), or on the fate of all those among the children of Israel who reproached Moses for the deaths of Korah and his retainers and his allies, whom God thereupon killed (14,700 in all) with a divine plague. Neither did Benjamin. Once one notices *all* of those who succumb, to God's earthquake, and His fire, and His pox, it becomes hard to see how the fate of Korah et al. exemplifies "bloodless" violence rather than bloody massacre.

Žižek asks us to reject attempts to render divine violence metaphysical, the equivalent of a "pure" bloodless event. "One should fearlessly identify divine violence with a positively existing historical phenomenon, thus avoiding all obscurantist mystification. . . . When those outside the structured social field strike 'blindly,' demanding *and* enacting immediate justice/vengeance, this is 'divine violence.' . . . Benjaminian 'divine violence' should thus be conceived as . . . the heroic assumption of the solitude of a sovereign decision." Žižek, *Robespierre*, x–xi. The point is well made. Violence is brought down to earth, "a decision (to kill, to risk or lose one's own life) made in absolute solitude, not covered by the big Other" (xi), that is, not covered by God. Still, in Turner's case we are dealing with someone whose introduction to divine violence—the spirit's injunction that he "fight against the serpent"—*was* covered by God. Precisely because of its visionary quality the divine violence Turner encountered "in the spirit" *could* be conceived as "pure event," and to that extent it could remain comfortingly metaphysical: unhistorical, unreal. Until, that is, God's intentions became clear.

What can the intimation of Turner's distress at the prospect of killing tell us about divine violence? It tells us we must grapple with Turner's dawning realization that "divine violence" was *not* something pure, something remote. Divine violence was real. It demanded *his* action. It demanded *his* decision (certainly reached in solitude) to become God's agent and to kill people amongst whom he lived. This is the prospect that causes him distress.

We know that Turner decided to obey God. We must not assume that the decision was easy, or that it is easily understood. To assume otherwise is to render Turner into something other than what he was. It is to discard the figure and the mentalité I have tried to unravel in chapter 2, and to substitute a different, flat, figure, one that David Scott has called a conscript of modernity, "a figure of enlightened sensibility and modern—indeed, modernist—political desire" a figure wrapped in "a modernist allegory of anticolonial revolution written in the mode of a historical Romance." See David Scott, *Conscripts of Modernity: The Tragedy of Colonial Enlightenment* (Durham, NC: Duke University Press, 2004), 59, 98. See also above, prologue, text at notes 156–61. See also Brown, *The Reaper's Garden*, 258: "Progressive narratives do little to explain popular politics within and beyond the world of slavery, where it is evident that the spiritual and supernatural inspired purposeful action."

4. Or, almost immediately. As the textual hinge swings toward death, Turner allows himself one final, perhaps wistful, perhaps sorrowful, glance backward to his former life: "Since the commencement of 1830, I had been living with Mr. Joseph Travis, who was to me a kind master, and placed the greatest confidence in me; in fact, I had no cause to complain of his treatment to me." *Confessions*, 11. Immediately thereafter, Turner describes preparations for the meeting at which the work of death will be set in motion. What was being asked of him, what was about to take place, he appears to be telling us, was of inestimably greater significance than any question of feelings that might arise from another man's personal kindness.

5. Walter Benjamin, "Goethe's Elective Affinities," in Bullock and Jennings, editors, *Walter Benjamin: Selected Writings Volume 1*, 354. Alain Badiou names such a break an "evental site," which he defines as "the ontological support of its own appearance. . . . It makes itself in the world, the being-there of its own being." Crucially, Badiou gestures toward the ephemerality, the instantaneity, of such a break. An evental site "is an ontological figure of the instant: it appears only to disappear." Badiou, *Logics of Worlds*, 363, 369. In Frank Kermode's terms (see above, chapter 2, note 63) this is the decisive ascendancy of the orthogonal apocalyptic instant (*kairos*) over time as waiting, unfulfilled time, empty duration (*chronos*). See also chapter 2, note 23. On the comparative temporality of "the instant" and of "duration," see Gaston Bachelard, *Intuition of the Instant* [1932] (Evanston, IL: Northwestern University Press, 2013); Christopher Tomlins, "Materialism and Legal Historiography, From Bachelard to Benjamin," in Maks Del Mar, Bernadette Meyler, and Simon Stern, editors, *The Oxford Handbook of Law and the Humanities* (Oxford: Oxford University Press, 2019).

6. *Confessions*, 19. "Fiend-like face" appears to allude to the serpentine Aron, in Shakespeare's *Titus Andronicus* (at 5.1.44–45): "Say, wall-eyed slave, whither wouldst thou

convey / This growing image of thy fiendlike face?" Gray uses the same adjective ("Not a single rumor of mercy was heard to break in upon the fiend-like track of these wretches) in his *Constitutional Whig* letter of September 26, 1831. See [Thomas Ruffin Gray, letter of September 17, 1831], *The Constitutional Whig*, Richmond, Virginia (September 26, 1831), in Tragle, *Southampton Slave Revolt*, 97.

7. *Confessions*, 4. On Gray's youthful contempt for religion, see above, Prologue, note 70. For the pervasive nineteenth-century American cultural idiom "which treated human transgression as a dark secret lying buried beneath the deceptively serene surface of American social life," see Halttunen, *Murder Most Foul*, 123. On melodrama and political theory, see Bonnie Honig, *Antigone, Interrupted* (Cambridge: Cambridge University Press, 2013), at 14, 80–81, 92–94. Melodrama is a recurrent genre in Southern depictions of the tragic necessities of slaveholder legality. For a superior example, see the judgment of Thomas Ruffin in *State v. Mann*, 13 N.C. 263 (1830), which begins as follows: "A Judge cannot but lament, when such cases as the present are brought into judgment. It is impossible that the reasons on which they go can be appreciated, but where institutions similar to our own, exist and are thoroughly understood. The struggle, too, in the Judge's own breast between the feelings of the man, and the duty of the magistrate is a severe one, presenting strong temptation to put aside such questions, if it be possible. It is useless however, to complain of things inherent in our political state. And it is criminal in a Court to avoid any responsibility which the laws impose. With whatever reluctance therefore it is done, the Court is compelled to express an opinion upon the extent of the dominion of the master over the slave in North-Carolina" (264).

8. Søren Kierkegaard, *Fear and Trembling: Dialectical Lyric*, C. Stephen Evans and Sylvia Walsh, editors (Cambridge: Cambridge University Press, 2006), 31–34. In Badiou's terms, Turner is a "subject," defined as "the *local* status of a procedure, a configuration in excess of the situation," without which an event cannot occur "within an evental site." He is "a militant of truth," in "active fidelity to the event of truth." Badiou, *Being and Event*, xvi, 412 (emphasis in original); Žižek, *In Defense of Lost Causes*, 386; see also above, preface, note 18. For examples, see Badiou, *Logics of Worlds*, 363–80; Heinrich Von Kleist, *Michael Kohlhaas* (1810), in *The German Classics: Masterpieces of German Literature*, Frances A. King, translator (New York: The German Publication Society, 1914), 4:308–415; Ernst Bloch, *Thomas Münzer als Theologe der Revolution* (München: Kurt Wolff, 1921); C.L.R. James, *The Black Jacobins: Toussaint L'Ouverture and the San Domingo Revolution* (New York: Vintage Books, 1989). See, generally, Toscano, *Fanaticism*. Oliver Feltham comments, "The 'and' of being and event . . . names the space of the subject, the subject of the work of change, fragment of a truth procedure—the one who unfolds new structures of being and thus *writes the event into being*." Oliver Feltham, "Translator's Preface," in Badiou, *Being and Event*, xxxii. On the conjuncture between Kierkegaard's philosophy of "the leap" of faith and Badiou's philosophy of the event, see Armen Avanessian and Sophie Wennerscheid, "Introduction: Kierkegaard's Intervention of the Single Individual as Model for Political Theory and Practice Today?"; Sophie Wennerscheid, "The Passage through Negativity, or From Self-Renunciation to Revolution? Kierkegaard and Žižek on the Politics of the Impassioned Individual"; and Sigi Jöttkandt, "No Three without Two: Badiou with Lacan with Kierkegaard"; all in Armen Avanessian and Sophie Wennerscheid, editors, *Kierkegaard and Political Theory: Religion, Aesthetics, Politics, and the Intervention of the Single Individual* (Copenhagen: Museum Tusculanum Press, 2014), at 10, 141–65, and 221–22, respectively. Kierkegaard, writes Žižek, makes clear that "Christianity is the first and only religion of the Event," the event as rupture, "when Eternity reaches into time." Slavoj Žižek, *Event: A Philosophical Journey Through a Concept* (Brooklyn: Melville House, 2014), 35–36.

9. Søren Kierkegaard, *Frygt og Bæven: Dialektisk Lyrik* (Copenhagen: C. A. Reitzel, 1843).
10. C. Stephen Evans, "Introduction," in *Fear and Trembling*, vii. And see Hebrews 11:1, 3, 17—"Now faith is the substance of things hoped for, the evidence of things not seen. . . . / Through faith we understand that the worlds were framed by the word of God, so that things which are seen were not made of things which do appear. . . . / By faith Abraham, when he was tried, offered up Isaac . . . his only begotten son."
11. Kierkegaard, *Fear and Trembling*, 18.
12. Hebrews 11:6. As we have seen Charles Talbert put it, "One does not know God's will and then decide whether to do it. Rather, one wills to be obedient to God's will first and then, and only then, discerns what it is." Talbert, *Reading Luke*, 39 (and above, chapter 2, notes 33–36 and accompanying text).
13. *Confessions*, 9.
14. Kierkegaard, *Fear and Trembling*, 39.
15. *Ibid.*, 24.
16. *Ibid.*, 49.
17. *Ibid.*, 52. Kierkegaard, says Badiou, "is for/against Hegel. . . . Kierkegaard turns a particular point, which sums up all the others, into the instance through which the subject comes back into himself so that he may communicate with God. In the pure choice between two possibilities, which are in fact two ways of relating to the world and to himself, the subject attains the being-there of what Kierkegaard names 'subjective truth' or 'interiority.'" Choice is "a cut in time." Attaining the eternity of truth as subjective truth ("having done with Hegel") means "reconstructing that moment of existence when we are summoned to a radical decision, which alone—and not the laborious becoming-subject of the Absolute—constitutes us in a manner worthy of the Christian paradox," which is "that eternity must be encountered *in* time." Badiou, *Logics of Worlds*, 425–26, 428; see also 513. Or as Robert Orsi puts it, the transcendent must break into time. Orsi, *History and Presence*, 48, 51.
18. Evans, "Introduction," xxv.
19. *Ibid.*, xxv; Kierkegaard, *Fear and Trembling*, 53. Dominik Finkelde writes of the intervention of the single individual in *Fear and Trembling*, "Kierkegaard develops . . . an understanding of autonomy that—as an unconditional singular universal—cannot be integrated in any traditional theory of the subject as a socially-mediated and, more important, socially dependent entity. It proves itself as unconditional without being psychotic. . . . Abraham is the placeholder for this singularity. He is presented as an individual with a stubborn attachment to a void that stands—as void, gap, or simply as an absurdity in the matrix of sense—against 'common sense.'" Dominik Finkelde, "Excessive Subjectivity: The Paradox of Autonomy in Hegel and Kierkegaard," in Avanessian and Wennerscheid, editors, *Kierkegaard and Political Theory*, 114, and see 138.
20. Slavoj Žižek, *For They Know Not What They Do: Enjoyment as a Political Factor* (London: Verso, 2008), lxxxix; and see lxxiii.
21. Kierkegaard, *Fear and Trembling*, 62 (emphasis added).
22. *Ibid.*, 70.
23. Turner tells four confidants (Hark, Nelson, Henry, and Sam) of "the great work laid out for me to do" but we do not know precisely what he told them (see above, chapter 2, note 208), or how they responded (see above, chapter 2, note 81). The only explicit articulation of motive that *The Confessions* offers other than Turner's elaborated discourse of faith is the single and entirely secular statement attributed to Will [Francis]: "I . . . asked Will how came he there, he answered his life was worth no more than others, and his liberty as dear to him." *Confessions*, 12. See also Breen, *Deluged in Blood*, 30. On the limitations inherent in a secular liberal discourse of "liberty or death," see Russ Castronovo, *Necro Citizenship: Death, Eroticism, and the Public Sphere in the*

Nineteenth-Century United States (Durham, NC: Duke University Press, 2001), 25–61; but see also Gordon, *Ghostly Matters*, 137–90. See also above, preface, note 13.

24. Kierkegaard, *Fear and Trembling*, 101–2.
25. Jacques Lacan, *The Other Side of Psychoanalysis, 1968-1969 Book XVII* (New York: W. W. Norton, 2007), 186, in Maria Aristodemou, "From Decaffeinated Democracy to Democracy in the Real," in Philippopoulos-Mihalopoulos, editor, *Law and Theory*, 361; Fredric Jameson, *Postmodernism, or, The Cultural Logic of Late Capitalism* (Durham, NC: Duke University Press, 1991), 51–54. See, generally, Maria Aristodemou, *Law, Psychoanalysis, Society: Taking the Unconscious Seriously* (Abingdon, UK: Routledge, 2014).
26. Aristodemou, "Decaffeinated Democracy," 361–62. And see Eelco Runia, *Moved by the Past: Discontinuity and Historical Mutation* (New York: Columbia University Press, 2014), 106–43. Walter Benjamin called this "find[ing] the constellation of awakening." Benjamin, *The Arcades Project*, 458; Stéphane Mosès, *The Angel of History: Rosenzweig, Benjamin, Scholem*, Barbara Harshav translator (Stanford: Stanford University Press, 2009), 103–9. And see Hinks, *To Awaken My Afflicted Brethren*, 232–33.
27. Alain Badiou, *Saint Paul: The Foundation of Universalism*, Ray Brassier, translator (Stanford: Stanford University Press, 2003), 9, 4–15, 75–85. Badiou cites Galatians: "Before faith came we were kept under the law . . . But after faith is come . . . There is neither Jew nor Greek, there is neither bond nor free, there is neither male nor female; for ye are all one in Christ Jesus" (Galatians 3:23, 25, 28).
28. Kierkegaard, *Fear and Trembling*, 93 (emphasis added); Ryan Johnson, "Kierkegaard and the Dialectic of Demonic Despair," *Postgraduate Journal of Aesthetics* 9, no. 3 (summer 2012): 29–30.
29. Richmond *Enquirer* (August 30, 1831), in Tragle, *Southampton Slave Revolt*, 45.
30. "At a court of Oyer and Terminer summoned and held for the County of Southampton on the 3d day of September 1831 for the trial of . . . Jack a negro man slave the property of William Reese decsd." Southampton County Court, *Minute Book* (1830–35), 90; "A detailed account of the late insurrection in Southampton, kindly furnished us by a gentleman well conversant with the scenes he describes" [Thomas Ruffin Gray, letter of September 17, 1831], *The Constitutional Whig*, Richmond, Virginia (September 26, 1831), in Tragle, *Southampton Slave Revolt*, 90–99, at 93.
31. Žižek, *Robespierre*, x. By "structured social field," Žižek means, essentially, "the way things are."
32. "I have nothing more to say." *Confessions*, 20.
33. Kierkegaard, *Fear and Trembling*, 97.
34. *Ibid.*, 99. Here we encounter the role assigned the black criminal in Jeannine DeLombard's gallows literature, to which she wishes (mistakenly, in my view) to annex the Turner of Gray's *Confessions*. See DeLombard, *In the Shadow of the Gallows*, 1–205.
35. Kierkegaard, *Fear and Trembling*, 105.
36. Evans, "Introduction," xxix.
37. *Confessions*, 20; Kierkegaard, *Fear and Trembling*, 93. Writing of the eighteenth century's Moravian-Methodist convergence (see above, chapter 2, text at notes 126–51), Frederick Dreyer notes that both Wesley and Zinzendorf appealed to the authority of the senses. Wesley warranted feeling ("sensible inspiration") to be "the 'main doctrine of the Methodists.' It was 'the substance of what we all preach.'" In Zinzendorf's case, feeling was "the 'concomitant' of evangelical truth . . . proof for our possession of faith. 'As long as you do not feel, you have not tasted the word of God.'" Dreyer, *Genesis of Methodism*, 80–81.
38. *Confessions*, 20.
39. *Ibid.*, 21.
40. Kierkegaard, *Fear and Trembling*, 106.

CHAPTER 4: THE WORK OF DEATH: MASSACRE, RETRIBUTION

1. Georg Wilhelm Friedrich Hegel, *The Phenomenology of Mind*, J. B. Baillie, translator (New York: Harper & Row, 1967), 232, 234 (emphasis in original), 236. See also Brennan, *History After Lacan*, 23 ("an objectifying projection is a condition of subjectivity"); Aristodemou, *Law, Psychoanalysis, Society*, 17 ("it is separation from the object in the first place that enables the subject to emerge as a subject.")
2. Hegel, *Phenomenology*, 234, 236, 237. Completion here does not refer to an ending, as in the end of a sentence, but to a self's sublating achievement of self-consciousness.
3. *Ibid.*, 237.
4. *Ibid.*, 237, 238. "This consciousness was not in peril and fear for this element or that, nor for this or that moment of time, it was afraid for its entire being; it felt the fear of death, the sovereign master. It has been in that experience melted to its inmost soul, has trembled throughout its every fibre, and all that was fixed and steadfast has quaked within it. This complete perturbation of its entire substance, this absolute dissolution of all its stability into fluent continuity, is, however, the simple, ultimate nature of self-consciousness, absolute negativity, pure self-referrent existence, which consequently is involved in this type of consciousness. This moment of pure self-existence is moreover a fact for it; for in the master it finds this as its object." (237–38).
5. *Ibid.*, 238, 239.
6. Andrew Cole, "What Hegel's Master/Slave Dialectic Really Means," *Journal of Medieval and Early Modern Studies* 34, no. 3 (fall 2004): 578.
7. *Ibid.*, 592, 594, 599–600; and see generally Cole's greatly expanded and augmented argument, *The Birth of Theory* (Chicago: University of Chicago Press, 2014). See also Hickman, *Black Prometheus*, 121–22, 126–28.
8. Cole, "Master/Slave Dialectic," 592. Cole does not make the historicist case dogmatically. In *The Birth of Theory*, he states: "To be clear, mine is not a task in historicizing Hegel so much as paying attention to the words he writes on the page, the terms and problems he takes up in his philosophy and which point to his historical present," a present decisively influenced by potent feudal remainders (xv). His argument is mainly with those who simply reject as "wrong" any attempt to locate the *Phenomenology* in history (82).
9. On the limitations of context, see above, prologue, notes 22–29, and accompanying text; Kunal M. Parker, "Context in History and Law: A Study of the Late Nineteenth-Century American Jurisprudence of Custom," *Law and History Review* 24, no. 3 (fall, 2006): 473–85, discussing Constantin Fasolt, *The Limits of History* (Chicago: University of Chicago Press, 2004).
10. See Susan Buck-Morss, "Hegel and Haiti," *Critical Inquiry* 26, no. 4 (summer 2000): 821–65, and *Hegel, Haiti, and Universal History* (Pittsburgh: University of Pittsburgh Press, 2009), 49 (claiming the dialectic for slave relations: "The idea for the dialectic of lordship and bondage came to Hegel in Jena in the years 1803–5 from reading the [news]papers"); David Brion Davis, *The Problem of Slavery in the Age of Revolution, 1770–1823* (New York: Oxford University Press, 1999), 558 (claiming the dialectic for revolutionary liberal modernity: "With the sound of Napoleon's thundering cannons in his ears, Hegel was completing a work that contained the most profound analysis of slavery ever written"); Alexandre Kojève, *Introduction to the Reading of Hegel: Lectures on the Phenomenology of Spirit* (assembled by Raymond Queneau), Allen Bloom, editor, James H. Nichols Jr., translator (Ithaca: Cornell University Press, 1980), 44 (claiming the dialectic for the completion of history).
11. "Self-consciousness is primarily simple existence for itself. . . . The presentation of itself, however, as pure abstraction of self-consciousness consists in showing itself as a

pure negation of its objective form, or in showing that it is fettered to no determinate existence, that it is not bound at all by the particularity everywhere characteristic of existence as such, and is *not* tied up with life." Hegel, *Phenomenology*, 231–32 (emphasis in original). Barry Hindess and Paul Hirst comment: "Hegel's text on 'Lord and Bondsman' in *The Phenomenology of Mind* has been recognised (in certain readings) as giving a unique dialectic to slavery. . . . Hegel's passage is justly famous but it has nothing to do with slavery and establishes no special relation of domination between master and slave. Hegel's object is the genesis of self-consciousness not the dynamics of slave systems. . . . For Hegel the social status of the occupants [of the two subject positions in the dialectic] is inconsequential, and the status of these [subject positions] in *The Phenomenology of Mind* is a function of its own object and its own logic." Barry Hindess and Paul Q. Hirst, *Pre-Capitalist Modes of Production* (London: Routledge and Kegan Paul, 1975), 114. See also Alex Callinicos, *Theories and Narratives: Reflections on the Philosophy of History* (Durham, NC: Duke University Press, 1995), 22–39. And Cole certainly acknowledges this in *The Birth of Theory*. "My positing a feudal frame . . . should not be misunderstood as an attempt to literalize Hegel's dialectical scenario or to forget this is a phenomenology, always already susceptible to allegory and transposition" (203n102). Compare Hickman, *Black Prometheus*, 117–67.

12. Slavoj Žižek, *Violence: Six Sideways Reflections* (New York: Picador, 2008), 152 (emphasis in original).
13. See, e.g., "At a court of Oyer and Terminer summoned and held for the County of Southampton at the courthouse on the 31st day of August 1831 for the trial of Daniel, a negro man slave the property of Richard Porter, Jack, the property of Everett Bryant, Moses, the property of Thomas Barrow, Tom, late the property of Caty Whitehead, Jack, late the property of Caty Whitehead, Andrew, late the property of Caty Whitehead, Davy, late the property of Elizabeth Turner, Stephen, the property of Thomas Ridley, and Curtis, the property of Thomas Ridley." Southampton County Court, *Minute Book* (1830–35), 72. On the deaths before trial of the twenty-five slaves and free persons of color, see below, text at note 165. One free person of color, Berry Newsom, was convicted at the Southampton Circuit Superior Court in April 1832, and hung.
14. On the irrelevance of the dialectic to the specificities of the master-slave relation, see above, notes 8–11 and accompanying text. My point here is simple: just because Hegel's lord/bondsman dialectic is not, in fact, about the specificities of relations between lords and bondsmen, or masters and slaves, but about the formation of self-consciousness, that does not mean it cannot be applied to a specific historical situation of relations between masters and slaves, particularly when the issue at hand is, *precisely*, understanding the formation of self-consciousness, of subjectivity.
15. See C. B. Macpherson, editor, *John Locke: Second Treatise of Government* (Indianapolis: Hackett Publishing, 1980), 18–30; Richard Teichgraeber, "Hegel on Property and Poverty," *Journal of the History of Ideas* 38, no. 1 (1977): 47–64, "Labor is the work of possession, an act of the will to shape one's surroundings"; Cole, *Birth of Theory*, 76.
16. *Confessions*, 12.
17. The phrase begins to appear with some degree of frequency in works in English in the second half of the eighteenth century, and increases in incidence in the nineteenth century between 1810 and 1840, before falling off somewhat thereafter. Its point of origin may well be Alexander Pope's translation of Homer's *Iliad*, first published 1715–20. See book VII, line 11–12: "Bold Paris first the work of death begun / On great Menestheus, Areïthous' son." In Samuel Johnson, *The Works of the Poets of England and Ireland* (London: Printed for Andrew Miller, 1800), VI, 61. The phrase is not biblical but it does appear in the Book of Mormon. See *Alma* 43:37, "And the work of death commenced on both sides . . ." See also *Alma* 43:38, 44:20, and 60:7; *Helaman* 4:5.

18. Noting the association of the phrase with the American Civil War, Drew Gilpin Faust writes: "Civil War Americans often wrote about what they called 'the work of death,' meaning the duties of soldiers to fight, kill, and die, but at the same time invoking battle's consequences: its slaughter, suffering, and devastation. 'Work' in this usage incorporated both effort and impact—and the important connection between the two. Death in war does not simply happen; it requires action and agents. It must, first of all, be inflicted; and several million soldiers of the 1860s dedicated themselves to that purpose. But death also usually requires participation and response; it must be experienced and handled. It is work to die, to know how to approach and endure life's last moments. . . . It is work to deal with the dead as well, to remove them in the literal sense of disposing of their bodies, and it is also work to remove them in a more figurative sense"—bereavement. Drew Gilpin Faust, *This Republic of Suffering: Death and the American Civil War* (New York: Vintage, 2009), xiv.
19. Genovese, "Evil, Redemption, and History," 210–11.
20. Allmendinger, *Rising*, 102–65.
21. *Ibid.*, 97, 171–72. For Allmendinger, Turner and his confidants "saw themselves mounting a revolution."
22. Paul Gilroy writes of "the simple fact that in the critical thought of blacks in the West, social self-creation through labour is not the centre-piece of emancipatory hopes. For the descendants of slaves, work signified only servitude, misery, and subordination." Paul Gilroy, *The Black Atlantic: Modernity and Double Consciousness* (Cambridge, MA: Harvard University Press, 1993), 40. But compare Sartre, "This irrepressible violence is neither sound and fury, nor the resurrection of savage instincts, nor even the effect of resentment: *it is man re-creating himself*." Jean-Paul Sartre, "Preface," in Frantz Fanon, *The Wretched of the Earth*, Constance Farrington, translator (Harmondsworth, UK: Penguin Books, 1967), 18 (emphasis added). See generally Homi K. Bhabha, "Foreword: Framing Fanon," in Frantz Fanon, *The Wretched of the Earth*, Richard Philcox, translator (New York: Grove Press, 2004), xix–xli; Homi K. Bhabha, "Foreword to the 1986 Edition," in Frantz Fanon, *Black Skin, White Masks*, Charles Lam Markmann, translator (London: Pluto Press, 1986), xxi–xxxvi. The writer and journalist John Waters observes, "The first thing the colonizer did, Fanon tells us, was to 'plant deep in the mind of the native population the idea that before the advent of colonialism their history was one which was dominated by barbarism.' Colonization is something the native ultimately does to himself, having been persuaded of his own inadequacy. For this reason, freedom cannot be regained by negotiation, but only by a redemptive act. The violent occupation of lands and minds can be answered only with violence of the heart and hand." John Waters, "Fanon's Warning," *First Things* (August 2018), at https://www.firstthings.com/article/2018/08/fanons-warning (last accessed February 22, 2019).
23. *Confessions*, 12.
24. *Ibid.*, 12.
25. *Ibid.*, 11–12. In Turner's description of the preparation of the dinner we encounter a final trailing echo of Luke (see above, chapter 2), in which, at 22:8–14 the evangelist provides a detailed description of preparations for the Last Supper. Christ dispatches Peter and John to make ready, "And when the hour was come, he sat down, and the twelve apostles with him."
26. *Confessions*, 12.
27. "At a court of Oyer and Terminer summoned and held for the County of Southampton on the 3d day of September 1831 for the trial of . . . Jack a negro man slave the property of William Reese decsd." Southampton County Court, *Minute Book* (1830–35), 90.
28. A later recruit, the free man of color Billy Artis, was reported to have "wept like a child" when first "pressed into service." See "A detailed account of the late insurrection

in Southampton, kindly furnished us by a gentleman well conversant with the scenes he describes" [Thomas Ruffin Gray, letter of September 17, 1831], *The Constitutional Whig*, Richmond, Virginia (September 26, 1831), in Tragle, *Southampton Slave Revolt*, 90–99, at 97. See also Allmendinger, *Rising*, 171 (reporting evidence suggesting that Hark Moore "shed tears" over the death of Mrs. Sarah Newsom in the attack on Elizabeth Turner's property, "she the sister of his Master"). Testimony of slaves from Jacob Williams's property, too, suggests initial perpetrator reluctance and trauma. See testimony of Stephen [Bell] a slave "At a court of Oyer and Terminer summoned and held for the County of Southampton on the 3d day of September 1831 for the trial of . . . Nelson, a negro man slave belonging to Jacob Williams." Southampton County Court, *Minute Book* (1830–35), 88: "The negroes . . . told Nelson to go with them he seemed unwilling to go . . . was forced to go with them—lagged behind when he was guarded." Cynthia [Williams], a slave, testified that Nelson, who seemed "very sick," said to her "Cynthia you do not know me. I do not know when you will see me again." Nelson remained with the group through the morning of August 23. He was sentenced to hang.

29. *Confessions*, 11; "A detailed account," 93. And see Jacques Semelin, "In Consideration of Massacres," *Journal of Genocide Research* 3, no. 3 (2001): 384: "Massacre is rarely spontaneous. It almost always has organisers. They are those who think through the mass crime and put it into practice precisely by playing on individuals' imagination."

    It is unclear whether the earlier July 4 date carried any pointed significance, beyond being known to those involved as a holiday. "Dates were a rare knowledge among slaves," writes Anthony Kaye, but "they made ample use of holidays as time markers." The highly literate Turner, however, did name dates by month, day and year (see, for example, *Confessions*, 11). See Anthony E. Kaye, *Joining Places: Slave Neighborhoods in the Old South* (Chapel Hill: University of North Carolina Press, 2007), 44, 46.

30. "A detailed account," 93. (The words "destruction and murder" and "insurrection" here are, of course, Thomas Ruffin Gray's.) See also "The Bandit—Taken! Extracts of Letters" [Thomas Ruffin Gray (?), undated letter], Richmond *Enquirer*, Richmond, Virginia (November 8, 1831), in Tragle, *Southampton Slave Revolt*, 138: "Nat states that there was no concert of an insurrection; that he did mention the subject to two persons about the months of April or May, but that no other persons knew anything about his plans until the day previous to the attack."

31. *Confessions*, 12. No attempt had been made to secure weapons in advance. At the outset the group relied on farm tools—"hatchets and axes." Richmond *Enquirer* (November 8, 1831), in Tragle, *Southampton Slave Revolt*, 137.

32. *Ibid.*, 12. According to testimony given in Jack Reese's trial, the men arrived at Travis's "on Sunday night" and were still there "a few hours after." See "trial of . . . Jack," 90. In the *Confessions*, Turner states the Cabin Pond meeting broke up at "about two hours in the night," which David Allmendinger interprets as 10 p.m. Allmendinger estimates the men arrived at Travis's shortly after 10 p.m. but did not break into the house until 1 a.m. on the morning of Monday 22. See *Confessions*, 12; Allmendinger, *Rising*, 166–67. On the relationship between alcohol and mass killing, see below, note 92.

33. "The Bandit—Taken! Extracts of Letters" [William C. Parker, letter of November 1, 1831], Richmond *Enquirer*, Richmond, Virginia (November 8, 1831), in Tragle, *Southampton Slave Revolt*, 136–37, at 137 (emphasis added).

34. *Confessions*, 12. Randall Collins notes, "The conventions of portraying violence almost always miss the most important dynamics of violence, that it starts from confrontational tension and fear, that most of the time it is bluster, and that the circumstances that allow this tension to be overcome lead to violence that is more ugly than

entertaining." Violence, Collins emphasizes, is hard. With a few exceptions, "people are . . . for the most part, not good at violence." Randall Collins, *Violence: A Micro-sociological Theory* (Princeton: Princeton University Press, 2008), 10, 20.

35. Moses [Moore], aged thirteen, was pressed into service by the rebels to hold horses, and would accompany the group throughout the day. Austin [Edwards] also joined the Cabin Pond group at Travis's, in what was quite likely a prearranged meeting, one of several signs that the original group had supporters waiting for them to act. (For example, in evidence given at the trial of Isham [Edwards], a slave witness, Henry [Edwards], testified "that on Saturday night preceding the day on which the insurrection broke out the prisoner told him that Capt. Nat was going to collect his company and rise and kill all the white people / and wanted witness to join." The witness declined. "At a court of Oyer and Terminer continued by adjournment and held for the County of Southampton on the 7th day of September 1831 for the trial of Hardy and Isham, negro men slaves the property of Benjamin Edwards." Southampton County Court, *Minute Book* (1830–35), 97–98. Similarly, in evidence given at the trial of Nelson [Williams], Caswell Worrell, an overseer, testified that on Thursday August 18th "the prisoner told the witness that *they* might look out and take care of themselves—that something would happen before long—that any body of his practice could tell these things." Both Worrell and Jacob Williams, the prisoner's owner, testified that on the morning of Monday 22 they suspected the prisoner had the intention to attack them. See testimony of Jacob Williams and Caswell Worrell, "At a court of Oyer and Terminer summoned and held for the County of Southampton on the 3d day of September 1831 for the trial of . . . Nelson, a negro man slave belonging to Jacob Williams." Southampton County Court, *Minute Book* (1830–35), 87–88.

36. *Confessions*, 12. "Those who have nothing have only their discipline." Filippo del Luchesse and Jason Smith, "'We Need a Popular Discipline': Contemporary Politics and the Crisis of the Negative, Interview with Alain Badiou," *Critical Inquiry* (02/07/07), at http://www.lacan.com/baddiscipline.html (last accessed February 22, 2019). "Military organization is the easiest place to trace the social techniques for overcoming our biological propensity not to be violent." Collins, *Violence*, 29.

37. *Confessions*, 12–13.

38. *Ibid.*, 13.

39. *Ibid.*, 13.

40. *Ibid.*, 13. Throughout the rebellion, and after until he was captured, Turner carried that same "small light sword" even though it had proven virtually useless as a weapon. Richmond *Enquirer* (November 8, 1831), in Tragle, *Southampton Slave Revolt*, 137. Alone among the synoptic gospels, Luke (22:36–38) represents Christ condoning his disciples arming themselves with swords prior to his betrayal on the Mount of Olives. Revelation 1:16, meanwhile, represents Christ as the bearer "out of his mouth" of "a sharp twoedged sword." The sword in Christ's mouth signifies the power of his words—an image frequently repeated. See Revelation 1:16; 2:12; 2:16; and particularly 19:15 ("out of his mouth goeth a sharp sword, that with it he should smite the nations") and 19:21.

41. For the best account of the order of recruitment, which must remain somewhat conjectural, see Allmendinger, *Rising*, 170–72.

42. *Confessions*, 13. On capture, Turner would deny any interest in acquiring money or property, reportedly exclaiming "You know that money was not my object." See "The Bandit—Taken! Extracts of Letters" [Thomas Ruffin Gray (?), undated letter], Richmond *Enquirer*, Richmond, Virginia (November 8, 1831), in Tragle, *Southampton Slave Revolt*, 138. Turner's object has been described in chapters 2 and 3. Others, however, clearly did seek money, or articles of clothing. See, e.g., Allmendinger, *Rising*, 170. On

the multiplicity of motivations among participants, see also above, preface, note 16–17, and accompanying text.

43. Notwithstanding the stated objective to "kill all the white people," numbers of whites along the path followed by Turner's group were left untouched. See, for example, Oates, *Fires of Jubilee*, 88. Rather than kill indiscriminately, the group was working its way methodically from one to the next home farm/plantation associated with its core members and their networks of kinship and acquaintance. As Allmendinger explains, twelve of the fifteen men present at Elizabeth Turner's had links to the first four households destroyed, and the remaining three were all linked to households—Porter's, Edwards's—against which they would move next. Allmendinger, *Rising*, 172, and generally 102–56.
44. *Confessions*, 13. Letter, August 24, 1831, in *Norfolk Herald* (27 August 1831).
45. *Confessions*, 13–14.
46. Katherine Whitehead's daughter Harriet hid in the house and survived—the only white person to survive any of the attacks to that point.
47. The recruits were Nat [Turner] and Joe [Turner]. In evidence given at the trial of Joe Turner, a slave witness, Hubbard [Whitehead], testified "prisoner appeared reluctant to go with the murderers but were told by them he should go and he went with them." See "Joe a negro man slave the property of John C. Turner who stands charged with conspiring to rebel and make insurrection," at a court of Oyer and Terminer held for the County of Southampton on the 19th day of September 1831. Southampton County Court, *Minute Book* (1830–35), 102.
48. *Confessions*, 14.
49. *Ibid.*, 14. Allmendinger argues the rebellion was most likely discovered as a result of the attack on Elizabeth Turner's plantation, and the noise of the gunshot there. But it is at least as likely discovery stemmed from the Whitehead attack where Turner had seen someone running from the house, given that the first patrol sent out from Jerusalem as a result of messages of alarm carried from the Cross Keys vicinity headed for the Whitehead property. Allmendinger, *Rising*, 176–77, 182–23.
50. *Confessions*, 14. Allmendinger reports several defections from the Doyles/Harris group, notably of Jack Reese, and of Davy [Turner] (recruited unwillingly at Elizabeth Turner's) and Joe Turner, recruited unwillingly at Whitehead's. Reese's defection was genuine. Davy and Joe may, however, simply have been engaged in a raid of their own devising on a neighboring householder, Elisha Atkins, in search of guns, ammunition, and recruits, intending to rejoin the main group. See Southampton County Court, *Minute Book* (1830–35), 102 (testimony of Christian [Atkins]); Allmendinger, *Rising*, 176.
51. Allmendinger, *Rising*, 179–80. Moses Moore testified that several slaves recruited at the Francis property "went unwillingly" and that three—Nathan, Tom, and Davy, all boys aged thirteen to fifteen—"were constantly guarded by negroes with guns who were ordered to shoot them if they attempted to escape." See "At a court of Oyer and Terminer continued by adjournment and held for the County of Southampton on the 6th day of September 1831 for the trial of Nathan, a negro man slave belonging to the estate of Benjamin Blunt, dcsd. & Nathan, Tom, and Davy, negro boys slaves belonging to Nathaniel Francis." Southampton County Court, *Minute Book* (1830–35), 93–95.
52. Allmendinger, *Rising*, 180–81. On the Francis and Barrow attacks, see also Thomas Ruffin Gray's commentary on Turner's narrative in *Confessions*, 19–20.
53. *Confessions*, 14. Allmendinger places the numbers at this point at no more than thirty, of whom several were under guard. See *Rising*, 183–84. Allmendinger emphasizes that recruitment occurred through networks of kinship and acquaintance. On properties where the rebels had no personal contacts they did not recruit well.

54. "butchered" and "mangled" were common descriptions of the bodies of those killed in the rebellion. See, for example, General Richard Eppes to Governor John Floyd, August 24, 1831 ("horribly mangled"), in the Richmond *Compiler*, Richmond, Virginia (August 27, 1831); Salon Borland to R. C. Borland, August 31, 1831 ("old women—girls—boys—infants of the smallest size butchered and mangled") in Alfred L. Brophy, "The Nat Turner Trials," *North Carolina Law Review* 91, no. 5 (June 2013): 1840–41; Governor John Floyd, "Narrative of the Insurrection," (Trajan Doyel "killed and mangled"), cited by James McDowell, of Rockbridge (speech of January 21, 1832), in Erik S. Root, editor, *Sons of the Fathers: The Virginia Slavery Debates of 1831-32* (Lanham, MD: Rowman & Littlefield, 2010), 233–54, at 250 [hereafter *VSD*]. See also below, note 104 (etymology of mangle) and accompanying text.
55. *Confessions*, 14.
56. *Ibid*., 14.
57. *Ibid*., 14.
58. John Hampden Pleasants, Senior Editor, dispatch to *The Constitutional Whig*, 25 August 1831, Richmond, Virginia (August 29, 1831), in Tragle, *Southampton Slave Revolt*, 51.
59. *Confessions*, 14–15.
60. Allmendinger, *Rising*, 187.
61. *Ibid*., 187–88; *Confessions*, 15.
62. *Confessions*, 15.
63. *Ibid*., 15. Allmendinger puts the numbers at thirty-three, the company constantly supplemented by both voluntary and coerced recruitments and then falling in number as those coerced quietly absconded. See Allmendinger, *Rising*, 188–89.
64. *Confessions*, 16. To return to the Lukan themes of chapter 2, "It is impossible to miss the importance of Jerusalem . . . for Luke. All of the major saving events of Jesus happen in Jerusalem." David Wenham, "The Purpose of Luke-Acts: Israel's Story in the Context of the Roman Empire," in Bartholomew et al., editors, *Reading Luke*, 79–103, at 91. Likewise, "Jerusalem dominates the structure of Luke's Gospel." Charles H. H. Scobie, "A Canonical Approach to Interpreting Luke: The Journey Motif as Hermeneutical Key," in Bartholomew et al., editors, *Reading Luke*, 327–49, at 341.
65. *Confessions*, 15.
66. Allmendinger, *Rising*, 182, 190; "A detailed account," 96.
67. *Confessions*, 15–16.
68. *Ibid*., 19.
69. *Ibid*., 15–16; Allmendinger, *Rising*, 190.
70. *Confessions*, 16.
71. *Ibid*., 16. General William Brodnax would report that "not a white family in many neighborhoods remained at home—many went to other counties, and the rest assembled at different points in considerable numbers for mutual protection." Brodnax to Governor John Floyd (August 27, 1831), in *VSD*, 249; John Hampden Pleasants described "the whole country" as "thoroughly alarmed; every man armed, the dwellings all deserted by the white inhabitants, and the farms most generally left in possession of the blacks. . . . Jerusalem was never so crowded from its foundation." Dispatch to *The Constitutional Whig*, August 25, 1831, in Tragle, *Southampton Slave Revolt*, 51. The Richmond *Enquirer* (August 30, 1831) reported the contents of a letter written from Jerusalem (August 24, 1831): "Every house, room and corner in this place is full of women and children, driven from home."
72. Allmendinger, *Rising*, 194–95.
73. *Confessions*, 16.
74. *Ibid*., 16–17.
75. *Ibid*., 17.

76. Whether measured by white fatalities (55) or total fatalities (99, not allowing for fatalities beyond the county line), the Turner rebellion was the most serious slave uprising in American history. The largest American uprising of the colonial era, South Carolina's Stono Rebellion (1739) resulted in some 65 total deaths, two-thirds slaves; the largest uprising of any era measured in numbers of participants, the German Coast Uprising (1811) in the New Orleans Territory, resulted in about 100 deaths, only two of whom were not slaves. By comparison, the largest uprising in any British colony in the Americas—Jamaica's "Baptist War" of December 1831–February 1832—involved vastly larger numbers of rebels (in the thousands), vastly greater destruction of property (£1.15 million), and about 550 total deaths, but only 14 dead whites. On Stono, see Robert Olwell, *Masters, Slaves and Subjects: The Culture of Power in the South Carolina Low Country, 1740-1790* (Ithaca, NY: Cornell University Press, 1998); on the German Coast, see Walter Johnson, *River of Dark Dreams: Slavery and Empire in the Cotton Kingdom* (Cambridge, MA: Harvard University Press, 2013), 18–22, and Daniel Rasmussen, *American Uprising: The Untold Story of America's Largest Slave Revolt* (New York: Harper, 2011); on the Baptist War, see Brown, *The Reaper's Garden*, 232–34. Cedric Robinson remarks, "In the vast series of encounters between Blacks and their oppressors . . . Blacks have seldom employed the level of violence that [Europeans] understood the situation required." Robinson, *Black Marxism*, 168.
77. *Oxford English Dictionary*, entry for "massacre," *n.* and *v.*, etymologies, at http://www.oed.com/view/Entry/114675?rskey=o2XdfY&result=1#eid, and http://www.oed.com/view/Entry/114676#eid37725283 (last accessed February 22, 2019). See also Semelin, "In Consideration of Massacres," 378; Mark Levene, "Introduction," in Mark Levene and Penny Roberts, editors, *The Massacre in History* (New York: Berghahn, 1999), 7–9.
78. Mark Greengrass, "Hidden Transcripts: Secret Histories and Personal Testimonies of Religious Violence in the French Wars of Religion," in Levene and Roberts, editors, *The Massacre in History*, 69–88; Natalie Zemon Davis, "The Rites of Violence: Religious Riot in Sixteenth-Century France," *Past & Present* 59 (May 1973): 51–91. See generally, Arlette Jouanna, *The St Bartholomew's Day Massacre: The Mysteries of a Crime of State* (Manchester: Manchester University Press, 2015). *Oxford English Dictionary* etymologies report scattered twelfth- and thirteenth-century usages associating massacre with the killing of large numbers of people.
79. Semelin, "In Consideration of Massacres," 379. See also Jacques Semelin, *Purify and Destroy: The Political Uses of Massacre and Genocide* (New York: Columbia University Press, 2007), 323, defining massacre as "a generally collective form of action, involving the destruction of non-combatants, men, women, children or disarmed soldiers." Randall Collins writes, "Fighters are mostly fearful and incompetent in their exercise of violence; when they are evenly matched they tend to be particularly incompetent. It is when the strong attack the weak that most violence is successful." Collins, *Violence*, 40.
80. See, for example, Alain Corbin, *The Village of Cannibals: Rage and Murder in France, 1870* (Cambridge, MA: Harvard University Press, 1992), 69, discussing the murder of Alain de Monéys as massacre ("The mob . . . had made up its mind to dispose of its victim in accordance with the traditional forms of massacre"); and see 88–97 on those "traditional forms" as expressed during the French wars of religion and, later, in the extravagant murders during the Revolutionary epoch of Joseph-François Foulon de Doué, Louis Bénigne François Bertier de Sauvigny, and Henri de Belsunce (all in July and August 1789), and Jean Féraud (1795). The ritualized and performative manner of their deaths recalls the elaborate executions of the regicides François Ravaillac (1610) and Robert-François Damiens (1757). See also Timothy Tackett, *The Coming of the Terror in the French Revolution* (Cambridge, MA: Harvard University Press, 2016), 57.

81. Committee of the Citizens of Southampton to General Andrew Jackson (August 29, 1831), in *VSD*, 250. John Hampden Pleasants used the same image, which suggests access to the Committee's deliberations: "A bloodier and more accursed tragedy was never acted, even by the agency of the tomahawk and scalping knife." See "Southampton Affair," *The Constitutional Whig*, Richmond, Virginia (September 3, 1831).
82. Semelin, *Purify and Destroy*, 70.
83. *Ibid.*, 77, and see, generally 22–51; Jacques Semelin, "Toward a Vocabulary of Massacre and Genocide," *Journal of Genocide Research* 5, no. 2 (June 2003): 196–98.
84. Semelin, *Purify and Destroy*, 92; and see also 266: "The collective practice of killing immediately transports the perpetrators into a sphere of omnipotence. They suddenly enter another world, created by the terror of their weapons alone. It is a world in which human beings entirely at their mercy have already ceased to exist, even as they reach the point where they become corpses."
85. *Ibid.*, 90–91, 92. See generally René Girard, *Violence and the Sacred* (Baltimore: The Johns Hopkins University Press, 1977).
86. Semelin, *Purify and Destroy*, 325. Note that contemporary descriptions of the Turner Rebellion dwelt on the destruction of households, referring to both persons and property. See, for example, the Richmond *Compiler*, Richmond, Virginia (August 24, 1831) reporting that "several white families had been destroyed"; the Petersburg *Intelligencer*, Petersburg, Virginia (August 26, 1831), reporting that "Between 25 and 30 families have already been entirely destroyed"; the Richmond *Enquirer*, Richmond, Virginia (August 26, 1831), reporting "that *thirty families* had been destroyed"; the *American Beacon*, Norfolk, Virginia (August 29, 1831), reporting "In the vicinity of the massacre we witnessed the greatest scene of devastation imaginable"; the Richmond *Constitutional Whig*, Richmond, Virginia (August 29, 1831), reporting "the rebels traversed a country of nearly twenty miles extent, murdering every white indiscriminately, and wrecking the furniture." See also *Confessions*, 13 ("general destruction of property"), 14 ("the property in the house they destroyed").
87. On proximities of slaves and slaveholders, see Kaye, *Joining Places*, 9–12. On "amity" see below, note 213, and accompanying text. Kaye notes that Turner's narrative of the rebellion was "a neighborhood story" (21)—the word appears nine times in *The Confessions*. See also Anthony E. Kaye, "Neighborhoods and Nat Turner: The Making of a Slave Rebel and the Unmaking of a Slave Rebellion," *Journal of the Early Republic* 27, no. 4 (winter 2007): 705–20. Randolph Scully describes Southampton County as "a community of small and medium farms" practicing a mixed agriculture "in which black men and women constituted a slight majority of the population but tended to live in small groups, in close proximity to their whiter masters and neighbors." This was "a place where people—white and black, free and enslaved, men and women—lived, worked, worshipped, preached, and played" alongside each other. Scully, *Religion*, 13, 14. On proximities in massacres, see Jan T. Gross, *Neighbors: The Destruction of the Jewish Community in Jedwabne, Poland* (New York: Penguin, 2001); Nicholas A. Robins and Adam Jones, editors, *Genocides by the Oppressed: Subaltern Genocide in Theory and Practice* (Bloomington: Indiana University Press, 2009); Mahmood Mamdani, *When Victims Become Killers: Colonialism, Nativism, and the Genocide in Rwanda* (Princeton: Princeton University Press, 2001), 5–6. Semelin notes that Rwandan peasants, with no prior military discipline or indoctrination, "were simply asked, during a crisis, to use a familiar farm tool, the machete, not to work in the fields but to go and chop up the Tutsi enemy." *Purify and Destroy*, 246. His point is that groups become killers "*in situ* and through action." See also Christopher R. Browning, *Ordinary Men: Reserve Police Battalion 101 and the Final Solution in Poland* (New York: Harper, 1993).
88. Semelin, *Purify and Destroy*, 240.
89. *Ibid.*, 266.

90. Wolfgang Sofsky, *Traité de la Violence* (Paris: Gallimard, 1998), 163, in Semelin, *Purify and Destroy*, 266.
91. Semelin, *Purify and Destroy*, 267; and see Saira Mohamed, "Of Monsters and Men: Perpetrator Trauma and Mass Atrocity," *Columbia Law Review* 115, no. 5 (June 2015), 1157–1216. Note the expressions of perpetrator trauma in evidence appearing in the Southampton County Court trial record, above, notes 27 and 28, and accompanying text.
92. On drinking and mass violence see Browning, *Ordinary Men*, 61, 68–69, 80–85, 100; Semelin, *Purify and Destroy*, 299. On the consumption of alcohol during the Turner Rebellion, see *Confessions*, 11, 12, 13, 14; Allmendinger, *Rising*, 185, 188–89.
93. Browning, *Ordinary Men*, 61–68. On participants absconding during the Turner Rebellion, see Allmendinger's meticulous account of the ebb and flow of recruitment in *Rising*, 166–98, and summary appendices at 281–85.
94. Semelin, *Purify and Destroy*, 254, 269.
95. *Ibid.*, 254–55. "It required not one but many hacks of a machete to kill even one person. With a machete, killing was hard work, that is why there were often several killers for every single victim." Mamdani, *When Victims Become Killers*, 6.
96. Semelin, *Purify and Destroy*, 186–89, 233, 246, 254, 273.
97. *Ibid.*, 269–70; Browning, *Ordinary Men*, 161.
98. Semelin, *Purify and Destroy*, 195, 210, 258. See, generally, Collins, *Violence*, 370–462.
99. Semelin, *Purify and Destroy*, 279–80. See, generally, Abram de Swaan, *The Killing Compartments: The Mentality of Mass Murder* (New Haven: Yale University Press, 2015).
100. Semelin, *Purify and Destroy*, 296. Inevitably, Semelin cites Levinas. "Killing while meeting the eyes of the other, and while gazing into his eyes seems almost impossible. On the contrary the performance of massacre confirms one of the strongest assertions made by the philosopher Emmanuel Levinas, namely that the recognition of our common humanity necessarily rests on meeting the other face to face." And see Emmanuel Levinas, *Totality and Infinity: An Essay on Exteriority* (Pittsburgh: Duquesne University Press, 1969), 187–219. On the severe limitation of Levinasian ethics, see Jason Caro, "Levinas and the Palestinians," *Philosophy and Social Criticism* 35, no. 6 (2009): 671–84.
101. "It was hardly in the power of rumor itself, to exaggerate the atrocities which have been perpetrated by the insurgents: whole families, fathers, mothers, daughters, sons, sucking babes, and school children, butchered, thrown into heaps, and left to be devoured by hogs and dogs, or to putrify on the spot." John Hampden Pleasants, dispatch to *The Constitutional Whig*, August 25, 1831, Richmond, Virginia (August 29, 1831).
102. Arjun Appadurai, "Dead Certainty: Ethnic Violence in the Era of Globalization," *Development and Change* 29 (1998): 917, 919.
103. *Ibid.*, 917, 919, 920.
104. To mangle is "to hack, cut, lacerate, or mutilate (a person or animal) by repeated blows; to reduce (a body, limb, etc.) by violence to a more or less unrecognizable condition." Mangle is derived from Anglo-Norman *mangler* or *mahangler*, which means to mutilate, and is likely related to *mahaignier*, to maim and perhaps the Middle Dutch *mangelen* which means to mingle, exchange, fight, come to grips with. *Oxford English Dictionary*, entry for "mangle," *v.*[1], etymology, at http://www.oed.com/view/Entry/113421?rskey=BJxxBA&result=4#eid (last accessed February 22, 2019).
105. Appadurai, "Dead Certainty," 920. Virginia Governor John Floyd summarized the reports he had received thus: "Men, women, and infants, their heads chopped off, their bowels ripped out, ears, noses, hands, and legs cut off, no instance of mercy shown." Charles H. Ambler, *The Life and Diary of John Floyd, Governor of Virginia, an Apostle of Secession, and the Father of the Oregon Country* (Richmond: Richmond Press, 1918), 158 (Diary entry for 3 September 1831).

106. Scully, *Religion*, 201–2. On the centrality of the outcast as "enemy" to Anglo-American colonization, see Christopher Tomlins, *Freedom Bound: Law, Labor, and Civic Identity in Colonizing English America, 1580–1865* (Cambridge: Cambridge University Press, 2010), 176–77. Interestingly, the meanings of "wretch" include both one who is an "exile," and one who is "sunk in deep distress, sorrow, misfortune, or poverty," both quite fitting in application to enslaved Africans in Virginia. *Oxford English Dictionary*, entry for "wretch," at http://www.oed.com/view/Entry/230654?rskey=OyxKCU&result=1&isAdvanced=false#eid (last accessed February 22, 2019).
107. Semelin, *Purify and Destroy*, 90. Murder becomes "a foundational practice" for "collective transcendence." The violence of massacre "regenerates the group through the sacrifice of those designated as being responsible for the crisis."
108. Hegel, *Phenomenology*, 239.
109. Richmond *Compiler*, Richmond, Virginia (August 24, 1831).
110. Petersburg *Intelligencer*, Petersburg, Virginia (August 26, 1831).
111. Richmond *Enquirer*, Richmond, Virginia (August 30, 1831).
112. *Ibid.*
113. *Ibid.*; *American Beacon*, Norfolk, Virginia (August 29, 1831).
114. Richmond *Compiler*, Richmond, Virginia (August 27, 1831).
115. Richmond *Constitutional Whig*, Richmond, Virginia (August 29, 1831).
116. *American Beacon*, Norfolk, Virginia (30 August 1831).
117. Richmond *Constitutional Whig*, Richmond, Virginia (August 29, 1831).
118. Fayetville *Journal*, Fayetville, North Carolina (August 31, 1831).
119. Richmond *Compiler*, Richmond, Virginia (August 27, 1831).
120. Hegel, *Phenomenology*, 237.
121. *Ibid.*, 232. It is of crucial importance to note that in what follows I will employ Semelin's term *insurrection* in Semelin's terms, as a "model" of one form of killing. We must remember that Turner rejected the term as it applied to the specific instance of the killings in Southampton County in August 1831 (see above, chapter 1, text at note 78; chapter 2, text at note 212).
122. Semelin, *Purify and Destroy*, 327.
123. *Ibid.*, 327–30.
124. *Ibid.*, 334–35.
125. As in English colonizing in North America, and U.S. wars of removal and eradication against American indigenous populations throughout the nineteenth century. See Tomlins, *Freedom Bound*, 133–83; Benjamin Madley, "Reexamining the American Genocide Debate: Meaning, Historiography, and New Methods," *American Historical Review* 120, no. 1 (February 2015): 98–139, and *An American Genocide: The United States and the California Indian Catastrophe* (New Haven: Yale University Press, 2016).
126. As in the Nazi invasion of the Soviet Union, June 1941, and in the "Final Solution of the Jewish Problem" resolved at the Wannsee Conference, January 1942.
127. Semelin, *Purify and Destroy*, 340–41. It is worth noting that the etymology of territory, derived from classical Latin *territorium*, which in turn is usually traced to *terra*, meaning earth or land, can better be traced to classical Latin *terrere*, meaning to frighten. "Since *-torium* is a productive suffix only after verbal stems, the rise of *terri-torium* is unexplained." Michiel de Vaan, *Etymological Dictionary of Latin and the other Italic Languages* (Leiden: Brill, 2008), 616. Territory hence includes within its meaning the idea of exclusion of unwanted others by means of threats intended to terrify.
128. Semelin, *Purify and Destroy*, 347.
129. Ariel Merari, "Terrorism as a Strategy of Insurgency," *Terrorism and Political Violence* 5, no. 4 (winter 1993): 213, 229, 230.
130. Semelin, *Purify and Destroy*, 347, 348–51.
131. See above, note 121 and accompanying text.

132. *Confessions*, 14, 15.
133. *Ibid.*, 15.
134. Consider the metrics devised by Anthony Oberschall, "Explaining Terrorism: The Contribution of Collective Action Theory," *Sociological Theory* 22, no. 1 (March 2004): 26–37, at 27: discontent; ideology-feeding grievances; capacity to organize; political opportunity. On each dimension Turner's rebellion can be considered a rational display of collective action.
135. See Genovese, "Meditation on Evil," 210–11; Genovese, "The Nat Turner Case," paragraph 11: "There is a limit to what may be claimed for a general who on the day before he marches does not know where he is marching to."
136. Donald Black, "The Geometry of Terrorism," *Sociological Theory* 22, no. 1 (March 2004): 14–25. Black's theoretical claim is that "terrorism arises intercollectively and upwardly across long distances in multidimensional social space" (19), and that "violence requires contact, and most occurs in limited areas of physical space where people are close in social space—within households, neighborhoods, and communities" (20). His empirical observation is that "for most of human history, social geometry largely corresponded to physical geometry. Social distances matched physical distances: The people closest in social space (relationally, culturally, and otherwise) were the closest in physical space, and those separated by the greatest social distances were separated by the greatest physical distances" (20). Rural slavery in Southampton County, however, placed the slaveholding population in intimate contact with the enslaved population on isolated farmstead properties where the population ratios favored the enslaved.
137. Michel de Certeau, *The Practice of Everyday Life*, Steven Rendall, translator (Berkeley: University of California Press, 1984), ix, xiv–xxii, 34–39.
138. *Ibid.*, xi–xii.
139. *Ibid.*, xiii–xiv. Hegel, *Phenomenology*, 234.
140. See Claude Levi-Strauss, *The Savage Mind* (Chicago: University of Chicago Press, 1966), 22–23, describing *bricolage* as a particular mode of production in which the *bricoleur* confronts particular material constraints: a closed "universe of instruments" and rules of the game that "are always to make do with 'whatever is at hand.'"
141. Semelin, *Purify and Destroy*, 252.
142. Alexander Laban Hinton, *Why Did They Kill? Cambodia in the Shadow of Genocide* (Berkeley: University of California Press, 2005), 30.
143. Certeau, *Everyday Life*, xix.
144. *Confessions*, 12–13 (emphasis added).
145. Certeau, *Everyday Life*, xix.
146. *Ibid.*, xix (emphasis added), 37 (emphasis in original).
147. *Ibid.*, 37.
148. *Confessions*, 11.
149. *Ibid.*, 11.
150. Certeau, *Everyday Life*, 37.
151. *Ibid.*, 35 (emphasis in original), 38–39. Many, beginning with Thomas Ruffin Gray, puzzled over the insurgents' apparently aimless "zigzag course" when plotted on a map. See Gray, letter of September 17, 1831, in *The Constitutional Whig* (September 26, 1831); Allmendinger, *Rising*, 102.
152. *Confessions*, 14 (emphasis added), 15, 16 (emphasis added).
153. *Ibid.*, 13 (emphasis added), 14 (emphasis added), 15 (emphasis added).
154. Certeau, *Everyday Life*, 38. According to a letter of August 24, partly reprinted in the Richmond *Enquirer* of August 30, 1831, "For many miles around their track the country is deserted by the women and children, but armed troops are in every mile in squads."

155. *Confessions*, 17.
156. Outside "the formalist dialectic of the post-Kantian systems" and its resolution in "the concept of synthesis," lies "another concept, that of a certain nonsynthesis of two concepts in another . . . another relation between thesis and antithesis is possible besides synthesis." Walter Benjamin, "On the Program of the Coming Philosophy," in Bullock and Jennings, editors, *Walter Benjamin: Selected Writings, Volume 1*, 100–110, at 106. See, generally, Susan Buck-Morss, *The Origin of Negative Dialectics: Theodor W. Adorno, Walter Benjamin, and the Frankfurt Institute* (New York: The Free Press, 1977). Compare Hickman, *Black Prometheus*, 126.
157. Kojève, *Introduction to the Reading of Hegel*, 46.
158. Orlando Patterson, *Slavery and Social Death: A Comparative Study* (Cambridge, MA: Harvard University Press, 1982), 99.
159. The circumspection of the black minority is evident in the failure of the rebels to recruit consistently, and to hold onto those they did recruit; its ambivalence is clear in the expressions of dismay of slaves caught in the crossfire of rebellion. See, for example, evidence given in the trials of Jack [Whitehead] and Andrew [Whitehead], "At a court of Oyer and Terminer continued by adjournment and held for the County of Southampton on the first day of September 1831 for the trial of . . . Jack late the property of Caty Whitehead, *Andrew* late the property of Caty Whitehead . . ." Southampton County Court, *Minute Book* (1830–35), 74–75.
160. Patterson, *Slavery and Social Death*, 99.
161. On accounts of white atrocities against the black population of Southampton County and the region, both at the time and since, and for an authoritative estimate of revenge killing, see Allmendinger, *Rising*, 289–99.
162. The theme of legal process emerged in commentaries on the rebellion more or less from the beginning. See the "Order of General Epps" [Richard Eppes], Jerusalem, August 28, 1831, in the Lynchburg *Virginian*, Lynchburg, Virginia (September 8, 1831): "A public execution in presence of thousands will demonstrate the power of the law, and preserve the right of property. The opposite course, while it is inhuman and therefore not to be justified, tends to the sacrifice of the innocent and the security of the guilty!" Richmond *Enquirer* (August 30, 1831): "The courts will discriminate the innocent from the guilty."
163. See, generally, Shaunnagh Dorsett and Shaun McVeigh, *Jurisdiction* (Abingdon, UK: Routledge, 2012); Kaye, *Joining Places*, 6–7. Oyer and Terminer jurisdiction for the county courts, "to take for evidence the confession of the party or the oaths of two witnesses or of one with pregnant circumstances, without the sollemnitie of jury, and the offender being found guilty as aforesaid, to pass judgment as the law . . . provides in the like case, and on such judgment to award execution," had been established for capital crimes of slaves in the late seventeenth century, and restated in the early eighteenth century. See "An act for the more speedy prosecution of slaves committing Capitall Crimes," (April 1691), and "An act for the speedy and easy prosecution of Slaves, committing Capitall Crimes," (October 1705), both in William Waller Hening, *The Statutes At Large; Being a Collection of all the Laws of Virginia from the First Session of the Legislature in the Year 1619* (Philadelphia: Printed for the Author, by Thomas DeSilver, 1823), 3:102–3, 269–70.
164. Certeau, *Everyday Life*, 36.
165. For a detailed summary of African American deaths consequential on the Turner Rebellion, see Allmendinger, *Rising*, 290–95. Governor Floyd followed the recommendations of commutation of the Southampton County Court in all instances but one, Jack Reese, tried the third and, by adjournment, the fifth of September, whom the governor, on the advice of his council, determined should hang. Reese's trial was one of the longest and most contentious before the court, and the court had been divided

in recommending commutation in his case. Reese was hanged on Monday September 12. Allmendinger comments: "Jack's sentence clarified the thinking of the judges and the governor. They would offer commutations or even acquittals if the accused had been forced to join the band, had separated from it, had not come under suspicion of committing a crime, and had shown no sympathy for the insurgents" (234).

166. For a summary record of the proceedings before the court, see Tragle, *Southampton Slave Revolt*, 229–45.

167. General Richard Eppes's "Order" of August 27 had announced establishment of "A sufficient force . . . for the security of the prisoners, and to sustain and enforce the sentence of the Courts, as well as to cause to be respected its judgments of dismissal" to be maintained "as long as there is the least appearance of necessity" and "as long as any portion of it can contribute to the restoration of peace and tranquility." Lynchburg *Virginian* (September 8, 1831), in Tragle, *Southampton Slave Revolt*, 75. In the first historical monograph published on the rebellion, William Sidney Drewry observed, inaccurately, "no trial was begun before the eighth of September. Ample time was given for excitement and passion to give way to order and reason. Never were more pains taken to give fair trials and justice to prisoners." William Sidney Drewry, *The Southampton Insurrection* (Washington: The Neale Company, 1900), 96.

168. On the matter of commutation, see above, chapter 1 note 40.

169. Isaac [Champion] and Jim [Champion], tried September 22 and sentenced to hang with no recommendation of commutation, had their sentences commuted by Governor Floyd. The two Champion slaves were originally among a dozen slaves put on trial in Sussex County on suspicion of sedition and conspiracy to make insurrection. The Sussex court divided on the question of the Champion slaves' guilt but transferred both to Southampton on the grounds that their cases belonged in that county because they had allegedly been heard planning insurrection at the property of Solomon Parker of that county. The Sussex trials took place over two days (September 12 and 13) and resulted in eight death sentences, three transfers to Southampton, and one discharge, all on the basis of testimony given by one enslaved girl, aged fifteen, Beck [Parker]. The other major incident of white suspicion directly stemming from the Turner Rebellion occurred in mid-September 1831, in Duplin and Sampson counties, North Carolina, where several slaves were tortured ("*very* severe punishment") into confessing to an alleged conspiracy. On the Sussex County, Virginia, and the Duplin County and Sampson County, North Carolina, incidents, see Brophy, "The Nat Turner Trials," 1849–54, 1864–67. The North Carolina incident follows the pattern of allegation, torture, and confession typical of many incidents of antebellum slave "conspiracy." See, for example, Johnson, *River of Dark Dreams*, 46–72 [Madison County, Mississippi, 1835]; Winthrop D. Jordan, *Tumult and Silence at Second Creek: An Inquiry into a Civil War Slave Conspiracy* (Baton Rouge: Louisiana State University Press, 1995) [Adams County, Mississippi, 1861]. The most famous such incident is the Denmark Vesey Conspiracy [Charleston, South Carolina, 1822], on which see Egerton and Paquette, eds., *The Denmark Vesey Affair*, and, on coercion and forced confession, Johnson, "Denmark Vesey and His Co-Conspirators," 915–76.

170. The Southampton Circuit Superior Court met in April 1832 to try four free men of color—Berry Newsom, Isham Turner, Exum Artist, and Thomas Hathcock—each remanded for trial by the County Court during September and October the previous year. Newsom was sentenced to death and hung, the others acquitted. See Brophy, "The Nat Turner Trials," 1829–30, note 93.

171. Allmendinger, *Rising*, 231.

172. Gray, letter of September 17, 1831, in *The Constitutional Whig* (September 26, 1831).

173. Fabricant, "A Critical Look," 343–52.

174. William Waller Hening, *The Virginia Justice Comprising the Office and Authority of a Justice of the Peace, in the Commonwealth of Virginia*, 4th ed. (Richmond: Printed for the author, Shepherd & Pollard, 1825), 200, in Fabricant, "A Critical Look," 350.
175. "At a court of Oyer and Terminer summoned and held for the County of Southampton on Saturday the fifth day of November 1831 for the trial of Nat alias Nat Turner a negro man slave the property of Putnam Moore an infant charged with conspiring to rebel and making insurrection." Southampton County Court, *Minute Book* (1830–35), 122.
176. Fabricant, "A Critical Look," 351.
177. As Fabricant acknowledges, "It was permissible in Virginia for a sitting justice to testify against the accused," nor was it illegal "to convict an accused based on his confession to an examining magistrate." *Ibid.*, 350.
178. *Ibid.*, 352, 353.
179. Brophy, "The Nat Turner Trials," 1842, 1847.
180. *Ibid.*, 1848, 1862. Of the thirty slaves convicted of capital crimes, eighteen had their sentences commuted by Governor Floyd. According to Brophy's count, of 22 slaves charged with conspiracy alone, 12 were found guilty (7 hanged, 5 recommended for transportation) and 10 not guilty. Of 21 charged with insurrection or murder—some with conspiracy as an additional count—18 were found guilty (12 to hang, 6 recommended for transportation) and 3 not guilty. Of these, Jack Reese, recommended for transportation, had the court's recommendation rejected by Floyd and was hanged; and Isaac Champion and Jim Champion, sentenced to hang, had their sentences commuted by the governor and were transported. On the role of clemency in capital punishment, see V.A.C. Gatrell, *The Hanging Tree: Execution and the English People, 1770–1868* (Oxford: Oxford University Press, 1994), 197–221.
181. Susanna L. Blumenthal, "Of Mandarins, Legal Consciousness, and the Cultural Turn in US Legal History: Robert W. Gordon. 1984. Critical Legal Histories. *Stanford Law Review* 36:57–125," *Law & Social Inquiry* 37, no. 1 (winter 2012): 176; Tomlins, "After Critical Legal History," 33–37.
182. *Confessions*, 3. On countersovereignty, see Honig, *Antigone, Interrupted.*
183. This is the Southampton County Court's generic death sentence.
184. "O God, the Creator and Preserver of all mankind, we humbly beseech thee for all sorts and conditions of men . . . that it may please thee to comfort and relieve them according to their several necessities." *Book of Common Prayer*, 814–15. For Allmendinger, the rebels' work of death was an announcement "that slaveholding was a capital crime that corrupted blood and for which there could be no plea of innocence." Allmendinger, *Rising*, 169. The Southampton County Court's work of death was, just as surely, punishment of slaves who would kill to free themselves from masters who claimed property in those in whom they had invested their will.
185. On law as a modality of rule, see Christopher L. Tomlins, *Law, Labor, and Ideology in the Early American Republic* (Cambridge: Cambridge University Press, 1993), 16, 29–34, 92–94, 294. See also Kaye, *Joining Places*, 166–72. See, generally, Saidiya Hartman, *Scenes of Subjection: Terror, Slavery, and Self-Making in Nineteenth-Century America* (New York: Oxford University Press, 1997).
186. Žižek, *Violence*, 153 (emphasis in original).
187. Benjamin, "Critique of Violence," 242 (emphasis added).
188. Norfolk *Herald*, Norfolk Virginia (November 14, 1831); Petersburg *Intelligencer*, Petersburg, Virginia (November 14, 1831). On the execution of Robert-François Damiens, see Michel Foucault, *Discipline and Punish: The Birth of the Prison*, Alan Sheridan, translator (New York: Vintage, 1979), 3–6; Gatrell, *The Hanging Tree*, 13–14.
189. See Shai J. Lavi, *The Modern Art of Dying: A History of Euthanasia in the United States* (Princeton: Princeton University Press, 2005), 5. Recall Adam Smith: "A brave man is not

rendered contemptible by being brought to the scaffold. . . . The man, on the contrary, who dies with resolution, as he is naturally regarded with the erect aspect of esteem and approbation, so he wears himself the same undaunted countenance; and if the crime does not deprive him of the respect of others, the punishment never will. He has no suspicion that his situation is the object of contempt or derision to any body, and he can, with propriety, assume the air, not only of perfect serenity, but of triumph and exultation." Adam Smith, *Theory of Moral Sentiments*, D.D. Raphael and A. L. Macfie, editors (Indianapolis: Liberty Fund, 1982), 60–61.

190. Louis Masur notes that on execution day condemned prisoners were expected "to enact the drama of penitence and redemption," and that "evidence of criminals refusing to act as they were expected to act is rare." Louis P. Masur, *Rites of Execution: Capital Punishment and the Transformation of American Culture, 1776-1865* (New York: Oxford University Press, 1989), 41, 43. See also above, works cited at chapter 1 note 16.

191. The description is Stuart Banner's. See Stuart Banner, *The Death Penalty: An American History* (Cambridge, MA: Harvard University Press, 2002), 44.

192. Hugh M. Milne, editor, *Boswell's Edinburgh Journals, 1767-1786* (Edinburgh: John Donald, 2013), entry for September 1, 1774, recounting a conversation with Alexander Monro, professor of anatomy at Edinburgh (emphasis in original).

193. A study of sixty-five hangings that took place in the United States during the years 1869–73 (that is, well after the "professionalization" of execution) found only six complete neck fractures and four partial fractures. See Alonzo Calkins, *Felonious Homicide: Its Penalty and the Execution Thereof, Judicially* (New York: Russell Brothers, 1873), 17, cited in Banner, *Death Penalty*, 47. English studies showed similar rates.

194. "It has been observed in the execution of criminals, that death takes place at different intervals of time after suspension. This difference is probably dependent on the greater or less degree of constriction produced by the ligature." Rapid death, brought about by the rupture or compression of the spinal cord, was "extremely rare" and "seldom met with in persons criminally executed." Death from hanging generally required "a few minutes," the exact period dependent on the strength of the person in question. One criminal executed under prison conditions in Albany N.Y. still had a heartbeat at "*nine minutes and a half* after suspension." Alfred Swaine Taylor, *The Principles and Practice of Medical Jurisprudence* (London: John Churchill & Sons, 1865), 650–51, 653 (emphasis in original). For Southampton County's hanging tree, see Drewry, *Southampton Insurrection*, 115; Tragle, *Southampton Slave Revolt*, 169.

195. Taylor, *Medical Jurisprudence*, 654–55.

196. John Greenleaf Whittier, "The Human Sacrifice," from *Songs of Labor and Reform*, in *The Complete Poetical Works of John Greenleaf Whittier* (Boston: Houghton Mifflin, 1904), 436–38, at 437.

197. Gatrell, *The Hanging Tree*, 30, and generally 29–55. See also Banner, *Death Penalty*, 44–47.

198. *An Act for Preventing the Horrid Crime of Murder* 25 Geo. II c. 37 (1751). See, generally, Peter Linebaugh, "The Tyburn Riot Against the Surgeons," in Douglas Hay et al., *Albion's Fatal Tree: Crime and Society in Eighteenth-Century England* (New York: Penguin Books, 1977), 65–117; Banner, *Death Penalty*, 76–80.

199. Drewry, *Southampton Insurrection*, 102. Turner's skull became separated from the rest of his skeleton, and appears eventually to have come into the possession of Richard Hatcher, first African American mayor of Gary, Indiana (1968–87), via the College of Wooster in Wooster, Ohio. See "Nat Turner's Skull Turns Up Far From Site of His Revolt," *Baltimore Sun* (June 15 2003); Greenberg, "Name, Face, Body," 20–21.

200. Gatrell, *The Hanging Tree*, 69, 257.

201. *Ibid.*, 256. "The ceremony began with the wiring of Corder's limbs to a battery to make them twitch."
202. *Ibid.*, 257 (Report of the Suffolk County Surgeon, emphasis in original).
203. *Ibid.*, 257 (*Bell's Life in London*, 24 May 1829).
204. *Ibid.*, 69.
205. *Ibid.*, 258. See https://www.moyseshall.org/your-visit/gallery.cfm (plate 4) (last accessed 27 July 2019).
206. See Karl Marx, *Capital: A Critique of Political Economy. Volume 1: A Critical Analysis of Capitalist Production*, Ben Fowkes, translator (London: Penguin Books, 1990), 280.
207. Certeau, *Everyday Life*, 140. In his autobiographical *Life of William Grimes, The Runaway Slave* (1825), William Grimes wrote from inside his own tortured body, "If it were not for the stripes on my back which were made while I was a slave, I would, in my will, leave my skin a legacy to the government, desiring that it be taken off and made into parchment and then bind the constitution of glorious, happy, and free America. Let the skin of an American slave bind the charter of American liberty!" William L. Andrews and Regina Mason, editors, *Life of William Grimes, The Runaway Slave* (New York: Oxford University Press, 2008), 103.
208. Robert Cover, "Violence and the Word," *Yale Law Journal* 95, no. 8 (July 1986): 1601.
209. Colin Dayan, *The Law Is a White Dog: How Legal Rituals Make and Unmake Persons* (Princeton: Princeton University Press, 2011), 39–112.
210. Kafka, *In the Penal Colony*, 11.
211. *Ibid.*, 14; Panu Minkkinen, "The Radiance of Justice: On the Minor Jurisprudence of Franz Kafka," *Social & Legal Studies* 3, no. 3 (September 1994): 358–59.
212. Certeau, *Everyday Life*, 139.
213. Appadurai, "Dead Certainty," 907. The quality of interracial "amity" in a slave society is, of course, distinctly strained. The point here is only to note that interracial violence in antebellum America does have similarities to the interethnic *communal* violence that is Appadurai's subject. It is plain from the Southampton County Court trial record that in St. Luke's Parish, everyone knew everyone else, whether enslaved or free.
214. Žižek, *Violence*, 178.
215. *Ibid.*, 178–205; Benjamin, "Critique of Violence," 236–52; Žižek, *In Defense of Lost Causes*, 161, 476–87; see above, chapter 3, note 3.
216. Markus Dirk Dubber, "Rediscovering Hegel's Theory of Crime and Punishment," *Michigan Law Review* 92, no. 6 (May 1994): 1583n33.
217. Closely paraphrasing Dubber, crime, for Hegel, is an attempt to posit a (new) law by negating right (violating another's external freedom). The law posited by the criminal act is the offender's subjectivity universalized. Punishment exposes the futility of the criminal's attempt to found law on his subjectivity rather than on right. Punishment attaches to the only place where the law posited by the criminal act has any existence, namely, the criminal's will. Punishment treats the criminal as a rational person capable of acting according to maxims that could be universalized to all rational persons. Because crime violates another's external freedom, the criminal, as rational, is treated as having acted according to the maxim that one *should* violate another's external freedom. Punishment merely applies this law to the criminal. Punishment therefore is also the criminal's right in that it results from the application of the criminal's universalized maxim to himself. By committing the criminal act the criminal has posited the law that compels punishment. In this sense, by acting the criminal has consented to the punishment. *Ibid.*, 1607–8.
218. "A truth is solely constituted by rupturing with the order which supports it, never as an effect of that order. I have named this type of rupture, which opens up truths, 'the event.'" Badiou, *Being and Event*, xv. And again, "There is no stronger transcendental

consequence than the one which makes what did not exist in the world appear within it. . . . *The maximally true consequence of an event's (maximal) intensity of existence is the existence of the inexistent*." Badiou, *Logics of Worlds*, 376–77 (emphasis in original).

219. Badiou, *Logics of Worlds*, 369.
220. Alain Badiou, "Is the Word 'Communism' Forever Doomed?" (November 2008) at http://www.lacan.com/essays/?page_id=323, paragraph 3 (last accessed February 22, 2019).

CHAPTER 5: ON THE GUILT OF FRAGILE SOVEREIGNS

1. *Confessions*, 10, 11–12. "By putting the right to take life in their own hands, the perpetrators of religious violence [make] a daring claim of power on behalf of the powerless, a basis of legitimacy for public order other than that on which the secular state relies. In doing so, they [demonstrate] to everyone how fragile the public order actually is, and how fickle the populace's assent to the moral authority of power can be." Juergensmeyer, *Terror in the Mind of God*, 218.
2. Honig, *Antigone, Interrupted*, 151. (Honig's book, at 92, supplies the title of this chapter.) As I have already noted (above, chapter 2, note 209, and accompanying text) Gray wrote that Turner had "expressed himself fully satisfied as to the impracticability of his attempt." *Confessions*, 18. The implication is that Turner acknowledged his "rebellion" had no chance of success. But "impracticable" also carries the connotation of that which requires faith rather than works. That which is impracticable—"in practice impossible"—is that which cannot be achieved except by an unmediated act of faith, or of God. See Martel, *Divine Violence*, 47–54, 59–64.
3. *Confessions*, 4.
4. Here I follow Honig in deploying Walter Benjamin's account of the Baroque *Trauerspiel* (Mourning Play) in *Ursprung des Deutschen Trauerspiels* (Berlin: Suhrkamp Verlag, 1963) [*Origin of the German Trauerspiel*]. Like Honig's, my deployment is indebted to James R. Martel, *Textual Conspiracies: Walter Benjamin, Idolatry, and Political Theory* (Ann Arbor: University of Michigan Press, 2013).
5. *Confessions*, 4. Turner's "account of the conspiracy" actually has relatively little to say about the process of conspiring other than its difficulties—"Many were the plans formed and rejected by us" (11). Turner's conspiracy as it appears in Gray's pamphlet is, rather, a "textual conspiracy," specifically a conspiracy between Turner and particular biblical texts. See Martel, *Textual Conspiracies*, 153.
6. *Confessions*, 5, 21.
7. *Ibid.*, 21. On the question of "humanity to the improvident slave" see Mark Tushnet, *The American Law of Slavery, 1810-1860: Considerations of Humanity and Interest*, 3–5, 50–54 (1981).
8. *Confessions*, 4, 18–19.
9. *Ibid.*, 3, 4, 19–20.
10. Thomas Ruffin Gray, letter of September 17, 1831, in *The Constitutional Whig* (September 26, 1831).
11. *Confessions*, 5, 6, 21.
12. *Ibid.*, 21.
13. *Ibid.*, 5.
14. St. George Tucker, *A Dissertation on Slavery: With A Proposal for the Gradual Abolition of it, in the State of Virginia* (Philadelphia: Printed for Mathew Carey, 1796), 9–10 (emphasis in original). See, generally, Alan Taylor, *The Internal Enemy: Slavery and War in Virginia, 1772-1832* (New York: W. W. Norton, 2013), 35–39, 85–89. Tucker was no radical abolitionist, but his public condemnation of slavery was unusual. Virginians were obsessed with

avoiding public discussion of the demerits of slavery, or its end. As the successor to Tucker's chair of law and police at the College of William & Mary, Thomas Roderick Dew noted in 1832, "We have heretofore doubted the propriety even of too frequently agitating, especially in a public manner, the question of abolition, in consequence of the injurious effects which might be produced on the slave population." Thomas Roderick Dew, *Review of the Debate in the Virginia Legislature of 1831 and 1832* (Richmond: Printed by T. W. White, 1832), 8.

15. James Monroe, of Loudoun, in *Proceedings and Debates of the Virginia State Convention, of 1829–30. To which are Subjoined, the New Constitution of Virginia, and the Votes of the People* (Richmond: Printed by Samuel Shepherd & Co. for Richie & Cook, 1830) 149. [Hereinafter *PDVSC*]. See also 248–49 (William B. Giles, who was the incumbent governor at the time). Compare 858 (John Randolph).

16. Might rumor of the convention's rumbling undercurrent of conflict over slaveholding—explored in detail in chapter 6—have been a factor in moving Turner from faith to demonic action? There is no trace of this in his account of himself. Yet if William C. Parker was correct in November 1831 that "it was not until rather more than a year ago" that Turner exchanged his quest for "superior righteousness" for "the idea of emancipating the blacks," we cannot discount the possibility. See letter attributed to William C. Parker, Richmond *Enquirer* (November 8, 1831), in Tragle, *Southampton Slave Revolt*, 137.

That the convention was the occasion for rumors among the enslaved over the future of slavery in Virginia is indicated by a report dated July 18, 1829, from Christopher Tompkins of Mathews County to then Governor William B. Giles, "Informing that the common belief among the negroes of his county was, that the State Convention had been elected to decide on the question of their emancipation. That emancipation would be proclaimed at the next August Court. In the case of failure, there were some who advocated insurrection." *Calendar of Virginia State Papers and Other Manuscripts, from January 1, 1808, to December 31, 1835)*, X (Richmond, 1892), 569. Anthony Kaye writes, "Slaves knew far more about politics than white people realized." Kaye, *Joining Places*, 24, and see also 173–75; Harding, *There is a River*, 74.

17. Whites deserted the countryside and congregated in centrally defended locations. "One account asserted that more than '15 hundred women and children' had taken refuge in Jerusalem." Breen, *Deluged in Blood*, 81.

18. *The Constitutional Whig*, Richmond, Virginia (October 14, 1831), in Tragle, *Southampton Slave Revolt*, 119–23, at 120, 122; Richmond *Enquirer* (December 20, 1831; January 7, 1832).

19. [Benjamin Watkins Leigh], *The Letter of Appomatox to the People of Virginia: Exhibiting a Connected View of the Recent Proceedings in the House of Delegates, on the Subject of the Abolition of Slavery: and a Succinct Account of the Doctrines Broached by the Friends of Abolition, in Debate: And the Mischievous Tendency of those Proceedings and Doctrines* (Richmond: Printed by Thomas W. White, 1832), 27.

20. Dew, *Review of the Debate*. Dew's *Review* is analyzed at length in chapter 6 below, notes 221–89 and accompanying text. And see Laurence Shore, *Southern Capitalists: The Ideological Leadership of an Elite* (Chapel Hill: University of North Carolina Press, 1986), 4, 24–28; James Oakes, "The Peculiar Fate of the Bourgeois Critique of Slavery," and Walter Johnson, "Commentary [on Oakes]," both in Winthrop D. Jordan, editor, *Slavery and the American South* (Jackson: University Press of Mississippi, 2003), 40–42; 49, 50.

21. See Žižek, *Event*, 91. One is reminded of MacHeath: "Grooch . . . you are an old burglar. Your profession is burglary. I wouldn't think of suggesting that your profession, in itself, is out of date. That would be going too far. Only in its form, Grooch, does it

lag behind the times. You are an artisan, a hack, and that's all there is to it. That class is on the wane—you can't deny that. What is a pick-lock compared to a debenture share? What is the burgling of a bank compared to the founding of a bank? What, my dear Grooch, is the murder of a man compared to the employment of a man? . . . Brute force is out of date. Why send out murderers when one can employ bailiffs? We must build up, not pull down; that is, we must build up for profit." Bertolt Brecht, *Threepenny Novel*, Desmond I. Vesey, translator (New York: Grove Press, 1956), 246–47.

22. Breen, *Deluged in Blood*, 5–8.
23. See Christopher Tomlins, "The Threepenny Constitution (and the Question of Justice)," *Alabama Law Review* 58 (2007): 1003.
24. William Edward Burghardt Du Bois, *The Souls of Black Folk* (New York: Penguin Books, 1996), 204.
25. Dew, *Review of the Debate*, 64 (emphasis in original). On Turner's impossibilism, see above, note 2. On failure, see Martel, *Textual Conspiracies*, 36 ("failure becomes refusal, resistance, subversion"); or Samuel Beckett, *Worstward Ho* ("Ever tried. Ever failed. No matter. Try again. Fail again. Fail better."); or Žižek, *In Defense of Lost Causes*, 392: "That the evental irruption functions as a break in time, introducing a totally different order of temporality (the temporality of 'the work of love,' fidelity to the event), means that, from the perspective of non-evental time of historical evolution, there is never a 'right moment' for the revolutionary event."
26. Dew, *Review of the Debate*, 64.
27. Pausânias, *Pausanias's Description of Greece*, J. G. Frazer, translator (London: MacMillan, 1913), 1:64.
28. *Sedet, aeternumque sedebit /Infelix Theseus* ("There sits, and to eternity shall sit, the unhappy Theseus"). Virgil, *Aeneid*, VI, line 617–18, quoted in Dew, *Review of the Debate*, 64.
29. To return to *Antigone, Interrupted*, the political parallel suggested here is that of Ismene's surreptitious unity in conspiracy with Antigone against Creon, which Honig explores in her chapter entitled "Sacrifice, Sorority, Integrity," 151–96, a chapter with many resonances (for example, on the nature and ethics of choice) for the politics of rebellion and endurance in slavery. Compare Michel-Rolph Trouillot, *Silencing the Past: Power and the Production of History* (Boston: Beacon Press, 1995), 70–107; Johnson, "Commentary [on Oakes]," 55.

CHAPTER 6: REVULSIONS OF CAPITAL: VIRGINIA, 1829–32

1. *Confessions*, 4.
2. *Confessions*, 4. Hinks, *To Awaken My Afflicted Brethren*, 139–45, 168–71. *Calendar of Virginia State Papers and Other Manuscripts, from January 1, 1808, to December 31, 1835)*, X (Richmond, 1892), 567–69 (Mathews, Gloucester, Isle of Wight, and adjoining counties). We should note that throughout the 1820s, Virginia's agricultural economy suffered a profound depression that would have had severe material repercussions for the slaves of indebted slaveholders, stoking resentments. See Haulman, *Virginia and the Panic of 1819*, 137–51. Only a few years earlier, during the War of 1812, Virginia's tidewater counties had seen mass flight of hundreds of slaves to British warships, many of whom returned to fight former masters as guides, pilots, sailors, and marines. See Taylor, *The Internal Enemy*. Memories of those years were awakened by the Turner Rebellion, when rumor among slaves had it "that the English were in the County killing white people." See "At a court of Oyer and Terminer continued by adjournment and held for the County of Southampton on the 7th day of September 1831 for the trial of Hardy and Isham, negro men slaves the property of Benjamin Edwards." Southampton

County Court, *Minute Book* (1830–35), 96, and see also 98 ("the British were in the Country killing the white people").

3. See, generally, Alison Goodyear Freehling, *Drift Toward Dissolution: The Virginia Slavery Debate of 1831-1832* (Baton Rouge: Louisiana State University Press, 1982). Description of eastern planters as an "aristocracy" belies the reality that most were smallholders who owned only a few slaves. However, "freeholder aristocracy" was a common form of tendentious political rhetoric during the 1829–30 Virginia Constitutional Convention debates, just as "peasantry" was an equally tendentious description of the population of the Trans-Allegheny west. See, for examples, John R. Cooke, of Frederick, in *PDVSC* (October 27, 1829), 54–62 ("aristocracy"); Benjamin Watkins Leigh, of Chesterfield, in *PDVSC* (November 3, 1829), 158 ("peasantry").
4. Freehling, *Drift*, 23–24.
5. Christopher Michael Curtis, *Jefferson's Freeholders and the Politics of Ownership in the Old Dominion* (Cambridge: Cambridge University Press, 2012), 1–16.
6. See, for example, Eric Hobsbawm and George Rudé, *Captain Swing* (London: Phoenix Press, 2001); K.D.M. Snell, *Annals of the Labouring Poor: Social Change and Agrarian England, 1660-1900* (Cambridge: Cambridge University Press, 1985); R. P. Boast, "The Ideology of Tenurial Revolution: The Pacific Rim 1850–1950," *law&history* 1 (2014): 137–57; Sally Engle Merry, *Colonizing Hawai'i: The Cultural Power of Law* (Princeton: Princeton University Press, 2000), 3–114; Brenna Bhandar, *Colonial Lives of Property: Law, Land and Racial Regimes of Ownership* (Durham, NC: Duke University Press, 2018); Wagner, *The Tar Baby*, 20–50, 74–124.
7. Dew, *Review of the Debate*. See below, notes 219–89 and accompanying text. Slaves had of course been treated as commodities since the first sale of the first slave. What is at issue here is the intensity of commoditization (such that commoditization defines slavery as it defines wage labor, vacating paternalism), its scale (progressing far beyond local credit networks to regional, national, and Atlantic networks), and the proliferation of forms (beyond hiring out and sale, to pledges against debt, loan collateral and mortgages, insurance contracts, and capital investment). For valuable studies of the nature and trajectory of commoditization in practice, see Bonnie Martin, "Silver Buckles and Slaves: Borrowing, Lending, and the Commodification of Slaves in Virginia Communities," and Karen Ryder, "'To Realize Money Facilities': Slave Life Insurance, the Slave Trade, and Credit in the Old South," both in Forret and Sears, editors, *New Directions in Slavery Studies*, 30–52, and 53–71. For the intensification, scale, and impact of commoditization that renders the nineteenth century "the century that enthroned the commodity," see Baucom, *Specters of the Atlantic*, 17, 3–112; Johnson, *River of Dark Dreams*; Johnson, *African American Religions*, 13–156; Anthony E. Kaye, "The Second Slavery: Modernity in the Nineteenth Century South and the Atlantic World," *Journal of Southern History* 75, no. 3 (2009): 627–50; Edward E. Baptist, *The Half Has Never Been Told: Slavery and the Making of American Capitalism* (New York: Basic Books, 2014); Sven Beckert, *Empire of Cotton: A Global History* (New York: Knopf, 2015); Sven Beckert and Seth Rockman, editors, *Slavery's Capitalism: A New History of American Economic Development* (Philadelphia: University of Pennsylvania Press, 2016).
8. Nathaniel Beverly Tucker, "Note to Blackstone's Commentaries," *Southern Literary Messenger* 1, no. 5 (January 1835): 228.
9. As such, of course, it was an exquisitely unequal transaction. For an example, see *Bailey v. Poindexter's Executor* 55 Va. 132 (1858), holding a testator's provision that slaves loaned to his wife for life shall have their choice on his death of being emancipated or sold publicly, the emancipation being made to depend on the slaves' election to be free, to be void and of no effect, slaves having no legal capacity to choose. For an extended commentary on *Bailey*, see Colin Dayan, *The Law Is a White Dog: How Legal Rituals Make and Unmake Persons* (Princeton: Princeton University Press, 2011), 138–76. For

commentary on the perpetuity of African American debt, surviving emancipation, see Hartman, *Scenes of Subjection*, 115–206. See also Christopher Tomlins, "Debt, Death, and Redemption: Towards a Soterial-Legal History of the Turner Rebellion," in David Cowan and Daniel Wincott, editors, *Exploring the 'Legal' in Socio-Legal Studies* (London: Palgrave, 2016), 50–52.

10. As the epigraph to this chapter indicates, Thomas Roderick Dew's *Review of the Debate* (at 68) employed "revulsion" in precisely this sense—not simply "the action or process of drawing back or away," or "a sudden violent change of feeling," as the *OED* defines it, but as Adam Smith uses the word in *Wealth of Nations*. "The new market and the new employment which are opened by the colony trade, are of much greater extent than that portion of the old market and the old employment which is lost by the monopoly. The new produce and the new capital which has been created, if one may say so, by the colony trade, maintain in Great Britain a greater quantity of productive labour, than what can have been thrown out of employment by *the revulsion of capital* from other trades of which the returns are more frequent." See Adam Smith, *An Inquiry into the Nature and Causes of the Wealth of Nations*, R. H. Campbell and A. S. Skinner, general editors (Indianapolis: Liberty Fund, 1981), 2:609 (emphasis added); see also 596. One can date white Virginia's revulsion (in both senses discussed here) from the mass absconsions of the War of 1812. See Taylor, *The Internal Enemy*; Kaye, *Joining Places*, 26–27.
11. Johnson, *River of Dark Dreams*, 1–17.
12. Freehling, *Drift*, 24. On "aristocratic" planters, see above, note 3.
13. John W. Green, of Culpeper, in *PDVSC* (27 October 1829), 63–64; Robert Stanard, of Spottsylvania, in *PDVSC* (14 November 1829), 306, 307; John Randolph, of Charlotte, in *PDVSC* (12 January 1830), 858.
14. Littleton W. Tazewell, of Norfolk Borough, in *PDVSC* (9 October 1829), 17.
15. Curtis, *Jefferson's Freeholders*, 100–101; Freehling, *Drift*, 16–17; Carter Goodrich, "The Virginia System of Mixed Enterprise," *Political Science Quarterly* 64, no. 3 (September 1949): 355–87, at 376. See also below, note 45, and accompanying text.
16. Freehling, *Drift*, 35.
17. Curtis, *Jefferson's Freeholders*, 101.
18. "An Act to declare who shall have a right to vote in the Election of Burgesses to serve in the General Assembly, for Counties; and for preventing fraudulent Conveiances, in order to multiply Votes at such Elections," Acts of Assembly, August 1736, Ch. II, in William Waller Hening, *The Statutes at Large: Being a Collection of all the Laws of Virginia from the first session of the Legislature, in the Year 1619* (Richmond: Printed for the Editor, At the Franklin Press, 1820) 4:475–78. Freehold amounting to 100 acres in two or more counties should be voted in the county where the largest portion lay.
19. Curtis, *Jefferson's Freeholders*, 19.
20. *Ibid.*, 77, and generally 71–78.
21. *Ibid.*, 86.
22. *Ibid.*, 14.
23. *Ibid.*, 14–15. Erik S. Root, *All Honor to Jefferson? The Virginia Slavery Debate and the Positive Good Thesis* (Lanham, MD: Rowman & Littlefield, 2008), 71–74.
24. Curtis, *Jefferson's Freeholders*, 124–25.
25. Although see above, chapter 5 note 16.
26. The constitutional convention opened on October 5, 1829, and concluded January 15, 1830. The new state constitution was ratified in April 1830. The first legislative election held under the new constitution occurred in October 1830 for the legislative session beginning December 6, 1830. The legislature for the session beginning December 5, 1831 was elected August 1, 1831. The Turner Rebellion took place August 21–23, 1831.

27. Root, *All Honor to Jefferson?* 71. For an oral history of reform agitation since 1790, concentrating on the Staunton Conventions of 1816 and 1825 (assemblies of delegates from western counties seeking apportionment and suffrage reform), see Philip Doddridge, of Brooke, in *PDVSC* (October 27, 1829), 81–83.
28. In 1817, following the first Staunton Convention, legislation was passed to equalize Virginia's senatorial districts and to apportion them on the basis of free white population according to the federal census of 1810. See Doddridge, *PDVSC*, 82–83; Richard O. Curry, *A House Divided: A Study of Statehood Politics and the Copperhead Movement in West Virginia* (Pittsburgh: University of Pittsburgh Press, 1964), 14.
29. Freehling, *Drift*, 36.
30. See the Virginia Auditor General's estimates of population, cited in *PDVSC*, 61–62.
31. Freehling, *Drift*, 41. See also Philip Doddridge, of Brooke, in *PDVSC* (October 27, 1829), 80 (declaiming against the long history of county subdivision in the Tidewater, creating a representation "so unequal," and consequences "so intolerable, as no longer to be borne with.")
32. It is important to note that the 1825 Staunton Convention also demanded greater access to bank credit and a program of state-sponsored internal improvements. See Curtis, *Jefferson's Freeholders*, 101.
33. Freehling, *Drift*, 45–47
34. *Ibid.*, 48.
35. Curtis, *Jefferson's Freeholders*, 101.
36. *Ibid.*, 101–2, 108–9; Christopher Michael Curtis, "Reconsidering Suffrage Reform in the 1829–1830 Virginia Constitutional Convention," *Journal of Southern History* 74, no. 1 (February 2008): 92, 106. For evidence of the same general transition in reformist white democratic consciousness from "locality" to "supralocality," see Laura F. Edwards, *The People and Their Peace: Legal Culture and the Transformation of Inequality in the Post-Revolutionary South* (Chapel Hill: University of North Carolina Press, 2009).
37. Philip Doddridge, of Brooke, in *PDVSC* (October 27, 1829), 82–83.
38. Alexander Campbell, of Brooke, in *PDVSC* (October 31, 1829), 123.
39. Report of the Committee appointed on the Legislative Department of the Government, in *PDVSC* (October 24, 1829), 39–40.
40. Benjamin Watkins Leigh, of Chesterfield, in *PDVSC* (October 24, 1829), 53 (declaiming against "a plan which proposes, in effect, to put the power of controlling the wealth of the State, into hands different from those which hold that wealth"; a plan foreign to Virginia's English ancestry, better known to "the rights of man held in the French school," and licensing the same "rapine, anarchy and bloodshed"; a plan based not "on the actual state of things as they are" but on "mere abstractions," and constituting "the most crying injustice ever attempted in any land"). See also Littleton Tazewell, of Norfolk Borough, in *PDVSC* (November 16, 1829), 331–32 ("Oppressed labor seizes power to redress its wrongs; capital endangered, must purchase power to protect its rights." Wise statesmen should resolve "these opposing forces into a third"—government—the object of which was to keep them checked, restrained, and balanced.)
41. Abel P. Upshur, of Northampton, in *PDVSC* (October 28, 1829), 74, 75.
42. Benjamin Watkins Leigh, of Chesterfield, in *PDVSC* (November 4, 1829), 173 (emphasis added).
43. John Randolph, of Charlotte, in *PDVSC* (November 14, 1829), 316.
44. Benjamin Watkins Leigh, of Chesterfield, in *PDVSC* (November 4, 1829), 172.
45. Abel P. Upshur, of Northampton, in *PDVSC* (October 28, 1829), 74. Western demands for state investment in internal improvements, and eastern resistance to those demands, are evident throughout the convention debates. See, for example, John W. Green, of Culpeper, in *PDVSC* (October 27, 1829), 63 (speaking in support of a "mixed basis" as protection against western eagerness for state borrowing and capital

investment in internal improvements); Richard Morris, of Hanover, in *PDVSC* (October 30, 1829), 114 (ridiculing "the people of the west" for their ambitions "to make some Appian, or some Flaminian way, or some Roman aqueduct, or some other such splendid work of Internal Improvement," and warning of the debts that would result); John Scott, of Fauquier, in *PDVSC* (October 31, 1829), 127–28 (noting that no interests were more distinct in the convention debates than the differences among the populations of different geographic divisions of the state on the question of internal improvements); Benjamin Watkins Leigh, of Chesterfield, in *PDVSC* (November 3, 1829), 154, 158 (warning against the "overweening passion for Internal Improvements" evident in the state's northern and western districts).

46. Chapman Johnson, of Augusta, in *PDVSC* (November 11, 1829), 257.
47. John R. Cooke, of Frederick, in *PDVSC* (October 27, 1829), 54–55; Philip P. Barbour, of Orange, in *PDVSC* (October 29, 1829), 94.
48. Philip P. Barbour, of Orange, in *PDVSC* (October 29, 1829), 94; Richard Morris, of Hanover, in *PDVSC* (October 30, 1829), 109.
49. Abel P. Upshur, of Northampton, in *PDVSC* (October 27–28, 1829), 69 (emphasis in original), 72, 78–79.
50. Benjamin Watkins Leigh, of Chesterfield, in *PDVSC* (December 5, 1829), 571.
51. Briscoe G. Baldwin, of Augusta, in *PDVSC* (October 29, 1829), 102; James Monroe, of Loudoun, in *PDVSC* (2 November 1829), 148; Benjamin Watkins Leigh, of Chesterfield, in *PDVSC* (November 3, 1829), 156; Philip N. Nicholas, of Richmond City, in *PDVSC* (November 16, 1829), 324; Benjamin Watkins Leigh, of Chesterfield, in *PDVSC* (November 21, 1829), 408–9; Briscoe G. Baldwin, of Augusta, in *PDVSC* (December 4, 1829), 566 (observing "I must notice a topic of the gravest character, which has been several times brought to our view, by Eastern members, in the course of debate. I mean a separation of the State—at one time gently insinuated—at another wrapt up in beautiful rhetorical language, and finally expressed in what has been emphatically called plain old English.")

Just as western demands for state investment in internal improvements are evident throughout the convention debates, so too is eastern anxiety at the implications of losing political ascendancy for the security of slaveholding. Erik Root has argued that the fears for slaveholding underlying the eastern attack on western suffragists' natural rights arguments were so pronounced that the convention was really not debating suffrage and representation at all, but actually debating the abolition of slavery. Root, *All Honor to Jefferson?* 72–124, particularly at 72. Root perhaps reads back too vigorously the Virginia slavery debate of 1831–32 onto the convention debate of 1829–30: suffragists were antagonistic to direct (federal basis) or indirect (mixed basis) acknowledgment of slaves in representation calculations rather than slavery per se. Suffragist leaders reassured slaveholders their property would be safe in a free white majority government. They noted—tepidly—that slavery was also growing west of the Blue Ridge, and that Pennsylvania and the states of the Old Northwest (Ohio, Indiana, Illinois) were increasingly hostile to runaways and free people of color. See Philip Doddridge, of Brooke, in *PDVSC* (October 27, 1829), 86–89. Still, it is clear that the convention's slave party was deeply apprehensive of the impact of suffragists' natural rights arguments on the legitimacy of slaveholding. See, for example, Philip P. Barbour, of Orange, in *PDVSC* (October 29, 1829), 91 ("At the threshold, we are met with a principle laid down in the Bill of Rights, *that all men are by nature, equally free*. . . . If you give to the language, all the force which the words literally import (and they are, I believe, but an echo of those in the Declaration of Independence,) what will they amount to, but a declaration of universal emancipation, to a class of our population, not far short of a moiety of our entire number, now in a state of slavery? And if you were to give to such a declaration, its full operation . . . you might as a natural consequence, soon expect to see realized here, the frightful and appalling scenes of horror and desolation, which were produced in St. Domingo by a declaration of much the same tenor, issued by the famous National Assembly of France"). See also Richard Morris, of Hanover, in *PDVSC* (October 30, 1829), 116 (arguing that the increased capitation taxes on slaves that the slave party claimed would be an inevitable consequence of white majority government would amount to a forced emancipation because slaveholders would not be able to afford to keep their slaves. "Perhaps some gentlemen may consider it a very desirable thing, that we should be reduced to such a necessity; but, Sir, let it once be known, that this separation of the master and his slave is not a voluntary thing on either side, but a matter of compulsion, produced by the agency of the Government: I care not, whether this agency be manifested by the passage of a law of emancipation, or a tax-law depriving the master of the power of holding his slave: and soon a sword will be unsheathed, that will be red with the best blood of this country, before it finds the scabbard. This thing between master and slave, is one which *cannot* be left to be regulated by the Government. Compensation for 400,000 slaves, *can not* be made. The matter must be left to the silent operation of natural causes" (emphasis in original).) See also Robert Stanard, of Spottsylvania, in *PDVSC* (November 14, 1829), 306, 307.

52. Thus, Benjamin Watkins Leigh, of Chesterfield, noted reluctantly that "it seems, plainly enough, to be the general opinion, that any effort to preserve a landed qualification of the Right of Suffrage must fail." *PDVSC* (November 20, 1829), 393.
53. Alfred H. Powell, of Frederick, in *PDVSC* (October 30, 1829), 105.
54. Philip Doddridge, of Brooke, in *PDVSC* (October 27, 1829), 89; William F. Gordon, of Albemarle, in PDVSC (November 2, 1829), 139; Charles F. Mercer, of Loudoun, in *PDVSC* (November 5, 1829), 189.
55. John Scott, of Fauquier, in *PDVSC* (December 16, 1829), 637, and (December 19, 1829), 685; Lewis Summers, of Kanawha, in *PDVSC* (December 16, 1829) 637.
56. Benjamin Watkins Leigh, of Chesterfield, in *PDVSC* (November 3, 1829), 158 ("In every civilized country under the sun, some there must be who labour for their daily bread, either by contract with, or subjection to others, or for themselves. Slaves, in the eastern part of this State, fill the place of the peasantry of Europe—of the peasantry or day-labourers in the non-slave-holding States of this Union. The denser the population, the more numerous will this class be. Even in the present state of the population beyond the Alleghany, there must be some peasantry, and as the country fills up, they will scarcely have more—that is, men who tend the herds and dig the soil, who have neither real nor personal capital of their own, and who earn their daily bread by the sweat of their brow. These, by this scheme [the white basis], are all to be represented—but none of our slaves. And yet, *in political economy*, the latter fill exactly the same place. Slaves, indeed, are not and never will be comparable with the hardy peasantry of the mountains, in intellectual power, in moral worth, in all that determines man's degree in the moral scale, and raises him above the brute—I beg pardon, his Maker placed him above the brute—above the savage—above that wretched state, of which the only comfort is the natural rights of man. I have as sincere feelings of regard for that people, as any man who lives among them. But I ask gentlemen to say, whether they believe, that those who are obliged to depend on their daily labour for daily subsistence, can, or do ever enter into political affairs? They never do—never will—never can.") See also Thomas R. Joynes, of Accomack, in *PDVSC* (November 5, 1829), 207. See, in reply, Charles F. Mercer, of Loudoun, in *PDVSC* (November 5, 1829), 183, 185.
57. Benjamin Watkins Leigh, of Chesterfield, in *PDVSC* (November 3, 1829), 158–59 ("Now, what real share, so far as mind is concerned, does any man suppose the peasantry of the west—that peasantry, which it must have when the country is as completely

filled up with day-labourers as ours is of slaves—can or will take in affairs of State? Gentlemen may say, their labourers are the most intelligent on earth—which I hope is true—that they will rise to political intelligence. But, when any rise, others must supply the place they rise from. What then, is the practical effect of the scheme of representation in question? Simply, that the men of property of the west, shall be allowed a representation for all their day-labourers without contributing an additional cent of revenue, and that the men of property of the east, shall contribute in proportion to all the slave-labour they employ, without any additional representation. Sir, I am against all this—I am for a representation of every interest in society—for poising and balancing all interests—for saving each and all, from the sin of oppressing, and from the curse of being oppressed.")

58. Chapman Johnson, of Augusta, in *PDVSC* (November 11, 1829), 265. In all Johnson's speech lasted 2½ days.
59. Chapman Johnson, of Augusta, in *PDVSC* (November 11, 1829), 270.
60. Robert Stanard, of Spottsylvania, in *PDVSC* (November 13, 1829), 295–300, (November 14, 1829), 301–12; John Randolph, of Charlotte, in *PDVSC* (November 14, 1829), 312–21. Stanard and Randolph spoke in succession immediately after the conclusion of Johnson's marathon speech.
61. The words ("bare majority" and "most respectable minority") are from Littleton W. Tazewell, of Norfolk Borough, in *PDVSC* (October 9, 1829), 17. See John Scott, of Fauquier, in *PDVSC* (November 17, 1829), 342 ("The gentleman from Brooke [Philip Doddridge] says, that though their majority in this House is small, it represents a large majority of the people of the State. However this may be, I am very sure of one thing: and that is, that the minority in this House represents a large majority of the freeholders of Virginia.")
62. The compromise led to further weeks of haggling over which counties would gain and lose delegates.
63. *The Memorial of the Non-Freeholders of the City of Richmond, respectfully addressed to the Convention, now assembled to deliberate on amendments to the State Constitution*, in *PDVSC* (October 13, 1829), 25–31.
64. *Ibid.* Similar petitions seeking suffrage extension were received from other nonfreeholder constituencies—of Shenandoah, and Rockingham. See *PDVSC* (October 15, 1829), 32.
65. See, for example, John R. Cooke, of Frederick, in *PDVSC* (October 27, 1829), 57, (November 16, 1829), 341; Richard H. Henderson, of Loudoun, in *PDVSC* (November 18, 1829), 354–55.
66. Richard H. Henderson, of Loudoun, in *PDVSC* (November 18, 1829), 358.
67. *The Memorial of the Non-Freeholders of the City of Richmond*, in *PDVSC* (October 13, 1829), 27–28.
68. Richard H. Henderson, of Loudoun, in *PDVSC* (November 18, 1829), 360.
69. Freehling, *Drift*, 72.
70. Philip N. Nicholas, of Richmond City, in *PDVSC* (November 18, 1829), 364, 366.
71. *The Memorial of the Non-Freeholders of the City of Richmond*, in *PDVSC* (October 13, 1829), 30.
72. Abel P. Upshur, of Northampton, in *PDVSC* (October 27, 1829), 68, (October 28, 1829), 73; Benjamin Watkins Leigh, of Chesterfield, in *PDVSC* (November 3, 1829), 161; Robert Stanard, of Spottsylvania, in *PDVSC* (November 14, 1829), 311.
73. Philip P. Barbour, of Orange, in *PDVSC* (October 28, 1829), 91–92; Benjamin Watkins Leigh, of Chesterfield, in *PDVSC* (November 3, 1829), 161.
74. Abel P. Upshur, of Northampton, in *PDVSC* (October 27, 1829), 68 ("And how can gentlemen venture to limit themselves to *white* population alone, and yet found their

claim on a law of nature that knows no distinction between white and black?" (emphasis in original)). See, in reply, Samuel McDowell Moore, of Rockbridge, in *PDVSC* (November 6, 1829), 227 ("The question . . . as to our right to exclude the free negroes from the rights of citizenship, is sufficiently answered by saying, that we choose to exclude them for reasons which must be obvious . . . and therefore need not be assigned.")

75. Benjamin Watkins Leigh, of Chesterfield, in *PDVSC* (November 20, 1829), 399 ("In Virginia, the great mass of intelligence and virtue resides in that stout and generous yeomanry, the freeholders of this land; that to them belongs not only all the real property of the Commonwealth, but almost all of the personal property also; that they are the class, who feed, who clothe, who educate all classes; who hold the greatest stake in society; who are the only persons who have any stake that may not be withdrawn at pleasure, in the twinkling of an eye; who, therefore, have, and actually take, the deepest interest in the public welfare.")
76. Richard Morris, of Hanover, in *PDVSC* (October 30, 1829), 111 (emphasis in original) ("when, in 1776, Virginia gave the control of her Government to *freeholders*, she granted it to *slave-holders*: nor could she have given to the latter a more effectual guarantee. The freeholder was himself a slave-holder").
77. Charles F. Mercer, of Loudoun, in *PDVSC* (November 23, 1829), 442.
78. William H. Fitzhugh, of Fairfax, in PDVSC (December 16, 1829), 639.
79. "And in case of two or more tenants in common, joint tenants or parceners, in possession, reversion or remainder, having interest in land, the value whereof shall be insufficient to entitle them all to vote, they shall together have as many votes as the value of the land shall entitle them to."
80. See *An Amended Constitution, or Form of Government for Virginia* (*adopted by the Convention January 14th, 1830*), Article 3.14, in *PDVSC* 900 (emphasis added). The following "Summary of the Right of Suffrage—Persons who have the Privilege of Voting under the New Constitution" appeared in the Richmond *Enquirer*, October 12, 1830: "1. All persons who were entitled to vote under the old Constitution, although their land may not be worth one dollar; 2. All white male citizens of the age of 21 years and upwards, who shall be entitled to land valued by the commissioner at $25, or a share in land, if his share is valued at $25, although the quantity of land be ever so small; 3. Those entitled to land valued by the commissioner at 50 dollars, or a share in land if his share is valued at $50, in which some other person has a life estate. Under the old Constitution these could not vote; 4. Those who shall be in possession of land leased to them for five years, of the yearly rent of 20 dollars, the agreement for which has been recorded 2 months before the election; 5. Those who are house-keepers and heads of families, and who shall have paid a state tax, in the county in which they shall offer to vote, for the preceding year. The tax must be a state tax, not a parish or county levy. Those who own a horse, or hire a slave, for instance, pay a state tax."
81. Curtis, *Jefferson's Freeholders*, 116.
82. Philip P. Barbour's speech of November 23 is notable in this regard. Extolling "landed qualification" as "the best surety for such a permanent interest in the community as justly entitles any citizen to the exercise of [the elective franchise]" Barbour stressed its intransience—"an attribute which has nothing to do with personal property" but "belongs to landed property alone." Landed estate was "visible, tangible, immovable." With no sense of irony or contradiction, Barbour then added another advantage of land: it was a commodity. "Must a man who owns a freehold to-day, own it forever? Does not this interest in the soil pass from hand to hand? Is it not actually changing every day and hour?" Suddenly, the principal virtue of the freehold suffrage was that it was a claim to power "based on a foundation as fluctuating as the waves of the

ocean." Any man might enjoy the franchise simply by buying it. Philip P. Barbour, of Orange, in *PDVSC* (November 23, 1829), 435, 436, 437.

83. Curtis, *Jefferson's Freeholders*, 122, 125.
84. *Ibid.*, 125. Here Benjamin Watkins Leigh, reluctant to see the end of property as an expression of vicinage, parted company from his slave party colleagues: "Mere personal property has no locality. Slaves without land to work them on, are more valuable in the South Western States than here." Benjamin Watkins Leigh, of Chesterfield, in *PDVSC* (November 20, 1829), 400.
85. Abel P. Upshur, of Northampton, in *PDVSC* (28 October 1829), 75.
86. *Ibid.* (emphasis in original).
87. *Ibid.*
88. Philip Doddridge, of Brooke, in *PDVSC* (October 27, 1829), 88.
89. See, for example, Thomas R. Joynes, of Accomack, in *PDVSC* (November 5, 1829), 206–11 (arguing that "the wealth of a country . . . depends upon the productive industry of that country," that "whether these productions arise from the labour of freemen, or of slaves, they add equally to the wealth of the community at large," and that the only criterion for representation should be that "those who pay the taxes ought to have complete control over those who have the power of laying the taxes"); William H. Fitzhugh, of Fairfax, in *PDVSC* (November 6, 1829), 219–20 (I would allow no man to participate in laying the taxes, who did not also participate in paying them.")
90. Abel P. Upshur, of Northampton, in *PDVSC* (October 28, 1829), 75 (emphasis added).
91. George L. Vose, *A Sketch of the Life and Works of Loammi Baldwin, Civil Engineer* (Boston: The Press of Geo. H. Ellis, 1885), 15, 16–18. Vose describes Baldwin as "the Father of Civil Engineering in America" (3).
92. Vose reports the interior dimensions of each dock as, at the top 86 feet in width and 253 feet in length, and at the bottom 30 feet in width and 228 feet in length. Each dock was 30 feet in depth. *Ibid.*, 16, 17.
93. *Ibid.*, 17. Vose reports the exact cost of the Charlestown dock as $677,090, and of the Norfolk dock as $943,676 (16, 17).
94. In construction of the Charlestown dock, Baldwin made use of convict labor. See Linda Upham-Bornstein, '"Men of Families': The Intersection of Labor Conflict and Race in the Norfolk Dry Dock Affair, 1829–1831," *Labor: Studies in Working-Class History of the Americas* 4, no. 1 (spring 2007): 77, 85.
95. This account of the Norfolk Dry Dock controversy is largely based on my essay, "In Nat Turner's Shadow: Reflections on the Norfolk Dry Dock Affair of 1830–1831," *Labor History* 33, no. 4 (fall 1992): 494–518. It is already well established that at moments of stress the labor relations characteristic of antebellum urban slavery would become sites of conflict and controversy, not least (as in this case) complaints by white workingmen about competition from slaves at work sites. For a careful study of the operation of a mixed urban labor market (Richmond, Virginia, at the turn of the nineteenth century), see Sidbury, *Ploughshares into Swords*, 184–219. What is notable about this case, aside from its coincidence with Turner's rebellion, is the extensive documentation that the controversy produced, and the painstaking analysis of the relative efficiency of slave and free labor that Baldwin undertook in his own defense, allowing one a clear image of the terms on which labor was undergoing commoditization at the time.
96. Henry Singleton to Commodore James Barron, April 27, 1830, in *Papers of Loammi Baldwin, Jr.*, in *Baldwin Collection,* Boxes 8, 17–23, Baker Library (Division of Historical Collections, Harvard Business School). Hereinafter *Baldwin Papers.*
97. Upham-Bornstein, "'Men of Families,'" 69–71.
98. Singleton to Barron, April 27, 1830, *Baldwin Papers.*
99. "Petition of the Inhabitants of Portsmouth and Persons Employed in the Navy Yard and Dry Dock, Presented to a Meeting of the Citizens of Portsmouth, Sept. 17, 1831,"

in *Baldwin Papers*. Project managers retorted that the number was 111 and that since the excavation phase they had employed no more than 150, averaging between one-quarter and one-third of the total labor force. Loammi Baldwin Jr. to the Honorable Levi Woodbury, Sept. 27, 1831, *Baldwin Papers*.

100. Baldwin to Woodbury, Sept. 27, 1831, *Baldwin Papers*.
101. Upham-Bornstein, "'Men of Families,'" 69.
102. John Rodgers to Loammi Baldwin, Jan. 23, 1830, *Baldwin Papers*.
103. Jefferies Wilkinson and eight others to the Honorable John Branch, Jan. 6, 1830, *Baldwin Papers* (emphasis in original). As "men of families" (and, in several cases, Upham-Bornstein shows, taxed slaveholders) protesting the subversion of white equality by the assignment of skilled work to hired slaves, the petitioning stonemasons were entering much the same civic protest against their "degraded condition" as the nonfreeholder citizens of Richmond in their memorial to the state constitutional convention. They were representing themselves as self-possessed productive laborers, entitled to respect as such. See above, notes 63–64 and accompanying text. See also Upham-Bornstein, "'Men of Families,'" 74.
104. Singleton would subsequently explain that "at the time slaves were first engaged Conl. Baldwin requested me to find some and put them upon the rolls at the ordinary wages saying he left that department exclusively to me because I lived here, knew the people well, had often employed great numbers at the several works in which I have been engaged and because I was better acquainted with the customs & practice relative to slave labour." Singleton to Barron, April 27, 1830, *Baldwin Papers*.
105. Loammi Baldwin Jr. to Commodore John Rogers, Jan. 29, 1830, *Baldwin Papers*.
106. William Jackson and two others to the Honorable John Branch, April 3, 1830, *Baldwin Papers*.
107. "No comment can be necessary upon the conviction which will arise in the mind of any man, upon a simple inspection of the foregoing table. The advantage of adopting slaves for this kind of work far exceeds my expectations, and I think I shall neglect my duty to Government, if after this evidence, *almost as strong as a geometric demonstration*, I do not adhere to my first plan of employing blacks. Indeed, I intend to hire no more whites, than are necessary, at hammering stone, & increase the number of slaves." Loammi Baldwin Jr. to Commodore James Barron, April 27, 1830, *Baldwin Papers* (emphasis added).
108. "Compare the two stones marked 'a' hammered by Whites, at an average cost of $18, with that hammered by the slave Wilson, which cost only $8.64. The average cost then of three 'b's hammered by White men is $12.33 while that of similar stones hammered by blacks is $8.28. The White man, Allen, hammered a stone 'e' at a cost of $13. When the negro James Sparrow, worked one for $7.56. So the cost of white labour on 'f' was $14 and $15 and that of the blacks, upon a similar stone $11.52. No account of the cost of tools is taken, in that would probably be the same, whether used by blacks or whites." Baldwin to Barron, April 27, 1830, *Baldwin Papers*.
109. John W. Murdaugh, a Portsmouth slaveholder, Norfolk County commissioner, and Virginia General Assembly representative, described Singleton as "universally esteemed in the society of this town, as a gentleman of great probity, honesty & industry," whose appointment by Baldwin had been considered "judicious and received the approbation of all who knew him." The complainants, in contrast, were "poor, ignorant, creatures," or worse, "worth-less & infamous scoundrel[s]," one of whom was not even a citizen. See John W. Murdaugh to Commander James Barron, April 28, 1830, *Baldwin Papers*. On Murdaugh, see Upham-Bornstein, "'Men of Families,'" 87.
110. Samuel Johnson to Commodore James Barron, April 28, 1830, *Baldwin Papers*.
111. Singleton to Barron, April 27, 1830, *Baldwin Papers*.

112. Patrick Gilday to Loammi Baldwin Jr., May 24, 1830; Charles Brownell to Loammi Baldwin Jr., Jan. 20, 1831; both in *Baldwin Papers.*
113. "A true Jackson man" to President Andrew Jackson, July 30, 1831, *Baldwin Papers.*
114. Lewis Warrington to Loammi Baldwin, Charlestown, Aug. 11, 1831, *Baldwin Papers.* See also Lewis Warrington to Henry Singleton and Samuel Johnson, Aug. 9, 1831, *Baldwin Papers.* Henry Singleton to Loammi Baldwin, Aug. 12, 1831, *Baldwin Papers.*
115. Samuel Johnson to Commodore L. Warrington, Aug. 11, 1831, *Baldwin Papers.* Johnson added, "there has been a saving of some thousands of dollars to the Government by employing and learning negroes."
116. John W. Murdaugh to Commodore Lewis Warrington, Aug. 13, 1830, *Baldwin Papers.* See also William Loyall et al. and Samuel Watts et al. all to Commodore Lewis Warrington, Aug. 12, 1831, *Baldwin Papers.* On the background of these local notables—virtually all slaveholders—see Upham-Bornstein, "'Men of Families,'" 87–89.
117. Henry Singleton to Loammi Baldwin Jr., Aug. 26, 1831, *Baldwin Papers.* His letter would have crossed with one from Baldwin stating that all Boston was "much interested in the frightful insurrection among the negroes in Southampton County. I hope that it is all silenced by this time, and that the murderers are in good keeping." Loammi Baldwin Jr. to Henry Singleton, Aug. 29, 1831, *Baldwin Papers.* On Norfolk's panicked reaction to the Turner Rebellion, see Tragle, *Southampton Slave Revolt*, 16.
118. H. Singleton to L. Baldwin, Aug. 29, 1831, and Sept. 3, 1831, *Baldwin Papers.*
119. Henry Singleton to Loammi Baldwin Jr., Sept. 7, 1831, and Loammi Baldwin Jr. to Henry Singleton, Sept. 12, 1831, both in *Baldwin Papers.* Baldwin's letter appears to refer to the detention of slaves employed on the dry dock. Unfortunately, the letter from "Mr. Campbell" from which Baldwin seems to have gained this information does not appear in Baldwin's preserved correspondence.
120. Henry Singleton to Loammi Baldwin Jr., Sept. 21, 1831, *Baldwin Papers.*
121. J. W. Wilson to Henry Singleton, Sept. 23, 1831, and Henry Singleton to Loammi Baldwin Jr., Sept. 24, 1831, both in *Baldwin Papers.* "Resolutions Passed at a Meeting of the Citizens of the Town of Portsmouth, Held at the Masonic Hall on Saturday Evening, September 17th 1831," in *Baldwin Papers.*
122. Upham-Bornstein, "'Men of Families,'" 88, 91.
123. "Petition of the Inhabitants of Portsmouth and Persons Employed in the Navy Yard and Dry Dock," in *Baldwin Papers.* Upham-Bornstein, "'Men of Families,'" 91.
124. "Petition of the Inhabitants of Portsmouth and Persons Employed in the Navy Yard and Dry Dock," in *Baldwin Papers* (emphasis in original).
125. Loammi Baldwin Jr. to the Honorable Levi Woodbury, Sept. 27, 1831, *Baldwin Papers*; Loammi Baldwin Jr. to Henry Singleton, Sept. 27, 1831, *Baldwin Papers.* Baldwin's clichéd description of the dry dock's "cheerful" slave laborers is contradicted by evidence discovered by Linda Upham-Bornstein in the autobiography of George Teamoh (born 1818, escaped slavery 1853) who worked as a water-bearer during the construction of the dry dock: "I have worked in every Department in the Navy Yard and Dry-Dock, as laborer, and the same might be said of vast numbers, reaching to thousands of slaves who have been worked, lashed and bruised by the United States government. . . . Justice and time points with significant finger to the first stratum of imbedded rock there deposited by the unrewarded labor of the slave. I have wrought upon these 'works' in common with my fellow bondsmen, receiving the same scanty ration as dealt out by the commissary." F. N. Boney, Richard L. Hume, and Rafia Zafar, editors, *God Made Man, Man Made the Slave: The Autobiography of George Teamoh* (Macon, GA: Mercer University Press, 1990), 81–82; Upham-Bornstein, "'Men of Families,'" 93–94.
126. Baldwin to Singleton, Sept. 27, 1831, *Baldwin Papers.*

127. Loammi Baldwin Jr. to Henry Singleton, Oct. 1, 1831, *Baldwin Papers* (emphasis in original).
128. Loammi Baldwin Jr. to Henry Singleton, Oct. 17, 1831, *Baldwin Papers.*
129. Early in October, Secretary of the Navy Levi Woodbury had replied to the petition to indicate that "the interest of the Government will be duly weighed as well as the rights of individuals considered." Quoted in Henry Singleton to Loammi Baldwin Jr., Oct. 7, 1831, *Baldwin Papers.*
130. See this chapter, section IV.
131. [Payrolls, *Baldwin Papers*].
132. Tommy L. Bogger, *Free Blacks in Norfolk, Virginia, 1790–1860: The Darker Side of Freedom* (Charlottesville: University Press of Virginia, 1997), 65–66, 76–77, 78.
133. *Journal of the House of Delegates of the Commonwealth of Virginia, Begun and Held at the Capitol, in the City of Richmond, on Monday, the Fifth Day of December, One Thousand Eight Hundred and Thirty-One* (Richmond: Printed by Thomas Ritchie, 1831), 9. So far as Floyd himself was concerned, the main import of his message had little to do with Turner's rebellion. The message was directed at the Jackson administration. It was "ultra States Rights," a "bold and strong" assault on the Federal Executive—"a weak and wicked administration to be stopped in its downward career." Charles H. Ambler, *The Life and Diary of John Floyd, Governor of Virginia, an Apostle of Secession, and the Father of the Oregon Country* (Richmond: Richmond Press, 1918), 170, 171 (Diary entries for November 28 and December 2, 1831).
134. See, generally, Ambler, *Life and Diary*, 9–118.
135. *Ibid.*, 86.
136. How to fill the office of governor had been another of the many issues over which the constitutional convention had fought. Western delegates had successfully proposed popular election of the state's governor, and had defended popular election until late in the convention, when the innovation was stripped out in favor of election by joint vote of the two houses of the General Assembly. See *PDVSC*, 464, 821–82.
137. *Journal of the House of Delegates of the Commonwealth of Virginia, Begun and Held at the Capitol, in the City of Richmond, on Monday, the Sixth Day of December, One Thousand Eight Hundred and Thirty* (Richmond: Printed by Thomas Ritchie, 1830), 8, 9. Floyd's sense of urgency speaks of the deep agricultural depression the state had suffered throughout the 1820s. See Haulman, *Virginia and the Panic of 1819*; Thomas Ritchie, Richmond *Enquirer* (March 1, 1828).
138. *Journal of the House of Delegates (1830–31)*, 9 (emphasis added).
139. *Ibid.*, 10. James River improvement had been yet another bone of contention at the constitutional convention: eastern delegates pointed to improvements desired by the west in the western region of the state as evidence of western profligacy and extravagance; western delegates pointed to improvements already made in the eastern region of the state as evidence of eastern hypocrisy—ready as anyone to run the state into debt when it was in their interests to do so. See John Scott, of Fauquier, in *PDVSC* (31 October 1829), 127; William F. Gordon, of Albemarle, in *PDVSC* (November 2, 1829), 143.
140. *Journal of the House of Delegates (1830–31)*, 9, 10.
141. *Ibid.*, 9, 14.
142. *Ibid.*, 14.
143. John Floyd to Colonel W. J. Worth. Commanding 1st Battalion U.S. 2nd Artillery, Norfolk, Virginia, in Tragle, *Southampton Slave Revolt*, 270–72, at 271–72.
144. Antagonism to any assumption of state indebtedness to fund western internal improvements had been one of the main motivations of eastern delegates to the constitutional convention. See John W. Green, of Culpeper, in *PDVSC* (October 27, 1829), 63.

145. John Floyd to James Hamilton Jr. (November 19, 1831), in Tragle, *Southampton Slave Revolt*, 275–76.

146. Although the Norfolk mechanics' petition makes no mention of emancipation, in its antagonism to both the slave and free coloured populations one may think of it as something of a forerunner to this later statewide agitation. On press petitions and memorials, see Root, *All Honor to Jefferson?* 136; Erik S. Root, "Introduction: Something Must be Done," in Root, ed., *Sons of the Fathers* [*VSD*], 1–23, at 5. The notice published in the Richmond *Enquirer* (November 15, 1831) was headed "To the Citizens of Virginia" and signed "A Native of Eastern Virginia." It reads in full: "A memorial is circulating amongst you, the object of which is to call the attention of the ensuing Legislature to the subject of the bond and free coloured population of this State, and to urge upon them the necessity of devising some means by which the blacks may be removed beyond our borders, and by which the number of slaves may be gradually diminished. If it be conceded that this is a subject which demands the exercise of Legislative power, it will not be denied that it ought to be acted on promptly, and that a more auspicious moment for action than the present can never arrive. And if this be admitted, the only question to be decided will be in what form it should be made to approach the Legislature, so as most effectually to secure the adoption of prompt and efficient measures. The form of memorial is deemed objectionable because it carries no authority with it; in ordinary cases it might suffice. But the subject now to be discussed and disposed of, is not of that character, and it is not to be presumed that your representatives without your special instructions, would take one step in a matter of such magnitude, and of so much importance in all its bearings. With a view then to avoid all unnecessary delay, it is proposed that meetings of the qualified voters be held in all the counties in this State, on their respective Court days in December—to deliberate upon this momentous subject, and to give such direction to it, as they in their wisdom may deem advisable."

147. Ambler, *Life and Diary*, 170. Floyd's diary entry for November 21, 1831, begins, "There are still demands for arms in the lower country. I could not have believed there was half the fear amongst the people of the lower country in respect to their slaves." The entry for November 26 notes "I have received more applications for arms." Ambler, *Life and Diary*, 170.

148. *Journal of the House of Delegates (1831-32)*, 10. As indicated in his November 19 letter to South Carolina governor James Hamilton (see above, text at note 145), which as well as mooting the emancipation proposal had given Hamilton advance notice of Floyd's intent to recommend laws that would "confine the Slaves to the estates of their masters—prohibit negroes from preaching—[and] absolutely to drive from the state all free negroes," Floyd's intention was to pursue security measures that would answer the fears provoked by Turner's rebellion, while simultaneously attempting to take advantage of those fears to advance a gradual emancipation plan against the interests of his political adversaries.

149. Ambler, *Life and Diary*, 170.

150. *Ibid.*, 172.

151. *Journal of the House of Delegates (1831-32)*, 10. Floyd's charge of listlessness stemmed from the previous session's failure to pass a loan bill to fund the improvements he had advocated in his December 6, 1830, message. See *Journal of the House of Delegates (1831-32)*, 43 (motion of Mr. Castleman), 157 (motion of Mr. Williams), 206 (motion of Mr Eppes "that the farther consideration of the said bill . . . be indefinitely postponed").

152. *Journal of the House of Delegates (1831-32)*, 10, 11, 13. Somewhat opportunistically, Floyd emphasized not only the "great commercial advantages" to be derived from the improvements he advocated, but also their solution to the present difficulty "of giving [military] aid to one region of the State, by drawing succor from a distance" (11).

153. *Ibid.*, 11.
154. Ambler, *Life and Diary*, 172 (entry for December 26, 1831).
155. *Ibid.* As Floyd's political opportunism underlines, one cannot attribute his zeal for abolition to any concern for the enslaved. So far as he was concerned, the only difference between slavery and freedom was that freed slaves could "wander at large." In all other respects, "They have for years occupied the position of laborers as they have felt nothing of slavery." Floyd to L.N.Q. (20 October 1831) in Ambler, *Life and Diary*, 166 (entry for October 20, 1831).
156. A full list of petitions received (beginning December 6, 1831, and ending February 20, 1832, all but one received before the end of January 1832) appears in appendix B to Eva Sheppard Wolf, *Race and Liberty in the New Nation: Emancipation in Virginia from the Revolution to Nat Turner's Rebellion* (Baton Rouge: Louisiana State University Press, 2006), 242–45. Note also the petition "of sundry inhabitants of the counties of Charles City and New-Kent, complaining of the practice of employing slaves and free negroes as millers in the county mills, and asking the passage of a law compelling the owners of mills to employ white millers" introduced December 27, 1832, by James Dandridge Halyburton, of Charles City and New Kent. *Journal of the House of Delegates (1831-32)*, 56.
157. Wolf, *Race and Liberty*, 242–45. An additional three petitions received sought state aid for colonization efforts, and one opposed any state action on the matter of abolition of slavery.
158. *Ibid.*, 198–206, 245–47.
159. *Ibid.*, 200–202.
160. *Ibid.*, 245–46 (Text A), 242–43 (four petitions). Both the petitions and the subsequent legislative debate showed the influence of the federal census of 1830. Both petitioners and legislators were alarmed by the census's record of rapid growth in Virginia's black population, free and enslaved. See, for example, "The Memorial of the Undersigned Citizens of Hanover County" (December 14, 1831), in *VSD*, 314–17; Samuel McDowell Moore, of Rockbridge (January 11, 1832), in *VSD* 31–35; William H. Brodnax, of Dinwiddie (January 13, 1832), in *VSD*, 78–79; Charles J. Faulkner, of Berkeley (January 14, 1832), in *VSD*, 102–3, 104; Thomas Marshall, of Fauquier (January 14, 1832) in *VSD*, 115–16; William H. Roane, of Hanover (January 16, 1832), in *VSD*, 124–25; George W. Summers, of Kanawha (January 17, 1832), in *VSD*, 155; John C. Campbell, of Brooke (January 23, 1832), in *VSD*, 259, 260–61.
161. Wolf, *Race and Liberty*, 246–47 (Text B), 243 (eleven petitions).
162. *Ibid.*, 207. *Journal of the House of Delegates (1831-32)*, 15. Chaired by William Brodnax, of Dinwiddie, the select committee had thirteen members: ten were from Tidewater and Piedmont counties (Brodnax of Dinwiddie, Cobb of Southampton, Newton of Westmoreland, Roane of Hanover, Fisher of Northampton, Stillman of Fluvanna, Anderson of Nottoway, Brown of Petersburg, Gholson of Brunswick, and Wood of Albemarle); three were from west of the Blue Ridge (Campbell of Brooke, Smith of Frederick, and Moore of Rockbridge). On December 31 Brodnax sought the enlargement of the committee. Eight new members were added: six were from Tidewater and Piedmont counties (Booker of Amelia, Bruce of Halifax, Bryce of Goochland, Marshall of Fauquier, Smith of Gloucester, and Witcher of Pittsylvania); two were from west of the Blue Ridge (Faulkner of Berkeley, and Keller of Washington in the far southwest).
163. *Journal of the House of Delegates (1831-32)*, 29; Wolf, *Race and Liberty*, 208–9.
164. Richmond *Enquirer* (December 17, 1831) reporting House of Delegates debate of December 14. See also the letter from P.Q.O. of Hanover in the Richmond *Enquirer* (December 10, 1831).

165. This was not all it enjoined. The legislature should also "adopt a new and enlightened system of Internal Improvements"; and it should proclaim support for President Jackson in the tariff war. Richmond *Enquirer* (December 20, 1831).
166. Richmond *Enquirer* (January 7, 1832).
167. Ambler, *Life and Diary*, 173 (entries for January 9 and 10, 1832). Floyd added in his January 9 entry: "It has been very adroitly brought about. Summers [Kanawha], Faulkner [Berkeley], Preston [Montgomery] and Berry [Jefferson], also Campbell [Brooke] and Brook[e] [Augusta], will be fast friends to the measure. They are talented young men and will manage this affair most excellently well." As the entry suggests, Floyd was relying on delegates from west and southwest of the Blue Ridge to manage the debate.
168. Richmond *Enquirer* (January 12, 1832); *VSD*, 25.
169. *VSD*, 25.
170. Richmond *Enquirer* (December 10, 1831); Thomas Jefferson to Jared Sparks (February 4, 1824), at http://web.archive.org/web/20110221130257/ and http://etext.lib.virginia.edu/etcbin/toccer-new2?id=JefLett.sgm&images=images/modeng&data=/texts/english/modeng/parsed&tag=public&part=274&division=div1 (last accessed February 22, 2019).
171. A key spur encouraging Randolph to move forward and outlining a strategy for him to do so appears in the form of a letter of December 29, 1831, from Edward Coles, formerly a Virginia slaveholder, sometime private secretary to James Madison, and correspondent of Thomas Jefferson on the subject of gradual emancipation. Coles pressed the grandson toward an initiative that the grandfather had been unwilling to champion. (Coles had left Virginia in 1819 and emancipated his slaves on crossing the Ohio River. As governor of Illinois, 1822–26, he had combatted proslavery interests in that state.) A proponent of colonization, Coles thought slavery's impact on cultivation "wretched and blighting," and African Americans a "pernicious" population, "ignorant, immoral & degraded." Randolph would follow his advice closely. See "Extract of a letter to Th: Jefferson Randolph, Member of the Virginia Legislature, dated Philadelphia, December 29, 1831," in "Letters of Edward Coles," *William and Mary Quarterly* 7, no. 2 (April 1927): 97–113, at 105–7; Louis P. Masur, *1831: Year of Eclipse* (New York: Hill & Wang, 2001), 58–62.
172. See James H. Gholson, of Brunswick (January 12, 1832), in *VSD*, 43.
173. William Goode, of Mecklenburg (January 11, 1832), in *VSD*, 25–27, at 26.
174. Samuel McDowell Moore, of Rockbridge (January 11, 1832), in *VSD*, 27–37, at 36.
175. Philip A. Bolling, of Buckingham (January 11, 1832), in *VSD*, 37–40, at 39, 40.
176. Thomas Jefferson Randolph, of Albemarle (January 11, 1832), in *VSD*, 40–41, at 41; Richmond *Enquirer* (January 19, 1832).
177. Ambler, *Life and Diary*, 173 (entry for January 11, 1832).
178. Forlornly, James Bryce, of Frederick, bade the House leave the matter with the select committee, behind closed doors, but he was more or less alone. See James G. Bryce, of Frederick (January 11, 1832), in *VSD*, 27.
179. Ambler, *Life and Diary*, 174 (entry for January 12, 1832). By "open doors" Floyd meant that the debate would be a public debate on the floor of the House of Delegates rather than secreted in committee.
180. James H. Gholson, of Brunswick (January 12, 1832), in *VSD*, 43–56, at 45, 46, 47, 49, 54–55 (all emphases in original); Richmond *Enquirer* (January 21 and 24, 1832). Gholson, like other slave party spokesmen, held that the debate was damning Virginia in the eyes of other slave states, causing them to consider barring Virginia slaves from the interstate slave trade. Louisiana had already done so; Kentucky, Tennessee, Georgia, Alabama, and the rest would follow (55). Emancipationists argued that in fact

other states were taking steps to shield themselves from the pernicious effects of a constantly expanding slave population, laid bare for all to see by Turner's rebellion. See Samuel McDowell Moore, of Rockbridge (January 11, 1832), in *VSD*, 27–37, at 35; William B. Preston, of Montgomery (January 16, 1832), in *VSD*, 134–40, at 139.

181. William M. Rives, of Campbell (January 12, 1832), in *VSD*, 56–60, at 58.
182. William H. Brodnax, of Dinwiddie (January 13, 1832), in *VSD*, 61–86, at 63, 66 (emphasis in original), 79.
183. Whether it was an "evil," however, had been challenged. See, for example, William Daniel Jr., of Campbell (January 14, 1832), in *VSD*, 95–99, at 97 (emphasis added): "You may prove, *if you can*, that slavery is immoral, unjust, and unnatural, that it originated in avarice and cruelty, that it is an evil and a curse, and you still do not convince me that our slaves are not property, and as such, protected by our Constitution." See also James H. Gholson, of Brunswick (January 12, 1832), in *VSD*, 49.
184. William H. Brodnax, of Dinwiddie (January 13, 1832), in *VSD*, 67, 68: "Is not the probability of increase, an essential constituent in the value of a female slave? Does not this prospect enter into the calculation of value, whenever one is purchased, or sold?"
185. *Journal of the House of Delegates (1831-32)*, 99.
186. See above, text at notes 48–49.
187. Charles J. Faulkner, of Berkeley (January 14, 1832), in *VSD*, 99–112, at 106, 107, 108 (emphasis in original).
188. Ambler, *Life and Diary*, 174 (entry for January 15, 1832).
189. Following Brodnax's speech on January 13, debate on the slave party side was dominated by members of the select committee, all of whom spoke in support of Brodnax's position. See Thomas Marshall, of Fauquier (January 14, 1832) in *VSD*, 112–18, William H. Roane, of Hanover (January 16, 1832), in *VSD*, 121–26, and Rice W. Wood, of Albemarle (January 16, 1832), in *VSD*, 126–34.
190. See, for example, William Daniel Jr., of Campbell, above, note 183. Rice Wood, of Albemarle (January 16, 1832), in *VSD*, 130, spoke of his "regret and surprise that many of the sons of our common mother [Virginia] believe her *fallen*—yes, some have said *degraded—degraded* because man holds his fellow man in slavery!" He believed "that the African was as much indebted to the master as the master to him. The obligation was mutual—they had reciprocal duties to discharge, and the debt of gratitude was mutual. The master loved the faithful slave, and in turn the faithful slave loved the master" (emphasis in original).
191. Bryce's preamble read as follows: "Profoundly sensible of the great evils arising from the condition of the colored population of this Commonwealth: induced by humanity as well as policy to an immediate effort for the removal, in the first place, as well of those who are now free, as of such as may hereafter become free: believing that this effort, while it is in just accordance with the sentiments of the community on the subject, will absorb all our present means; and that a further action for the removal of the slaves should await a more definite development of public opinion: *Resolved, &c.*" Richmond *Enquirer* (January 17, 1832). The amendment was withdrawn on the understanding that its addition might be debated by the House prior to final action on the report.
192. Richmond *Enquirer* (January 17, 1832).
193. *Journal of the House of Delegates (1831-32)*, 99.
194. William B. Preston, of Montgomery (January 16, 1832), in *VSD*, 134–40, at 138 (emphasis in original), 139, 140. Preston estimated Virginia's decennial exportation of slaves at 85,000.
195. Alexander G. Knox, of Mecklenburg (January 17, 1832), in *VSD*, 141–49, at 141, 147–48. Both the inevitability of subordination in human society, and the inevitability of state division should eastern property rights in human capital not be respected, were

themes familiar from the Virginia state convention, notably from Benjamin Watkins Leigh. See above, notes 51 and 56–57, and accompanying text.

196. John T. Brown, of the town of Petersburg (January 18, 1832) in *VSD*, 169–84, at 174–75, 178, 179.

Brown's speech is also significant, as were others delivered by the slave party, in seeking to minimize Turner's rebellion: "The tragedy of Southampton, is held up to our view as an argument that admits of no refutation, and is sufficient to outweigh any conclusions to which our minds might be brought by reason and reflection. It was indeed an appalling occurrence—not from its importance or consequences—but from the deep-toned atrocity that characterized it. Yet, it has happened only once, in the course of near sixty years, which have elapsed since we became an independent people. And is this solitary calamity—so brief and rare—to change the whole tenor of our lives and uplift the very foundations of society? To allow a single disaster to outweigh the long security of years would be as absurd as to deduce the principles of philosophy from the eccentricities of nature, instead of her customary habits. All that human wisdom can do is to calculate the chances of evil, and abide by that which is comparatively remote. Vesuvius labors, perhaps, once in a century, and cities are buried under its burning lava. Yet the peasant who dwells at its foot feels a comfortable sense of security" (183–84). See also William H. Brodnax, of Dinwiddie (January 13, 1832), in *VSD*, 76: a "danger . . . entirely of a temporary character" (Brodnax was also reported by several others to have called the rebellion "a petty affair." See, for example, Charles J. Faulkner, of Berkeley (January 14, 1832), in *VSD*, 111). See also James H. Gholson, of Brunswick (January 12, 1832), in *VSD*, 46: "alarm and excitement have subsided . . . society is restored to its ordinary current and repose"; Rice W. Wood, of Albemarle (January 16, 1832), in *VSD*, 129: "a tale of fancy has been created . . . which may do very well to frighten naughty children"; John E. Shell, of Brunswick (January 19, 1832), in *VSD*, 203: the Southampton insurrection was a "single isolated" incident in which (referencing the final confrontation at Dr. Blunt's) the "mighty General, and his *formidable* army" had been demolished and overthrown by "*three men and two boys*" (emphasis in original); William O. Goode, of Mecklenburg (January 24, 1832), in *VSD*, 277: "This momentary feeling; this evanescent excitement." As Thomas Marshall, of Fauquier, commented (January 14, 1832), in *VSD*, 116, "Gentlemen assure us that the danger of insurrection has blown over—that the massacre of Southampton was a small affair." So too Samuel M. Garland, of Amherst (January 18, 1832), in *VSD*, 189: "The melancholy catastrophe in Southampton has been called a little affair." The slave party's minimization of the rebellion was of a piece with its claim that the debate itself was the real threat to Virginia's interests, endangering the state's free and unrestricted access to domestic slave markets. See above, note 180 and accompanying text.

197. William O. Goode, of Mecklenburg (January 24, 1832), in *VSD*, 279.

198. Freehling, *Drift*, 155.

199. Thomas J. Randolph, of Albemarle (January 20, 1832), in *VSD*, 215–224, at 216, 217, 223; see also *Speech of Thomas J. Randolph, in the House of Delegates of Virginia, on the Abolition of Slavery* (Richmond: Printed by Samuel Shepherd & Co., 1832); Coles to Randolph (December 29, 1831), in "Letters of Edward Coles," at 106: "It is well known that a great number have been annually sent out of the State [by] . . . owners of estates whose chief profit arose from rearing & selling slaves to the cotton & sugar planters of the South."

200. Ambler, *Life and Diary*, 174 (entry for January 20, 1832).

201. James McDowell, of Rockbridge (January 21, 1832), in *VSD*, 233–54, at 241–42 (emphasis in original).

202. James D. Halyburton, of Charles City and New Kent (January 23, 1832), in *VSD*, 255.

203. Ambler, *Life and Diary*, 174–75.

204. William O. Goode, of Mecklenburg (January 24, 1832), in *VSD*, 285. See Alexander G. Knox, of Mecklenburg (17 January 1832), in *VSD*, 148; John E. Shell, of Brunswick (January 19, 1832), in *VSD*, 209.
205. *Journal of the House of Delegates (1831–32)*, 109 (January 25, 1832).
206. *Ibid.*
207. *Ibid.*, 110 (January 25, 1832). Ambler, *Life and Diary*, 175 (entry for January 25). In fact, debate resumed on the topic of colonization. On January 27 William Brodnax, of Dinwiddie, introduced proposals from the select committee for compulsory colonization of free people of color. The proposals were debated on February 6 and 7 and rejected in favor of voluntary colonization of free people and mandatory colonization of manumitted slaves. See Freehling, *Drift*, 177–83.
208. Ambler, *Life and Diary*, 175 (entry for January 25). Floyd elaborated in a later entry: "Goode, of Mecklenburgh, said to me the day the debate closed upon the 'slave question' as it was called, that the Eastern and Western people were not at all the same people, that they were essentially a different people, that they did not think alike, feel alike, and had no interests in common, that a separation of the State must ensue, and rather than have the subject of abolition again debated he would be glad for a separation." See Ambler, *Life and Diary*, 177 (entry for February 3).
209. *Journal of the House of Delegates (1831–32)*, 131 (February 3, 1832); Richmond *Enquirer* (February 4, 1832).
210. *Journal of the House of Delegates (1831–32)*, 131–32 (February 3, 1832), and compare 109–10 (January 25, 1832).
211. Ambler, *Life and Diary*, 177 (entry for February 3). Following the defeat of the second resolution, Joseph C. Cabell, of Nelson, submitted a resolution calling for the incorporation of a James River and Kanawha River company to improve the line of navigation between the James and the Ohio and assume ownership of existing improvements already undertaken at state expense. Sixty percent of the corporation's capital stock was to be raised by private subscription, and 40 percent subscribed by the state, whose stake was to include stock issued to the value of the transferred assets. *Journal of the House of Delegates (1831–32)*, 132 (February 3, 1832). "The General Assembly are now devising a law to give up the public improvements finished by the State into the hand of individual companies" Floyd observed—a final dagger in the back of his hopes. Ambler, *Life and Diary*, 178 (entry for February 7). The House agreed to Cabell's resolution on February 10. *Journal of the House of Delegates (1831–32)*, 142 (February 10, 1832).
212. Richmond *Enquirer* (February 4, 1832), subsequently published as *The Letter of Appomatox to the People of Virginia*.
213. *Letter of Appomatox*, 4, 6, 7 (emphasis in original), 11, 14, 18–20, 22.
214. *Ibid.*, 21–22, 46.
215. *Ibid.*, 27 (emphasis in original).
216. *Ibid.*, 13, 14, 24–25.
217. *Ibid.*, 28 (emphasis in original).
218. Ambler, *Life and Diary*, 178–206. Thus, Floyd took no obvious notice of the only legislation the legislature actually passed in regard to the state's African American population—bans on African American preaching, controls on slave movement and assembly, and harsh restrictions on the legal status of free people of color (trials transferred to the courts of oyer and terminer in cases of larceny and felony; prohibitions on gun ownership; restrictions on the purchase of slaves by free blacks). Wolf, *Race and Liberty*, 233, and see generally 229–33.
219. "Professor of History, Metaphysics, and Political Law," is how Dew identifies himself on the title page of his *Review of the Debate*, and of his *Lectures on the Restrictive System, Delivered to the Senior Political Class of William and Mary College* (Richmond: Printed by

Samuel Shepherd & Co., 1829). His full title at William and Mary was "Professor of History, Metaphysics, Natural and National Law, Government, and Political Economy." See Lowell Harrison, "Thomas Roderick Dew: Philosopher of the Old South," *Virginia Magazine of History and Biography* 57, no. 4 (October 1949): 390–404, at 391. In the "Preface" to the *Lectures*, dated September 14, 1829, Dew disclaims attachment to any party or political position. "I have wished as far as possible to avoid mingling in the politics of the day, being convinced it is the great duty of the Professor to inculcate upon the mind of the Student those general principles alone, which may form the basis of his future opinions and actions" (iv). Insofar as the *Lectures* revealed Dew's personal opinions on matters of contemporary moment (suffrage extension, taxation, slavery), however, they were largely those of eastern Virginia. See below, notes 283 and 286.

220. Floyd and Dew were acquainted, and Floyd was well aware of Dew's support for his advocacy of internal improvements, which Dew expressed in a series of articles published in the Richmond *Enquirer* (December 30, 1831–January 19, 1832). See Stephen S. Mansfield, *Thomas Roderick Dew: Defender of the Southern Faith* (Ph.D. Diss., University of Virginia, 1968), 48–51; Ambler, *Life and Diary*, 167 (entry for October 24, 1831). In his commentary, Ambler notes (92) that Floyd wrote to Dew in April 1832, "inviting his attention to the subjects of slavery and abolition as set forth in the debates of the Assembly of 1831–1832."

221. Thomas Roderick Dew, "Abolition of Negro Slavery," *The American Quarterly Review* 12, no. 23 (September 1832): 189–265.

222. Thomas R. Dew, "Preface," in Dew, *Review of the Debate*.

223. *Ibid.* Dew's *Review* was also published unabridged in Duff Green's Washington-based *Political Register* 2, no. 25 (October 16, 1833), 769–831.

224. Drew Gilpin Faust, "Introduction," in Drew Gilpin Faust, editor, *The Ideology of Slavery: Proslavery Thought in the Antebellum South, 1830-1860* (Baton Rouge: Louisiana State University Press, 1981), 8–9; Eugene D. Genovese, *Western Civilization through Slaveholding Eyes: The Social and Historical Thought of Thomas Roderick Dew* (New Orleans: The Graduate School of Tulane University, 1986), 1, 5–6. But see also below, notes 284–89 and accompanying text. For an examination of Dew's place in the development of an affirmative antebellum Southern jurisprudence of slavery "based on economics, religious teachings, and empirical observation," see Alfred L. Brophy, *University, Court, and Slave: Pro-slavery Thought in Southern Colleges and Courts and the Coming of the Civil War* (Oxford: Oxford University Press, 2016), xix, 34–47.

225. In the process of composition Dew drew liberally on both the House debates, published in the Richmond newspapers and also in the form of pamphlets published by debate participants, and on Benjamin Watkins Leigh's *Letter of Appomatox*. His stadialist history was of a piece with his political economy, which, as Genovese writes in *Western Civilization*, at 4, "self-consciously followed the Scottish Enlightenment." Dew's political economy was classical in the tradition of Adam Smith, but deeply influenced by Smith's English revisers, David Ricardo and Thomas Malthus. The influence of Ricardian comparative advantage theory, for example, persuaded Dew to reject Smith's reliance on home trade preference in analyzing efficient allocation of labor and capital. For stadialism in the Scottish Enlightenment, see Adam Smith, *Lectures on Jurisprudence*, R. L. Meek, D. D. Raphael, and P. G. Stein, editors (Indianapolis: Liberty Fund, 1982), 14–16; Parker, *Legal Thought before Modernism*, 50–57. For Dew on Ricardo and Smith, see his *Lectures on the Restrictive System*, 14–19. Michael O'Brien, who writes of Dew as "a sort of bourgeois accountant, a man in a black frock-coat who . . . [kept] the books for an irregular world," identifies the University of Edinburgh's William Robertson as the principal influence on Dew's theory of history, no doubt because the *Review of the Debate* cites Robertson by name on twenty occasions in its text and several more in its notes. See Michael O'Brien, *Conjectures of Order: Intellectual Life and*

the American South, 1810-1860 (Chapel Hill: University of North Carolina Press, 2004), 2:943, 946. For Robertson's relationship to the Scottish Enlightenment's conjectural history and political economy, see Poovey, *A History of the Modern Fact*, 215, 219–26. For additional sources influencing Dew's proslavery arguments, see Brophy, *University, Court, and Slave*, 40–41.

226. Here Dew was restating and improving on arguments made three years earlier at the state constitutional convention by Benjamin Watkins Leigh and Abel Upshur (see above, notes 56, 57, and 86, and accompanying text). Here too we see the influence of David Ricardo, notably Ricardo's argument that "the natural price of labour is that price which is necessary to enable the labourers, one with another, to subsist and perpetuate their race, without either increase or diminution." David Ricardo, *On the Principles of Political Economy, and Taxation* (London: John Murray, 1817), 90. Ricardo, of course, was addressing wages, but his reasoning could as easily be applied (as Dew did) to the "price" (subsistence) of slave labor accruing to the slaveholder in a production function. Ricardo also distinguishes natural price from market price—"the price which is really paid for [labour] from the natural operation of the proportion of the supply to the demand" (91)—but here too Ricardo's reasoning was applicable to markets for slave labor as a factor of production. Thus Dew could (and did) fashion arguments for the fungibility of labor from the political economy of an abolitionist. For the centrality of Ricardo's *Principles* to "the framework within which mainstream political economists worked" on both sides of the Atlantic for the next half century, see Sklansky, *The Soul's Economy*, 79.
227. Dew, *Review of the Debate*, 106.
228. *Ibid.*, 5.
229. *Ibid.*, 5.
230. *Ibid.*, 6, 7 (emphasis in original), 8. From the outset, Dew frames the abolition debate as the slave party had in the legislature—a completely irrational response to a momentary disorder. See above, note 196.
231. *Ibid.*, 64. Ironically, three years earlier John Randolph had assailed the state convention for considering the imposition of minimum age requirements on state senators (30 years) and delegates (24): "Sir, who ever heard a whisper, *ab urbe condita* to this day, that the Senators of Virginia were too youthful? I never heard such a sentiment in my life. And in the House of Delegates, what man ever heard that the members . . . were too young?" John Randolph, of Charlotte, in *PDVSC* (November 14, 1829), 313. See also Thomas M. Bayly, of Accomack, in *PDVSC* (November 26, 1829), 462: "Has a single or solitary instance been quoted, where the Commonwealth has received any injury from the very numerous number of young men of great merit and promise, which the people, the freeholders, have introduced into their two Houses of General Assembly?"
232. *Ibid.*, 9–46.
233. *Ibid.*, 9, 10.
234. Thus, the last lines of the pamphlet: "Let us reflect on these things, and learn wisdom from experience: and know that the relations of society, generated by the *lapse of ages*, cannot be altered in a *day*." *Ibid.*, 130 (emphasis in original).
235. *Ibid.*, 28.
236. This is both classic stadialism (see above, note 225) and Lockean political philosophy. See John Locke, *Second Treatise of Government*, C. B. McPherson, editor (Indianapolis: Hackett, 1980), 18–30 (chapter V, "Of Property").
237. Dew, *Review of the Debate*, 13.
238. *Ibid.*, 18–19 (citing Grotius, Pufendorf, Rutherforth, Bynkershoek, Vattel, and Locke). See also Tomlins, *Freedom Bound*, 420–23, and see also 372–73, 434–35.

239. Blackstone "denies the right to make prisoners of war slaves; for he says we had no right to enslave unless we had the right to kill, and we had no right to kill, unless 'in cases of absolute necessity, for self-defence; and it is plain this absolute necessity did not subsist, since the victor did not actually kill him, but made him prisoner.'" Blackstone, says Dew, speaks here "of slavery in its pure unmitigated form, 'whereby an unlimited power is given to the master over the life and fortune of the slave.'" But slavery in this form—essentially a continuance of a state of war—existed almost nowhere. Moreover, Blackstone misunderstood the nature of the justification for slavery in law of nations civilian writing on the law of war, it being well-established there that slaughter of captives in war arises not from "absolute necessity" but from retaliation (*lex talionis*). Enslavement of captives, hence, was the law of war's means to avoid atrocity. Dew, *Review of the Debate*, 19, citing St. George Tucker's edition of Blackstone's *Commentaries on the Laws of England* (Philadelphia: William Young Birch and Abraham Small, 1803), 2:423.
240. Dew, *Review of the Debate*, 20, 21.
241. "Call them by what name you please." *Ibid.*, 21 (emphasis in original).
242. *Ibid.*, 22. So powerful was the predilection to accumulate, Dew observed, that he was inclined to assign habits of property priority over the customs of war in the production of slavery. See also Genovese, *Western Civilization*, 6.
243. Dew, *Review of the Debate*, 23.
244. *Ibid.*, 24.
245. *Ibid.*, 25, 26. Here one sees Dew assimilating slavery to a transaction, precisely as Nathaniel Beverly Tucker would two years later (see above, text at note 8). In the "impure" slavery of real life, labor was the pragmatic quid pro quo of the master's protection and provision. As we have seen, this was also Governor Floyd's view. See above, note 155. On the political economy of subsistence, see above, note 226.
246. *Ibid.*, 26–27.
247. *Ibid.*, 27. The correctness of Dew's observation was confirmed by contemporary law and, thirty-five years later, by the Thirteenth Amendment's "convicted criminal" exception. See Dayan, *The Law Is a White Dog*, 58–69.
248. Dew, *Review of the Debate*; 27.
249. *Ibid.*, 28, 29, 29–36, 36. On the "escape from drudgery" see Shore, *Southern Capitalists*, 17–18 (referencing Edmund Ruffin). Here, Dew is responding to "the dire implications of Ricardian [and Malthusian] economics" for the generation and distribution of wealth by representing slavery as a means of escape into white plenitude. Henry Carey would soon begin a career dedicated in like fashion to the development of a "positive" political economy of abundance from America's unique factor endowments. See Sklansky, *The Soul's Economy*, 7, 83, 80–89. For Southern successors of Dew, notably Henry Hughes and George Fitzhugh, see Sklansky, 6–7, 93–103.
250. Dew, *Review of the Debate*, 38, 39.
251. *Ibid.*, 39–46, 46 (emphasis in original). British responsibility for the slave trade, and for slavery in Virginia, had been a common refrain of the abolition debate. See, for example, James H. Gholson, of Brunswick (January 12, 1832), in *VSD*, 49. As we have seen, it had also been heard during the state convention. See above, chapter 5, text at notes 15–16. For additional examples, see Samuel McDowell Moore, of Rockbridge, in *PDVSC* (November 6, 1829), 226; William B. Giles (Governor), of Amelia, in *PDVSC* (November 10, 1829), 248.
252. Dew, *Review of the Debate*, 46. As we have seen, the slave party's assault on abstraction had been a common feature of both the state convention representation and suffrage debates and the legislature's abolition debate. For examples, see above text at notes 47–49, and 195, 201.

253. *Ibid.*, 47–48. These were the figures generally used and accepted during the abolition debate. See, for example, Alexander G. Knox, of Mecklenburg (January 17, 1832), in *VSD*, 142. Dew is allowing a 30,000 increase in slave population 1830–32, which is in excess of his estimate of increase in the state's entire black population of 6,000 p.a. (48).
254. Dew, *Review of the Debate*, 48. Dew's valuation was from 1817 (see *PDVSC*, 178). See also John T. Brown, of the town of Petersburg (January 18, 1832) in *VSD*, 170. Others during the state convention debates estimated current land values at less than half their 1817 valuation—$90 million—and total capitalization of slave labor at $67.5 million (see *PDVSC*, 625). It is likely the 1817 valuation was a reasonable approximation of 1832 values. John Majewski argues that land values in the Piedmont between 1819 and 1838 were essentially stagnant. See John Majewski, *A House Dividing: Economic Development in Pennsylvania and Virginia before the Civil War* (Cambridge: Cambridge University Press, 2000), 17–18.
255. Dew, *Review of the Debate*, 48.
256. *Ibid.*, 48. Again this was a figure commonly used in the legislative debate. See William H. Brodnax, of Dinwiddie (January 13, 1832), in *VSD*, 80–81 (6,000); Thomas Marshall, of Fauquier (January 14, 1832) in *VSD*, 117 (6,000). It was, however, at variance with Dew's estimate of a 30,000 increase in slave population 1830–32. Later in the pamphlet Dew offers a third possible variation, estimating a slave population birth rate of 20,000 per annum but offering no mortality estimate (63).
257. Dew, *Review of the Debate*, 48–49. Recall that Governor Floyd's reported state treasury surplus for 1831 was $106,000. See above, text at note 152.
258. *Ibid.*, 49–50 (emphasis in original), 62, 64.
259. *Ibid.*, 51.
260. *Ibid.*, 52.
261. *Ibid.*, 54, 55, 56–57. Dew variously estimated white emigration to be between 1,000 and 2,000 per annum (61), and more than 3,000 (121).
262. *Ibid.*, 57 ("When one is torn away, another succeeds." Virgil, *Aeneid*, VI, line 143). As James Oakes observes, "The novelty of Dew's argument against colonization was his Malthusian analysis of the problem." See James Oakes, "Bourgeois Critique of Slavery," 34, 36–37.
263. Dew, *Review of the Debate*, 62, 63 (emphasis in original). For the same critique of government, see *Letter of Appomatox*, 14 ("There is not a man that ever bestowed a thought upon such subjects, who does not know, that property in the hands of the public, is worse managed, and more unprofitable, than property of the like kind in the hands of individuals; and slave property let out to hire under the management of public agents, having no other interest than to enhance to the utmost, the expenses of their agency, will be peculiarly unproductive.")
264. Dew, *Review of the Debate*, 64, 66, 68, 69.
265. *Ibid.*, 81.
266. *Ibid.*, 82, 85, 86. Here Dew echoes Floyd's "ultra States Rights" politics. See above, note 133.
267. *Ibid.*, 87.
268. *Ibid.*, 87 (emphasis in original), 88.
269. *Ibid.*, 93–94.
270. *Ibid.*, 97–99, 98 (emphasis in original).
271. *Ibid.*, 105. See also 54. Dew's reference here, of course, is to Mary Wollstonecraft Shelley, *Frankenstein, or, The Modern Prometheus* (London: Printed for Lackington, Hughes, Harding, Mayor, & Jones, 1818).
272. *Ibid.*, 106, 107.
273. *Ibid.*, 106–8.

274. *Ibid.*, 111, 112, 113.
275. *Ibid.*, 126. This meant that the English laborer was superior to the slave, the Irish no more than the slave's equal, the Spanish and Italian inferior.
276. *Ibid.*, 127–29.
277. *Ibid.*, 126. Dew would underline his conviction of the "blessings [of slavery] in southern latitudes" in correspondence with William H. Harrison of Amelia County. See Thomas Dew, Williamsburg, Virginia to William H. Harrison, principal of the Academy at the Wigwam in Amelia, Virginia (18 October 1837), in Series 1, Folder 4, *Office of the President: Thomas Roderick Dew Records, 1830-1967*, Swem Library, Special Collections, College of William & Mary.
278. *Ibid.*, 126. One should recall, however, that earlier Dew had explained that slavery was introduced to Virginia because it suited the Chesapeake's "sultry" and "warm" climate, "so congenial to the African constitution" (39).
279. *Ibid.*, 119, 120.
280. *Ibid.*, 120, 121 (emphasis in original).
281. *Ibid.*, 121, 122.
282. *Ibid.*, 123 (emphasis in original).
283. *Ibid.*, 124 (emphasis in original). Dew's endorsement of a "judicious" system of internal improvements (122) took the particular form of praise for the Virginia Legislature's incorporation of the James River and Kanawha Company, which he though "almost certain of success" (123). We have already noted (above, note 211) that the company's incorporation came at the expense of (and unaccompanied by) legislative support for direct state investment in improvements in the form of state borrowing. In Dew's system, "judicious" meant private investment, not public investment underwritten by taxation. Like the tariff, he argued, the history of internal improvements in America was "a melancholy exemplification" of the distortions of rational allocation of resources induced by government. *Lectures on the Restrictive System*, 176. See also 183 (attacking the injustice of "taxes laid on a minority by a majority, secured by a combination of sectional interests.")
284. Genovese, *Western Civilization*, 1. See also above, note 224.
285. In fact, evidence of such a "turn" had been bubbling up throughout the 1820s. See, for example, Edwin C. Holland, *A Refutation of the Calumnies Circulated Against the Southern & Western States, Respecting the Institution and Existence of Slavery Among Them. To Which is Added, a Minute and Particular Account of the Actual State and Condition of Their Negro Population . . . By a South-Carolinian* (Charleston: Printed by A. E. Miller, 1822), and works cited by Brophy, *University, Court, and Slave*, 41, and 306–7, notes 100–109. In Virginia, the structural conditions for such a turn had been set in place by the War of 1812. See Taylor, *The Internal Enemy*, 4–10; Irons, *Origins of Proslavery Christianity*, 87–90. James Oakes has argued that a "bourgeois critique" stressing that slavery was an economic evil, "intrinsically inferior to free labor" and damaging to agriculture, had attained near consensus by the late eighteenth century and would maintain intellectual sway "among leading Americans" through the early 1830s. See Oakes, "Bourgeois Critique," 34, 36–37. See also Shore, *Southern Capitalists*, 24. Certainly evidence of this critique can be found in both the Virginia State Convention debates and in the House of Delegates' gradual emancipation debate. See, for example, above, text at note 42, text at note 164, text at notes 174–76, also above chapter 5, text at notes 14–16. But in Virginia at least the prevalence of the bourgeois critique is challenged by evidence of deep proslavery sentiment. See Fredrika Teute Schmidt and Barbara Ripel Wilhelm, "Early Proslavery Petitions in Virginia," *William and Mary Quarterly* 30, no. 1 (1973): 133–46 (discussing petitions submitted to the October 1784 and 1785 sessions of the Virginia legislature in opposition to Revolutionary era antislavery agitation). We have also seen that proslavery "positive good" sentiments were distinctly in evidence in the

House of Delegates' debate. One may conclude that Dew materially *advanced* "positive good" arguments by theorizing (intellectualizing) them before a national audience in a scientific language, but not that his essay invented those arguments.

286. There is evidence to this effect in Dew's *Lectures on the Restrictive System*, which considered that in a nation composed of 500,000 freemen and 500,000 slaves, were the population considered to amount to a million individuals then slavery would have to be considered disadvantageous, because the economic benefits to the 500,000 freemen from the labor of the 500,000 slaves could never outweigh the costs to the latter. "But if you throw [the slaves] entirely out of the estimate, and suppose only the 500,000 freemen to compose the nation, slavery might be advantageous to such a country, in an economical point of view, and this is the light in which I am now considering the subject. . . . The happiness, rights, &c. of the slave, are in this case supposed to be merged completely in those of the master" (10). See also 153–55 (warning both of the dangers of "*esprit de corps*"—collective consciousness—bred by the massing of operatives in manufacturing districts, and of their vulnerability to manipulation by their employers in elections. Dew's publication of this observation coincided with the Virginia suffrage debate).

287. The views of government that Dew brought to his *Review of the Debate* are well on display in his *Lectures on the Restrictive System*. "The vigilant eye of government is not required to watch over any of the departments of industry." Costs of production regulated price, and demand regulated supply; "the proper application of labour and capital" adjusted accordingly (5). Men were governed by their interests; government could not know any man's interest better than he did himself; it could not produce "a better employment" of labor and capital than was produced by the sum of individual allocations. Interest alone accounted for "the immense improvements which we witness in the world" (7). Government's sphere was to secure the individual from crime and aggression, not "procure for us any positive good" (8). Government that exceeded its designated sphere "becomes a *usurper*" (180 emphasis in original).

288. Dew, *Lectures on the Restrictive System*, 153, and see also 156: "There is nothing in the employment of manufactures, which should cause us to wish their premature introduction. On the contrary, there are evils attendant on them, which under an equal choice of labour, would lead us to prefer agriculture. Better far, therefore, that we should leave every department of industry to itself. Manufactures will arise when our country is filled up with a denser population, and capital has been more extensively accumulated. They are necessary then to keep in lucrative employ the redundant capital and population, and they will arise without the guardian protection of the Legislature."

289. Dew, *Review of the Debate*, 130: "The power of man has limits, and he should never attempt impossibilities. . . . The deep and solid foundations of society, cannot be broken up by the vain *fiat* of the legislator" (130, emphasis in original). We might contrast Dew's secular evasion of "impossibility" to Turner's faithful embrace of "impracticability." See above, chapter 5 note 2.

290. See, for example, William Daniel Jr., of Campbell (January 14, 1832), in *VSD*, 98: "We have already struck a chord, which may vibrate with the most fearful discord throughout this Commonwealth for some time to come"; John C. Campbell, of Brooke (January 23, 1832), in *VSD*, 255: "We were shorn of our rights . . . under the [plea] of necessary protection for this same slave property, the freemen of the West suffered a political disenfranchisement."

291. Abel P. Upshur, of Northampton, in *PDVSC* (October 28, 1829), 75.

292. "Destroy agriculture, destroy tillage, and the ruin of the farmer will draw down ruin upon the mechanic, the merchant, the sailor, and the manufacturer—they must all flee together from the land of desolation." Dew, *Review of the Debate*, 68, 69.

293. *Ibid.*, 124.
294. Majewski, *A House Dividing*, 3; Goodrich, "Virginia System," 366–69, indicates a significant upswing in state commitments to internal improvements beginning around 1833.
295. Majewski, *A House Dividing*, 8–11, 12–36, 59–70, 124–40.
296. Richmond *Enquirer* (January 10, 1854), quoted in Majewski, *A House Dividing*, 131, and see generally 124–40.
297. Goodrich, "Virginia System," 367 (table 1), 371–74; Majewski, *A House Dividing*, 131.
298. Majewski, *A House Dividing*, 136 (table 5.4), 136–38.
299. Dew, *Review of the Debate*, 61; Phillips, *Life and Labor*, 177 (Virginia slave prices bottomed at $400, 1825–29, before beginning their climb toward $1100 in 1836–37); John C. Campbell, of Brooke (January 23, 1832), in *VSD*, 259.
300. William B. Preston, of Montgomery (January 16, 1832), in *VSD*, 139; Henry Berry, of Jefferson (20 January 1832), in *VSD*, 230; John C. Campbell, of Brooke (January 23, 1832), in VSD, 259; Thomas Marshall, of Fauquier (January 14, 1832) in *VSD*, 116.
301. Thomas J. Randolph, of Albemarle (January 20, 1832), in *VSD*, 215–24, at 221, 223. Randolph apparently preferred to sweat his labor rather than sell it. John Majewski cites him as an example of a slaveholder "ambitious . . . to squeeze out the last ounce of toil and labor." See Majewski, *A House Dividing*, 71–72.
302. Figures are from Michael Tadman, *Speculators and Slaves: Masters, Traders, and Slaves in the Old South* (Madison: University of Wisconsin Press, 1989), 12 (table 2.1). The estimate is based on comparing the "share" of the total increase in southern state slave populations attributable to Virginia with the actual increase in the state's slave population recorded by the census. The difference between the two figures is held to be the sum of forced departures. This is the method used in Frederic Bancroft's classic study, *Slave Trading in the Old South* (1931; reprint New York: Frederick Ungar, 1959), see 382–86. For an assessment of Tadman's methodology, and a valuable analysis of recent scholarship on domestic slave trading, see Richard Bell, "The Great Jugular Vein of Slavery: New Histories of the Domestic Slave Trade," *History Compass* 11/12 (2013): 1150–64.

The method assumes that all slave state populations shared the same decennial rate of natural increase, and hence could properly be inferred to be growing at the same rate as the overall slave population: 31.2 percent between 1820 and 1830; 23.8 percent 1830–40; 27.8 percent 1840–50; and 23.4 percent 1850–60. Birth and death statistics were collected by the census in 1850 (the only census year slave population vital statistics were collected), but are considered unreliable. If one were to assume consistency in the methodology of their collection (i.e., that their inaccuracies are consistent), 1850's vital statistics would indicate that Virginia had one of the lowest rates of natural increase of all southern state slave populations. Only Louisiana, with a negative rate of increase, was lower. If one adjusts the "share" of the total increase in southern state slave populations attributable to each state according to the state's 1850 rate of natural increase, weighted by the state's population at the beginning of each decade, Virginia is estimated to have accounted for 18.10 percent of total population increase in 1820–30 (88,299); 14.97 percent in 1830–40 (72,196); 11.71 percent in 1840–50 (77,353, omitting Texas); and 9.63 percent in 1850–60 (72,239). These estimates of attributable increase translate into the following lower-bound forced departure estimates: 1820–30, 42,478; 1830–40, 90,279; 1840–50, 52,410; 1850–60, 52,401.

The method I have adopted obviously does not provide any measure of the local or intrastate slave trade. However, county-level census data do allow one to compare the dynamics of regional populations within states. It is likely that the intrastate trade was at least as high as the interstate trade, and probably substantially higher.

See Thomas Russell, "South Carolina's Largest Slave Auctioneering Firm," *Chicago-Kent Law Review* 68 (1993): 1241–82, and "Articles Sell Best Singly: The Disruption of Slave Families at Court Sales," *Utah Law Review* 4 (1996): 1161–1209.

303. Using a similar method to that described above (note 302), but different rates of natural increase, Charles Irons estimates an annual average of 3,500 slaves sold or sent out of the state in the 1810s, 3,000 in the 1820s, 10,000 in the 1830s, and 6,000 in the 1840s and 1850s. See Irons, *Origins of Proslavery Christianity*, 125, 304–5n86.

304. On slave and cotton price movements, see Phillips, *Life and Labor*, 177 ("Prices of Slaves in Four Markets and of Cotton at New York, 1795–1860"). On Virginia's crop price movements and the relative prosperity of its agricultural economy, see Majewski, *A House Dividing*, 2, 17–25, 68–72, 166–67.

305. See John J. Clegg, "Capitalism and Slavery," *Critical Historical Studies* 2, no. 2 (2015): 281–304. Adopting Robert Brenner's definition of capitalism as generalized market dependence, Clegg comments, "Insofar as it is capable of being either hired or purchased slave labor is like any other capitalist commodity. The presence of a specialized class of slave traders in the antebellum South ensured that slave markets were exceptionally liquid. Evidence of their allocative efficiency can be found in the estimated net transfer, from 1820 to 1860, of more than half a million slaves from the less productive plantations of the Old South to the more productive plantations in the New South via the domestic slave trade alone." He concludes, "there is something pristinely capitalist about the total commodification of labor under slavery" (301–2).

306. John C. Campbell, of Brooke (January 23, 1832), in *VSD*, 259 (describing the remarks of John E. Shell, of Brunswick, four days earlier); and see above, note 196. Dew, *Review of the Debate*, 125 (emphasis in original).

307. John T. Brown, of the town of Petersburg (January 18, 1832) in *VSD*, 169–84, at 170.

EPILOGUE: DEMONIC AMBIGUITIES

1. *The Confessions of Nat Turner* . . . (Baltimore: Lucas & Deaver, print., 1831), 5–6.
2. Max Weber, "Science as a Vocation," in H. H. Gerth and C. Wright Mills, editors, *From Max Weber: Essays in Sociology* (New York: Oxford University Press, 1958), 155, 156.
3. Walter Benjamin, "Capitalism as Religion," in Bullock and Jennings, editors, *Walter Benjamin: Selected Writings, Volume 1*, 289.
4. Along with photographic developers, Benjamin also uses the metaphor of the kaleidoscope, "which with every tum of the hand dissolves the established order into a new array." Benjamin, *The Arcades Project*, 339.
5. *Confessions*, 6.
6. The common law meaning of "full faith and credit" is evidentiary, attesting (for example) the confidence one may have in an agent's representation of a principal. Stephen E. Sachs, "Full Faith and Credit in the Early Congress," *Virginia Law Review* 95 (2009): 1217–20. At issue here is not the use of the phrase but the words *in* the phrase. For law's "double form," at once œconomic and sacral, see Peter Goodrich, "Specters of Law: Why the History of the Legal Spectacle Has Not Been Written," *UC Irvine Law Review* 1 (2011): 773–812.
7. Weber, "Science as a Vocation," 156; Michael Löwy and Robert Sayre, *Romanticism against the Tide of Modernity*, Catherine Porter, translator (Durham, NC: Duke University Press, 2001), 35. See also Poovey, *A History of the Modern Fact*, 29–91.
8. Thomas Kemple, *Intellectual Work and the Spirit of Capitalism: Weber's Calling* (New York: Palgrave Macmillan, 2014), 160–65, 173–76. Although Kemple is skeptical of the

possibility that Weber's acting/waiting dichotomy expresses the eschatological tension of Parousia's now/not yet (175), one may observe that it is precisely such a moment over which Weber's demon presides. See above, chapter 2, note 23.

9. Werner Hamacher, "Guilt History: Benjamin's Fragment 'Capitalism as Religion,'" *Cardozo Law Review* 26 (2004–5): 900.
10. "Ambiguity is the appearance of dialectic in images, the law of dialectics at a standstill." Walter Benjamin, "Paris the Capital of the Nineteenth Century (Exposé of 1935)," in Benjamin, *The Arcades Project*, 3–13, at 10. And see Tiedemann, "Dialectics at a Standstill," 929–44. For the meaning of phantasmagoria and armature, see below, notes 48 and 49, and accompanying text.
11. See above, chapter 3.
12. Boer, *Criticism of Heaven*, 62; Benjamin, "On the Concept of History," 396. Stéphane Mosès puts it thus: "When the social compact no longer rests on anything but the disenchanted awarenesss that nothing essential will ever change, that is, on the frustration of all hopes, the utopian energy that henceforth has no object will be invested completely—as if in compensation—in eschatological daydreams, in the expectation of the final catastrophe that will destroy the world so that a new humanity may rise from its ruins." Mosès, *The Angel of History*, 5. See also Richard Eldridge, *Images of History: Kant, Benjamin, Freedom, and the Human Subject* (New York: Oxford University Press, 2016), 102–49.
13. Benjamin, "On the Concept of History," 396.
14. *Confessions*, 20 (emphasis in original).
15. Tragle, *Southampton Slave Revolt*, 221–23.
16. *Confessions*, 20–21. Benjamin writes of such acts that they occur within an order (law) "which is merely a residue of the demonic stage of human existence"—the stage of nature, of the creaturely, of myth and fate, of "the endless pagan chain of guilt and atonement" prior to "the purity of the man who has expiated his sins, who is reconciled with the pure god." Fate shows itself "in the view of life . . . as having essentially first been condemned and then become guilty. Goethe summarizes both phases in the words 'the poor man you let become guilty.' Law condemns not to punishment but to guilt. Fate is the guilt context of the living. It corresponds to the natural condition of the living." Walter Benjamin, "Fate and Character," in Bullock and Jennings, editors, *Walter Benjamin: Selected Writings Volume 1*, 203–4.
17. Thus, according to Anaximander (ca. 610–546 BC) "Whence things have their origin, thence also their destruction happens, according to necessity; for they give to each other justice and recompense for their injustice in conformity with the ordinance of Time." See http://en.wikipedia.org/wiki/Anaximander (last accessed February 22, 2019). Hamacher, "Guilt History," 887–89. Lest one think this a philosophy too esoteric for the antebellum republic, let us note its articulation by no less a progenitor than James Madison: "If the earth be the gift of *nature* to the living, their title can extend to the earth in its *natural* state only. The *improvements* made by the dead form a debt against the living, who take the benefit of them. This debt cannot be otherwise discharged than by a proportionate obedience to the will of the Authors of the improvements." James Madison to Thomas Jefferson (February 4, 1790), in Ilan Wurman, *A Debt Against the Living: An Introduction to Originalism* (Cambridge: Cambridge University Press, 2017), 3 (emphasis in original).
18. Walter Benjamin, "Zur Geschichtsphilosophie. Historik und Politik," in Rolf Tiedemann and Herman Schweppenhäuser editors, *Walter Benjamin, Gesammelte Schriften* (Berlin: Suhrkamp Verlag, 1977), 6:92, translation by Werner Hamacher, in Hamacher, "Guilt History," 890. See also Eldridge, *Images of History*, 156–58. Hamacher explains: "Whatever is prior has had something taken from it by that which follows; or,

whatever is prior has withheld something from that which follows it. Every 'having' is thus declared as a having from something else that previously had it—as in the *debere*, the *de habere* of debt. If guilt is a genealogical category, it is 'the highest category of world history' insofar as it is the category of genesis itself and the only category that can account for occurrences in a homogenous sequence. Whatever happens, it happens from another and *toward* yet another, and is therefore indebted to these other occurrences. It is, however, also indebted in the sense that whatever happens in the line of descent occurs as a theft in which something is torn away, leaving a lack in the place of its origin. Guilt accordingly designates the reason of an absence, a failure, a deficit. Everything that happens is guilt. This is why guilt is 'the highest category' of history" (889–90).

19. Hamacher, "Guilt History," 893.
20. Benjamin, "Fate and Character," 203.
21. Hamacher, "Guilt History," 893 (emphasis added). On Christianity's guilt-economy, see Juster, *Sacred Violence*, 19–22. For an empirical account of the interaction between guilt-economy and debt-religion, see Mark A. Peterson, *The Price of Redemption: The Spiritual Economy of Puritan New England* (Stanford: Stanford University Press, 1997).
22. Michael Löwy notes, "The title of the fragment is directly borrowed from Ernst Bloch's 1921 *Thomas Münzer as Theologian of the Revolution*, which denounces Calvinism for having 'completely destroyed Christianity', replacing it with the elements of a new religion, 'capitalism as religion [*Kapitalismus als religion*]', or the Church of Mammon." Michael Löwy, "Capitalism as Religion: Walter Benjamin and Max Weber," in Michael Löwy, *On Changing the World: Essays in Political Philosophy, from Karl Marx to Walter Benjamin* (Chicago: Haymarket Books, 2013), 190. See also Löwy and Sayre, *Romanticism*, 176–77; Toscano, *Fanaticism*, 184–91.
23. Benjamin, "Capitalism as Religion," 288 (emphasis added). Benjamin is referencing Max Weber, "The Protestant Ethic and the 'Spirit' of Capitalism," for which see Baehr and Wells, editors, *Protestant Ethic*.
24. Weber, *Benjamin's -abilities*, 265–66. "The Christianity of the Reformation period did not favor the growth of capitalism; instead it transformed itself into capitalism." Benjamin, "Capitalism as Religion," 290.
25. Benjamin, "Capitalism as Religion," 288.
26. *Ibid*., 288. [Bullock and Jennings follow the *Gesammelte Schriften* in rendering the quotation "*sans rêve et sans merci*"—without dream and without mercy. Hamacher (897n19) prefers *sans trêve et sans merci*—without rest and without mercy. Benjamin's corpus sustains both possibilities.]
27. Benjamin, "Capitalism as Religion," 288.
28. Hamacher, "Guilt History," 895. Here again we see "Fate and Character" deployed to expand on "Capitalism as Religion."
29. Benjamin, "Capitalism as Religion," 288–89.
30. In Weber, "Protestant Ethic," 70.
31. *Ibid*., 70–71.
32. *Ibid*., 75 (original emphases). See, generally, Giorgio Agamben, *The Kingdom and the Glory: For a Theological Genealogy of Economy and Government* (Stanford: Stanford University Press, 2011).
33. Weber, "Protestant Ethic," 77.
34. *Ibid*., 79. See above, chapter 2 note 53.
35. Benjamin, "Capitalism as Religion," 288. "Worries: a mental illness characteristic of the age of capitalism. . . . A condition that is so bereft of hope causes guilt feelings. 'Worries' are the index of the sense of guilt induced by a despair that is communal, not individual and material, in origin" (290).

36. Matthew 6:12. In the *Luther Bibel* (1545) the verse reads *Und vergib uns unsere Schuld, wie wir unseren Schuldigern vergeben.* In German, as we have seen, "Schuld" means both guilt and debt simultaneously.
37. Benjamin, "Capitalism as Religion," 289 (emphasis in original).
38. Hamacher, "Guilt History," 909, 904–5.
39. Benjamin, "Capitalism as Religion," 289. Hamacher notes that Benjamin "interprets the historical process that transforms the one mode of production into the other as a debt-progression according to the metaphors of interest and compound interest, and thereby interprets history in the age of capital religion as debt history. The socialism projected by Marx can only become a more advanced state in the debt history of capital." Hamacher, "Guilt History," 906.
40. Benjamin, "Capitalism as Religion," 289.
41. Hamacher, "Guilt History," 915. Hamacher is referencing Benjamin's philosophy of origin, as expressed in a famous passage from *Ursprung des Deutschen Trauerspiels* [*Origin of the German Trauerspiel*], here in the translation by Samuel Weber in *Benjamin's -abilities*, 88–89: "Origin, although an historical category through and through, has nevertheless nothing in common with emergence [*Entstehen*]. In origin what is meant is not the becoming of something that has sprung forth [*das Werden des Entsprungenen*] but rather the springing-forth that emerges out of coming-to-be and passing away [*dem Werden und Vergehen Entspringendes*]. Origin stands in the flow of becoming as a maelstrom [*Strudel*] that irresistibly tears [*reißt*] the stuff of emergence into its rhythm. In the bare manifestation of the factual, the original is never discernible, and its rhythm is accessible only to a dual insight. It is recognizable on the one hand as restoration, as reinstatement, and on the other, precisely therein as incomplete, unfinished." See also Christopher Tomlins, "Of Origin: Toward a History of Contemporary Legal Thought," in Justin Desautels-Stein and Christopher Tomlins, editors, *Searching for Contemporary Legal Thought* (Cambridge: Cambridge University Press, 2017), 23–42. Compare Alain Badiou's philosophy of the event, above chapter 3, notes 5 and 8; and chapter 4, notes 218–20.
42. Hamacher, "Guilt History," 915–16.
43. Walter Benjamin, "The Meaning of Time in the Moral Universe," in Bullock and Jennings, editors, *Walter Benjamin: Selected Writings Volume 1*, 286–87. See also Howard Eiland, "Translator's Introduction," in Walter Benjamin, *Origin of the German Trauerspiel*, Howard Eiland translator (Cambridge, MA: Harvard University Press, 2019), xix, and Benjamin's text at 254.
44. *Ibid.*, 287. The image is, of course, immediately recognizable as that made famous in the ninth thesis of "On the Concept of History," 392. See also Benjamin, "Critique of Violence," discussed above, chapter 3, note 3.
45. Samuel Weber, *Targets of Opportunity: On the Militarization of Thinking* (New York: Fordham University Press, 2005), 115.
46. *Ibid.*, 120.
47. *Ibid.*, 123.
48. Weber, *Benjamin's -abilities*, 270, 277. On Benjamin's concept of "phantasmagoria" see Martel, *Divine Violence;* Martel, *Textual Conspiracies*; James R. Martel, *The One and Only Law: Walter Benjamin and the Second Commandment* (Ann Arbor: University of Michigan Press, 2014); and Margaret Cohen, "Benjamin's Phantasmagoria: The *Arcades Project*," in David S. Ferris, editor, *The Cambridge Companion to Walter Benjamin* (Cambridge: Cambridge University Press, 2004), 199–220.
49. Weber *Benjamin's -abilities*, 278. And see Andreas Philippopoulos-Mihalopoulos, *Spatial Justice: Body, Lawscape, Atmosphere* (Abingdon: Routledge, 2015), 2–7; Tomlins, "Materialism and Legal Historiography," 10–13. In Philippopoulos-Mihalopoulos's

terms, visibilizing the framework is the work of culling *the lawscape* out of *atmosphere*, rendering it open to view. In light of the work cited in this note and note 48 above, not to mention elsewhere in this book, Andrew Cole's pronouncement that "Benjamin's dialectical image is the traditional historicist one" is hard to understand. See Cole, *Birth of Theory*, 161.

50. However, not too much risk. Note, for example, *The Liberator*'s response to the news from Southampton County (September 3, 1831): "Wo to this guilty land, unless she speedily repents of her evil doings! The blood of millions of her sons cries aloud for redress! IMMEDIATE EMANCIPATION can alone save her from the vengeance of Heaven, and cancel the debt of ages!"
51. Hartman, *Scenes of Subjection*, 79–163. Prior to emancipation, the African American *is* only as a criminal; after, as both criminal and debtor (debtor because eternally indebted to white America for paying the blood-debt of emancipation in warfare).
52. *Confessions*, 20.
53. Hamacher, "Guilt History," 900.
54. *Confessions*, 11 (emphasis added). Note the importance of a temporality of instantaneity to Hamacher's "immanent rebound."
55. "And I saw a great white throne, and him that sat on it, from whose face the earth and the heaven fled away; and there was found no place for them." Revelation 20:11.
56. Revelation 1:21–22; 20:12–15. And see Walter Benjamin, "Theological-Political Fragment," in Eiland and Jennings, editors, *Walter Benjamin: Selected Writings, Volume 3*, 305–6.
57. Hamacher, "Guilt History," 907. We can return to Hamacher's text at 915–16 (above at note 41)—"The nothing of this counter-history is time itself as the time to come"—and consider the first half of Turner's confession precisely as the counter-history that reveals the "not" of his "not guilty" as "time itself as the time to come." Hence the triple significance of his response, "was not Christ crucified" (above chapter 2, notes 84 and 89 and accompanying text): the statement repudiates the allegation of self-delusion—Christ's crucifixion was no divine "error"; it confirms Turner's sacrificial innocence—like Christ, Turner will die for others; and it is predictive—Turner's execution, like Christ's, signifies messianic forgiveness (time to come).
58. Walter Benjamin, "Goethe's Elective Affinities," in Bullock and Jennings, editors, *Walter Benjamin: Selected Writings, Volume 1*, 297–360, at 346. On freedom as ethico-legal universal, see above, chapters 3 and 4.
59. *Confessions*, 18.
60. *Ibid.*, 19.
61. See Aristodemou, *Law, Psychoanalysis, Society*, 51: "Reality, knowledge, and existence dwell in the realm of the symbolic, that is, in the register of language, of what is said and sayable. Our emphasis on reality, therefore, rather than affording us access to truth, functions as a defense against the truth of what cannot be represented. . . . There is always a gap, therefore, between reality, which the subject can try to know and represent, and the Real, which . . . stuns, transforms, and indeed destroys the subject." See also 78–79.
62. Orsi, *History and Presence*, 5; Žižek, *Event*, 108–9. Thomas Parramore properly notices the intensity of the relationship between Gray and Turner, but interprets it as solidarity, in my view mistakenly. See Parramore, "Covenant in Jerusalem," 74–76.
63. *Confessions* (title page). And see above, chapter 1.
64. *Confessions*, 3, 4, 5.
65. Weber, "Science as a Vocation," 155.
66. *Ibid.*, 138, 139 (emphasis in original).

67. *Confessions*, 21.
68. See Allmendinger, "Construction," in Greenberg, editor, *Nat Turner*, 25–36.
69. Ambler, *Life and Diary*, 155.
70. *Ibid.*, 157, 158.
71. *Ibid.*, 159; Floyd to Worth, in Tragle, *Southampton Slave Revolt*, 271–72.
72. "It was the slaves," says Cedric Robinson, citing W.E.B. Du Bois, "who had mounted the attack on capitalism." It was "from the periphery and not the center that the most sustained threat . . . materialized." Robinson, *Black Marxism*, 314.
73. "Where thinking suddenly comes to a stop in a constellation saturated with tensions, it gives that constellation a shock, by which thinking is crystallized as a monad. The historical materialist approaches a historical object only where it confronts him as a monad. In this structure he recognizes the sign of a messianic arrest of happening, or (to put it differently) a revolutionary chance in the fight for the oppressed past." Benjamin, "On the Concept of History," 396. For commentary, see Gordon, *Ghostly Matters*, 65–66: "This oppressed past is neither linear, a point in a sequential procession of time, nor an autonomous alternative past. In a sense, it is whatever organized violence has repressed and in the process formed into a past, a history, remaining nonetheless alive and accessible to encounter. . . . To fight for an oppressed past is to make this past come alive as the lever for the work of the present." For Gaston Bachelard the monad is "the space-time-consciousness complex . . . the triple essence of atomism . . . affirmed in its triple solitude—without communication with other things, other times, or other souls." Bachelard, *Intuition of the Instant*, 21; and see Tomlins, "Materialism and Legal Historiography," 8–9.
74. The classic statement is as follows: "In simple circulation [C-M-C], the value of commodities attained at the most a form independent of their use values, *i.e.* the form of money. But now, in the circulation M-C-M, value suddenly presents itself as a self-moving substance which passes through a process of its own, and for which commodities and money are both mere forms. But there is more to come: instead of simply representing the relations of commodities, it now enters into a private relationship with itself, as it were [M-M]. It differentiates itself as original value from itself as surplus-value, just as God the Father differentiates himself from himself as God the Son, although both are of the same age and form, in fact one single person; for only by the surplus value of £10 does the £100 originally advanced become capital, and as soon as this has happened, as soon as the son has been created, and through the son, the father, their difference vanishes again, and both become one, £110. Value therefore now becomes value in process, money in process, and, as such, capital. . . . Lastly, in the case of interest-bearing capital, the circulation M-C-M′ presents itself in abridged form, in its final result and without any intermediate stage, in a concise style, so to speak, as M-M′, i.e. money which is worth more money, value which is greater than itself. " Marx, *Capital*, I, 256–57.
75. *Ibid.*, 919 (emphasis in original).
76. Hamacher, "Guilt History," 902–3.
77. *Ibid.*, 903.
78. Floyd to Worth, in Tragle, *Southampton Slave Revolt*, 272 (emphasis added).
79. Hamacher, "Guilt History," 903.
80. Floyd to Worth, in Tragle, *Southampton Slave Revolt*, 271. Tragle notes (427) how "all questions pertaining to Turner's rebellion became, so to speak, 'business transactions.'"
81. Weber, "Science as a Vocation," 156.
82. Dew, *Review of the Debate*, 8.
83. *Ibid.*, 7, 8 (emphasis in original), 50, 64.

84. See above, text at note 82 (Dew), and at chapter 1, note 54, and chapter 2, note 79 (Turner).
85. This does not mean that they thought about numbers in the same way. As Mary Poovey notes, "Numbers have come to epitomize the modern fact, because they have come to seem preinterpretive or even somehow noninterpretive at the same time they have become the bedrock of systematic knowledge. Historically, however, there was no necessary connection between numbers and this peculiarly modern epistemological assumption, nor have number always seemed free of an interpretive dimension." Poovey, *A History of the Modern Fact*, xii.

    Dew thought populations, their increase, their value, and the cost of reducing them in size of unsurpassable importance. For his part, as we have seen (see above, chapter 2, note 191), Turner thought the numbers 6,000, 30,000, and 80,000 of particular significance. Their compound may have been an attempt to determine the spiritual resources at his disposal. Alternatively (more prosaically) they may have been his attempt to determine the forces arrayed against him—the white population of "the country." See Parramore, "Covenant in Jerusalem," 62. It is unclear what Turner took "the country" to be—Southampton County, the cross-border region (southside Virginia, northern North Carolina), the state of Virginia, or the federal union. If 6,000 was his approximation of the county's white population (6,573 at the 1830 U.S. Census) it was a shrewd one. For Dew, meanwhile, 6,000 was both the estimated annual increase of Virginia's slave and free colored populations, and the estimated number of slaves "exported" elsewhere." Dew, *Review of the Debate*, 122. As we have seen (above, chapter 6, notes 299–304 and accompanying text) in at least the second aspect Dew's powers of approximation were inferior to Turner's.
86. Dew, *Review of the Debate,* 62 (footnote), and compare Turner, text at chapter 2, note 81.
87. *Ibid.*, 57.
88. *Ibid.*, 62 (footnote).
89. *Ibid.*, 47–48.
90. See above, chapter 6, text at note 152.
91. James W. C. Pennington, *The Fugitive Blacksmith; or, Events in the History of James W. C. Pennington, Pastor of a Presbyterian Church, New York, Formerly a Slave in the State of Maryland, United States* (London: Charles Gilpin, 1849), iv.
92. Dew, *Review of the Debate,* 64 (emphasis in original).
93. On simultaneity, time, and fulfillment (messianic time), see Walter Benjamin, "*Trauerspiel* and Tragedy," in *Walter Benjamin: Early Writings, 1910-1917*, Howard Eiland et al., translators (Harvard University Press, 2011), 241–44; Benjamin, "On the Concept of History," 396, 397.
94. Herman Melville, *Pierre; or, The Ambiguities* (New York: Harper & Brothers, 1852), 178–84, 181, 183.
95. *Ibid.*, 182; Gaston Bachelard, *Earth and Reveries of Will: An Essay on the Imagination of Matter*, Kenneth Haltman, translator (Dallas, TX: The Dallas Institute, 2002), 148.
96. Orsi, *History and Presence*, 38.
97. Gray died on August 23, 1845, of malaria. He was attended by the Reverend Vernon Eskridge of the Methodist Episcopal Church. "O, that I could be permitted strength to go abroad but for an hour," this remorseful "vilest of sinners" reportedly told Eskridge on his deathbed. "I would cover myself with dirt and ashes and cry aloud to sinners to repent and flee from the wrath to come." See Allmendinger, *Rising*, 278–79.
98. Melville, *Pierre*, 182.
99. Stephen John Hartnett, *Executing Democracy, Volume II: Capital Punishment and the Making of America, 1835-1843* (East Lansing: Michigan State University Press, 2012), 211, 212; William Butler Yeats, "The Second Coming," *The Dial* 69 (November 1920), 466. See also Michael Paul Rogin, *Subversive Genealogy: The Politics and Art of Herman Melville*

(Berkeley: University of California Press, 1985), 159. For Rogin, "there is no liberation in Melville's fiction." *Pierre* registers "the claustrophobic gloom and the portents of explosion" that inhabit the politics of the 1850s. See generally 155–220.

100. See above, chapter 6, text at note 283; Christopher Tomlins, "Why Law's Objects Do Not Disappear: On History as Remainder," in Philippopoulos-Mihalopoulos, editor, *Law and Theory*, 365–86, particularly 376–80. Although not, unlike Thomas Ruffin Gray, a scoffer at religion (he was an Episcopalian), Dew's exposition of political economy is noticeably "scientific," free of the "moral and Christian dimensions" of the subject. See O'Brien, *Conjectures of Order*, 2:888, 943, 955.

101. As M. R. James put it in his ominous tale of gothic guilt and foreboding, "quis est iste qui venit" [who is this who is coming]? See Montague Rhodes James, "Oh, Whistle, and I'll Come to You, My Lad," in *Ghost-Stories of an Antiquary* (London: Edward Arnold, 1905), 181–225. James is referencing Isaias 63:1 in the *Biblia Sacra Vulgata* (the *Vulgate*), the principal Latin version of the Bible (revised 1592). In the King James Version, Isaiah 63:1–4 reads: "Who is this that cometh from Edom, with dyed garments from Bozrah? This that is glorious in his apparel, travelling in the greatness of his strength? / Wherefore art thou red in thine apparel, and thy garments like him that treadeth in the winefat? / I have trodden the winepress alone; and of the people there was none with me: for I will tread them in mine anger, and trample them in my fury; and their blood shall be sprinkled upon my garments, and I will stain all my raiment. / For the day of vengeance is in mine heart, and the year of my redeemed is come."

102. Dew, *Review of the Debate*, 68. He continues, "Destroy agriculture, destroy tillage, and the ruin of the farmer will draw down ruin upon the mechanic, the merchant, the sailor, and the manufacturer—they must all flee together from the land of desolation" (69). And see chapter 6, note 290 (William Daniel Jr., of Campbell).

103. Bachelard, *Earth and Reveries of Will*, 175.

104. Tiedemann, "Dialectics at a Standstill," 944.

105. Bachelard, *Earth and Reveries of Will*, 149, and see generally 141–79.

106. Mary Boykin Chesnut, in Isabella D. Martin and Myrta Lockett Avary, editors, *A Diary from Dixie, as Written by Mary Boykin Chesnut, Wife of James Chesnut, Jr., United States Senator From South Carolina, 1859-1861, and Afterward an Aide to Jefferson Davis and a Brigadier-General in the Confederate Army* (New York: D. Appleton and Company, 1905), 38 (entry for April 13, 1861).

107. O'Brien, *Conjectures of Order*, 2:945.

108. Aimé Césaire, "Et les Chiens Se Taisaient" ("And the Dogs Were Silent"), from *Les Armes Miraculeuses* (Paris: Gallimard, 1946), in *The Complete Poetry of Aimé Césaire*, Bilingual Edition, A. James Arnold and Clayton Eshleman, translators (Middletown, CT: Wesleyan University Press, 2017), 225.

109. Walter Benjamin, "The Dialectical Image," in "Paralipomena to 'On the Concept of History,'" in Eiland and Jennings, editors, *Walter Benjamin: Selected Writings Volume 4*, 405; Daniel Heller-Roazen, "Editor's Introduction: To Read What Was Never Written," in *Potentialities: Collected Essays in Philosophy*, by Giorgio Agamben (Stanford, CA: Stanford University Press, 1999).

INDEX

italic pages refer to figures and tables